UNIVERSITY OF ST. THOMAS LIBRARIES

The publisher gratefully acknowledges the generous contribution to this book provided by the Ahmanson Foundation Humanities Endowment Fund of the University of California Press Foundation.

The Emerging Female Citizen

STUDIES ON THE HISTORY OF SOCIETY AND CULTURE
Victoria E. Bonnell and Lynn Hunt, Editors

The Emerging Female Citizen

Gender and Enlightenment in Spain

THERESA ANN SMITH

University of California Press
BERKELEY   LOS ANGELES   LONDON

University of California Press, one of the most distinguished university presses in the United States, enriches lives around the world by advancing scholarship in the humanities, social sciences, and natural sciences. Its activities are supported by the UC Press Foundation and by philanthropic contributions from individuals and institutions. For more information, visit www.ucpress.edu.

Parts of chapter 3 appeared originally in Theresa Ann Smith, "Fashioning the Enlightenment: The Proposal for a Female National Dress in Eighteenth-Century Spain," *Dieciocho: Hispanic Enlightenment* 23, no. 1 (Spring 2000): 76–85. Parts of chapter 6 appeared originally in Theresa Ann Smith, "Writing out of the Margins: Women, Translation, and the Spanish Enlightenment," *Journal of Women's History* 15, no. 1 (Spring 2003): 116–43; reprinted with the permission of Indiana University Press.

University of California Press
Berkeley and Los Angeles, California

University of California Press, Ltd.
London, England

© 2006 by The Regents of the University of California

Library of Congress Cataloging-in-Publication Data

Smith, Theresa Ann, 1971–
   The emerging female citizen : gender and enlightenment in Spain / Theresa Ann Smith.
    p. cm. — (Studies on the history of society and culture ; 53)
   Includes bibliographical references and index.
   ISBN 0-520-24583-0 (cloth : alk. paper)
   1. Women—Spain—History—18th century. 2. Sex role—Spain—History—18th century. 3. Women—Spain—Intellectual life. 4. Women—Spain—Social conditions. 5. Feminism—Spain—History—18th century. I. Title. II. Series.
   HQ1693.S64 2005
   305.42'0946—dc22   2005016606

Manufactured in the United States of America

15 14 13 12 11 10 09 08 07 06
10 9 8 7 6 5 4 3 2 1

This book is printed on New Leaf EcoBook 60, containing 60% postconsumer waste, processed chlorine free; 30% de-inked recycled fiber, elemental chlorine free; and 10% FSC-certified virgin fiber, totally chlorine free. EcoBook 60 is acid-free and meets the minimum requirements of ANSI/ASTM D5634–01 *(Permanence of Paper).*

To my husband, John,

for his intelligence, love, and wit,

and to our son, Joseph,

for his smiles

Contents

List of Illustrations	ix
Acknowledgments	xi
Introduction	1

PART I. DEVELOPING IDEOLOGIES OF CITIZENSHIP

1.	The Woman Question	17
2.	Admitted Equals: Art and Letters	40
3.	On Equal Terms? Membership in the Economic Society	74

PART II. ENACTING CITIZENSHIP

4.	Negotiating a Female Public: Writers and Reformers	111
5.	Public Works: Female Citizens as Mothers and Workers	148
6.	Between Reason and Passion: Citizenship in Translation	178
	Conclusion	197
	Notes	201
	Selected Bibliography	257
	Index	299

Illustrations

FIGURES

1. Francisco de Goya, *Maja desnuda*, 1797–1800 ?
2. Faraona María Magdalena Olivieri, *Self-Portrait*, circa 1759 57
3. Mariana Urries y Pignatelli, *Cupid*, circa 1775 60
4. Francisco de Goya, *The Marquise of Villafranca Painting Her Husband*, 1804 63
5. María Ramona Palafox y Portocarrero, *Virgin with Child*, circa 1790 65
6. Francisca Efigenia Meléndez, *Virgin with Child*, circa 1791 70
7. María Josefa Caron, *D. Diego de Villanueva*, circa 1761 72
8. Española and Carolina, dress designs, 1788 83

TABLES

1. Women Admitted as *Académicas* to the Real Academia de Bellas Artes de San Fernando, 1752–1808 54
2. Nonacademic Female Artists Who Exhibited at the Real Academia de Bellas Artes de San Fernando, 1785–1808 67
3. Classes of Women Suggested in M.O.'s Female National Dress Proposal 85
4. Dress Guidelines Suggested According to Class in M.O.'s Female National Dress Proposal 86
5. Members of the Women's Council, 1786–1811 137
6. Topics on Women's Education Presented by the Countess of Trúllas for Discussion by the *Junta de Damas* in 1795 152

Acknowledgments

The roots of this book stretch back to those teachers who first helped me to develop an interest in history. Jack Benson and Fred Engel opened my eyes to how dynamic a discipline history can be. A number of excellent teachers at the University of California, Berkeley, sustained my enthusiasm, including Richard Herr, who introduced me to the history of Spain, and Paloma Fernández Pérez, who taught me so much about researching women in the early modern world. At the University of California, San Diego, various faculty members helped advance my knowledge of women's studies, including Christine Hünefeldt, Susan Kirkpatrick, and Susan Smith. In its earliest incarnation, this project grew out of the seminar "Women in the Age of the French Revolution," led by Cynthia Truant. For helping me to find this topic and for her enthusiastic encouragement, I am grateful. Pamela Radcliff offered her critical eye as a reader in the earliest stages of this project, and I am indebted to her for her careful and always thought-provoking reading. David Ringrose, my thesis advisor, helped shape this project by providing valuable advice at all stages. His warmth and encouragement were a wonderful gift.

This project made the transition from dissertation to book during my tenure as a visiting assistant professor at Claremont McKenna College and as an Ahmanson-Getty Postdoctoral Fellow at the William Andrews Clark Memorial Library and the Center for Seventeenth- and Eighteenth-Century Studies at the University of California, Los Angeles. I am grateful to Peter Reill and Kirstie McClure for connecting me with the dynamic community of scholars at the Clark, and to the wonderful staff, especially Jennifer Schaffner and Bruce Whiteman, for making it such a welcoming place to rethink my work. Particularly valuable during this stage of my project was my friend and colleague Lisa Cody, whose comparative perspective and sheer brilliance enabled me to see my research in new and exciting ways.

A number of institutions made the completion of the research component of this project possible. I owe thanks to archivists and staff at numerous Spanish libraries and archives, including the Archivo Histórico Nacional, the Archivo de la Real Academia de Bellas Artes, the Archivo de la Real Academia Española, the Archivo de la Real Academia de la Historia, and the Biblioteca Nacional. Special thanks go to the personnel at the Archivo de la Real Sociedad Económica Matritense de Amigos del País who allowed me after-hours access to materials when I was pressed for time during a busy research year, and to Pilar Ríos Izquierdo, who oriented me in the archive. The resourcefulness and patience of the interlibrary loan staff at both UCSD and UCLA enabled me to access a range of rare materials from home. The Department of History at UCSD; the Program for Cultural Cooperation between Spain's Ministry of Culture and U.S. Universities; and the Tinker Foundation (administered through the Center for Iberian and Latin American Studies at UCSD) provided generous funding for overseas research.

The warmth, insight, and generosity of fellow *hispanistas* at all stages of this project cannot be overstated. Jesús Cruz and Andrés Úbeda de los Cobos provided assistance in navigating Spanish archives, and Jodi Campbell offered daily support over coffee at the Biblioteca Nacional. I thank the members of the Society for Spanish and Portuguese Historical Studies and the Southwestern Spanish History Consortium for providing productive and friendly forums for me to discuss my research. This book builds on the exemplary work of many scholars in Spanish historical and literary studies. Though they are too numerous to mention here, their works fill the pages of my bibliography. I would like, however, to express particular gratitude to Helen Nader and Betsy Perry, who have inspired me with both their scholarship and their kind words of support, and to Elizabeth Lehfeldt and Lisa Vollendorf, who both generously shared their works in progress and read portions of the manuscript.

I also thank Lynn Hunt for encouraging me in the submission process, and my editor Sheila Levine, who selected wonderful readers for the manuscript. Suggestions from David Gies, Betsy Perry, and an anonymous third reader helped to make this a better book.

Friends new and old have helped me to celebrate and at times endure the process of writing this book. Barnet Hartston, Kathy McKee, Kristine Puich, Paul Morsink, and even my cat, Zilia, provided welcome encouragement. My writing partner, Phoebe Kropp, gave freely of her talents, her time, and her friendship. Without her encouragement and persistence, this book would never have been finished.

Deepest gratitude goes to my family. My parents, Shirley and Phyllis Smith, supported me in my earliest academic pursuits, and their encouragement and love continue to sustain me. I dedicate this book to my wonderful husband, John Ferrari, and our son, Joseph, whose love and companionship give greater meaning to everything I do.

Introduction

Perhaps the most famous image of a woman from eighteenth-century Spain is Francisco de Goya's *Maja desnuda* (1797–1800). A portrait of a nude woman stretched out on a green, pillow-covered chaise, arms tucked behind her head and eyes staring intently at the viewer, Goya's canvas alarmed contemporaries and startles viewers even today (see figure 1). Its perceived licentiousness led the Inquisition to summon the famed artist before their tribunal in 1815, though Goya ultimately escaped prosecution. The question of who posed for such a scandalous portrait has long consumed scholars, as well as descendants of the Duchess of Alba—the woman often considered the work's most likely subject—who studied her exhumed body in the twentieth century to prove she did not shed her clothing for the controversial painting. The love affair between Goya and Alba even made it to the big screen in 1959's *The Naked Maja*, starring Ava Gardner.[1] The flurry *Maja desnuda* created can in part be explained by its subject's departure from acceptable norms of female comportment. In addition to being an immodest woman who dared to pose nude for an artist and his viewers, Goya's *maja* challenged the ideal of female subjection with her bold, confident gaze.[2]

As alarming as this behavior may appear on the canvas, however, women in eighteenth-century Spain were far bolder with the brush than as its object. As artists, writers, and reformers, Spanish women took up pens, joined academies and economic societies, formed literary circles, and became active in the burgeoning public discourse of the Enlightenment. Talented female artists gained membership in Spain's Royal Academy of Fine Arts of San Fernando; women such as Ana Meléndez, María Prieto, and Ana María Mengs stood among the more than 8 percent of all artists admitted between 1752, when the academy opened its doors, and 1808, the year Napoleon invaded Spain. In the 1780s and 1790s, the Count-Duchess of Benavente

Figure 1. Francisco de Goya, *Maja desnuda*, 1797–1800. Oil on canvas, 98 x 191 cm. Catalog no. 742. Courtesy of the Museo del Prado, Madrid.

and her good friends the Countess of Montijo and the Marquise of Fuerte-Híjar hosted *tertulias,* small gatherings similar to French salons in which male intellectuals and select women assembled to discuss politics, art, and literature. In 1787, Rita López de Porras, the Countess of Carpio, and the Marquise of Ayerbe joined others in forming a women's council to the Madrid Royal Economic Society of Friends of the Country. Women's admission to this influential institution, which worked toward the cultural and economic regeneration of the nation, was achieved thanks in part to the skillful argumentation of the Aragonese writer Josefa Amar y Borbón. The women's council, which met weekly during its most active period, from 1787 to 1811, undertook a number of ambitious projects, including reforming Madrid's foundling home, analyzing the state of female education, and administering lace-making schools for young girls. These activities suggest that women contributed meaningfully to Spain's cultural, political, and economic life in the eighteenth century.

Documenting the lives of these remarkable women is important in and of itself, and part of my aim here is to expand knowledge of the range and depth of women's accomplishments during this era. Indeed, along with Dena Goodman's French *salonnières* and the subjects of Linda Kerber's *Women of the Republic,* Spanish women and their achievements should take their place amid the now rich scholarship on women in the age of Enlightenment.[3] However, while the work that follows reveals the broad reach of women's thought and activity in eighteenth-century Spain, its larger goal is to explain what their new visibility meant in the Spanish context. Women's expanding public activities coincided with two important trends in Spain: the emergence of new institutions of sociability and discourse, and a push by leading Spanish intellectuals to reinvent the Spanish nation. In other words, women's participation went hand in hand with the development of a significant community of thinkers devoted to basic Enlightenment tenets of reason and progress.

In the past several decades, historians have demonstrated the vibrancy and scope of this community, though it has been difficult to completely overturn the portrait of eighteenth-century Spain as a fading empire lagging behind the rest of Europe economically, socially, and politically.[4] The Franco dictatorship and Spain's late embrace of democracy contributed to the persistence of this myth, but this portrait of Spain is nothing new. Eighteenth-century Spanish intellectuals themselves were obsessed with overcoming their country's miserable reputation. European sentiment typically dismissed Spain as a backward realm with undeveloped industry and a culture stagnating in the grip of the Catholic Church and its notorious Inquisition. Partly to overturn this judgment, Spain's emerging liberal elite developed a sweeping agenda for the creation of a modern state in Spain, one rooted firmly in Enlightenment principles. The question of how women would contribute to Spain's regeneration and the question of women's place in the new citizenry became key topics for discussion. Moreover, women's presence and their often eager participation in new Enlightenment institutions affected the intellectual consideration of "the woman question" to a profound degree. This book examines the social debates by and about women—how intellectual discourse and women's actions worked together to define women's roles in the emerging nation in eighteenth-century Spain.

Making sense of the Spanish story has proven difficult, in part because much of the language historians use to describe and analyze women's history today was born in the 1980s and 1990s by scholars of France, England, and the United States. Aiming to move beyond the mainly recuperative and celebratory "herstory" of the 1960s and 1970s, these historians modified theoretical frameworks that promised to at once broaden and deepen historical inquiry on women and gender. The shift from documenting women's contributions in the past to analyzing the gendered basis of a broad number of historical institutions and transformations allowed historians of women to move beyond the perception that theirs was a minor subfield and make gender a central category of analysis.[5] Yet, as historians have moved from women's to gender history, the field has remained steeped in Franco-British concerns, and for scholars of other national contexts, the language of the discipline has been an uncomfortable fit.

Take, for example, debates over undoubtedly the most influential theoretical construct in women's history in the past twenty years: Jürgen Habermas's public sphere.⁶ Originally published in 1962 and translated into English in 1989, Habermas's *The Structural Transformation of the Public Sphere: An Inquiry into a Category of Bourgeois Society* articulated a space between society and the state in which the public organized itself to participate in discourse and formulate public opinion. This model promised to revolutionize discussions of women's political lives. For feminist scholars, Habermas's theory seemed to provide a useful language with which to explore the relegation of women to private, domestic life as well as to analyze their struggle to define themselves in the public and political realms. As Mary P. Ryan explained in 1992, the concept "freed politics from the iron grasp of the state, which, by virtue of the long denial of the franchise to women and their rare status as public officials, effectively defined the public in masculine terms."⁷ Taking Habermas as a starting point, many feminist theorists have accepted some tenets of his model but also have criticized its idealization of the public sphere as a completely inclusive space, its tendency to devalue the private sphere, and its failure to recognize the fluid connections between public and private.⁸ Habermas's public sphere, refashioned to varying degrees with these issues in mind, has become the dominant explanatory model for understanding women's new visibility in public life in eighteenth-century France, England, and the United States. As such, it presents a compelling path for considering the similar emergence of women into new arenas of sociability and political action in the Spanish context.

However, the public sphere model may have outlived its utility. This scholarship has remained imprisoned in old, often inflexible, notions of liberalism, equality, and the Enlightenment, which makes its application to the Spanish case particularly problematic. A major debate in French historiography demonstrates the model's shortcomings. As French scholars have endeavored to understand women's presence in the public sphere in pre-Revolutionary France, they have turned to the rise of liberal ideology as the most plausible explanation, creating a debate that has consumed scholars for over a decade. The pivotal question: did liberal ideology allow for the broadening of women's roles in this period, or were pre-Revolution liberal assumptions inherently patriarchal? In broader terms, what is the relationship between liberal ideology and gender construction?

Until recently, scholars have tended to divide themselves into two camps. The first camp, perhaps best exemplified by the work of the political theorist Joan Landes, argues that liberal ideology is inherently masculinist—in other words, that women's exclusion was a given from the start. Landes finds that the shift from an absolutist monarchy, where all subjects—both male and female—were subordinate to the king, to a liberal state based on ideals of masculine reason and female virtue actually weakened women's status. For scholars like Landes, the only possible outcome of the rise of liberal political theory is a gendered polity that excludes women.[9] The second camp has challenged this interpretation, arguing that liberal ideology did provide women with a basis to claim rights within the public sphere. I agree with this assertion—the emergence of an ideology based on assumptions about natural equality and universal rights undeniably fostered women's participation in new activities. As Lynn Hunt explains, "It made the exclusion of women into an issue."[10] But women did eventually find themselves excluded, so the absence of women from politics in the early nineteenth century, after the flowering of liberal ideology, begs an explanation. This second camp links women's exclusion to the upheaval of the French Revolution, providing a political (and national) rather than an ideological explanation for women's exclusion from the new citizenry.[11]

Yet part of the limitation of this debate is in the very narrow usage of the terms it embraces. The representation of liberal ideology as antithetical to absolute monarchical rule is one facet of the problem. In France, where calls for liberty and equality formed part of a revolutionary challenge to a tyrannical monarch, this distinction is at least understandable, even though it crystallizes old notions of absolutism that recent scholarship has challenged. Historians have convincingly shown that absolutist governments entailed much more negotiation between monarch and subject than the term belies.[12] Yet in Spain, where the Enlightenment elite entertained discussions that challenged the notion of royal sovereignty, called for a more rational economic policy, and touted liberty of thought and writing—all within royal institutions and sometimes even from the position of royal advisors—the dichotomy between liberal ideals and absolutist rule severely hinders understanding of the nation's political developments. Still, the notion that the discourse of the public sphere, defined by its liberal rationality, must pose a direct challenge to absolute rule remains enshrined in dominant usage of the term.

The idea that liberal rationality entails the wholesale rejection of religious passion is another persistent myth, one that is particularly problematic in the case of Spain. When measured against a French yardstick, the virtual absence in Spain of the strident religious critiques made by key French philosophes has led many to emphasize Spain's lack of Enlightenment spirit. The work of American political theorists such as James Madison and

Thomas Jefferson, who during the same century forged a new nation with a founding document that clearly articulated the separation between church and state, has provided yet another measure of Spain's backwardness. This constructed dichotomy between religious faith and reasoned inquiry has been a major mark against the existence of a Spanish Enlightenment, not least because this division is embedded in prevalent definitions of the public sphere. After all, the public sphere is supposed to be a site of rational, critical debate, which by its very essence would challenge received knowledge and impassioned faith.

Recent scholarship, however, has begun to interrogate the role of religion in the Enlightenment, a key point where both Spain and women are concerned. This work has led historians to rethink the dominant view that the Enlightenment constituted "the rise of modern paganism," as Peter Gay titled the first volume of his hallmark *The Enlightenment: An Interpretation* in 1966.[13] In contrast to this old paradigm, scholars such as J. G. A. Pocock, David Sorkin, and Anthony La Vopa have shown the complex relationship between reasoned inquiry and religious faith in Enlightenment Europe.[14] Their work suggests a multifaceted past featuring, as Pocock explains, "Enlightenments" rather than *the* Enlightenment. Having moved away from the study of France as the classic example of Enlightenment, this new approach has identified multiple Enlightenments within one particular country as well as highlighted distinct national characteristics.[15] *The Emerging Female Citizen* contributes to this scholarship by challenging the old dichotomy between reason and faith. Spanish women and men often understood the relationship in more complementary and complex ways that the typical view of Enlightenment logic has obscured. In this book I eschew terminology created to describe France, England, and the United States and in its place use the language of eighteenth-century men and women in an attempt to recover the language of Spanish Enlightenment debates.

The need for scholars to develop their own vocabulary when discussing Spanish women has only recently come to light. Following on the heels of those studying the French and English, historians in Spain in the 1970s and 1980s began to find evidence for women's history in the archives.[16] Only in the 1990s did this basically commemorative history give way to a more theoretical approach shaped to a great extent by work being done in France and England. This historiographical shift accompanied a major revisionist wave in scholarship on Spain. Scholars began to refute the mainstream view of Spanish history as a story of decline and failure in which economic difficulties and lack of political modernization explained the rise and persistence of the Franco dictatorship. In contrast to this teleological story, more recent scholarship on Spain argues, the social, political, economic, and cultural transitions occurring west of the Pyrenees did not diverge so dramatically from what was happening in the rest of Europe.[17] This desire to fit Spain into the European mold has had its own limitations, however, for historians of Spain and of women alike.

In the past decade, feminist historians and literary scholars have done much to flesh out our understanding of the changing ideas on and roles of women in eighteenth-century society. Sally Ann Kitts's detailed study of essays, pamphlets, and treatises on women, for example, documents the debate on the woman question that permeated Spain's periodical press and reformist circles.[18] Recent literary scholars have analyzed the increased presence of female authors in the literary world.[19] In addition, work has flourished on notable female intellectuals such as Josefa Amar y Borbón.[20] Perhaps the most insightful study of eighteenth-century Spanish women, Mónica Bolufer Peruga's *Mujeres e ilustración: La construcción de la femininidad en la Ilustración española*, skillfully analyzes the complexity of male and female intellectuals' beliefs about the nature and role of women in eighteenth-century Spain.[21] In her analysis, Bolufer Peruga emphasizes connections between the Spanish Enlightenment and the Enlightenment in Europe at large, as she utilizes debates about women to show that broader Enlightenment concerns echoed throughout Spain and in this particular debate.

The Emerging Female Citizen advances this growing body of scholarship by adopting a unique approach to studying eighteenth-century Spanish discourse on women. My work breaks new ground in Enlightenment studies by embracing a methodology that affirms women's central role in the Spanish Enlightenment. Through analysis of women's presence in academies, economic societies, and *tertulias*, as well as through a critique of women's literary and intellectual activities, this book interrogates more directly the interplay between views on women and women's actual lived experience than previous scholarship. Emerging discourses on women altered women's actual place in society, but key to the story I tell is how shifting gender roles in turn shaped broader discourses. In addition, my work approaches the Spanish case on its own terms and in doing so demonstrates that gender was at the heart of Enlightenment in Spain. This book argues that gender debates are not merely a window through which scholars today can view Enlightenment principles at work, but rather that these debates were central to reconfiguring Spain as an enlightened nation. In the eyes of those who witnessed it, redefining gender identities was critical to Spain's political, social, and economic modernization.

As scholars of the eighteenth century have endeavored to show that Spaniards embraced the new laissez-faire economics of Scottish Enlightenment thinkers or contemplated the nature of political rule alongside French philosophes, they have been forced to accept histories shaped by very distinct contexts. This latter example is especially instructive, as Spain's dynastic history differed substantially from that of its neighbors. Like the French thinkers and revolutionaries who articulated the rights of the *citoyen* and *citoyenne*, Spanish intellectuals formulated their own definitions of citizenship as a central part of the discussion about moving Spain toward modern nationhood. Some envisioned this new nation as a constitutional monarchy (the kind the Constitution of Cádiz defined in 1812), while others saw a country led by an enlightened monarch who would listen earnestly to the voices of his subjects. In either case, this nation would be composed of inhabitants who felt a sense of duty not to their king or the church but to the nation. Cultivating this duty in female citizens constituted a key point of concern, and thus the connection between discourses on women and on citizenship is crucial to understanding women's shifting political, social, and cultural roles in eighteenth-century Spain.

Some historians may be reluctant to use the term *citizenship* in the context of eighteenth-century Spain. This may be particularly true of French scholars for whom the notion of citizenship is tied precisely to claims made during the French Revolution for concrete political rights. It may initially seem incongruous to say that anyone could have been a citizen or enjoyed the rights of citizenship in an absolutist country like early modern Spain. Yet a discussion of citizenship focused solely on the attainment of political rights bespeaks our modern bias: an emphasis on rights, rather than the duties and responsibilities, of citizens.[22] Spaniards demonstrated an acute awareness of their responsibilities to the nation in their discussions of social, economic, and cultural reform. Intellectuals constantly referred to the *utilidad pública*, or public utility, of the programs they proposed, describing at length how these programs would have a widespread and lasting effect on the nation. These effects might not have included a broadening of the franchise or freedom from taxation, which French revolutionaries demanded; however, to limit citizenship rights to legal rights is to perpetuate a very narrow notion of politics. This is particularly problematic in discussing women's history, as feminist scholars for over a decade have argued for the need to consider politics much more broadly in discussing groups who fall outside the realm of official politics.[23] By broadening the terms of this discussion, I hope to open up women's history beyond the mainstream cases of

France, Britain, and the United States and suggest the inadequacy of existing terminology in the study of those cases.

Spain has its own story to tell, and understanding my application of *citizenship* to Spain requires consideration of the political and social milieu in which women took on these new political roles. One of the key features of the political landscape in eighteenth-century Spain was the cooperation between the monarchy and Spain's enlightened elite that characterized much of the century. That this cooperation occurred seems natural considering the history of monarchical rule in Spain. Philip du Borbonne, the grandson of the French King Louis XIV, inherited the Spanish throne after the death of Charles II in 1700. The accession of a French Bourbon king to the Spanish crown led to the War of the Spanish Succession (1702–1713). Since Philip could not rely on the support of the aristocracy, which saw the Bourbon accession as a threat to its own local power, he turned to the group of reform-minded elite, many of whom were part of Spain's bureaucratic, or *letrado*, class, which had emerged in the waning days of Charles II's reign. In this way, Philip broadened his power base and helped secure his place as king. Ironically, the installation of a French king thus occasioned a more tight-knit partnership between Spain's reformist elite and their monarch, markedly different from the frequently antagonistic relationship between philosophes and the crown in France. This new Spanish elite became highly influential in shaping the nature of the Bourbon monarchy during the reigns of Philip V (1700–1746) and his sons Ferdinand VI (1746–1759) and Charles III (1759–1788). The expansion of the European economy and the growth of Atlantic trade provided funds for the realization of part of this group's reform agenda.

Scholars outside Spain often question how "enlightened" royal-sponsored institutions could be. After all, the monarch's influence would seem to limit the possible ideas intellectuals could express within those institutions. The Economic Societies provide compelling evidence that royal influence did not hinder Spain's Enlightenment thinkers. These societies—royal-sponsored institutions designed to promote the cultural and economic regeneration of Spain—played a key role in eighteenth century discourse and reform. Part of the reason for these institutions' importance was that they created a forum for discussing issues central to Spain's future. Mónica Bolufer Peruga and Isabel Morant Deusa have said of the Economic Societies: "They also created a public sphere for discussion and, if generally limited by collaboration with enlightened absolutism, they sometimes fostered debate which went further in its critical implications. In fact, some of their most radical members considered them to be, in some way, a kind of political assembly which would contribute, through its advice, to legitimate the king's power to govern and reform."[24] In creating a space for public discourse, these royal societies moved beyond state institutions and helped intellectuals to formulate their reform agenda. More than simply groups of aristocrats in collusion with the crown, these were thriving institutions that fostered public debate beyond their walls.

This collaboration, which reached a height during the reign of Charles III, nearly disintegrated when his son Charles IV ascended the throne in 1788. The full-blown revolution that broke out next door created a climate of anxiety at court. Fears about the uprisings in France led Charles to quash information coming in from across the Pyrenees, though internal channels of Enlightenment continued to operate into the 1790s. In 1790, Charles began to undermine the influence of enlightened thinkers, such as Gaspar Melchor de Jovellanos, in the government's operations, and, in 1792, he dismissed the Count of Floridablanca, who had been a pivotal figure in encouraging collaboration between the monarch and Spain's Enlightenment elite. There is some evidence that this last decision resulted from a personal vendetta on behalf of the king's wife, María Luisa. Suspected of having an affair with the royal guardsman Manuel Godoy, María Luisa may have harbored resentment against Floridablanca for advocating the dismissal of her lover. Spaniards became even more concerned when Charles IV appointed Godoy as his first secretary late in 1792, suggesting his role as "the willing cuckold."[25] As Charles declared war on France in 1793 and stepped up measures to keep knowledge of the events in France from seeping into the country, the flow of French propaganda and information on the Revolution continued unabated, particularly as émigrés began to flood the country.

Richard Herr has argued that this constant stream of information, however, proved unimportant, as Spaniards en masse showed that they were not behind the revolutionaries. Herr explains, "The Spanish people, by their attachment to the monarchy and the Catholic religion, were poorly prepared to approve of the events in France."[26] While Herr paints this as the product of a successful propaganda campaign on behalf of the church and monarch, what it truly shows is how the productive collusion of crown and intellectual had shaped the Enlightenment project in Spain. In fact, the French Revolution, with its chaos and bloodshed, did not represent the kind of peaceful and cooperative transition that Spanish intellectuals themselves had been developing and implementing. And even those who did embrace the rhetoric of the Revolution and called for a French victory in the war against Spain following Godoy's appointment did not truly sympathize with the revolutionary cause. As Herr himself has written, "The desire they repeatedly expressed for a French victory was a symptom rather of their exasperation with Godoy and María Luisa than of true sympathy for the French Republic."[27] When the war ended in August 1795, Enlightenment reformers had already picked up where they had left off. The French Revolution had not brought an end to Spain's Enlightenments.[28]

That Spanish thinkers did not always agree on what shape the nation should take became painfully clear when Napoleon invaded Spain in 1808. After over a century of Enlightenment discourse, it was only natural that distinct visions of Spain's future eventually emerged, creating deep fissures in Spanish society. These divisions did not develop overnight, nor in response to any one event; rather, they resulted from ongoing negotiation and debate among Spanish intellectuals. As reformers increasingly embraced liberal ideals, traditional forces, particularly the church, became concerned about the extent to which they might be excluded in this vision of a new Spain. When more liberal forces dominated the national Cortes—called in 1810 to determine how to proceed after Napoleon's forces had overtaken the Spanish monarch—and formulated a very radical constitution in 1812, the split became even more pronounced. The attempt to realize in the constitution much of the Enlightenment elites' agenda for reform was cut short by the restoration of Ferdinand VII in 1814. Spain's new monarch, eschewing the tradition of cooperative rule forged by his predecessors, threw out the constitution and dismissed the Cortes. This exacerbated the divisions already apparent in Spanish society, contributing to a tumultuous and unstable interval in the nineteenth century.

It is tempting to look to the French Revolution or the Napoleonic invasion to answer the question of why women, present in much of Spain's political discourse beginning in the 1740s, disappeared from most public institutions in the early nineteenth century. After all, as noted above, many scholars have seen the French Revolution as a pivotal moment in women's exclusion from the polity in France. And clearly, the Revolution played a role in Spanish politics at large. Yet women's relegation to the domestic sphere in the early nineteenth century began in liberal debates long before the storming of the Bastille. Liberal ideology was not inherently masculinist. But, in practice, many Enlightenment elites in Spain came to define women's citizenship in the emerging liberal nation in a way that limited women's role and thus confined them to the domestic realm. A careful assessment of Spanish debates over women's role in the nation indicates that male intellectuals even at the high tide of Enlightenment sentiment defined women's contribution to the nation according to gender and rank.

The responses of women to this vision of circumscribed citizenship varied. A number of women capitalized on their inclusion and, in the face of the imposed limitations, forged their own female space for civic action. That is, they carved out a sphere of activity for women based on concerns purportedly unique to the female sex. However, for the most part, their strategies for forging a more active citizenship role for women moved them away from universalist political arguments and often underscored women's difference from, rather than equality to, men. Thus, while the presence of liberal ideology helped facilitate women's entry into the realm of public debate, the context in which they were forced to maneuver prevented their sustained presence in political life. The evolution of this dialogue between enlightened women and men shows how the process of gendering the polity as male was neither an ideological given nor the result of a single event no matter how momentous.

Part 1 of my book tracks the debates and events that shaped women's entry into Spain's emerging world of letters. This section shows that the terms of the debate quickly shifted from a broadly framed universalist political discourse to an emphasis on men's and women's different social roles and potential contributions. Chapter 1 argues that the relationship between the woman question and women's everyday lives took on new meaning in the eighteenth century with the creation of a larger reading public and wider arenas of public debate. This is exemplified in the intense debates on women and society in Spain in the 1720s and 1730s, particularly the discussion of the question of female equality spurred by the 1726 publication of Fray Benito Jerónimo Feijoo y Montenegro's *Defense of Women*. This renewed and widespread attention to the woman question paralleled contemporary discussions in other parts of western Europe.

Chapter 2 argues that by the 1740s and 1750s much of Spain's intelligentsia had accepted the idea that women were rational and thus equal beings. Key to this assessment was women's participation in two leading Enlightenment institutions in Spain: the Academy of Fine Arts of San Fernando and the *tertulia*, a gathering similar to the French salon. The acceptance of women as both contributors to and facilitators of Spain's burgeoning world of letters suggests changing notions of women's status in society. Once female equality was established and women's status began to change, a new debate over women's proper role in society occupied intellectuals in the 1760s and 1770s.

Much of this debate centered on the question of female admission to the Economic Society of Madrid, the topic of chapter 3. The intense debate over women's admission to the Madrid branch spanned more than a decade, lasting from 1775, when the organization was founded, to 1786, when the king agreed to create a *junta de damas*, or women's auxiliary. An analysis of the arguments for women's membership in the organization suggests that even male members in favor of women's admission did not envision women as active participants. This vision of women as passive members of the association is particularly apparent when the arguments of two female intellectuals who contributed to the debate are contrasted with the views of their male counterparts. This chapter locates the discussion of women's place in this organization and in society at large in the context of Spanish intellectuals' calls for national reform. It argues that the architects of a new Spain focused on the particular obligations of female citizens, thereby limiting the role they would play in the new nation. In addition, it contends that intellectuals posited a status-specific definition of female citizenship. They differentiated between working-class women, who would serve the nation as producers, and elite women, who would be good consumers.

Part 2 analyzes how women responded to the vision of limited female citizenship that came out of the debates of the 1760s and 1770s. Although women's strategies had definite short-term success, they contained detrimental long-term implications for women's place in Spanish society. Chapter 4 explores how women carved out their own space in the realm of public debate by focusing on two cases: censorial appeals from female writers for publication of their texts; and debates over the statutes of the *junta de damas* and its relationship to the larger organization of the Economic Society. These two examples suggest the seemingly contradictory ways that women defined their roles in response to the circumscribed citizenship that male intellectuals articulated. At times, women's censorial appeals implicitly acknowledged their right to equal access to a public audience. At other times, female authors asserted their unique position as women writers to their advantage. In the case of the *junta de damas*, women both emphasized their integration in the larger society to gain certain rights and pointed to their relegation to a separate council as a sign of their independence. While the strategies female authors and female council members adopted enabled their participation in Spain's Enlightenment reform, the long-term effects of these mixed appeals ultimately made women's position in public life less tenable.

Chapter 5 argues that many women conceived of their public activities as part of a uniquely female sphere of action. This was true of many female authors who concerned themselves with issues they considered unique to the female sex and who often addressed their works to a female audience. The conception of this female sphere is clearest in the agenda that the *junta de damas* established for itself. The members of the women's council saw themselves as mothers to the nation, and, in line with the doctrine of Republican Motherhood that they and other writers espoused, they worked to educate women to fulfill their proper roles as citizens. As did many male intellectuals, the women of the *junta de damas* adopted a class-based vision of female citizenship, focusing on preparing elite women for their role as mothers and poorer women for their role as workers.

The book's final chapter investigates the work of women translators and suggests how some women, in creating their own sphere of action, interpreted liberal discourse. Women's use of translation as a safer means to express their views in print evidences women's pursuit of a place in the public discourse, not dissimilar to the struggles of women writers or members of the *junta de damas*. However, discussion of their texts shows that some prominent translators underscored women's passion at the same time they claimed that women possessed innate reason. This method of argumentation proved an awkward fit; it undermined the attempt to make women equal citizens of a liberal state based on rational, public debate. Thus the story of women in eighteenth-century Spain is one of gains and losses. While women capitalized on the new vision of equality inherent in Enlightenment discourse, their efforts to establish a prominent place for themselves among Spain's reform elite ultimately excluded them from it altogether. This was not a foretold conclusion, but one that the interplay of gender discourse and social change ultimately produced.

PART I

Developing Ideologies of Citizenship

1 The Woman Question

> In an immense imbroglio I place myself. It is not only against the ignorant commoner with whom I enter contest: to defend all women comes to be the same as to offend almost all men, since rare is he that is not interested in building up his sex at the expense of the other.
>
> BENITO JERÓNIMO FEIJOO Y MONTENEGRO, *Defensa de la mujer*

The prophetic opening lines of Fray Benito Jerónimo Feijoo y Montenegro's *Defensa de la mujer* (Defense of Women), published in 1726, provoked contemporary readers.[1] Antagonizing and shocking some, persuading and rousing others, Feijoo's landmark essay sparked a heated debate on the nature of women that continued well into the 1730s. Published in the first volume of Feijoo's eight-volume compendium *Teatro crítico universal* (1726–1740), the *Defense* questioned the long-standing view of women as inferior creatures whose nature dictated their lowly station. That the writings of a single monk essentially revolutionized the discussion about women in Spain may seem surprising to modern readers, but scholars have uncovered at least twenty-one direct responses to Feijoo's *Defense*, suggesting his contemporaries found his ideas on women highly provocative.

Feijoo's writings, which often prompted this kind of public debate, came to occupy a central place in Enlightenment discourse.[2] His *Teatro crítico* can be likened to Diderot's widely read *Encyclopédie* (1745–1772) in terms of both its attempt to take on a broad philosophical agenda and its place as a defining text in the minds of his contemporary readers. Printers issued twenty editions—more than three thousand copies—of the *Teatro crítico* between 1726 and 1787 alone, and the text became an essential point of departure for the aspiring intellectual in Spain.[3] As Richard Herr observes, "Only one work rivaled Feyjóo's [sic] in popularity, and that was the ever-loved *Don Quixote*."[4] Outside Spain, Feijoo's essay on women became one of his best-known texts in the 1700s. Not only did excerpts with commentary appear in the French periodicals *Mercure de France* and *Mémoires de Trévoux* in the 1730s, but by century's end his work also had enjoyed translation into French and English and partial translation into Italian and Portuguese.[5]

In part because of its popularity, Feijoo's essay on women helped engineer a significant shift in the relationship between gender discourse and women's lives in Spain. As in other European countries, in Spain the role women should play in society had been fodder for discussion for centuries. However, during most of the early modern period, the woman question remained principally theoretical. While writings prescribing women's appropriate station in society solidified traditional views of inequality and submission into the 1700s, these views did not define women's lives. Rather, a wide gap existed between women's lived experience in fifteenth-, sixteenth-, and seventeenth-century Spain and the doctrine of female enclosure and inferiority that dominated early modern Spanish writings.

The publication of Feijoo's essay, however, raised the woman question among a wider circle of intellectuals than had considered it before. The incorporation of more minds—including an unprecedented number of female authors—into the debate over women's place in society helped move these discussions off the page and into real life by building the base for genuine social change. By the time the furor surrounding Feijoo's essay on women fizzled out in the late 1730s, a significant number of Spain's intellectual elite were convinced by the Benedictine's assertion of female equality. As these young reformers began to reimagine Spanish society and create institutions focused on improving the nation, their newfound belief in women's natural equality and potential intellectual capabilities led them to include the female sex in their blueprint for reform.

THE WOMAN QUESTION IN EARLY MODERN SPAIN

To understand the nature of these eighteenth-century debates on women, it is instructive to look back at the development of the woman question in early modern Spain, perhaps beginning with the marriage of Ferdinand and Isabel in 1469, which has long been the starting point for histories of Spain. After all, this historic union created Spain as we know it today, through the unification of the crowns of Aragon and Castile. Less often considered is how the marriage gave the woman question a new force and urgency with the ascension of the strong-willed and intelligent Isabel to the throne. When Isabel took the throne in 1474, discussion on the place of women in society was in full swing throughout Europe. Estimates figure an astounding one thousand works concerned with the nature and role of the female sex were written in Europe in the fifteenth and sixteenth centuries, not counting reprints and translations.[6]

In varying ways, these writings aimed to challenge or shore up the dominant view on women derived from the Bible and the writings of early church fathers. As this existing paradigm explained, women, the descendents of Eve, were at once manipulative and sinful, gullible and frail. While some authors would challenge this notion of women as evil and weak, it would remain the dominant gender ideology in Spain into the 1700s. Nevertheless, texts promoting women's enclosure and praising male rule—two antidotes to women's capricious nature—more likely constituted reactions to, rather than shapers of, women's behavior. Isabel and countless other Spanish women lived more public and more active lives than promoters of patriarchy desired.

In the half century before Isabel's reign, some writers had already begun to seriously challenge the underpinnings of the dominant misogynist discourse. One of the earliest critiques in Spain of the portrait of women as weak and wicked came in Enrique de Villena's 1417 *Doce trabajos de Hércules*. Villena devoted an entire chapter of his work to the merits of women, noting that their natural virtues helped inspire the best in men.[7] Villena's departure from the prevailing image of Eve corrupting man became a common trope of pro-female writers. Similarly, Juan Rodríguez del Padrón's 1443 *Triunfo de las donas* elucidates women's strengths and argues for female superiority. Along with more mainstream arguments about female chastity and beauty, Rodríguez del Padrón introduced a rather bizarre line of reasoning. He contended that the fact that women's genitalia are more concealed than men's points to their moral superiority.[8] Rather than argue for female superiority, Álvaro de Luna, in his 1446 *Libro de las virtuosas y claras mugeres*, claimed that society must recognize the many women who behave virtuously. His text, which lists such noteworthy women, revised the negative view of the female sex, which he believed was based on the behavior of a few misguided women. These three works exemplify the variety of defenses of the female sex that fifteenth-century thinkers composed in the face of the predominant anti-female view.[9] These early defenses focused on reversing the notion of women's inherent weakness and sinfulness, but did little to consider how this reversal might alter women's social roles.

Isabel's first year as queen shows the difficulties not only of negotiating this dynamic and evolving gender landscape but also of capitalizing on the possibilities that the proliferation of pro-female texts provided.[10] Isabel's reign proved a challenge from the start, since her right to succession was highly contested. The dispute over who should inherit the throne of Castile left vacant by the death of Enrique IV in December 1474 involved two main contenders: Enrique's daughter Juana—the rightful heir—and Enrique's half-sister Isabel. A large portion of the nobility, exasperated by Enrique's rule, rejected Juana. It did not help Juana's case that a prominent rumor made her the illegitimate daughter of Enrique's wife, Juana, and the court advisor Beltrán de la Cueva, earning her the nickname "Juana la Beltraneja."[11] Repulsed by a supposed bastard daughter and a cuckolded king, some nobles looked to Isabel to return strong rule to Spain.[12]

Isabel immediately proved that she was up to the task. When she learned of Enrique's death, Isabel took matters into her own hands and staged an acclamation ceremony—without Ferdinand—proclaiming herself the rightful ruler of Castile. Studies of chroniclers' reactions to this ceremony show that her supporters and critics focused on her highly symbolic use of an unsheathed sword in the procession. Her supporters defended her right to use this very masculine symbol of justice by pointing out that she, the sovereign ruler of Castile, needed to restore order at a time when questions over the succession could throw the kingdom into crisis. Meanwhile, her critics blasted her use of the sword as an unacceptable usurpation of Ferdinand's role as both her husband and the king. As Elizabeth Lehfeldt explains, "The action seemed to them a foolish display of a wife ostentatiously taking on the attributes of her husband."[13] Martín de Córdoba, in his 1468 advice manual *Jardín de las nobles doncellas*, which he presented to Isabel on the eve of her marriage to Ferdinand, made clear that the role she should play was very different from that of her spouse. In his account, "the husband/king was father, judge, and sword, while the queen was mother, advocate, and shield."[14] Worried about the weak nature of women, Córdoba warned Isabel to be dutiful and faithful.

This was advice she only partly followed. When Ferdinand and his troops initially retreated from battle against the warring supporters of Juana at Toro in 1474, Isabel publicly dressed him down for his defeat. Often compared to the speech England's Elizabeth I gave to her troops at Tilbury in 1588, Isabel's words dismissed the notion that her female body hindered her from judging the soldiers' performance: "Whether women lack discretion to know, and the courage to dare, and the tongue to speak, I have found that we have eyes to see."[15] Isabel, whose library included writings by Christine de Pizan and other proto-feminist writers, emerged as a strong leader and formidable challenge, even to her husband, Ferdinand.[16] The strength she displayed helped her to counter the image of a weak monarch left behind by the effeminate Enrique.

At the same time, however, Isabel had to take care that her sexuality was not impugned the way Enrique's had been. Isabel's chroniclers emphasized her marriage to Ferdinand and portrayed her as, if not the consummate wife, the ideal mother. By likening her to the Virgin Mary, Isabel's chroniclers cast the queen's sexualized female body in positive terms and tried to counter the negative portrayal of women that focused on the figure of Eve. As Lehfeldt explains, "Mary had offered the world the ultimate redemption: the son of God. Isabel offered a similar redemption. She gave Castile an indisputable male heir who stood in a direct line to the throne."[17] The careful image that Isabel constructed, as well as the consternation that her presence on the throne produced for some contemporaries, shows that despite developing critiques of traditional views on the female sex, the old misogynistic discourse still dominated views on women in fifteenth-century Castile.

Isabel, however, was not the only woman who successfully negotiated a place of power in this highly patriarchal society. The dynamism of a society in the throes of imperial expansion presented numerous women with opportunities for empowerment. In the southern city of Seville, near the thriving port of Cádiz, for example, the years surrounding 1492 witnessed dramatic demographic change, a flourishing economy, and colonial expansion that thrust Sevillian women into a new, more public role. Partly because of the emigration of many of the city's men to the Americas, women assumed increasing responsibility for crucial family and business decisions. They bought, sold, and rented property; they negotiated marriages for their children; and they even pursued commercial ventures.[18] Andres Navagero, the Venetian ambassador to Spain, remarked on women's shifting place in Sevillian society in 1525, when he described the city as being "in the hands of women."[19] Not surprisingly, women's increased power created anxiety, particularly among the clergy. As Mary Elizabeth Perry explains, "Gender beliefs that women required special protective enclosure seemed to be even more strongly invoked as men's preoccupation with wars and colonizing required women to participate more actively in the life of the city."[20] In this case, the proliferation of texts praising women's enclosure actually bespoke women's active presence in public life.

This dynamic environment extended into the colonies themselves, and more than one woman found a degree of liberation in the Americas. Among the most outrageous examples is Catalina de Erauso, a woman who shed the privileges attached to her noble birth, and her nun's habit, and headed to the colonies. Donning men's clothing, Erauso became a fierce warrior and something of a ladies' man. When her cross-dressing was discovered and Erauso was forced to return to Europe, she successfully gained a papal dispensation to wear men's clothing and a regular pension from the king of Spain in gratitude for her military service. Erauso's behavior could be forgiven, even celebrated, because it proved male superiority in the very lengths a woman would go to in order to become a man.[21]

A number of women in early modern Spain also found power from within the confines of the convent. Many nuns and abbesses enjoyed economic sway, based on their control over large estates.[22] Administering the often diversified properties that these elite institutions held involved mastery of complex financial transactions. Nuns oversaw production on landed estates, sold goods in the marketplace, collected rents on urban properties, served as creditors, collected taxes or annuities based on bestowed privileges, filed lawsuits, and became skilled bookkeepers. Handling many of these affairs took nuns outside the convent's walls. Rather than living truly apart from the secular world, women in convents resided in "permeable cloisters," as Elizabeth Lehfeldt demonstrates in her 2005 study of convents in early modern Valladolid.[23] As founders and patrons of religious houses, aristocratic women—often as widows—forged female communities that became centers of female learning and independence while also demonstrating their wealth and prestige in a highly corporate society.[24] And, of course, the Carmelite nun Santa Teresa de Jesús of Avila (1515–1582), who founded seventeen religious houses and wrote numerous spiritual works during her lifetime, helped shape the character of female monastic life throughout Castile.[25] Even after the Council of Trent, generally seen as a negative turning point for female religious, women in Spanish convents enjoyed positions of prominence in local communities.[26]

Some aristocratic women even found religious enclosure a useful position from which to exercise influence over national politics. The most well-documented case of this involves two women related to Philip III who resided at the Convent of the Descalzas Reales in Madrid: Empress María, Philip's grandmother, and her daughter Margaret of the Cross. Along with Philip's wife, Margaret of Austria, who lived at court, these women forged political networks that allowed them to influence Philip's decisions to such a degree that his favorite advisor, the Duke of Lerma, pushed for the court's relocation to Valladolid in 1601, far from the reaches of the Madrid-based convent. The cloistered world of the Descalzas Reales enabled Empress María and her daughter to have extended visits with Philip III and other influential relatives in seclusion, away from the eyes and ears at court.[27]

While certainly only a small number of women influenced state policy from inside the convent, women successfully negotiated the strict legal and inquisitorial barriers of early modern Spanish society. Noble women, drawing on the limited power over family property that partible inheritance laws offered, sought to advance their families' power and prestige in the kingdom in myriad ways, from commissioning paintings to arranging marriages.[28] *Beatas*, spiritual laywomen affiliated with religious orders, led independent lives away from priests, husbands, and other male watchdogs. Women like Mariana de Jesús and Lucía de Jesús, who rejected their fathers' intentions to marry them off, and María Pérez de Ocampo, who fled her domineering stepfather, found freedom and spiritual fulfillment among other women.[29] Non-Christian women, bound to have even less power than their Christian counterparts, also found ways to elude patriarchal control. By preserving religious traditions in the home, including those concerning dress, food, and Sabbath rituals, Jewish women sidestepped the Inquisition's aim to regulate their beliefs. In fact, as the Inquisition thrust non-Christian religious observance out of the public realm, women's role in the home became even more important.[30] Extensive research in notarial and judicial archives in the past twenty years has demonstrated how women of varying ranks and classes manipulated the legal system to their advantage.[31]

Women's lived experiences aside, the dominant gender paradigm remained one that made women the charges of men, both their subjects and their defining characteristic. Women's enclosure in either convents or marriage was considered essential to uphold their virginity or virtue and thus, by extension, the honor and reputation of their male relatives. Lotario, a character in Miguel Cervantes's *Don Quixote*, explains, "As the flesh of the wife is one with the flesh of the husband, the blemishes which fall on her or the defects she incurs recoil upon the flesh of the husband, although, as I have said, he may be in no respect the cause of the trouble."[32] In Spain, where seven centuries of Christian, Jewish, and Muslim cohabitation resulted in heightened fears about miscegenation, controlling women's reproductive bodies was of critical social importance. Christian families endeavored to keep their family lines "clean," to ensure *limpieza de sangre*, or "purity of blood," meaning no traces of Jewish ancestry in their family trees. As laws excluding those with unclean blood from holding state and church offices codified the importance of racial purity in the late fifteenth and the sixteenth centuries, it would not do to leave women, considered easily duped and naturally lustful, unguarded.

Two conduct books written for women in the sixteenth century illustrate this negative view of the female sex: Juan Luis Vives's *De institutione feminae christianae*, commissioned by the English queen Catherine of Aragon for her daughter Mary Tudor and first printed in 1523; and Fray Luis de León's 1583 *La perfecta casada*. These books are worth looking at in depth partly because of the tremendous circulation they enjoyed, both in their day and beyond.³³ Vives's and León's texts constituted the chief authorities on women's comportment in early modern Spain and were certain to figure in the limited education of any elite woman. Not surprisingly, both of these texts followed the traditional Christian tale of women as being easily corrupted and prone to evil. For example, in arguing that women should not be teachers, Vives resorts to the age-old condemnation of Eve:

> For Adam was created first, then Eve, and Adam was not seduced but the woman was seduced and led astray. Therefore, since woman is a weak creature and of uncertain judgment and is easily deceived (as Eve, the first parent of mankind, demonstrated, whom the devil deluded with such a slight pretext), she should not teach, lest when she has convinced herself of some false opinion, she transmit it to her listeners in her role as a teacher and easily drag others into her error, since pupils willingly follow their teacher.³⁴

La perfecta casada, presented as a wedding present for León's niece María Varela Osorio, concurs in Vives's negative description of women. When León comments on "the good wife" in chapter 1, for example, it is to note that such a woman "is a rare thing."³⁵

Vives and León believed women to be highly susceptible to outside influences and prone to evil, so they stressed the necessity for women to be subject to their husbands. Vives explains, "The woman is still the daughter of the man and weaker, and for that reason needs his protection. And when she is bereft of her husband, she is alone, naked, exposed to harm."³⁶ Likewise, León makes no mistake about the inferior status of wives in marriage when he writes, "The state of the wife, in comparison to the husband, is a humble state."³⁷ Women's humble state relegated them to the home. *La perfecta casada* explains, "As men are made for public, women are made for enclosure; and as men are made to speak and go outside, women are made to enclose and cover themselves."³⁸

Being a good woman not only meant staying at home but also meant managing domestic affairs. Vives, for example, ranked skill in household governance as being among the most important traits of a Christian woman: "If to the two virtues of chastity and great love for one's husband there is added skill in governing a household, then marriages become happier and more harmonious."³⁹ León's manual outlined so many household responsibilities for women that one twentieth-century commentator jibed that the book should be renamed "the perfect prisoner, enslaved by one thousand chores."⁴⁰ For Fray Luis, the relationship between a woman and her home was something special and unique. He explains, "It has to be understood that her house is a body and she is its spirit."⁴¹ Both León's and Vives's texts imbued women's domestic responsibilities and private enclosure with importance, perhaps in order to keep women in their place.

The need to enclose women at home stemmed from the need to safeguard them. As Vives explains, "An unmarried young woman should rarely appear in public, since she has no business there and her most precious possession, her chastity, is placed in jeopardy."[42] For a single woman, Vives explains, virginity is the ultimate virtue; but a married woman need conform to an even longer set of rules. She must be loyal, dedicated, and obedient to her spouse; she must dress appropriately, covering her face in public; she must not allow any man into her house without her husband's permission. While a wife's obedience and dedication to her spouse determined her honor, a husband's honor stemmed from his ability to control his wife and ensure she remained virtuous. Vives expresses this rule in his rhetorical query "But who can have respect for a man who he sees is ruled by a woman?"[43] Not surprisingly, Vives's text for husbands, *De los deberes del marido*, fills less than half the pages of his advice book for women and focuses substantially on selecting and governing a good wife rather than detailing how a husband should behave in his own right.

Legal codes reinforced the views expressed in Vives's and León's works. For example, the law made adultery a civil crime for women but not for men, and a husband who found his wife committing adultery could kill her without fear of punishment. For men, bigamy constituted the only comparable crime, and even if a man were found guilty it was the authorities, not a jealous wife, who doled out his punishment.[44] Clearly, in early modern Spain, wives' and daughters' actions, rather than men's own, determined male honor and reputation. Accordingly, women had to be constantly scrutinized; their behavior, suitably controlled.

While women like Isabel and Catalina de Erauso challenged these rules in their everyday lives, a small group of female authors began to oppose them in print. By far the most outspoken critic of patriarchy in seventeenth-century Spain was the author María de Zayas y Sotomayor (b. 1590), most celebrated for her composition of two novella collections, *Novelas amorosas y ejemplares* (1637) and *Desengaños amorosos* (1647).[45] An elite woman whose presence in Madrid's literary circles between 1621 and 1647 earned her the respect of first-class playwrights like Lope de Vega, Zayas devoted much of her writing to exposing the flaws inherent in Spain's gender system. Her critique came at a crucial time for women. While the rise of humanism had opened up some opportunities for elite women's education in sixteenth-century Spain, the Counter-Reformation questioned the merits of training women in the classics and further entrenched traditional gender relations.[46] Zayas lamented women's lack of education and called into doubt the ability of a patriarchal society to truly protect women as it proposed to do. Her collections, published in more than ten Spanish editions and numerous translations and adaptations, were contemporary best-sellers and remained popular into the nineteenth century.[47] Even the English diarist Samuel Pepys had one of Zayas's books in his library.[48]

In her writings, Zayas questioned the notion that women were inherently inferior to men. Through a female protagonist, she contends, "Whether this matter that we men and women are made of is a bonding of clay and fire, or a dough of earth and spirit, it has no more nobility in men than in women, if our blood is the same, if our senses, our powers, and the organs that perform their functions are all the same; our souls the same, for souls are neither male nor female."[49] Here Zayas's character expresses the view that it was not women's bodies, but their upbringing, that handicapped them. However, in arguing for women's intellectual capabilities, Zayas hesitates to fully commit to a new paradigm of physical equality. She writes, "The real reason why women are not learned is not a defect in intelligence but a lack of opportunity[,] because if, in our upbringing, our parents gave us books and teachers instead of putting cambric on our sewing cushions and patterns in our embroidery frames, we would be as fit as men for any job or university professorship. Since intelligence consists of the damp humor, we might even be sharper because we're of a colder humor."[50] By claiming both that a proper education would make women men's equals and that female anatomy suggests women's mental superiority, Zayas's text reveals just how difficult it could be to break free from entrenched notions of the sexes, even for a radical-minded author like Zayas.

In addition to arguing for women's education, Zayas also critiques a society that blamed women for men's actions: "Because men preside over everything, they never tell about the evil deeds they do, they tell only about the ones done to them. If you think about it, men are really the ones at fault and women go along with them, thinking they must be right."[51] Her stories of male violence and female victims highlight some of the problems she identified in Spain's honor system. One story, "Mal presagio casar lejos," details the deaths of four wives murdered by their husbands. Victims of false accusations of marital infidelity, these characters suffer cruel and violent deaths. Zayas's graphic text reads like a modern-day crime novel: "Her husband came in through the dressing room door and with her own hair, which was very beautiful, he made a noose around her neck and strangled her. Then he poisoned the little boy, saying that he didn't want a child of questionable background to inherit his estate."[52] Even more disturbing are

Zayas's depictions of the female victims. For example, in one story, when the main character Camila confides to her husband that she was raped, he poisons her to avenge his honor. The narrator describes Camila's victimized body: "Her whole body [swelled] monstrously: her arms and her legs looked like huge pillars and her stomach distended at least a rod from her waistline."[53] Through her gruesome descriptions, Zayas crafted a critique of a social code that victimized women and children by placing their lives in the hands of conniving and cruel men.

By way of solution, Zayas pointed women toward each other. In female friendship and often in the separate world of the convent, Zayas suggested, women could escape the brutality of a misogynistic society. As the literary scholar Lisa Vollendorf explains, "Like other women writers—such as Christine de Pizan, Hélisenne de Crenne, Moderata Fonte, and Margaret Cavendish—Zayas depicts women's friendship and an all-female environment as antidotes to male-dominated society."[54] This comes through in the ending of *Desengaños amorosos* when Zayas's main narrator, Lisis, reveals her decision to forego her impending nuptials and enter the convent instead. With this plot twist, Zayas thwarts the convention of her adopted genre, the *maravilla* (enchantments), patterned in the style of Cervantes's 1612 *Novelas ejemplares*. While these stories traditionally ended with a marriage, Zayas has her heroine, Lisis, run off to the convent. According to Vollendorf, "Lisis urges men to change their ways and she urges other women to follow her to safety so they will not meet the same fate as the raped, tortured, and dead women whose stories have been told throughout the collection."[55]

Zayas provides a biting critique of feminine victimization in seventeenth-century Spain. Her pro-woman writings, grounded in a larger trajectory both in and outside of Spain, put into print a challenge to patriarchy that many women voiced in their everyday lives. The solution of female solidarity and seclusion Zayas posited shows just how dire she judged women's situation to be. For many women in Spain in the decades that followed, Zayas's texts provided an important catalyst for action. For example, when Clara Jara de Soto requested permission to print her manuscript *Las tertulias murcianas* in 1790, she explained that her work was fashioned after that of Zayas.[56] The rejection letter she received from Antonio de Capmany y de Montpalau revealed his dislike of her chosen exemplar: "I certify that in one of the meetings celebrated by the said [Royal] Academy [of History], the member of the Academy to whom it was assigned to examine the work titled *Las tertulias murcianas*, read the judgment that he had formed of its content[s], and he explained them to be some stories that the author composed [using] those of Doña María de Zayas for a model, [stories that,] with less refined style and less imagination, have all the defects of those of Zayas." The list of problems with *Las tertulias murcianas* went on and on: it was neither educational nor entertaining, it failed to observe traditional theatrical norms, it contained weak dialogue, it presented unbelievable and undeveloped characters, and it was driven by an awkward plot.[57] Not surprisingly, the academy, Capmany explained, saw no utility in publishing such a work. While Zayas's influence on writers like Soto may have been profound, her popularity did not necessarily signify her acceptance among Spain's intellectual elite. It was another, more masculine, voice that would lead Spain's most prominent thinkers to reconsider their views on the female sex.

FEIJOO AND FEMALE EQUALITY

When Benito Jerónimo Feijoo y Montenegro (1676–1764) published his *Defense of Women* in 1726, he sparked anew the debate on women that had begun in Spain centuries earlier. In his essay, Feijoo set out to prove women's moral, physical, and intellectual equality to men.[58] In doing so, he incorporated the works of recent European theorists into the old *querelle des femmes* (woman question), serving to shift the debate into new terms. As a student and then professor of theology, Feijoo devoted a serious portion of his time to reading foreign books largely unknown in Spain, texts like Francis Bacon's *Novum Organum* (1620), Nicolas Malebranche's *De la recherche de la vérité* (1674–75), and Pierre Bayle's *Dictionnaire historique et critique* (1697). Shaped by the dismal portrait of his native land found in many European texts, Feijoo set out to improve the level of knowledge in his own country with his *Teatro crítico universal*. From the age of fifty to eighty-eight, Feijoo endeavored through his writings to acquaint Spanish intellectuals with recent mental giants like René Descartes, Isaac Newton, and even Jean-Jacques Rousseau.[59]

Feijoo's *Defense* resonated with a number of these newly influential European thinkers, particularly Bacon. One of Feijoo's major goals in writing the *Defense* was to show the flaws of Aristotelian-based scholasticism. In contrast to this old method of inquiry, in which thinkers generalized truths from speculative reasoning, Feijoo advocated reasoning based in empiricism. He expresses his early emphasis on experiential knowledge in one of his childhood remembrances:

> When I was a boy, everyone said that it was very dangerous to eat anything right after the [morning] hot chocolate. My mind, for some reason

which I could not then perhaps have explained very well, was so skeptical of this common apprehension that I decided to make [an] experiment.... Immediately after my chocolate, I ate a large quantity of fried salt pork, and I felt fine that day and for a long time thereafter, wherefore I had the satisfaction of laughing at those who were possessed by this fear.[60]

This underpinning of Feijoo's thinking comes through in his argument against women's physical inferiority. First, he sums up the dominant view, which labeled woman "an imperfect and even monstrous creature, affirming that the design of nature in the work of generation always intends a male, and only by error or defect in either matter or faculty produces a female."[61] Here, Feijoo confronts a common belief, since not until much later in the eighteenth century did scientists contend that men and women were actually two different sexes, rather than perfect and imperfect forms of the same sex.[62]

In Spain, the notion that women's bodies spoke to their inferiority was well established in the writings of the humanist scholar Huarte de San Juan, notably his 1575 *Examen de ingenios*. Feijoo ridicules the idea that women are imperfect creatures by means of a series of rhetorical questions that suggest the inadequacy of the current view. Since nature relies on the existence of both sexes for its propagation, he states, how can anyone say that a female is simply a mistake? And since more females than males are born, he continues, are we to assume that nature is more often incorrect? And how do we explain the birth of supposedly lowly creatures from perfectly healthy and strong parents, he muses. These sorts of observations led Feijoo to dismiss the notion that women were physically inferior.

In addition to attacking this paradigm in the abstract, Feijoo also directed his critique at particular theorists. One of his main victims was the twelfth-century Parisian doctor Almarico, who posited that, if man had continued in a state of innocence, every human would have been born a man from the hands of God himself. Feijoo mocks Almarico, whom he calls "a blind follower of Aristotle," for drawing erroneous conclusions from Aristotle's own diatribes against women. Similarly, Feijoo criticizes Augustine for his belief that "in the Universal Resurrection this imperfect work would be perfected, changing all women into the male sex."[63] Here again, Feijoo's critique shows the problems with speculative reasoning and argues for the value of Bacon's empirical approach. With these examples, Feijoo questions both the erroneous beliefs and irrational methodologies of those who supported doctrines of female inferiority.

That Feijoo was reacting to the negative view of women that continued to dominate both within and outside of Spain during the early modern period is clear throughout the *Defense*. Feijoo continually references the "infinite books" that served as invectives against the female sex, the kind that women like Pizan and Zayas railed against. He points to the hypocrisy of their authors, citing among his examples Euripides, who, Feijoo explains, derided women in his plays but idolized them in private. He also suggests a more nefarious rationale for some authors' negatives views on women: "It may likewise be from revenge, at having met with rejection, for some men have been known to say a woman has bad character only because she would not stain her virtue by complying with his desires."[64] By way of example, Feijoo tells the story of an Irish beauty, Madame Douglas, who was labeled a traitor and put to death all because she would not give into the "appetite" of Guillermo Leout. The man scorned can be a forceful enemy of women.

Feijoo does not let women off the hook completely for bad behavior. He writes, "I do not deny the vices of many women." However, he refuses to accept that women are morally inferior to men. First, he points to male culpability in many cases of female immorality. He adds emphatically, "But, oh! If we were to throw light onto the genealogy of their disorderliness, how many of them will have their very origin in the perfidious impulses of individuals of our sex! Let him who would have all women good, set about converting all men."[65] He also refutes the image of wicked women based on the existence of biblical passages that deride women's lack of virtue. Feijoo explains that such scriptural diatribes against women refer to those who act immorally, not all women in general. After all, he queries, how could this scripture be interpreted as describing all women, when the church itself had declared women "devout," and important Catholic intellectuals had indicated that more women would be saved than men?

Even as he admits the existence of immoral women, Feijoo launches into his defense of the female sex. A major component of this defense is his attack on the rationale of those who considered women "the cause of all evil."[66] Feijoo works to dismantle the two central beliefs that perpetuated this view "inculcated at every pass among even the very lowest of the people that Caba brought the ruin of Spain, and Eve of all the world."[67] This first crime attributed to women stemmed from the history of the Muslim invasion of Spain in 711. Spain's foundation myth begins with Count Julian, the governor of the North African port city Ceuta, who sent his daughter Florinda Caba to reside at the court of King Roderigo of Spain, as was the custom of nobility at the time. While at court, Caba was raped by Roderigo, so she dutifully wrote a letter to her father notifying him of the offense against her. After deceiving Roderigo into sending Caba back to Ceuta, Julian conspired with Muza, an Arabian general, and led an attack on Spain that brought over twelve thousand Muslim men onto the peninsula, thus initiating the Muslim conquest of Iberia.

To debunk the popular sentiment that Caba was to blame, Feijoo argues that "Count Julian was the person who brought the Moors over to Spain, without being in the least persuaded by his daughter, who did nothing more than inform her father of the injury done to her. Wretched women, if in the case that they are trampled insolently, they have to keep quiet and fear confiding in their fathers or spouses!" Feijoo shows contempt for those who would blame the victim and instead points the finger at her avenger, suggesting the revenge enacted was excessive. Feijoo's critique of Caba's male avenger had considerable import in a country whose honor system relied heavily on retribution. Similarly, Feijoo dissects the story of Eve, not content to blame the fall of man on female frailty and vulnerability. Rather than pointing to Eve's susceptibility to the serpent, as most of his contemporaries did, Feijoo argues that Adam was actually the weaker party. After all, he explains, it took an angel to con Eve into disobeying God's orders, but only a mere mortal to convince Adam to sin. In short, Feijoo derides those who blamed women for either Spain's or humanity's problems.

Having discredited the general notion that women are flawed beings, Feijoo proceeds with his argument that women are men's equals. Women might not have the same levels of strength, fortitude, and prudence as men, Feijoo admits, but they had other qualities that measured up to these: beauty, gentleness, candor, and above all, modesty. In addition, he argues, their skill in activities traditionally deemed masculine was borne out by history. For example, Feijoo catalogues female rulers, from the fabled Semiramis, whose firm governance enabled her to rule from Ethiopia to Judea, to Spain's own Isabel, who achieved glory for her country with the discovery of the Americas. That this last triumph was the product of Isabel's, not Ferdinand's, rule, Feijoo leaves no doubt: "It is certain that we would not have achieved it without Isabel's magnanimity having conquered Ferdinand's apprehensions and indolence."[68]

Feijoo's celebration of women's success in politics did not mean he wished to completely overturn the tradition of male rule. He explains, "Nevertheless, the usual practice of nations is more in line with reason, as correspondent to the divine decree, signified to our first mother in Paradise, when subjection to men was imposed on her, and all of her daughters in her name." However, so convinced of women's abilities to govern was Feijoo that he ridicules the fear of female rule:

> The impatience which the people often levy toward a female government when the laws bring them under it should be corrected, and like-

wise that preposterous conceit of our sex, by which, a weak child has been preferred for the sovereign to an adult woman; and the Persians carried this partiality to a ridiculous excess, that on the occasion that a widow of one of the kings was left pregnant, having been advised by the magi that the embryo was a male, they placed a crown on the queen's belly, and proclaimed the fetus king, giving him the name of Sapor, before he was born.[69]

Feijoo ends the section on political women with this story—no analysis needed. For him, the idea that anyone would support the rule of a fetus over a capable woman was absurd.

Not only did Feijoo see women as skilled in politics, but he found them skilled in other traditionally male fields as well. He reminds his reader that women are adept at economics, often better household managers than their male counterparts. He tells numerous stories of their courage and heroism, emphasizing contemporary Spanish examples. His list culminates in stories of the Amazons, those warrior women who, whether or not they truly existed, attest to the strength of women throughout Europe, Asia, and the Americas. Finally, he argues that, contrary to common beliefs, women can keep secrets, even under the most harsh torture.

The last task that Feijoo tackles in his *Defense* is to argue for women's intellectual equality with men. Feijoo announces the enormity and import of this topic in his opening to this section: "Let us now come to the grand battle, which is the question of understanding in which I confess that[,] if reason does not support me, I have little to expect from authority, for writers on this subject (except for a rare one or two) are so wedded to the common opinion, that they almost uniformly speak of female understanding with disdain."[70] Feijoo explains that these views on women's intelligence were shaped by the fact that men, rather than women themselves, wrote books on the female sex. He remarks, "If women had written them, we [men] would be at the bottom."[71] Feijoo proceeds to discredit the oft-employed argument that women's current state of ignorance reflected their natural abilities. He criticizes the method those who doubt female intelligence used to draw this conclusion: "They see that on the whole [women] do not know other than those domestic employments for which they have been trained, then from there they infer . . . that they are not capable of anything else. Even the most limited thinker knows that the absence of the act does not imply the absence of the power, and thus, women not knowing more does not imply that they do not have talent for more."[72]

In arguing for women's mental abilities, Feijoo once again rejects physiological explanations of female inferiority. For example, he questions the premises behind the French philosopher Malebranche's theory that women's intellect is limited because the fibers of their brains are softer and more impressionable.[73] Malebranche based his conclusions on Aristotle's humoral theory, which deemed women's bodies more moist. Malebranche deduced that women's moist bodies would make their brains softer. Feijoo counters this assumption with the example of ice, which he points out has both moist and hard properties. In addition, Feijoo playfully turns the French thinker's false conclusion on its head. Drawing on other writings by Malebranche himself, Feijoo suggests that a softer, more impressionable brain might actually be better suited to mental operations than a firmer one. After a lengthy proof, Feijoo explains that he does not hold this opinion but simply aimed to illustrate the ease with which this sort of false view could be constructed. He explains:

> Every one philosophizes according to his fancy; and if I were to write from adulation, humor, or to display my wit, I could easily, by deducting a chain of consequences from received principles, elevate women's intelligence above our own. But this is not my goal; all I intend is to declare my mind, and I therefore aver, that neither Father Malebranche, nor any other writer hitherto, knows the precise mode or specific mechanism, by which the organisms of the head assist the faculties of the soul. We know not yet how fire burns, or water freezes, though both objects are within sight and touch; yet Father Malebranche, with the other Cartesians, would persuade us that they have seen clearly into all that passes in the most secret recesses of the rational soul.[74]

Feijoo's defense of female intelligence also reveals his own skepticism of Cartesian rationalism. A Baconian at heart, Feijoo questioned the human capacity to deduce scientific laws based on observation.

To evidence women's mental acuity, Feijoo looked to history, thus employing the standard argument used by many texts in the woman-question debate: the list or catalogue. A large portion of his text, more than one-fifth of the *Defense*, is devoted to recording numerous examples of intelligent women, from Italy's Laura Cereta to Spain's own Oliva Sabuco de Nantes.[75] In detailing the life of Sabuco, Feijoo laments the failure of her contemporaries, particularly fellow Spaniards, to recognize her many accomplishments, and even suggests that she was the true author of some principles of Cartesian rationalism: "It further appears that this eminent woman was prior to the celebrated René Descartes in the opinion that the rational soul resided in the brain."[76] To this list of intelligent women, Feijoo adds a brief catalogue of illustrious female artists, painters like Sofonisba Anguissola and Irene de Spilimberg, whose accomplishments speak to women's talent in the fine arts.

In closing, Feijoo tackles the ultimate argument against women: that God would not have placed women in subjection to men if they were not lower creatures. Feijoo's response is threefold. First, he questions the feasibility of establishing a definitive meaning of chapter 3 of Genesis, the scriptural passage contemporaries pointed to as proof of God's will, because of the competing versions of the text. However, even if the reader were to accept the scriptural version that supported women's subjection to men, Feijoo states, he still does not see how this proves men's natural superiority. For his second argument, Feijoo contends that the injunction of female subordination came about as a penalty for Eve's role in the fall from grace, not as a result of some natural inequality between men and women. Finally, Feijoo insists that subordination does not necessarily imply intellectual inferiority. He explains that, "even if God originally invested man with an authoritative superiority over women, that does not indicate man's intellectual superiority: the reason is, that though both be equal in talents, it is necessary for the government of the house that one of the two be the head, as otherwise it would have been a scene of confusion and disorder."[77] While Feijoo could only guess at God's motivations in selecting man, rather than woman, to be at the helm, his text conveys his firm belief that this system ensured order and stability in the household.

That Feijoo did not mean to overturn this order becomes even clearer in the final chapter of his *Defense*. He explains the two main motives behind his text. The first was, simply, to uncover the truth, which for Feijoo was a worthwhile goal in itself. The second motive was to raise the level of moral behavior. If men did not feel they were superior to women, he explains, they would not try to trick and deceive women. Conversely, if women did not consider themselves the inferior sex, they would not be so ready to blindly follow their male seducers. Feijoo envisions that happier marriages would result once people revised their incorrect view of the female sex. Equality would breed gentle husbands and faithful wives, since husbands would no longer degrade their wives for their stupidity and wives would no longer be enticed by the sweet nothings of prospective lovers. With this ending, Feijoo might assuage the fears of his contemporaries that his *Defense* opened the door to a doctrine of female superiority or a world run by women. Feijoo hoped to improve the lives of men and women and ensure moral behavior, but he did not imagine significant alterations in the social order.

Regardless of Feijoo's rather modest hopes, some contemporaries passionately rejected his *Defense*.[78] The publication of Feijoo's text provoked a debate, beginning with Laurencio Manco de Olivares's *Contradefensa crítica a favor de los hombres* (1726).[79] Manco de Olivares's opening anecdote reveals his concern over the kind of female rebellion Feijoo's treatise would engender. Among his reasons for writing his *Contradefensa*, Manco de Olivares explains, "is finding myself insulted and vilified by a woman, being her instrument, not the force of subtle arguments from you[,] most reverend [Feijoo,] with which she would have been victorious with myself shown to be defeated, but the force of blows of the *Teatro crítico*, which emboldened by the vengeful ire of her impulse, she did not stop until it became undone on my head."[80] Manco de Olivares's response to this fictional beating is a misogynistic diatribe that portrays women as weak creatures incapable of any real accomplishments.

Manco de Olivares employs a range of old-style arguments in refuting Feijoo. A case in point is his reaction to the Benedictine's defense of Eve. In contrast to Feijoo's assertion that it took an angel to beguile Eve, Manco de Olivares relies on the traditional explanation of the fall as the fault of inherently weak woman. Invoking the old arguments of female inferiority that Feijoo was trying to dismantle, Manco de Olivares reminds the reader that, since Eve was crafted in Adam's image, rather than in God's own as Adam was, she was naturally inferior to Adam. Similarly, Manco de Olivares casts doubt on all the historical examples of great women that Feijoo employed in his *Defense*. Of Feijoo's talented female rulers, for example, Manco de Olivares spitefully surmises that they must have taken credit for the accomplishments of their male subjects. And as far as female intelligence goes, he contends that if women truly were capable of more, they would already have accomplished more, including authoring works and achieving university degrees.

Once Manco de Olivares fired the opening salvo, authors on both sides of the debate launched critiques of their own. Feijoo's critics cited numerous reasons to mistrust his assertions. That Feijoo really intended to prove women's superiority to men, rather than their equality, constituted a common concern among his opponents. In his 1734 *Crisol crítico theológico*, for example, Salvador José Mañer explains with disapproval, "[Feijoo] intends to prove not only that they [women] equal us, but that they surpass us."[81] Mañer suggests that rather than being equal, as Feijoo maintained, men and women had distinct qualities suited to their respective roles in society. Another chief concern of Feijoo's critics centered on the Benedictine's suggestion that women be educated. Jaime Ardanaz y Centellas, for example, rejected Feijoo's proposal in his *Tertulia histórica y apologética* (1727).[82]

Ardanaz bemoaned his own wife's excessive interest in books and learning after she had read Feijoo's *Defense of Women*. Swayed by Feijoo's ideas on the female intellect, Ardanaz complains, his wife now spent her days quoting Descartes and studying foreign languages. Ardanaz blames Feijoo for turning the perfect wife into an unruly woman whose fancy for learning caused her to neglect her domestic responsibilities. A number of Feijoo's contemporaries worried that the *Defense* would lead to a complete breakdown in male-female relations.

The fear and anger this potential breakdown engendered came out in critics' works. The historian Mónica Bolufer Peruga points out that the pseudonymous Tiburcio Cascajales employed warlike imagery, referring to a "regular army of female knights-errant" and "the authority that controlled the squadrons of beardless faces."[83] Like Manco de Olivares and others, Tiburcio Cascajales (pseudonym of Cristóbal Medina Conde) worries about the fierce female rebellion that Feijoo's *Defense* might provoke. These anxieties frequently devolved into satirical asides and sharp jabs aimed at the Benedictine himself. Ardanaz labels the *Defense* a "senseless undertaking," and wonders maliciously about why a pious monk would write a defense of women at all.[84] Juan Antonio Santareli describes Feijoo in his deceptively titled *Estrado crítico en defensa de las mugeres* as "Narcissus himself, because he is so enamored with his own writing that he hardly forms a clause if a large share of it does not emit self-love."[85] These sorts of personal attacks reveal the level of anxiety that Feijoo's *Defense* produced in some of his contemporaries.

Feijoo's defenders fired back with equally witty and belittling asides aimed at refuting Manco de Olivares and company and providing further support for Feijoo's assertions. Ricardo Basco Flancas, for example, jumped into the skirmish in 1726 with a text whose very title reveals his position: *Apoyo a la defensa de las mujeres que escrivió el R.mo P. Fr. Benito Feyjó y crisis de la contra-defensa crítica que a favor de los hombres, y contra las mugeres, dió a luz temerariamente Don Laurencio Manco de Olivares, en dictamen que da de ella a una señora* (Support for the Defense of Women Written by the Reverend Father and Friar Benito Feijoo and Crisis of the Critical Counter-defense in Favor of Men and against Women, which with much Trepidation Don Laurencio Manco Brought to the Light of Day and Presented to a Lady). Written as a dialogue between two men reading Manco de Olivares's work, the *Apoyo a la defensa* refutes the criticisms Manco de Olivares levied against Feijoo line by line. In his critique, Basco Flancas mercilessly mocks Manco de Olivares. Early in the work, he quotes a popular verse whose last line allows him to play on the double meaning of

Manco de Olivares's last name: "Es MANCO el entendimiento." Manco, literally "crippled," here implies defective and faulty: "His understanding is faulty."[86]

Throughout the work, Basco Flancas describes his opponent in unflattering terms. For example, he writes, "I return to confirm my judgment . . . that the author is a poor Vadulaque, who without understanding what he reads, does nothing more than speak loudly."[87] Basco Flancas interweaves these continual damning references to Manco de Olivares's inability to comprehend Feijoo's ideas with arguments to counter his assertions. In closing, Basco Flancas suggests Manco de Olivares should be incarcerated in an insane asylum, left only with a few listed works: *The Romance of El Cid, Doze pares, The History of the Marqués de Mantua,* and his own *Contradefensa*. He proposes that a sign be tacked up on his cell that reads in big letters: "Manco is here without honor,/Because he offended women,/And if he proceeds in this thinking,/His punishment will be greater. /No girl with looks/Will marry such a man,/Since he will have to say to each one/With reason, hand over the club."[88] This rhyming verse ridiculed Manco de Olivares, turning the critic into a dishonorable man by questioning his very masculinity.

Other proponents of Feijoo provided meatier defenses. The anatomist Martín Martínez, for example, jumped into the skirmish with his *Carta defensiva* (1727), which supported Feijoo's contention that there was no anatomical rationale to suggest women had less intellectual potential than men did. Martínez drew on his knowledge and position to verify Feijoo's assertion that men's and women's brains were physically the same. He writes, "At the least, I, as an Anatomy Professor, can say, the [physical] arrangement that differentiates the two sexes not being instrumental to thought[,] . . . I am led to believe that in aptitude for the Sciences the functions are not unequal since the organs are not different."[89] Similarly, Miguel Juan Martínez y Salafranca's *Desagravios de la muger ofendida* (1727) provided further support for Feijoo's arguments by listing even more exemplary women whose achievements suggested women's talents and capabilities.[90]

Some authors tried to establish a compromise between Feijoo's *Defense* and Manco de Olivares's invectives. Such was the case with the anonymous *La razón con desinterés fundada*, published in 1727, which scholars have described as a "conciliatory essay."[91] In *La razón*, the author argues simultaneously for women's domesticity and intellectual capabilities. In addressing the question of Eve, the author negotiates between the traditional view that inferior Eve was made from Adam's rib and a novel argument that supports Feijoo's assertion of equality. The author explains that, since Eve came from Adam's side, not his head or his feet, she was his equal companion, neither his superior nor his subordinate. However, *La razón* did little to halt the ongoing battle between opponents and proponents of Feijoo's *Defense*. That same year, Manco de Olivares composed a second screed, titled *Defensiva respuesta a favor de los hombres* in which he directly attacked Basco Flancas, Martínez y Salafranca, and his other critics. And even Feijoo himself incorporated responses to his critics in his later works. Feijoo's 1729 *Ilustración apologética* suggests his impatience with the ongoing debate. Addressing Mañer's lengthy assertion that men are physically stronger than women, Feijoo sneers, "What time well spent! Who would refute it?"[92]

As the varied responses to Feijoo's *Defense of Women* suggest, not all Spanish intellectuals were ready to accept women's natural equality as a given. The resurgence of traditional discourses on women in the years following the *Defense* suggests just how threatening Feijoo's propositions were to certain contemporaries. Hoping to channel a growing body of female readers awakened by Feijoo's essay, José Clavijo y Fajardo, for example, suggested Juan Luis Vives's *De institutione feminae christianae*, Fray Luis de León's *La perfecta casada*, and François Fénelon's *Traité de l'éducation des filles* (1687) as guides to proper female comportment.[93] Not coincidentally, Vives's work was reprinted in Spanish in Madrid in 1792 and again in 1793. Similarly, *La perfecta casada* reappeared in Valencia in 1765 and 1773, in Salamanca in 1773, and in Madrid in 1786 and 1799.

While the debate over women's nature and place in society continued throughout the century, Feijoo's text represented a key starting point. The increasing participation of women in Spain's growing world of letters during the second two-thirds of the century remained integrally linked to Feijoo's *Defense of Women* in the minds of contemporaries. Dr. D. Joseph de Rada y Aguirre expresses this connection in his prologue to María Catalina de Caso's 1755 four-volume translation titled *Modo de enseñar y estudiar las bellas letras, para ilustrar el entendimiento, y rectificar el corazón*. Rada y Aguirre's prologue praises Caso's translation and describes the woman as a talented and knowledgeable author. The prologue closes by stating, "If the Reverend Father Master Feijoo were printing now a supplement to the *Theatro crítico*, he would put this woman in the appendix for her erudite and solid treatises of the Defense of Women." By likening Caso to one of Feijoo's celebrated women, Rada y Aguirre showed that the Benedictine's essay remained a significant marker of women's potential and achievement.

The questions that Feijoo's *Defense of Women* raised were far from settled in the eighteenth century, and they were arguably more unsettled than they had ever been in Spanish society. Feijoo introduced Spaniards to a new mode of inquiry that led them down a path of Enlightenment and reform. As Juan Sempere y Guarinos explained of Feijoo in 1785: "The works of this man produced a useful fermentation, they made us begin to doubt, they made known other books very different from those there were in the country, they aroused curiosity, and they opened to reason the door which had been closed by indolence and false knowledge . . . for they are in the hands of everyone."[94] Indeed, Feijoo spawned a new generation of thinkers who, skeptical of authorities and armed with empirical reasoning, were open to all kinds of new possibilities, including the possibility that educated women could contribute to the nation's reform. It was not long before this group endeavored to move women's ideas out of the realm of the abstract and to translate them into concrete activities and policies. As Spain's world of letters became increasingly institutionalized, the debate over women's nature and role in society took on a new character. It was no longer a theoretical debate, but one that would have a real effect on Spain's emerging Enlightenment institutions.

2 Admitted Equals

Art and Letters

Immediately following publication of Feijoo's *Teatro crítico universal*, Spain's devoted intellectuals delved into a whole slew of social and political debates, producing in the 1740s and 1750s a swift proliferation of Enlightenment culture and institutions. On the pages of new periodicals and in hastily written books, Spain's *ilustrados* (enlightened thinkers) churned out texts in unprecedented numbers. With equal enthusiasm, a growing reading public devoured these new publications. Nigel Glendinning estimates that there were between one and two million readers in Spain by the middle of the eighteenth century, with about fifty thousand of them located in Spain's capital city of Madrid.[1] These new readers and writers—men and women—circulated books, periodicals, and manuscripts and enjoyed lively exchanges at the cafés located on Madrid's newly widened, tree-lined boulevards. This growing world of letters found another home in the *tertulias*, regular gatherings like salons that became focal points for Spain's Enlightenment elite. In *tertulias*, Enlightenment thinkers circulated and criticized manuscripts, shared recent letters and news, and debated a whole range of social, cultural, and political matters.

Spanish intellectuals also collaborated in the creation of royal-sponsored state institutions designed to further foment social and cultural activities. As noted earlier, the Enlightenment elite and Spain's monarch worked in partnership for much of the century. One of the early collaborative projects between reformers and the crown were the royal academies. In 1713, Philip V founded the first royal academy in Spain: the Real Academia Española de la Lengua. Patterned after France's Académie Française of 1635, the Royal Spanish Language Academy was charged with standardizing the Castilian language, in part through its compilation and publication of an immense dictionary and comprehensive guides to orthography and grammar. The creation of a number of other academies in Madrid followed over the course of the century: the Real Academia de la Historia in 1736, the Real Academia Médica Matritense in 1738, the Real Academia de Bellas Artes de San Fernando in 1752, and the Real Academia de Jurisprudencia de Santa Bárbara in 1763.

Women's entry into these prominent institutions of Enlightenment sociability, in particular Madrid's *tertulias* and the Royal Academy of Fine Arts of San Fernando, demonstrates their centrality to this nascent Republic of Letters. While these two institutions may seem quite different from each other, they both represent the degree to which women's abilities had come to be respected in the 1750s. As the founders and hosts of Madrid's most important *tertulias*, women shaped the character of intellectual debate among Spain's foremost thinkers. For these select women, whose upbringing and education had already prepared them to take an active role in a world of letters, the *tertulia* constituted an effective tool for participating in and influencing social debate. Female artists enjoyed similar benefits in Madrid's Royal Academy of Fine Arts. After successfully completing an application process that mirrored the one utilized for male applicants, talented female artists joined the ranks of the academy. Their membership signaled public recognition of real artistic achievement and afforded women access to a community of distinguished painters, sculptors, and engravers. The academy's annual public exhibitions provided both accomplished and aspiring female artists with a public audience for their work.

Women's presence in both the unofficial and the official worlds of Enlightenment inquiry suggests the degree to which the debates spurred by Feijoo's *Defense of Women* had transformed predominant views on the female sex by the 1740s and 1750s. Less than twenty years after Feijoo's *Defense* first appeared in print, many, if not all, of Spain's intelligentsia had accepted the idea that women were rational and thus equal beings. No longer were women solely thought of as innately inferior creatures whose biological limitations determined their status. Rather, the writings of early Enlightenment thinkers like Feijoo made clear that women's potential contribution to society depended on how that society nurtured and prepared them. The existence of new opportunities for women within the nation's emerging Enlightenment institutions confirms that a newfound confidence in women's intellectual capacity and belief in their natural equality had taken root.

WOMEN AND *TERTULIAS* IN MADRID'S REPUBLIC OF LETTERS

The vital role of women in European salons has become a mainstay of historical thought in the last decade. The work of scholars such as Joan Landes,

Dena Goodman, and Deborah Hertz has convinced historians of the sway women held over Enlightenment discourse in their capacity as *salonnières*, especially in the case of France, which has received the most study.[2] This new research has dismantled the old portrait of salon women as unfit judges who made a mockery of themselves in trying to comment on their male contemporaries' intellectual pursuits. It has also recast *salonnières'* motives. Rather than seeing *salonnières* as women who sought to gain fame and power through their salons, scholars now emphasize the importance of these gatherings to the educational and intellectual objectives of both the men and women involved.

This characterization of the *salonnières* and their goals extends as well to the women who hosted four influential *tertulias* in Madrid in the 1740s and 1750s: Josefa de Zúñiga y Castro, the widowed Countess of Lemos and Marquise of Sarría; María Josefa Alonso-Pimentel Téllez-Girón, the Count-Duchess of Benavente and Osuna; María Francisca de Sales Portocarrero, the Countess of Montijo; and María Lorenza de los Ríos, the Marquise of Fuerte-Híjar.[3] By surrounding themselves with writers and thinkers who shared similar interests, the heads of Madrid's *tertulias* aimed to further both their own intellectual pursuits and the reformist agenda of Madrid's intelligentsia.[4]

The idea that Spain's *ilustrados* centered their Republic of Letters in an institution organized and controlled by women seems unlikely considering the lack of female education in early modern Spain. The novelist and amateur historian Carmen Martín Gaite has called into question how prepared Spain's women were to take on such a vital intellectual role: "Women had the right to some enjoyment, to an exchange of ideas. But did it actually serve these ends? Or better said, were Spanish women in the eighteenth century prepared to converse and exchange ideas? Did they have any, on any subject? It soon became obvious that they did not."[5] Since women were not prepared to partake in rational discourse, in Martín Gaite's estimation, the *tertulias* they hosted could not have been centers of serious intellectual inquiry: "There are many indications that the conversations presided over by women—and this type of gathering was predominant—were characterized, in general, by total inconsistency. The main theme was fashion, and its main derivatives—gossip and maids—did not do much for the mind."[6] Martín Gaite doubts that women's upbringing prepared them for more than idle chitchat. However, this categorization of Spain's *ilustradas* neglects the fact that many elite women did gain relatively good educations by midcentury. The poet Mariana Alderete, the Marquise of the Rosa del Monte, for example, mastered Latin, Greek, French, rhetoric, and philosophy at an early age.[7] And the translator María Catalina de Caso succeeded in learning six languages and studying the traditionally male disciplines of mathematics and military architecture during her youth.[8]

That many of the women who participated actively in Madrid's burgeoning Republic of Letters were members of the titular nobility is not surprising. Rather, it bespeaks the increased access to education available to women of a higher rank. María Josefa Alonso-Pimentel Téllez-Girón, for example, was not only the Count-Duchess of Benavente and Osuna but also the Duchess of Béjar, of Gandía, and of Arcos, the Marquise of Javalquinto, and the Princess of Anglona. Benavente was a direct descendent of the noble House of Pimentel as well as connected, through her marriage to her first cousin Pedro de Alcántara Téllez-Girón y Pacheco, to the Houses of López de Zúñiga and Ponce de León. In short, Benavente was not only one of the wealthiest but also one of the most well-situated women of her day. While not all the women who appeared as central figures in Spain's Enlightenment were as high up on the social ladder as the Count-Duchess of Benavente, most were aristocrats. The Duchess of Arcos, the Marquise of la Espeja, and the Countess of Benalúa, for example, were among the many women of varying noble rank who pursued Enlightenment activities.

Those women who did not hold titles themselves often came from important families and tended to have fathers or husbands who were influential court figures and members of Spain's rising *letrado* class. The writer María Rosa Gálvez de Cabrera, for example, was the adopted daughter of Antonio Gálvez de Málaga. The Gálvez family contained a number of powerful members, including Bernardo de Gálvez, the former governor of Louisiana and the viceroy of Mexico, and José de Gálvez, the secretary of the Council of the Indies.[9] Similarly, the writer and translator Josefa Amar y Borbón was the daughter of the court physician José Amar Arguedas and Ignacia Borbón y Vallejo de Santa Cruz, who was herself the daughter of the celebrated Aragonese doctor Miguel Borbón. In addition, Amar y Borbón was married to Joaquín de Fuertes Piquer, a judge for the Real Audiencia of Aragon.[10]

Having the kinds of family connections that women like Benavente and Gálvez enjoyed provided women with vital opportunities, not the least of which was access to education. In the case of Amar y Borbón, for example, her father's appointment as court physician for Ferdinand VI in 1755 brought her to the dynamic world of Madrid. As a young girl at court, she found a tutor in the king's librarian, Rafael Casalbón. In addition to studying Latin, French, and literature under Casalbón's guidance, Amar y Borbón availed herself of the ample reading material she discovered on the shelves of the royal library. Although Amar y Borbón returned to her native Aragon in 1772 and resided there for the remainder of her life, her connection to the intellectual world of Madrid remained strong.[11] Thus, Amar y Borbón's temporary move to court provided her with an avenue to education and played a role in shaping her subsequent intellectual development. María del Rosario Cepeda y Mayo also found a path to learning through family connections. The daughter of an important professor in Cádiz, Cepeda y Mayo put her learning on display in a public examination in September 1768.[12] During this proceeding, Cepeda y Mayo demonstrated her mastery of numerous disciplines, including Greek, Latin, Italian, French, history, and literature. As these examples suggest, the women of Spain's Enlightenment elite were highly educated individuals.[13]

Many of these women obtained the bulk of their education in convent schools, which often demanded costly tuition and maintained highly exclusive entrance requirements. While convent curriculums were focused primarily on preparing female students to be pious Catholics and devoted wives and mothers, they also entailed instruction for women in other subjects, particularly foreign languages. After all, the convent had long served as a retreat for women interested in academic pursuits.[14] María Manuela Pignatelli de Aragón y Gonzaga, the Duchess of Villahermosa, received such an education. The daughter of Joaquín Pignatelli de Aragón y Moncayo, the Count of Fuentes, and María Luisa Gonzaga y Carracciolo, the Duchess of Solferino, Villahermosa never lived with her parents, who left Spain soon after her birth to take up an ambassadorial post in Turin. From the age of four to fifteen, Villahermosa resided in the Real Monasterio de Monjas Salesas, where she received her early training.[15] Likewise, the Countess of Montijo received a convent education. Montijo's father, Cristóbal Antonio Portocarrero, the Marquis of Valderrábano, died in 1757, when Montijo was merely three years old. In his will, Valderrábano made clear his desire to procure the best possible education for his daughter. Accordingly, Montijo was sent to live in the Real Monasterio de Monjas Salesas in 1758.[16] Women who did not attend convent schools generally received their education from private tutors whom their families hired. Both Rafael Casalbón, as mentioned above, and Antonio Berdejo tutored Amar y Borbón. Juan Antonio González Cañavares provided much of Cepeda y Mayo's instruction.[17] Amar y Borbón and Cepeda y Mayo both exemplify the fine education a willing student could receive from a private tutor.

Women could also amass invaluable knowledge from their travels. In particular, a number of women had connections to France that led to their residence abroad.[18] The Duchess of Villahermosa's life provides a compelling example of how time spent on the other side of the Pyrenees served as an educational experience. As a young woman of sixteen, Villahermosa moved to Paris to be with her mother, the Countess of Fuentes. During this time, Villahermosa not only learned French but also became familiar with the active intellectual life of eighteenth-century Paris. Because of her family status, Villahermosa gained admittance to the most celebrated Parisian salons. She attended gatherings hosted by the Duchess of Choiseul and Madame Geoffrin, among others.[19] When Villahermosa returned to Spain in 1772 at the age of nineteen, she had accumulated a wealth of education and experience that led her to host her own regular gatherings of intellectuals, reunions much like those she had attended in Paris.

Through formal and informal means, women gained sufficient education to participate in the expanding world of letters. The *tertulia* provided a wonderful opportunity for women who had gotten a taste for learning early on. By bringing together select individuals on a regular basis, the *tertulia* enabled women to foster Enlightenment exchange in a way that supported their own intellectual growth. Not surprisingly, women catered their *tertulias'* membership and discussions to fit their own intellectual pursuits. Take, for example, the *tertulia* hosted by the Marquise of Sarría between January 9, 1749, and April 29, 1751.[20] Nicknamed the Academia del Buen Gusto (Academy of Good Taste), Sarría's salon became one of the capital city's most active literary groups.[21] A student of eighteenth-century Spanish literature could quickly identify the chief purpose of those who gathered at Sarría's palace on the Calle del Turco from a survey of the membership roster: the composition and study of poetry.[22] In fact, poets so dominated Sarría's salon that some contemporaries referred to it as the Academia Poética.[23]

Records of the group's activities reveal that poetry was by far the topic most often discussed. A typical meeting would include the reading and discussion of various types of poetry, such as sonnets, romances, and epic poems. On June 18, 1750, for example, the salon heard and discussed two sonnets by Agustín de Montiano y Luyando and a sonnet and a heroic poem both by José Antonio Porcel y Salablanca. The number of works discussed at any one meeting varied widely, partly depending on whether the works were short poems like sonnets or excerpts from longer works such as epic poems. While on May 7, 1750, the salon focused all its attention on one idyll by Ignacio de Luzán, on February 19, 1750, it had one of its busiest meetings, discussing fifteen sonnets, two odes, five romances, one psalm, and one *décima* (a poem with stanzas of ten octosyllabic lines).

There was also some interest in theatrical works, as exemplified by Montiano's publication of *Virginia,* Luzán's translation *La razón contra la moda,* and the representation of Francisco de Zamora's comedy *Castigando premia amor* in Sarría's residence. There was also minor interest in fables, which were presented by the Count of Torrepalma, the Count of Saldueña, and Antonio Nasarre y Ferriz on various occasions.[24] One scholar has summed up the significance of the group's literary pursuits: "The Academia del Buen Gusto was something much more than a frivolous court salon: it was the start of a new direction, a place where important indications of the future of poetic philosophy could be found."[25] By surrounding herself with poets, Sarría facilitated both her own literary education and the development of poetic discourse in Enlightenment Spain.

Sarría's *tertulia* set an example for other prominent female intellectuals in Madrid. During the remainder of the century, women continued to host Spain's Enlightenment elites at regular weekly gatherings. The Marquise of Fuerte-Híjar, in particular, took much from Sarría, dedicating her own *tertulia* to literary pursuits. Rather than poetry, however, Fuerte-Híjar's love of the theater dictated the nature of her group, which met at her residence on the Plazuela de Santa Catalina. There is little extant information to document the central players in Fuerte-Híjar's circle, but scholars do know that the tenor Manuel García and the playwright Nicasio Álvarez de Cienfuegos were frequent fixtures at her salon.[26] Fuerte-Híjar's role as host to many of Madrid's talented playwrights, actors, and musicians undoubtedly contributed to her own composition of two *comedias*, *El engreído* and *La sabia indirecta*, toward the end of the century.[27]

The Countess of Montijo likewise counted a wide circle of prominent Spanish intellectuals as guests and correspondents. As the British traveler Lady Holland describes her, "Mde. de Montijo has the reputation of being the cleverest and best informed woman in Spain. Her society is the best in Madrid, and was composed of the most remarkable men: the unfortunate but estimable Jovellanos is her intimate friend."[28] Montijo's friendship with Jovellanos remained a well-known and fulfilling connection throughout her life. As Richard Herr explains, "Her house was among the first in Madrid where Jovellanos had been seen as a young man, fresh from the university of Alcalá, with his flowing hair and black garb strangely out of place among the gay clothes and powdered wigs of the court. Twenty years later, during his exile in Asturias, Jovellanos still corresponded with this lady."[29] Montijo's relationship with Jovellanos exemplifies the strong ties she had to key contemporary intellectuals. Various figures, from the engraver Juan Antonio Salvador Carmona to the chemist Pedro Gutiérrez Bueno, visited Montijo at her palace to engage in stimulating conversations on an array of topics, including the latest books. Montijo was always anxious to discuss the new volumes appearing in the bookstores of Joaquín Ibarra or Antonio Sancha or those she had recently received from her French suppliers Thévin or Copin.³⁰ Without doubt, Montijo herself was at the center of Spain's Enlightenment circle.

While she was a woman of vast interests, Montijo chose to center her *tertulia* on religious reform. In contrast to the literary pursuits of Sarría and Fuerte-Híjar, the narrow focus of Montijo's *tertulia* reflected her desire to revive and reform Catholicism in Spain. Accordingly, Montijo gathered important ecclesiastical intellectuals and reform-minded scholars to attend regular reunions at her palace, including Antonio Palafox, the Bishop of Cuenca, and Juan Meléndez Valdés, an esteemed professor at the University of Salamanca.³¹ Many of these guests shared Montijo's interest in rethinking religious practice in Spain and helped shape her desire to transform the existing religiosity, which she saw as fanatical and superstitious, into true piety.³² As a result of its focus on religious change, Montijo's *tertulia* was labeled Jansenist by the Inquisition. This was not a surprising charge to be levied against her. Jansenism, a movement that aimed to curtail the power and wealth of the Catholic Church and to strengthen bishops by limiting the power of the pope and the Inquisition, became an umbrella term for religious reformers the Inquisition found threatening. In addition, the Inquisition undoubtedly considered Montijo's gatherings in the context of her translation of *Introducciones sobre el matrimonio*, a French work by Nicolás Tourneaux that was itself suspect for its Jansenist leanings. While not much came of these accusations in Spain, the mark this made on her reputation, combined with a later skirmish between herself and Carlos IV's minister Manuel Godoy, led to Montijo's banishment from Madrid in 1805.³³ Forced to give up her salon, she retired to her lands in Logroño and resided there until her death in 1808. Clearly, for her, this *tertulia* was much more than an idle diversion. It was a place to shape discussion on a topic that she felt was crucial to Spain's future.

The relatively specialized agendas of Sarría's, Fuerte-Híjar's, and Montijo's *tertulias* stand in sharp contrast to the varied intellectual circle that the Count-Duchess of Benavente sponsored. Benavente surrounded herself with every type of *ilustrado*, from economists to playwrights. This diverse group reflected her wide-ranging interests, and any number of topics were suitable for discussion at her *tertulia*. Benavente's biographer describes the numerous issues the hostess and her guests took up: "In these gatherings they discussed the latest book to arrive from France, popular musical pieces, the bullfighter in vogue, a renowned actress and the most recent political misfortunes. . . . This small group of intelligent men and some select women became engrossed in long literary discussions or considered the performances that were soon to be presented in the theater."³⁴ The quantity of

Benavente's interests did not harm the quality of her gatherings. With Jovellanos, Tomás de Iriarte, Ramón de la Cruz, and Leandro Fernández de Moratín as regular attendees, she hosted arguably four of the most important individuals to contribute to Spain's intellectual life in the eighteenth century.

The site of Benavente's *tertulia*—the family's newly built palace at the Alameda de Osuna—undoubtedly helped to attract these prominent *ilustrados*.[35] Benavente bedecked the palace in the latest French style, importing carpets, tapestries, furniture, and other accouterments from France. While she valued this French aesthetic, she also celebrated Spain's own artistic creations. As Lady Holland explains Benavente's purchases, "She has acquired a relish for French luxuries, without diminishing her national magnificence and hospitality."[36] For instance, the Count-Dukes of Benavente commissioned Spain's own Francisco Goya to create the paintings that would adorn the new palace, making themselves one of the first noble families to have a relationship with the renowned artist.[37] Amid these fine furnishings and exquisite paintings was the all-important library, which boasted an amazing collection. Because of the duke's exemption from normal importation procedures, they were able to collect all sorts of national and foreign works—even those condemned by the Inquisition—to fill the shelves of their library.[38] The music section of the library, for example, was so complete that professors at the University of Salamanca frequently asked the duchess to lend them some of her treasures.[39]

But it was Benavente herself, not the splendid palace with its fine library, who created such a thriving *tertulia*. Benavente's impressive network of artists and thinkers made her a natural center of Enlightenment discourse. The countess's correspondence, for example, includes discussions with important musicians and composers, numerous queries from writers on the literary works they sent for her perusal, and dialogue on scientific innovations that intrigued her.[40] One of her most interesting correspondents was the encyclopedist Charles Pougens, who frequently sent her large crates of recent editions of French periodicals, including Le Journal des Débats and Le Journal des Modes, or the latest works from the shelves of Parisian booksellers.[41] As Lady Holland wrote in her 1804 journal, the "Duchess of Osuna [Benavente] . . . is the most distinguished woman in Madrid for her talents, worth, and taste. . . . Her revenues are even greater than the D. of Osuna's, who is a very tolerably sensible man and of considerable knowledge."[42] Benavente's clear thirst for intellectual exchange and her renowned ability to facilitate it among others made her salon among the most successful and animated gatherings in Madrid.

The guests who attended these various *tertulias* recognized the importance of the women involved in shaping the character of these meetings. In the case of Sarría's *tertulia*, for example, the records indicate that she presided over every meeting of the academy during its more than two-year run. Although the group's vice president, treasurer, and secretary were reelected every four months, Sarría's position as president was a permanent one. As the host, Sarría selected who would participate in her group. A poem dedicated to her in 1750 suggests the key role that she played in determining who was admitted to the salon.[43] In the poem, titled "To Her Excellency the Señora Marquise of Sarría So That She Will See Fit to Admit Me in the List of Members of Her Poetic Academy," the author entreats Sarría to allow him to attend her gatherings: "My scant and meager inspiration,/at every word it falters,/not achieving its desire./But I am inspired/when I contemplate,/that I am something,/for then I know to aspire/to be a member of this assembly."[44] In addition to asking for admittance, the author also explains how participation in the salon would have a positive effect on his work: "If you, my lady, grant me/even your mere disregard,/you will see how you can form a new Apollo/from such raw material./What you toss away/shall serve to instruct me/and I even believe that I might be swayed/by reason of vanishing;/and I will be able to fear falling/if I rise so far."[45] Here the poet refers to the instruction that he will receive at the gatherings of the salon. This poet recognized both the intellectual advantages of membership in the *tertulia* and the position that Sarría held as the host.

Members of Benavente's *tertulia* also recognized the importance of her role in their intellectual growth. The clearest example here is Iriarte. Iriarte's relationship with Benavente was a long-lasting and close friendship based on common intellectual pursuits. Besides attending Benavente's salon in Madrid, Iriarte dedicated a number of poems to her, each of which expounded on her positive attributes. In 1780, she had portions of Iriarte's manuscript of the *Fábulas literarias* copied for her own study. Although Iriarte moved to southern Spain in 1790, he maintained an active correspondence with Benavente.[46] During a stay in the port town of Sanlúcar de Barrameda, Iriarte composed the play *El don de gentes* for her. According to one literary scholar, "In this play his intention was to present the perfect type of woman—intelligent, pleasant, and discreet. It is significant that he should dedicate such a play to the one woman whom he very much admired and who had helped him in various ways."[47] He also wrote another play for her, *Donde menos se piensa salta la liebre*. Benavente built a theater for the production of these two plays and was very active in their staging in order to ensure that Iriarte's works came to life as he conceived of them. Their relationship exemplifies the intellectual exchange of her *tertulia*, one where both host and guest benefited.

While most of the attendees at Madrid's four main *tertulias* were men, select women did join in these gatherings. Clear evidence remains for the presence of women at Sarría's *tertulia*, including the Duchess of Santisteban, the Marquise of Estepa, and the Duchess of Arcos, perhaps the most active female participant at these gatherings.[48] A number of these women were authors in their own right, and the records indicate that the group discussed their works as well. Like the male members, these women were predominantly poets. The Marquise of Castrillo, for example, composed and presented various romances for the group.[49] Although Castrillo died before completing her largest undertaking, an epic poem titled *Las glorias de Salamanca*, Porcel wrote a sonnet incorporating excerpts of Castrillo's poem and read it in Sarría's salon as a tribute to the lost poet.[50] This evidence suggests that women's role in Spanish *tertulias* was not limited to acting as host; they were guests and participants as well.

Sarría, Benavente, Fuerte-Híjar, and Montijo were all educated women whose own interests dictated the nature of their *tertulias*. Sarría's role as host to Madrid's Academia de Buen Gusto in the late 1740s opened up an important path for educated female elites who wanted to make their mark on Enlightenment society. As one of the primary institutions of sociability, the *tertulia* remained at the center of intellectual exchange throughout the century. The acceptance of women as creators and leaders of this vital institution speaks to the shift in overall attitudes toward women, to the growing recognition of their mental capabilities. These regular meetings became a place where women like Sarría and Montijo could shape and contribute to the developing discussions in Enlightenment Spain, a place where they could prove their mental acumen alongside other intellectual giants.

THE REAL ACADEMIA DE BELLAS ARTES DE SAN FERNANDO

As Sarría's poetic gatherings drew to a close, to be carried on in spirit by the dynamic circles of Fuerte-Híjar, Montijo, and Benavente, the Real Academia de Bellas Artes de San Fernando constructed its home on the Calle de Alcalá. Practically from its inception in 1752, this royal-sponsored center of artistic education and excellence opened its doors to the nation's women. Women's involvement in Spain's preeminent academy of fine arts signaled a shift in views on the female sex, just as their important role as hosts and participants in some of the nation's most prominent *tertulias* had done. Women did not participate substantially in Spain's earliest academies, such as the Real Academia Española de la Lengua, founded in 1713, or the Real

Academia de la Historia and Real Academia Médica Matritense, both founded in the 1730s. However, by the time the monarch established the Real Academia de Bellas Artes de San Fernando in 1752, the shift in attitudes toward women led to their almost immediate inclusion in the Enlightenment's latest center of research and learning. Their presence there would continue unabated through the century.

The admission of a significant number of women to a royal academy of fine arts appears to have been a uniquely Spanish phenomenon. The French academy limited the number of female members to four at any given time, and the only female members recorded in the eighteenth century were Rosalba Carriera (1675–1757), Elisabeth Vigée LeBrun (1755–1842), and Adélaïde Labille-Guiard (1749–1803).[51] Similarly, the English academy remained fairly closed to female artists, admitting only Mary Moser (1744–1819) and Angelica Kauffmann (1741–1807) during the course of the 1700s.[52] This small number of women recorded as members of European fine arts academies has led scholars to discount the seriousness of women's involvement in the early life of Madrid's Academy of San Fernando. Such is the case with one of the earliest discussions of these female academicians, found in José Parada y Santín's 1902 *Las pintoras españolas*. In this work, Parada y Santín argues that the acceptance of women in the academy had little to do with their artistic merit: "Many of them had the honor of being admitted as academics, something which in truth they owed more to their social position, to their beauty and to the excessive practice of gallantry and courtesy in that era, than to the merit of their works."[53] Parada y Santín does recognize some important results of the participation of these women in the art academy, such as the spread of artistic knowledge to a wider group and the increased attention given to the training of young artists. However, he concludes: "The gallant spirit of that era and the type of sensualism that ruled all the expressions of judgment and the customs of that time could not do less than to allow participation to the most important of the Spanish ladies, who were the most beautiful ornaments in the salons of the Academy of Fine Arts of San Fernando."[54] For Parada y Santín, these women were more like the academy's paintings and less its artist-members. Thus, he determines that the admission of women to Madrid's art academy in the eighteenth century was an honor based on decorum, not artistic merit.

More recently, Estrella de Diego, one of the most influential scholars in the development of feminist art historical studies in Spain, followed Parada y Santín's lead and dismissed the early participation of women in Spain's art academy by stating that it was purely honorary. In making this assertion, Diego relied heavily on Parada y Santín's discussion of these female academicians and provided little evidence of her own to discount their activities. Diego emphasizes women's exclusion from drawing classes, teaching appointments, and academy contests as evidence of the honorific nature of women's membership, and she argues that they were being rewarded not for artistic talent but for their social status. In Diego's view, serious female participation in the academy did not occur until the nineteenth century.[55]

Diego is correct to suggest that the involvement of women in Spain's academy in the eighteenth century differed significantly from their participation in the institution in the nineteenth century. For example, 1818 marked the first year in which women could attend formal drawing classes in the academy. In addition, eighteenth-century women did not gain appointments to the most important offices in the governing structure of the organization, and they did not participate in official academy prize competitions. But these exclusions do not tell the whole story. The records of the Real Academia de Bellas Artes de San Fernando suggest that women played a more active role in the life of the academy than these formal restrictions imply or than scholars such as Diego have assumed.

The ability of female artists to participate in the academy had important implications for their artistic development. Entrance to the academy was significant both in terms of the training available to an artist and the opportunities open for an artist to gain patronage. After their formation, academies became the center of the art world, controlling not only access to artistic training that previously had been made available in workshops but also dictating style and creating a hierarchy of artistic forms. Academies began to control commissions, and academy accolades became increasingly important components of a professional artist's resume.[56] Academy connections provided important assistance in improving the social position of the artist. It was the academy that granted an artist prestige. Desirous of both this recognition and the opportunity to develop their artistic talents within a community, female artists considered the academy an ideal place for themselves. Although many aristocratic women learned to paint as part of an appropriate education for young ladies, the admission of women into the academy created a new identity for women: the female artist with a public audience.

Established in 1752, Madrid's Academy of Fine Arts formed part of a wave of art academies founded in European cities in the eighteenth century, including Vienna, Copenhagen, London, and St. Petersburg.[57] These academies all patterned themselves after Paris's Académie de Peinture et Sculpture, which was founded more than a century earlier, in 1648. This was not the first time that artists in Madrid had attempted to form an academy. In fact, the municipal council, following a royal order from Philip II, began to consider the issue as early as 1584, but for unknown reasons the idea was quickly abandoned.[58] A similar effort at the beginning of the seventeenth century, this time spurred by painters themselves, was equally short-lived. The creation of the Academy of San Fernando in the eighteenth century was also preceded by some difficulties. The painter Francisco Antonio Meléndez presented the idea to the king in 1726.[59] A preliminary council began to consider the specifics of organizing the proposed academy on July 18, 1744, but it was not until April 12, 1752, that the academy commenced operations. Scholars attribute this eight-year lag to a protracted debate over how to formulate the institution's statutes.

In the end, the Academy of San Fernando followed the organizational lines of its Parisian counterpart. The 1757 statutes of the academy defined three types of academics.[60] The academy bestowed the first title—*académico de honor*—on those of high social status who were great connoisseurs of any of the three branches of art: painting, sculpture, or architecture. These members were chosen mainly for the prestige that they would bring to the academy, particularly when their names appeared in the membership list in academy publications.[61] For example, such prominent individuals as the Duke of Osuna and the Marquis of Ayerbe were admitted as *académicos de honor*. The remaining two levels of membership were reserved for talented artists. The academy awarded the title of *académico de mérito* to individuals who demonstrated they deserved accreditation as artists. In order to be elected an academic of merit, an artist had to present an example of his work—be it a painting, a sculpture, or an architectural model—to the academy. Then, the academy would vote on whether the artist's work showed that he or she merited distinction. If the candidate was an enrolled student at the academy, he or she had to receive a majority of votes to become an academic of merit. If not an enrolled student, the prospective academician needed a two-thirds majority. Artists who demonstrated significant artistic talent, but whose work had not attained the exceptional quality associated with an academic of merit, were named *supernumerarios,* the third level of academy membership.

Between 1752 and 1808, there were 175 academics of honor, 208 academics of merit, and 54 supernumeraries. Some *socios* occupied more than one category of membership, and the actual total number of academics during this period was 412.[62] In my research in the Archive of the Royal Academy of Fine Arts of San Fernando, I found evidence that thirty-four of these academics were women. Institutional records suggest that the academy judged women on an individual basis and decided their membership by considering their standing as artists, not women. And those female artists won appointments to all three categories of academy membership (see table 1).

TABLE 1. *Women Admitted as* Académicas *to the Real Academia de Bellas Artes de San Fernando, 1752–1808*

Year Admitted	Name of Artist	Titles Awarded
1752	Bárbara María de Hueva	Supernumerary
1753	Angela Pérez Caballero	Supernumerary
1759	Ana Meléndez	Supernumerary
	Faraona María Magdalena Olivieri	Academic of merit
1761	Catherina Cherubini Preciado	Academic of merit
	María Josefa Caron	Academic of merit
1766	Duchess of Huéscar y Arcos, Mariana de Silva Bazán y Sarmiento, Marquise of Coria, Countess of Oropesa	Academic of honor Honorary director
1769	María Prieto	Academic of merit
	Ana Gertrudis de Urrutia	Academic of merit
1771	Francisca de Cevallos Guerra	Academic of honor Academic of merit
1772	Faustina Mosti	Academic of merit
	Manuela Mosti	Academic of merit
	Gertrudis Bertoni	Academic of merit
	Clara Menéndez	Supernumerary
1773	María Luisa Carranque	Academic of honor Academic of merit
1775	Mariana Urries y Pignatelli, Marquise of Estepa	Academic of honor Honorary director
1776	Isabel de Ezpeleta	Academic of honor Academic of merit
1781	María Agustina de Azcona y Valanza	Academic of honor
1782	Marquise of Santa Cruz	Academic of honor Honorary director
1785	Marquise of Villaverde	Academic of honor
	Luisa Sanz de Cortes y Konock	Academic of honor Academic of merit
1788	Princess of Listenois Beaufremont, Antonia de Lavauguyon	Academic of merit Honorary directory

(continued)

TABLE 1. *(continued)*

Year Admitted	Name of Artist	Titles Awarded
1790	Ana María Mengs	Academic of honor
		Academic of merit
	María Lucia Gilabert	Academic of honor
		Academic of merit
	María Ramona Palafox y Portocarrero, Countess of Contraminz	Academic of honor
		Academic of merit
	María Ana Sabatini	Academic of honor
		Academic of merit
1791	Juana Regis Armendaríz y Samaniego, Marquise of Portago	Academic of honor
	Francisca Efigenia Meléndez	Academic of merit
	María Juana Hurtado de Mendoza	Academic of merit
1793	Elena Goughi y Quilty	Academic of merit
1802	Infanta Doña María Isabel	Academic of honor
		Academic of merit
1805	María Jacoba Costilla y Jaraba	Academic of merit
	Marcela de la Valencia	Academic of merit
	Marquise of Villafranca	Academic of merit

SOURCES: Archivo de la Real Academia de Bellas Artes de San Fernando, Legajos 40-4/1, 49-10/1, 82-8/4, 81-10/4, 3/14, 3/15, 3/18, 3/19, 3/81, 3/82, 3/83, 3/84, 3/85, 3/86, 3/87, 3/88, 3/121, 3/122, 3/124, 3/126, 55-2/1, CF-1/2, CF-2/17; and *Distribución de los premios* for the years 1754, 1760, 1763, 1766, 1769, 1772, 1778, 1784, 1790, 1793, 1796, 1802, 1805, and 1832. Also, Juan Agustín Ceán Bermúdez, *Diccionario histórico de los más ilustres profesores de las Bellas Artes en España* (1800; reprint, Madrid: Reales Academias de Bellas Artes de San Fernando y de la Historia, 1965); Frick Art Reference Library, *Spanish Artists from the Fourth to the Twentieth Century: A Critical Dictionary* (New York: G. K. Hall and Company, 1993); Alfonso E. Pérez Sánchez, "Las mujeres 'pintoras' en España," in *La imagen de la mujer en el arte español: Actas de las terceras jornadas de investigación interdisciplinaria*, ed. Universidad Autónoma de Madrid, Seminario de Estudios de la Mujer (Madrid: Ediciones de la Universidad Autónoma de Madrid, 1984), 73–86; Leo R. Schidlof, *La miniature en Europe aux 16e, 17e, 18e, et 19e siècles*, vol. 2 (Austria: Akademische Druck—u. Verlagsanstalt, 1964); Maxwell William Stirling, *Annals of the Artists of Spain* (London: John C. Nimmo, 1891); Diego Ignacio Parada, *Escritoras y eruditas españolas (ó apuntes y noticias para servir á una historia del ingenio y cultura literaria de las mujeres españolas, desde los tiempos más remotos hasta nuestros días, con inclusión de diversas escritoras portuguesas é hispano-americanas* (Madrid: Establecimientos Tipográficos de M. Minuesa, 1881); and José Parada y Santín, *Las pintoras españolas* (Madrid: Imprenta del Asilo de Huérfanos del S.C. de Jesús, 1902).

The most telling appointments in terms of women's artistic abilities are the twenty-four academics of merit and the four supernumeraries. The records of the academy show that the institution judged these female artists, like their male counterparts, by a complete evaluation of their work as stipulated in the statutes. This suggests that they were taken seriously as artists, not simply rewarded for their social status. The evaluation of female artists in this way was a precedent set from the date of the first admission of a woman to the academy. Juan Agustín Ceán Bermúdez, who compiled a dictionary of Spanish painters in 1800, describes the decision to admit Barbara María de Hueva:

> The day of June 13, 752 [sic], in which was celebrated the inaugural council of the royal academy of S. Fernando, she presented in the council some drawings by her own hand that merited the approbation of the directors and many acclamations from those present. Then the vice-protector who presided over it said in a loud voice: "Señores, the drawings that we have just finished seeing reveal so much progress by their creator, who even without benefiting from the privileges of sex, the academy grants for her merit the honorable title of academic, hoping that with it the celebrated will aspire in the name of other renowned female professors." From that point she retained the title of supernumerary academic, and it was the first title that the establishment bestowed.[63]

This practice of judging works continued. Faraona María Magdalena Olivieri submitted two portraits in her bid for membership, one of her husband, the architect Santiago Marquet, and one self-portrait (see figure 2). The academy voted unanimously to include her as an academic of merit on December 18, 1759. A letter sent to Olivieri from the secretary of the academy described the reasons why the academy chose to admit her, noting in particular her exceptional use of colors.[64]

When Isabel de Ezpeleta displayed a pencil drawing of a young girl to the academy in 1776, the organization "celebrated the delicacy and skill with which she handled the pencil" and named her an academic of honor and merit.[65] The academy explained that María Prieto was admitted in 1769 "in recognition of the success and skill with which she had executed the pencil drawings that she presented to the Academy."[66] Similarly, the academy records indicate admission of Gertrudis Bertoni in 1772 based on an evaluation of a portrait she composed in red pencil, and María Juana Hurtado de Mendoza in 1791 based on a study of her pencil drawing of Minerva. These examples demonstrate that the admission of women into the academy of San Fernando as members of merit or as supernumeraries was not hon-

Figure 2. Faraona María Magdalena Olivieri, *Self-Portrait*, circa 1759. Pastel, 56 x 45 cm. Catalog no. 94. Courtesy of the Museo de la Real Academia de Bellas Artes de San Fernando, Madrid.

orary. Rather, it was based on the demonstration of talent and the presentation of a worthy piece of art.

Also indicative of the serious nature of female appointments are the contents of women's bids for admission. The letters women sent requesting admission to the academy emphasized their artistic training and skill. Elena Goughi y Quilty wrote a letter to Isidoro Bosarte on July 12, 1793, requesting admission to the academy: "My Dear Sir: Having a strong affection for the study of the three fine arts and having made these days the design that I include, I ask that you grant me the favor of presenting it to the Royal Academy, anxious that it will merit its approbation and achieve some level of distinction with which the institution is known to encourage those people who hold it in high esteem."[67] By emphasizing the drawing that accompanied her letter, Goughi y Quilty indicated that she wanted to be considered for membership based on her displayed talent. The academy considered her request at their *junta general* the following day. On July 18, they informed her that she had been admitted as an academic of merit after a study of her drawing.

María Jacoba Costilla's application letter, sent to the academy on January 5, 1805, followed a similar pattern by stressing her past artistic activities: "Having dedicated myself from a tender age to drawing, I have had the honor of receiving awards in two contests sponsored by the Academy of Fine Arts established earlier in Toledo; following the force of my desire to draw, I have executed the one that I present to you, making at the same time, as it is the most efficacious moment, a reverent plea for you to grant me the honor of presenting it to the Royal Academy of Arts."[68] Like Goughi y Quilty, Costilla emphasized her proven artistic ability so that the academy would judge her as a serious artist. She referred to her past studies and previous awards in Toledo as well as submitted concrete evidence of her skill in drawing: a copy of a painting of the Virgin by Anton Raphaël Mengs. On January 6, the academy considered Costilla's bid for membership. As a result of her demonstrated skill, by a vote of nineteen in favor and two against, Costilla was admitted as an academic of merit. In her acceptance letter to the academy, dated January 19, she thanked her supporters for recording her achievements and encouraging her artistic talent: "Full of gratitude for the honor which the Royal Academy has deemed worthy to grant me by naming me Academic of merit in painting, I will always look at this distinction as a powerful stimulus that should impel me to dedicate myself to my work and to devote myself to the noble and skillful art of drawing."[69] For Costilla, academy admission was an important indicator of her achievements as an artist as well as an encouragement to continue her work.

María Agustina de Azcona y Valanza's petition for admission is very similar to those of Goughi y Quilty and Costilla. In a note to the academy dated January 13, 1781, Azcona y Valanza expressed her desire to be a member of the academy and described the accompanying drawing she hoped would prove her talent: "The inclination that I have always had toward the Noble Arts, and especially drawing, has inspired in me the desire to be a member of this Royal Academy, to which end I have completed the enclosed copy of a figure of Anibal Caraci, which I send to you to do me the favor of presenting it at the Academy."⁷⁰ Apparently, the academy did not find Azcona y Valanza's copy to be of the necessary quality to appoint her as either an academic of merit or a supernumerary. However, wanting to recognize her dedication to the arts, they selected her to be an academic of honor. This placed Azcona y Valanza in a group with three other women appointed solely as academics of honor: Mariana Urries y Pignatelli (see figure 3), the Marquise of Villaverde, and Juana Regis Armendariz y Samaniego.⁷¹ The fact that not all women were awarded the same title suggests that an assessment of a woman's artistic work was an essential determinant of whether she would be admitted to the academy and, more precisely, what rank in the academy she would hold.

In addition to being regular members, four of the women admitted to the academy in the eighteenth century were named honorary directors, a distinction generally reserved for artists of great skill who had the support of the king. The four women granted this title were the Duchess of Huéscar, the Marquise of Santa Cruz, the Princess of Listenois Beaufrement, and the Marquise of Estepa. In the 1766 *Distribución de los premios*, the academy wrote of the Duchess of Huéscar's selection as an honorary director:

> The Academy recognized that the drawing in itself, and without respect to the hand that formed it, merited the same praise as that of the most perfect and accomplished Professor: with which we could not refuse to you the same rank that would be given to him. In those terms and in those of the most rigorous judgment, you by unanimous acclamation, in the Council of July 20, were created and declared *Academic of Honor and Honorary Director of Painting* with voice, vote, and a preeminent seat in both classes, in all of the Councils that you attend, and with the option of holding whatever posts you would like to exercise.⁷²

Past scholars have erroneously dismissed the granting of this title to four aristocratic women, assuming that it must have been an empty honor.⁷³ Academy records suggest that these women were earnestly involved in the life of the organization. Santa Cruz and Listenois, for example, presented paintings numerous times at academy functions, suggesting this appointment both allowed and represented more than yet another honorific title for these aristocrats, encouraging their active, even leading, roles in the institution.⁷⁴

Academy records provide two central reasons for why the institution decided to admit women, rationales that mirrored female applicants' own reasons for joining. Among the more frequently cited explanations is academicians' desire to reward talented female artists. When María Luisa

Figure 3. Mariana Urries y Pignatelli, *Cupid,* circa 1775. Oil on canvas, 33 x 26 cm. Catalog no. 500. Courtesy of the Museo de la Real Academia de Bellas Artes de San Fernando, Madrid.

Carranque submitted her drawing, the academy records stated: "All of the Professors praised highly the skill, intelligence, and quality with which the pastel was worked; and in attention to this and due to the distinguished quality of this Señora, the Señor Viceprotector proposed her for Academic of honor and merit in Painting. And the Council by acclamation and unanimous consent of all its Voices, created and declared her as such Academic of honor and merit in Painting with voice and vote."[75] In addition to applauding already accomplished female artists, the academy wanted to further encourage women in the arts. The institution's response to Faustina and Manuela Mosti's applications for academy membership illustrates this goal in its assessment of the submitted works: "Seen by the Señores Professors, they were applauded highly, and the Academy felt it was an opportune moment to encourage their [Faustina's and Manuela's] application to and strong liking for the arts, to distinguish these Señoras with some title: to which end the Señor Viceprotector proposed them for Academics of Merit in Painting, and by acclamation and unanimous consent they were created and declared Academics of Merit in Painting."[76] Here, the two explanations go hand and hand. Talented female artists would find encouragement to continue their work by receiving a stamp of approval from the academy.

While the process of admission demonstrated the opportunities for female artists, the fact that most of the women who petitioned the academy for admission presented portraits is an important indicator of the limits on female artists in this era. Several factors produced artists' inclination toward portraiture, still lifes, and miniatures. First, during the early modern period, women were prohibited from studying life drawing. This limitation seriously hindered their development as artists, because it essentially barred them from the world of history painting and the production of major works of art. The feminist art historian Linda Nochlin has compared women's exclusion from life drawing to denying a medical student the opportunity to examine or dissect a human body.[77] Nochlin points to Johann Zoffany's 1772 painting *The Life Class at the Royal Academy* as a contemporary illustration of the absence of women from life classes at the art academy in London. The institution's two female members, Angelica Kauffmann and Mary Moser, are represented in Zoffany's painting with their portraits on the wall, since they could not be portrayed among the members of the class.[78] In fact, it was not until 1893 that women in England's academy were allowed to draw from nude models, and even these had to be partially draped.[79] Restrictions on the study of the human nude affected female artists in Spain as well. The notable absence of female artists from registration lists of art courses on the human form until at least 1894 points to restrictions similar to those found in the rest of Europe. Without the ability to study the human body, women could not paint great historical themes as prize competitions warranted.

Other factors also limited women's artistic choices. The art historian Mireia Freixa indicates that the choice to work in a certain medium was motivated by economic considerations: the need to choose a technique that used less expensive materials. For example, painting with pastels or watercolors was much more economical than painting in oils.[80] Further, the greater amount of time involved in mixing oil paints, as well as the complexity of the process, may also have been a factor in restricting women to certain mediums. Among female artists involved in the academy, the dominant mediums were pastel, pencil, and watercolor. The records contain evidence of only one female academician before 1815 who regularly used oil paints: the Marquise of Villafranca (see figure 4). Further, few women worked outside of painting. No aspiring female members presented sculptures or architectural models as examples of their talent. Factors such as women's lack of training in life classes and their restriction to certain types of materials, compounded by notions that certain genres were more appropriate for women, relegated female artists to less-respected artistic forms.[81]

While the prevalence of portraits and miniatures does point to limitations in female artistic production, the fact that many of the women presented copies does not suggest that their works lacked originality or skill. Rather, it documents their participation in what contemporary artists considered a vital step in artistic training at the academy. As Carl Goldstein explains, the practice of copying was an important component of an academic education dating back to the Renaissance.[82] Copying became a regular part of teaching at the academy as artists copied selected works considered to embody the ideal. Thus, the fact that women worked on copies suggests that they were being trained according to normal academic methods, just as other students were. Many of the women were skilled at reproducing other artists' works. In fact, a compilation of the academician María del Carmen Saíz's engravings based on copies of works by Rafael de Urbino was sold as a practice book in 1816.[83]

Female artists also participated in various academy-sponsored exhibitions. The display of their work in a public forum represented another key aspect of their participation in the life of the academy. In the fall of 1793, the academy decided to open its doors for two weeks every summer "in order to encourage a taste and liking for the three Fine Arts and for the esteem and goals of the institution of the Academy."[84] These public exhibitions, open from 9 A.M. to 2 P.M. and 4 P.M. to 6 P.M., were much like the famous salons

Figure 4. Francisco de Goya, *The Marquise of Villafranca Painting Her Husband*, 1804. Oil on canvas, 195 x 126 cm. Catalog no. 2448. Courtesy of the Museo del Prado, Madrid.

of Paris that the French academy held annually. Madrid's public exhibitions frequently featured the works of female artists. In fact, at the first exhibit, seven women—Mariana Sabatini, Luisa Sanz Cortes y Konock, Ana María Mengs, Elena Goughi y Quilty, Dorotea Michel, María Juana Hurtado de Mendoza, and María Ramona Palafox y Portocarrero (see figure 5)—exhibited their works alongside the creations of four men. The year 1793 was not an exception. At least fifty-two women presented their works in the academy's public exhibitions during the period between 1793, when these exhibitions began, and 1808, when they were suspended as a result of the French invasion.[85]

These were not women's exhibitions; they were full-fledged academy exhibitions in which both male and female artists displayed their works. For example, the skilled royal engraver Antonio Salvador Carmona and the well-known Francisco Goya exhibited their works alongside those of female artists. The academy also welcomed women as attendees at the official ceremonies that accompanied these public exhibitions. At the August 4, 1790, *junta pública*, for example, the Marquise of Santa Cruz, the Princess of Listenois Beaufremont, and Luisa Sanz Cortes y Konock witnessed a competition that included the work of four other female artists.[86] Thus, the participation of women in these public exhibitions is an important indicator of their real participation in the life of the academy.

Female artists also presented their works at the meetings of the academy, often in order to obtain the opinion of academy professors on their style or technique. At the October 5, 1794, *junta ordinaria*, the council members examined a pencil drawing by María Gertrudis de la Cueva y Alcedo. According to the record of that meeting, the *socios* who were present remarked on Cueva y Alcedo's artistic skill: "They celebrated her application to and achievements in this noble art."[87] Some artists exhibited their works frequently in the academy in order to chart their artistic progress. Notable is María del Carmen Saíz, who presented works to the academy eighteen times between 1803 and 1806.

Not all the women who displayed their works in the public exhibitions or the meetings of the academy were members of the institution (see table 2). For example, Dorotea Michel, daughter of the famed court sculptor Pedro Michel and one of the women mentioned above for participating in the 1793 public exhibition, does not appear on any of the lists of *académicas*. In fact, there were at least thirty-eight women, including Michel, who presented works to the academy as nonmembers in the years before 1808. This is very much in line with the practices of the French salons, which also allowed nonmembers to exhibit.[88] Perhaps the restrictions for membership were

Figure 5. María Ramona Palafox y Portocarrero, *Virgin with Child*, circa 1790. Pencil, 24 cm. diameter. Catalog no. P/2330. Courtesy of the Museo de la Real Academia de Bellas Artes de San Fernando, Madrid.

more rigorous than those for participating in public exhibitions. Regardless, the participation of these artists indicates that the academy facilitated the artistic development of, and offered access to an audience for, an even larger group of women in the eighteenth century.

The fact that some of Madrid's female academicians gained a reputation for their artistic endeavors is also noteworthy. In particular, Juan Agustín Ceán Bermúdez included a number of these female academics in his *Diccionario histórico de los más ilustres profesores de las Bellas Artes en España*, originally published in 1800. Ceán Bermúdez includes short entries praising the talents of Ana Meléndez, María Prieto, Barbara María de Hueva, and the Duchess of Huéscar.[89] One of his lengthier entries describes the life and works of Ana María Mengs. Mengs had been admitted to the academy as a member of merit on August 29, 1790, after presenting a pencil drawing titled *Madonna de la segiola* and three portraits in pastel—one of her father, the artist Anton Raphaël Mengs; one of her husband, the engraver Manuel Salvador Carmona; and another of her eldest daughter.[90] In his entry, Ceán Bermúdez recounted a bit of her biography as well as commended her excellent work in portraiture. He listed the numerous subjects she had painted, including the Infante Don Luis, the Marquise of Valdecarzana, Juliana Morales, and her own family. For Ceán Bermúdez, the fact that Mengs was a woman made her artistic achievements even more noteworthy. He includes details that highlight her accomplishments in light of her sex, such as: "Educated by that father and teacher who did not deny her being a student in spite of the inconveniences posed by her sex and her marriage"; and "Although she added to the burden with seven births, and the care and education of her children, she did not stop painting miniatures and pastels with good taste and intelligence."[91] Ceán Bermúdez portrays Mengs as an artist able to create in spite of the limits of her sex. His celebration of Mengs emphasizes that she embraced her responsibilities as a wife and mother but still found time for her art.

Ana María Mengs's fame went beyond Bermudez's acclaim. For example, in 1793 the academy organized an exhibition of the works of Mengs to commemorate the first anniversary of her death. At this exhibition, the Alcalá gallery displayed four of her pastels, along with works by Zacarías González Velázquez and other academic painters of her time.[92] The academy added to this commemoration in the 1793 *Distribución de los premios* by including a short piece on Mengs's life and works. This article detailed her marriage to Manuel Salvador Carmona in Rome in 1777 and her subsequent move to Spain. Of her works and talent, the academy wrote:

> The Academy paid deserved respect to this Señora, not simply for the merits of Don Antonio Mengs, but also for having made her own legacy. She cultivated painting in miniature and in pastel with great enthusiasm. Of those two genres, she presented works to Their Majesties, who had the satisfaction of accepting them with pleasure. She did various portraits at the behest of Señor Infante Don Luis: one of her Excellency the Señora Marquise of Valdecarzana, and another of the Señora Doña Juliana Morales. She also painted a portrait of her husband, Don Manuel Carmona, and presented it to the Academy, where it was always seen as original and deserving of applause: because in its likeness and level of painting you could hardly hope for anything better. Other various works of her hand are preserved by the family.[93]

TABLE 2. *Nonacademic Female Artists Who Exhibited at the Real Academia de Bellas Artes de San Fernando, 1785–1808*

Name of Artist	Exhibitions
Princess Luisa María	*Junta ordinaria* of April 3, 1785
Matilde de Gálvez	*Junta ordinaria* of August 4, 1793
Dorotea Michel	Public exhibition 1793
	Junta general of July 11, 1793
	Junta ordinaria of June 5, 1796
	Junta pública of June 5, 1796
María Magdalena de Enrile y Alcedo	*Junta ordinaria* of September 8, 1793
	Public exhibition 1794
	Junta ordinaria of April 6, 1794
Josepha Desvallo Coronela	Public exhibition 1794
María Gertrudis de la Cueva y Alcedo	Public exhibition 1794
	Junta ordinaria of April 6, 1794
	Junta ordinaria of October 5, 1794
Antonia Quintanilla	Public exhibition 1796
Isidora Villarino	Public exhibition 1797
María Magdalena Fernandez de Cordóva	Public exhibition 1799
Catalina Martin y Abril	*Junta ordinaria* of October 5, 1800
María Dolores Valenzuela y Pizarro	Public exhibition 1800
	Public exhibition 1802
María Ignacio de Texada Hermoso y de la Buria	Public exhibition 1801
	Public exhibition 1802
	Public exhibition 1803
	Public exhibition 1804
	Public exhibition 1805
	Public exhibition 1807
	Public exhibition 1808
Josepha Marsilla de Teruel y Montezuma	Public exhibition 1801
María Dolores Escobedo y Velasco	Public exhibition 1801
	Public exhibition 1802
	Public exhibition 1803
	Junta ordinaria of September 8, 1805
María Teresa de Arteaga y Palafox	Public exhibition 1801
	Public exhibition 1803
María Manuela Ybañez de la Rentería	Public exhibition 1802
	Public exhibition 1803
	Public exhibition 1804
	Public exhibition 1805
	Public exhibition 1806

(continued)

TABLE 2. *(continued)*

Name of Artist	Exhibitions
María Manuela Ybañez de la Rentería *(continued)*	Public exhibition 1807 Public exhibition 1808
Juana Antuner de Velasco	Public exhibition 1803
María Francisca Priego	Public exhibition 1803
Francisca Bernaldo de Quiros	Public exhibition 1803
Josepha Novales	Public exhibition 1803 Public exhibition 1804 Public exhibition 1805 Public exhibition 1806
Francisca Sabatier	Public exhibition 1804 Public exhibition 1805
María del Carmen Macía	Public exhibition 1804 Junta ordinaria of May 6, 1804 Junta ordinaria of June 3, 1804 Junta ordinaria of November 4, 1804 Junta ordinaria of March 3, 1805 Junta ordinaria of May 5 1805 Public exhibition 1805
María Casilda de Lezo y Garro	Public exhibition 1805 Junta ordinaria of July 25, 1805 Public exhibition 1806
Cipriana Durán	Public exhibition 1805
María Paula Miret	Public exhibition 1805
María Luisa García	Public exhibition 1805 Public exhibition 1807
Rita Martin de Retamora	Public exhibition 1806 Public exhibition 1807
María de la Quadra	Public exhibition 1806 Public exhibition 1807
María Josefa de Frías	Public exhibition 1807
María Concepción Justiniana y Peñaflorida	Public exhibition 1807 Public exhibition 1808
Luisa Soto y Urgujo	Public exhibition 1807
Duchess of Medinaceli y Santistevan	Public exhibition 1807
María Concepción Prada	Public exhibition 1807
María Campuzano	Public exhibition 1807
María Domingo Carbonero	Public exhibition 1807
Ana María Galazzo	Public exhibition 1807
María del Pilar Vizurrun de Azanza	Public exhibition 1808
Manuela Girón	Public exhibition 1808

While even in this tribute Mengs could not escape the connection with her father, these celebrations of her talent suggest that her contemporaries appreciated her artistic abilities above and beyond her family connections.

That Mengs's relatives included prominent artists did not make her unique among female academicians. In the words of the art historian Germaine Greer, "The single most striking fact about the women who made names for themselves as painters before the nineteenth century is that almost all of them were related to better-known male painters, while the proportion of male painters who were *not* related to other painters is nearly as high as the proportion of women who were."[94] The fact that a number of the women admitted to the academy were related to artists indicates the means women had to receive artistic training in early modern Europe. Put simply, women who did not receive artistic training within their families generally did not receive it at all. While access to training for women not related to artists did increase throughout the eighteenth century, the number of academicians related to artists is still striking. Mengs, the eldest of four daughters, received most of her artistic training from her father. Her mother, Teresa Concordia Marón (1725–1806), was also an excellent miniaturist and may have provided some instruction as well.[95] The Meléndez family presents another telling example. Both Ana Meléndez and Clara Meléndez received their artistic instruction as part of a family of artists. The daughters of the painter Francisco Antonio Meléndez (b. 1682), Ana and Clara were also related to other artists: the court painter Miguel Jacinto Meléndez (1679–1734, named court painter in 1712) was their uncle, and the still life painter Luis Meléndez (1716–1780) and the miniaturist Josef Agustin Meléndez (b. 1724) were their brothers. Their cousin, Francisca Efigenia Meléndez, the daughter of Miguel Jacinto Meléndez, undoubtedly owes her artistic training to her family lineage as well (see figure 6).

Aside from the issue of access to training, being related to an artist had both negative and positive effects on female artists. One of the major difficulties of family tutelage occurred when an artistic father pushed his apprentice daughter to mimic his style rather than develop her own. It was practically impossible for women to overcome the style and subject matter of their male teachers without risking losing the technical training they coveted.[96] Conversely, being related to an artist may have allowed some women access to training in genres not generally considered suitable for women. For example, the fact that María Prieto's husband and father were both engravers gave her the opportunity to learn and experiment in the medium of engraving when very few women artists did so.[97]

Only a few of the works produced by these female academicians have

70 / *Developing Ideologies of Citizenship*

Figure 6. Francisca Efigenia Meléndez, *Virgin with Child*, circa 1791. Oil on canvas, 21 x 18 cm. Catalog no. 465. Courtesy of the Museo de la Real Academia de Bellas Artes de San Fernando, Madrid.

survived.[98] Records suggest that female artists donated some of their works to the academy and that these works became part of the academy's permanent collection. For example, in 1790 the Marquise of Santa Cruz gave the academy a miniature pastel portrait that she had painted (presumably a copy) of Rubens with one of his wives. In an inventory of works donated to the academy, the listing for this item recorded the following note to the Marquise: "There is no one who would not give the highest praise to the exactitude, grace, and diligence with which you have composed this work, and all of us applaud your constant application and notable progress in this branch of fine arts."[99] The academy also seemed happy to receive two donations from María Lucia Gilabert. When she offered them a pencil drawing with an engraved frame on August 5, 1794, they thanked her and noted they would hang it in a distinguished location.[100] Similarly, they received with pleasure her August 13, 1799, donation of a self-portrait in pastel that she had exhibited at the *junta pública* of July 13. An early nineteenth-century inventory of the academy also indicates its ownership of works by Ana Meléndez, Faraona María Magdalena Olivieri, Catherina Cherubini, María Josefa Caron (see figure 7), Ana María Mengs, Francisca Efigenia Meléndez, and María Lucia Gilabert.[101] An 1817 inventory includes works by Rosa Ruiz de la Prada, María Luisa Carranque, Marcela de la Valencia, Clementina Bouligni del Pizarro, the Marquise of Villafranca, and the Marquise of Estepa.[102] The fact that these works, and others donated by eighteenth-century female artists, were accepted as part of the academy's permanent collection suggests a certain importance placed on the work of the institution's female members.[103]

Female artists may have been members of other art academies throughout Spain as well. Parada y Santín quotes evidence to assert that Micaela Ferrer was elected to the Academia de San Carlos in Valencia as an academic of merit on April 13, 1777.[104] He also lists Casilda Bisbal (August 9, 1789); María Vicenta Ramón y Ripalda (July 12, 1801); Eulalia Gerona (July 22, 1802); María Josefa Miranda, the Marquise of la Bóveda (June 6, 1815); and Ana Torres as members of the Valencian academy. Parada y Santín indicates that the Academia de San Carlos named Engracia de las Casas as both an honorary director and an academic of merit on October 23, 1774. Similarly, Josefa Mayans y Pastor (October 21, 1776) and María Caro y Sureda (December 18, 1779) were named honorary directors. Manuela Mercader y Caro, the Baroness of Cheste (December 18, 1779), was named an honorary director and academic of merit based on an evaluation of her pastel portrait of San Francisco.[105] Parada y Santín asserts that María Eugenia Miñano y Ramírez was named to the Academy of Noble Arts in Valladolid on April 7, 1799.[106] This information suggests that women's participation in Madrid's Real Academia de Bellas Artes de San Fernando was not an exceptional case.

Through their involvement in the life of the academy and as hosts of Madrid's prominent *tertulias*, women helped shape the new institutions of Enlightenment sociability that sprang up in the 1740s and 1750s. The accep-

Figure 7. María Josefa Caron, *D. Diego de Villanueva*, circa 1761. Pastel, 55 x 45 cm. Catalog no. 40. Courtesy of the Museo de la Real Academia de Bellas Artes de San Fernando, Madrid.

tance of female intellectuals and artists as central participants in this broad arena of cultural discourse evidences the degree to which predominant views on female intellectual capacity had changed by the 1750s. The relative acceptance of Feijoo's more open views on women enabled elite women to take full part in Spain's dynamic social and cultural transformations. Just as Feijoo's essay had reopened the age-old debate on the nature of women, the public visibility of Spain's *ilustradas* forced the question of their place in an enlightened society to the forefront of eighteenth-century debates.

As Spanish intellectuals worked to reshape some of their social and cultural institutions and to reform the nation's political and economic order, the question of how women should be involved in this regeneration became a central one. Women's leadership in *tertulias* and their admittance to Spain's newest academy had seemingly occurred without much controversy. At midcentury, male literati and academics embraced, and even seemed to encourage, female intellectual and artistic pursuits. Yet as their presence in these central and very public Enlightenment institutions made the question of their status impossible to ignore, the relatively calm waters of change would become increasingly murky.

3 On Equal Terms?

Membership in the Economic Society

In October 1775, Manuel José Marín posed a question to the newly formed Real Sociedad Económica Matritense de Amigos del País (Madrid's Royal Economic Society of Friends of the Country): should the group permit women to join? As Marín presented his arguments for female membership to his fellow Economic Society associates at the October 21 meeting of the general council, he made a telling reference to women's now twenty-year stint in the ranks of the Academy of Fine Arts of San Fernando in Madrid. Citing the case of the Duchess of Huéscar y Arcos, whom the academy named an academic of honor and an honorary director of painting in 1766, Marín asked his peers: "If a woman of such elevated position . . . has not considered it contrary to her greater enlightenment to risk staining her fingers with pencil, with what reasoning can we doubt that many Ladies of all the nobility, in so much as they are able and their brightness and circumstances permit them, will dedicate their attentions to the growth of Industry, to the reestablishment of Agriculture, and to the advance of the Arts?"[1] As Marín pointed out, women's presence in one key center of Enlightenment life begged the question of their participation in another.

Still, answering his deceptively simple query took no less than twelve years.[2] Marín's initial proposal for female membership in the Economic Society in Madrid and its eventual acceptance, culminating in women's admission to the organization in 1787, reveals the degree to which beliefs about the nature of the female sex and women's abilities had begun to change. The protracted debate that intervened, however, suggests just how tenuous the shift had been. The very fact that the inclusion of previously excluded groups surfaced as a topic requiring real deliberation suggests the force of calls for universal rights, even those as carefully couched as Marín's. Once women formed part of other realms of Enlightenment sociability, such as *tertulias* and the Real Academia de Bellas Artes de San Fernando, their absence from other institutions became noticeable, a matter for discussion.

That the topic would arise as a vital one in the inaugural decade of the Economic Society was logical, as women were slated to take on key roles in members' plans for reform. And here, the debate over *whether* women should participate in such institutions came to encompass *how* women could contribute and *what* their participation would mean to the nation. A number of Society members felt women's increased presence in industry was in fact crucial to placing Spain on the road to economic and political modernization, something they all desired. As these architects of a new Spain called for poorer women to become robust producers, they looked to elite women to become constant consumers. In this rank-based division of the female citizenry, elite women were to remain somewhat passive, their role in the nation tied to their pocketbooks. This vision extended to their participation in the Economic Society, where even *socios* who supported women's admission outlined a very limited role for prospective *socias*. Only the two female writers who publicly participated in the debate argued, often in frustration, that women who were to be admitted deserved an equal standing with men. The intense debate that took place in the chambers of the Economic Society and on the pages of Madrid's thriving periodicals showed just how fragile was women's claim to equal participation and men's acceptance of their equal status.

WOMEN IN INDUSTRY: A LARGER DEBATE

The arguments over women's incorporation in the Economic Society represented pieces of a larger discussion on how to modernize Spain. The Economic Societies were at the heart of this debate, since many Spaniards believed that developing the nation's industry was the key to its future success. The idea for the Economic Societies, born out of a gathering of Basque men organized by Javier María Munive e Idiáquez, the Count of Peñaflorida, originated in the lively intellectual exchange Peñaflorida witnessed during his youth in France.[3] When he returned to Spain in 1746, he hoped to see the same level of discourse flourish in his own country. So, in 1753 he organized an informal society of Basque intellectuals. In 1764, this group petitioned the king to be declared an official organization, and their request was granted one year later. The Sociedad Bascongada de los Amigos del País (the Basque Society of Friends of the Country) was born. From its inception, the group took on a wide variety of challenging tasks. Vowing to encourage agriculture, industry, commerce, and the arts and sciences, the group provided instruction in everything from Latin to experimental physics, sponsored contests to encourage industrial innovation, supported local agriculture and manufacturing, and built an impressive library of both Spanish and foreign works.

This flurry of activity attracted national attention, and the idea to create similar organizations in other parts of the country soon surfaced. The creation of an Economic Society in the country's capital city of Madrid in 1775 strengthened the connection between Spain's most influential reformers and these fledgling economic institutions. Though not the first of its kind, Madrid's Economic Society provided a model for other cities' reform efforts and its statutes formed the basis for the other fifty-four similar Societies founded throughout Spain between 1775 and 1789.[4] Thanks to its location in Madrid, the Sociedad Económica Matritense embodied the active partnership between Spain's reform-minded elite and the new Bourbon dynasty and quickly became the most influential of its type in the country.[5]

One of the issues members of the Economic Society immediately took up was women's role in the nation's economy. The crux of this issue became jump-starting Spanish industry, and a number of the solutions that contemporaries devised included incorporating women in various capacities. Several Spanish economic theorists, themselves members of the Madrid Economic Society, pointed to women's purportedly idle hands as a potential resource for industrial expansion. Failing to recognize that the time of all but the most elite women was taken up with unpaid domestic labor, these thinkers sought in women's work a panacea for Spain's industrial weakness. The prominent economist Pedro Rodríguez Campomanes (1723–1803), for example, argued that female idleness was hurting the nation, and he encouraged an increase in the participation of women in light industry. In both his 1774 *Discurso sobre el fomento de la industria popular* (Treatise on the Promotion of Popular Industry) and his 1775 *Discurso sobre la educación popular de los artesanos y su fomento* (Treatise on the Popular Education of Artisans and Its Promotion), Campomanes points to the idleness of wives and daughters, who put an added burden on male workers. He celebrates a past era when, in contrast, women and children worked, not only augmenting the family's income, but also supplying the nation with products that it currently had to import from abroad: "The wife and daughters of the worker busied themselves in laboring and spinning wool, and we did not have foreign wool, estamines, serge, flannels, and cordillas among us."[6] Campomanes extols the work of women in Spain's coastal regions like Galicia and Asturias who did everything from going out on fishing boats to weeding, planting, and harvesting crops. Unlike the inactive creatures that women had become, he explains, women in the past had been vital contributors to the nation's economy.

To emphasize his point, Campomanes calculates the number of idle women on the peninsula and surrounding islands whose work could help Spain's economy. He estimates that, if the 4 million able-bodied Spanish women were put to work spinning yarn, they could each spin 1 and 1/2 *reales*' worth of yarn per day.[7] In total, these women could add over 1 billion *reales* (80 million pesos) per year to Spain's industrial output. Antonio de la Quadra presents similar calculations in a memorandum to the Economic Society on October 14, 1775, in which he addresses the question of idle women in Madrid.[8] Perhaps inspired by Campomanes's calculation of the idle women in Spain, Quadra presents his own figures on the output that Madrid's idle women could achieve. He starts with an estimated 65,000 women in Madrid and eliminated 8,000 who were sixty years or older, 9,000 who were eight years or younger, 15,000 who were already employed, and 8,000 who were members of the upper classes. According to his computations, this left 25,000 women who were unnecessarily idle. As an example of what they could accomplish if they were put to work, Quadra contemplates the production of these women as spinners. He estimates that each woman could produce six ounces of yarn per day and thus, as a group, could produce thirty million ounces per year (based on two hundred work days per year). This work, he indicates, would produce a value of 15,820,312 *reales* and 17 *maravedis* (a Spanish coin worth $\frac{1}{34}$ of a *real*) per year.[9] With their calculations, both Campomanes and Quadra seem to demonstrate that the inclusion of currently idle women in the workforce would "add a vast sum to the nation's wealth."[10]

Economic theorists explained that female idleness was rooted in various social conventions. Much like French physiocrats and in the spirit of Adam Smith, they argued that these artificial restrictions needed to be removed in order to harness this potential female workforce. Campomanes, for example, blames the prevalence of female idleness in Spain on the persistent influence of Moorish culture, contrasting the assumed enclosure and idleness of women in Islamic society with the industrious lives of ancient Spanish women: "The moors and orientals have women enclosed in idleness. These customs do not agree with European practices."[11] Here, Campomanes clearly links Spain to the dominant European culture. Referring to the active women of the coastal regions, he writes, "The ancient Spanish women up to the eighth century of the Christian era all lived industrious lives, and their current apathy is a bad custom derived from the Arabs."[12]

It is significant that Campomanes refers here to two of Spain's northernmost regions. First, there was a myth of matriarchy in the north tied in part to the existence of matrilineal inheritance practices in some northern provinces. This provided him with something to draw on in presenting his view of how women lived there in the past. Also, the Muslim influence was felt to have been more pronounced in southern Spain. In particular, Asturias was the home of Pelayo, a Christian leader who waged a successful battle against the Moors in Covadonga in 722. Pelayo's victory marked the beginning of the reconquest, which was fought by the subjects of Pelayo's successors in Asturias and Galicia. Spaniards like Campomanes considered themselves the descendants of Pelayo. Thus, for Campomanes, the success of Spain relied on expunging Islamic practices brought to the peninsula with the invasion from North Africa in 711 and realigning Spaniards with the European practices of their past. The eradication of female idleness, an undesirable remnant of Spain's Muslim past, was essential to improving Spanish society in the future.[13]

While Campomanes viewed the enclosure of women as a remnant of "Moorish" influence, Jovellanos blamed guilds for having severely restricted female life. In a speech to the Economic Society on November 9, 1785, Jovellanos explains the importance of Charles III's efforts to remove guild restrictions affecting women's freedom to participate in industry.[14] According to Jovellanos, the guilds "have frustrated the liberty to work of half of the people who adopted them; they have separated women almost completely from the exercise of the arts, and they have reduced to idleness hands that nature created deft and flexible for the perfection of work."[15] The guilds, he argues, were artificial regulations that disturbed the natural order of the economy and society.

Anticipating the way that nineteenth-century liberals like John Stuart Mill would argue for women's political rights, Jovellanos maintains that natural limitations alone should determine the bounds of women's place in industry. Referring specifically to the 1779 royal decree, he explains that "the royal warrants establish a general rule, and they permit women to do all work that is not included as an exception. With that, if something remains to be verified, it is only which labors are loathsome to womanly decency and strength."[16] Jovellanos believed that women would not participate in work that was contrary to their nature. Utilizing the example of a female-owned tailor shop, he points out that no woman would herself go to a man's house to take measurements or to have him try on clothes, as "each sex knows what agrees with its decency."[17] Thus, Jovellanos did not see the rationale behind laws that restrict women's participation, as women would naturally restrict themselves. In the example of the tailor shop, he particularly attacks restrictions on women in the needle trades since, as he points out, "the very exercise of sewing is more suited to women than to men; so why cheat women of work with which they can earn a living without diminishing their honorableness?"[18] Jovellanos did not see men and women as completely equal; rather, he felt that natural limitations instead of artificially imposed restrictions should shape the range of male and female activities.

Women's inadequate education constituted another social barrier to female participation in industry. Thus one more step in ending the assumed idleness of women was educating them. Both Campomanes and Jovellanos, in particular, emphasized the importance of female education.[19] Following Feijoo's lead, Campomanes indicates that women's capacities are naturally equal to men's: "Women have the same use of reason as men do: the neglect that it suffers in their education is the only difference, no fault of their own."[20] Jovellanos did not consider women to be naturally lazy and weak; rather, he saw this as the product of their upbringing. He explains how the notion that women's education should be shaped by the goal of creating ornaments for men's pleasure hinders women. According to Jovellanos:

> The Creator fashioned women to be companions to men in all the occupations of life, and although he endowed them with less vigor and strength so that they would never be ignorant of the subordination that he imposed on them, he certainly did not make them useless for work. We were the ones who, against the design of Providence, made them weak and delicate. Accustomed to looking at them as born simply for our pleasure, we have segregated them from the study of all active professions, we have enclosed them, we have made them idle, and in the end we have combined the idea of their existence with the idea of debility and weakness, which education and custom have deeply rooted in our spirits more and more every day.[21]

Jovellanos contrasts the idleness of women in his society with the active role that they played in "primitive societies." He looks to an ideal past when woman was "the inseparable companion of man, not only in the house, but also in the forest, on the beach, in the field, hunting, fishing, herding, cultivating the earth, and pursuing all of the rest of the activities of life."[22] But this was not merely something from some mythic past "only existing in the imagination of poets"; Jovellanos points to places both in other countries and in Spain itself where, even during his own time, "the women busied themselves with the most difficult and arduous tasks; where they were breadmakers, bakers, weavers of wool and sackcloth, where they traveled to distant markets, and carried commercial goods on their heads, and in a word, where they worked together with men in all occupations and professions."[23]

For Jovellanos, these examples proved that women were naturally equipped to work in a variety of areas.

The obvious flaw in Jovellanos's and other theorists' economic models remained their presumption of female idleness, a theoretical idea that neglected the still dominant mode of the family workshop and that was far removed from the reality of most of Spain's women. This presumption led to their insistent calls for women's education. Confident that women had a natural capacity for work, theorists like Jovellanos and Campomanes saw education as essential to prepare women for their role in the workforce and to ready them for their role in the family. In the words of Campomanes: "If education is not commonplace, the wives and daughters of artisans will remain idle, and they will not be able to inspire industrious conduct in their children and husbands."[24] Campomanes explained that women especially needed to be educated in their capacity as mothers, "since both [boys and girls] receive their first impressions from the explanations and examples of their mothers."[25] This was not an expression of the kind of Republican Motherhood that figures like Mary Wollstonecraft espoused. Rather, these mothers were responsible for instilling a strong work ethic in their children, for making them industrious rather than idle. They were creating future workers, not active citizens. Thus, Campomanes considered female education to be crucial to Spain's regeneration: "None of the concerns of the Economic Societies is more urgent than that of examining the ways to solidly improve the education of women in our Spanish provinces."[26] For both Jovellanos and Campomanes, the issues of women's education and women's contribution to Spain's economy and culture were central to the project of national regeneration.

While the idea of women contributing to national wealth as spinners and tailors focused largely on the lower strata, and the idea of women as mothers educated to inculcate industriousness in their children encompassed the whole of female Spain, economic theorists imagined different roles for women of the elite. A 1788 treatise proposing a female national dress suggests how economic theorists like Jovellanos and Campomanes might have anticipated high-ranking women's contribution to the nation's economy.[27] Purportedly written by a female author who signed simply with the initials "M.O.,"[28] *Discurso sobre el luxo de las señoras y proyecto de un traje nacional* (Treatise on the Luxury of Ladies and the Project of a National Dress) explained the importance of enlisting women in the project of curbing luxury.[29] M.O. described the economic and demographic problems that women caused through their efforts to dress luxuriously and suggested that the solution was a uniform dress code for women. Accordingly,

M.O. outlined such a dress code, including a complex system by which a woman's attire would be dictated by her place in society. M.O. was not alone in pointing to the deleterious social effects of women's penchant for elaborate dressing in eighteenth-century Spain. A number of contemporary writers—from José Clavijo y Fajardo, whose essay-periodical *El Pensador* (The Thinker) was one of the most productive of its time, to Cristóbal Romea y Tapia, whose less well-known *El Escritor sin Título* (The Writer without a Title) was very short-lived—harped about fashion as a useless distraction that caused women to neglect their maternal duties and led to marital discord.[30] However, M.O.'s unique solution to adopt a female national dress was among the most interesting expressions of how female consumption could become a patriotic act.

In her treatise, M.O. maintains that women's luxury spending presented a national crisis. By quoting directly from a 1783 sumptuary law mandated by Christiano VIII, the king of Denmark, M.O. explains the two key problems the law aimed to solve: first, that the desire for luxury goods was driving the consumption of foreign products, in turn draining the nation's wealth and limiting the development of domestic industry; and second, that massive spending on luxury goods, spurred by a desire to emulate the rich, was reducing families to poverty. M.O. suggests that these two problems also existed in Spain. She describes the attempts of many Spanish women to emulate the dress of rich ladies. Sympathizing with the poor husbands and fathers whose wives and daughters spent far more than they could possibly earn, she paints a disjointed picture of hungry families dressed to the nines: "There is nothing more common than seeing entire families reduced to eating coarse and unhealthy meals in order to save for the cost of a new gown; such stories we hear daily from the mouths of many supplicants who, in order to arouse pity, confess to the daily hunger they suffer, while at the same time they and their wives are dressed in garments so far superior to their position that they deny their necessities, expose their pride, and deafen their misery."[31] As in Denmark, the author explains, this was not simply a problem for the family who could not support such high levels of spending. The problem was of national concern because of the tremendous importation of foreign products needed to feed this clothing frenzy. M.O. writes, "Everyone knows that the delicate crêpes, laces, embroideries, and brocades that principally drive the luxury of the Ladies are articles that come to us from outside the kingdom."[32] In fact, she calculates that an estimated 5.5 million Spanish women spent one centavo daily, for a total of 118,088,235 *reales*, on foreign luxury goods per year.[33] According to M.O., such a large sum spent on foreign goods was ruining the domestic industry. Thus, the author shows how these individual clothing purchases affected Spanish industry as a whole.[34]

In addition to the issue of the importation of so many foreign goods, the author points to demographic problems caused by the high consumption of luxury clothing. The author suggests that many men were not marrying because of the high cost of maintaining a wife.[35] According to M.O., "The number of marriages that are not contracted each year for this reason cannot be calculated, no matter how much we want to reduce to a number the men who we know have not dared to marry for fear of the expenditures their wives would bind them to without contributing the funds to support them."[36] M.O. warns that a drop in marriages would lead to low birthrates, suggesting the population crisis that female luxury spending would occasion.[37] She even points to low growth rates in urban centers, which she describes as centers of *luxo*, as indicative of these dangerous demographic trends.

At the end of this first chapter, the author reinforces the severity of this crisis by pointing to the Persian, Greek, and Roman empires as examples of amazing civilizations that were "victims of luxury." With this reference she apparently hopes to spur Spaniards to action before it is too late. She ends the chapter with a passionate cry against the evils of luxury: "No plan would be too rigorous when it deals with the rejection of an enemy that debilitates the heart, seduces the spirit, buries the virtues, foments passion and vice, impoverishes the State, debilitates the population, and annihilates and destroys the Monarchy. Those are the effects of the luxury that we waste in dressing. To say it is serious to the State is an understatement. Truth and the accuracy of language demand that we call it the corruption and the plague of Spain."[38] With this strong image, M.O. completes her analysis of the ramifications of women's luxury spending. In short, she identifies it as being among the gravest problems Spain faced.

After outlining the problems that women's drive for luxury goods created, M.O.'s treatise showed how women could play a key role in solving those problems. In this way, the dress code proposal seemed to assign women great importance in bringing about the nation's well-being. By appealing to women to adopt a uniform dress code for the benefit of the nation, M.O. seemed to show faith in women's citizenship potential. From the very first lines of the treatise, she positioned herself as a female patriot. She refers to "the patriotic spirit that animated me in the very moment that I took up my pen to write this essay."[39] In turn, she says, she felt that other women would be impelled by their love for the Spanish nation: "I see all of these women ready to make, from the homes of their families, a service that

Figure 8. Española (left) and Carolina dress designs from *Discurso sobre el luxo de las señoras*, 1788. Courtesy of the Fine Arts Library, Harvard College Library.

is more important to their country than that which it would receive from an army that would conquer another province for it."⁴⁰

This patriotic spirit finds expression in the dress designs that the author proposes in a later part of the treatise. These three proposed designs she names the Española, the Carolina, and the Borbonesa, or Madrileña. All these names, referring to the nation, its monarchy, and its capital city, were intended to evoke national sentiments. Ironically, the hand-tinted engravings of M.O.'s proposed dresses that accompanied the text may have been the product of a French couturier (see figure 8).⁴¹

Both the materials used to make the dresses and the dresses themselves were to be made in Spain.⁴² Thus, the project not only would provide women with a way of curbing luxury spending but also would permit them to make a concrete contribution to the development of Spanish industry. Further,

M.O. portrays women's adoption of this project as one with worldwide ramifications. According to her, "Indeed, this sensational era will be one of the most noted chapters in present history, one which many nations will later imitate, recognizing its advantages and confessing that they owe to Spain a lesson that is of widespread importance."[43] Thus, M.O.'s plan seemed to present women with a way to be crucial historical actors. By adopting the project of a national dress, they not only would help Spain but also would set a shining example for the rest of the world to follow.[44]

It is clear from M.O.'s treatise that her project was directed toward women of high rank. First, the dress designs that she proposed ensured the visibility of rigid social distinctions. M.O. did not simply create three dress types in order to assign patriotic names that would evoke women's national sentiment. Rather, the three dress styles were part of a complex plan in which rank dictated women's attire. In this scheme, the Española, made of the most exquisite fabric and adorned with luxurious trimmings, was also to have the most elegant design. The Carolina was to be less costly, and the Borbonesa, or Madrileña, was to be simple and inexpensive. In addition, each of these three dress styles was to be divided into three categories based on subtle differences in the quality or color of the fabric or decoration. Which dress design a woman wore would be based on a strict hierarchy that corresponded to the woman's place in society.

M.O.'s treatise detailed the social groups that would dictate a woman's attire (see table 3) and the appropriate dress corresponding to each rank (see table 4).[45] Her classifications determined a woman's status by the occupation or station of the woman's husband, father, or brother. The author suggests that women in a given rank should have three outfits: one for very ceremonious occasions such as a royal audience *(besamanos)*, another for less formal events, and another one to be used for street clothing. In addition, the dresses should carry some insignia identifying a woman's position. For example, a woman married to a doorkeeper *(portero de oficina)* would have a red silk ribbon two fingers wide sewn on the edges of both sleeves of all her dresses.[46] The wives of certain high-ranking military personnel, the author suggests, would wear the same sign of distinction that their husbands wore, whether that be epaulettes on the shoulders or stripes on their boots.[47] Once women were outfitted in these literal uniforms, their social status would be unmistakable.

M.O. does propose one deviation from the strictly rank-based dress code. The author suggests that if a woman were to merit special distinction, either "for her social virtues, or for a glorious deed, or an individual work of merit that she has done for the State," she should be honored by being

TABLE 3. *Classes of Women Suggested in M.O.'s Female National Dress Proposal*

Class 1	Grandees
Class 2	Wives, daughters, mothers, and sisters of those who have the title of His Excellency or Most Illustrious, and ministers of the royal chamber
Class 3	Wives, daughters, mothers, and sisters of those who have the title of Your Lordship, such as the titled of Castile, those of the counsels of the king, officers of the foreign secretary, jurisdictional superintendents, provincial intendants, and accountants and treasurers of the first class of the army
Class 4	Wives, daughters, mothers, and sisters of the commissaries of war, lieutenant colonels, sergeant majors, treasurers of the second and third classes of the army, accountants and treasurers of court revenues, governors of the rural guard of Madrid, the general administrators, accountants, and treasurers of the provinces, and the chief customs and market officers, as well as all other employees who are at the same rank
Class 5	Wives, daughters, mothers, and sisters of captains and their lieutenants, and those of the general offices of accounting and treasury in the court, and those of the provincial administration and customs offices, and those of the county administration, subordinate to the principal administration, and general commandants of the rural guard
Class 6	Wives, daughters, mothers, and sisters of second lieutenants of the army, and those of accountants, auditors, inspectors, customs officials and market officers of the county administration, other officials particular to the county, and lieutenant commanders
Class 7	Wives, daughters, mothers, and sisters of sergeants, inspectors and their lieutenants, guard commanders, corporals, and notaries of the patrol, and doorkeepers/porters
Class 8	The wives of military officers of sea and land, from second lieutenants to colonels

given permission to wear a loop of red ribbon on each shoulder that extended to the elbow. As with the military, this would allow a woman a special badge of distinction as a reward for her conduct. Women wearing this ribbon without sanction, the author continued, would receive grave punishment. Although this seems to provide women with a path to prestige beyond rank, the very use of the phrase "social virtues" raises questions about how available this distinction would be to lower-class women. The fact that poorer women were not included in the proposed social hierarchy, and that all the dress designs, even the most casual Borbonesa or Madrileña, were quite elaborate, suggests that M.O. did not envision poorer women as

TABLE 4. *Dress Guidelines Suggested According to Class in M.O.'s Female National Dress Proposal*

Class	Ceremonious Occasions	Less Formal Events	Street Clothing	Details of Attire
1	Española 1	Carolina 1	Borbonesa 1	Silver embroidery on both sleeves
2	Española 2	Carolina 1	Borbonesa 1	Silver embroidery on right sleeve
3	Española 3	Carolina 2	Borbonesa 2	Silver embroidery on left sleeve
4	Carolina 1	Carolina 3	Borbonesa 2	A braid of silver two fingers wide on the edge of both sleeves
5	Carolina 2	Carolina 3	Borbonesa 2	A braid of silver two fingers wide on the edge of the right sleeve
6	Carolina 3	Carolina 3	Borbonesa 3	A braid of silver two fingers wide on the edge of the left sleeve
7	Borbonesa 2	Borbonesa 2	Borbonesa 3	A red silk ribbon two fingers wide on the edge of both sleeves
8				The same decoration worn by their husbands

participants in her project; she apparently did not conceive of them as patriotic citizens at all.

M.O.'s proposal outlined a role for women not so far from what other Economic Society members envisioned. In fact, M.O.'s treatise would be directed to female members shortly after their admission to the Economic Society as a potential project they might consider implementing. Male reformers considered women to be key to Spain's modernization, but they hoped to channel women's participation into gender- and rank-appropriate activities. Women could help foster Spanish industry—aristocratic women by altering their consumption patterns, and poorer women by engaging in productive labor. By assigning women these roles, Enlightenment intellectuals seemed to accept women as citizens who could influence Spain's future. However, their discussion centered on what female citizens—as women—could do to help build a stronger economy and thus a new Spain.

That distinction found expression in the debate over female admission to the Economic Society, where gender and social position continued to shape how male intellectuals envisioned female participation in the nation.

WOMEN IN THE ECONOMIC SOCIETY: A CONTENTIOUS DEBATE

It was in the midst of discussions on the relationship of women to industry that Madrid's *socios* raised the question of women's membership in the ranks of the Economic Society. This debate comprised two stages. In the first stage, three proponents of female admission—Marín, Campomanes, and Luis de Imbille—spoke out on the vital role that women could play in realizing the goals of the Society, particularly in industry.[48] After these three men expressed their thoughts on the introduction of female members, the Society dropped the issue.[49] Almost ten years later, the president of the Economic Society, Pedro de Alcántara Téllez-Girón y Pacheco (Marquis of Peñafiel, Duke of Osuna), revived the debate by proposing the admission of María Isidra Quintina Guzmán y la Cerda to the Society on January 21, 1786. In turn, Ramón Carlos Rodríguez proposed the admission of the Countess of Benavente, Osuna's wife and a prominent *salonnière*.[50] The Society voted to admit both women on January 24, 1786. The admission of two women forced the question of female membership once again to the surface. In this second stage of the debate, the question became a topic of public discussion, occasioning comment from those who belonged to the Society and those who observed its actions. José de Guevara Vasconcelos, Jovellanos, Francisco Cabarrús, Josefa Amar y Borbón, Madame Levacher de Valincourt, and Ignacio López de Ayala all voiced their views on female admission. The publication of Jovellanos's, Cabarrús's, Amar y Borbón's, and Levacher's opinion papers in the periodical press widened the admission debate and made it a public matter that necessarily entailed questions about women's place in the nation as well as the Economic Society.

In both stages of the debate, the arguments fell along gendered lines. Whether proponents or opponents of women's admission, male contributors emphasized the utility of female membership. They suggested that women had an important role to play in the nation and that an elite group of female participants in the Society could help shape Spain's female citizenry. However, in defining women's roles in the nation, Society members proposed that women occupy a place different from that of their male counterparts. These thinkers assigned women a kind of passive citizenship that insulated them from total participation in public debates. Female participants agreed that women's involvement had tremendous public utility, but, unlike their male counterparts, they formulated arguments that emphasized equality and women's capacity to be full participants, and they ridiculed concerns over their public presence. Their participation in the debate not only reveals the limits of the arguments put forth by male contributors of the Society but also evidences women's actual presence in a very public and very prominent discussion.

On September 2, 1786, Ignacio López de Ayala read the last treatise regarding women's admission to the organization.[51] Since women were officially admitted before Ayala presented his speech to the Society, his text served mainly as a rearguard approbation of women's admission. Ayala posed the question of women's admission in terms of making women useful citizens of the Spanish nation:

> It amounts to determining if Spanish women, that is, if half of Spain, will remain useless as up to now; or if, on the contrary, they are to be furnished enlightenment and knowledge in order to help men and to govern their fortunes and families with intelligence. It amounts to determining if this sex can prove useful or if it is a reprobate assembly that should be abandoned to caprice, uselessness, idleness and whimsy; it is this issue we address when we ask if they should form part of the Economic Societies.[52]

Ayala's statement distills much of the debate over female admission. By couching the debate in terms of social utility, Ayala expressed the main rationale that his contemporaries embraced in order to admit women into their ranks. Simply put, advocates for female admission argued that women should be members insofar as their presence might be a step toward constructing a modern Spain. At the same time, Ayala's words reflect the patriarchal paternalism that would pose a real obstacle to women's achieving total equity within the organization. By casting men as the real actors in determining women's future—those who would furnish women with enlightenment and knowledge—Ayala's comment bespoke the passive role most *socios* envisioned for female members.

That these members felt women could be useful citizens implied their assimilation of Enlightenment views on women's character and capabilities. Ayala, for example, had read his Feijoo, and he affirms women's natural equality and explains women's idleness as a product of society. In particular, Ayala emphasizes that men's role in making women idle and keeping them ignorant was pervasive: "It is necessary to say it: men are those who have corrupted the other sex."[53] Thus, Ayala argues that, by providing women with knowledge and opportunities, they could finally contribute fully to

Spanish society as patriotic citizens: "Until now they have not known what the nation is; they should not have known and it is impossible that it could have been the object of their affection. If their passion, so much more vehement than ours, was directed at an object that for so many qualities is worthy of affection, what utility could they not bring to the nation and how much could they not deprive foreign ones?"[54] Ayala envisions a Spain in which all its citizens, both male and female, work together to eradicate idleness and increase productivity. Marriages would increase, the population would thrive, industry would prosper, the arts would flourish—these were just some of the benefits that would come from utilizing the half of the population that was currently idle. For Ayala, the decision to allow women to join the Society was a step toward a more modern world: "The world is new. The centuries of barbarity, Roman ambition, the cruelty of the Septentrions, the brutal enthusiasm of the Muslims have all passed. As a result of these lamentable experiences, Europe now knows that the happiness of nations does not consist of either the splendor of empires winning battles or the destruction of provinces, but rather in the cultivation of their possessions and arts by making all of their citizens useful."[55] As Ayala's speech suggests, advocates of female admission to the Society viewed the debate as part of the larger question of defining the nature of female citizenship.

In his speech of 1775, Marín had pointed to national examples of accomplished women in order to demonstrate that the participation of women in such activities was not unprecedented in the Spanish context. As noted earlier, he invoked Spain's medieval past, suggesting that distinguished women were not excluded from assemblies and other decision-making bodies in past eras. And, in a more contemporary example, he referenced women's participation in the Academy of Fine Arts. With these precedents, Marín hoped to convince his fellow Society members that the idea to admit women was not an outlandish one.

It was not hard to see, the proponents of female admission argued, that women could make a concrete contribution to society. Marín, for example, presented various examples to show that even women's private actions could affect the nation. He cited a case in Boston in 1768 in which, after an anonymous writer appealed to women to use only products made in the Americas, the women of the city stopped consuming European goods. Like M.O., Marín suggested that women could make a difference by simply altering their spending habits. Similarly, he pointed to the way in which French women had spurred literary production by themselves taking an active interest in books and writing. He asked his fellow members to imagine what a group of women dedicated to the goals of the Society could accomplish.[56]

As Marín's examples suggest, the proponents of female admission lobbied for the participation of a select group of elite women in their organization, not women in general. In turn, they expected that these high-ranking women would animate the wider female population and thus help eradicate female idleness. As Marín explains, "If we had in Spain equal prosperity such that henceforth reading, judgment, and appreciation of good books would substitute in the *estrados* of our ladies and the *tertulias* of both sexes, the frequent conversations on feminine adornments and other frivolous and costly diversions, the effects would not be minor, and before long, we could promise ourselves rapid progress in the Arts, in Industry, and in Agriculture."[57] For his contemporaries, Marín's mention of the *estrado*, a raised platform furnished with cushions and set off with a wooden railing that provided a protective sanctuary for married women, undoubtedly brought to mind an image of idle noblewomen. As Martín Gaite has written of the *estrado*, "For those women, seated in the midst of velvet, surrounded by their maiden servants busy with their needlework, there flowed, from the day of their marriage, a lifeless time that aged them, that detached them inexorably from all pursuits of an active existence."[58] Marín wanted to energize these women. He hoped that, at the very least, the appearance of women's names in the catalogue of members would spur other women to action: "By only seeing the names of some Spanish ladies placed on the list of the Economic Society of Friends of the Country, popular industry, agriculture, and crafts will be driven toward exceptional advancements; because those advancements created both directly or indirectly in the said way by the effort or mere entertainment of the ladies of the first nobility will move the rest of their sex to admirably emulate in order to be worthy of the applause with which they hear the ladies justly celebrated."[59] Marín's words point to how a female presence in the organization would encourage women to be industrious, thus advancing popular industry, agriculture, and the like.

Similarly, Jovellanos argues that the involvement of a select group of women in the Society would motivate Spanish women to embrace their social and domestic responsibilities: "Inspiring love for social duties and regard for domestic obligations in all, we will make this sex aware that there is no true pleasure nor real glory outside of virtue."[60] More concretely, Jovellanos, Campomanes, Marín, and others suggested that female participants in the organization could be important in spearheading the larger participation of women in industry and, thus, in the rejuvenation of the Spanish economy. Drawing on earlier Society debates about the importance of educating working women in industries appropriate to their sex, these proponents drew a clear link between women's involvement and the educational efforts of the Society.

Besides seconding the practical benefits of women's admission that Marín had emphasized in his own treatise,⁶¹ Campomanes also argues that admitting women was the just course of action. Campomanes claims that ultimately the issue of women's admission should not need debate at all, that his colleagues should agree simply because "women have an equal right to be admitted to the Society."⁶² In asserting this, he goes much further than Marín and others, who emphasized the social utility of admitting women. For Campomanes, this was not merely a question of utility but also a question of justice: "My opinion grants that admission is not only just, it is also convenient and necessary."⁶³ With his joint appeal to utility and justice, Campomanes anticipated the arguments for female suffrage articulated by nineteenth-century liberals like John Stuart Mill.

Thus, many of the male proponents of female admission emphasized both the utility and the justice of allowing women to join the ranks of the Economic Society. What they did not emphasize was female equality. Nor did male members' arguments aim to liberate women. While those like Campomanes spoke strongly in favor of women's equal "right" to be admitted, their discussions of the practical matters that were involved in incorporating women into the organization stopped short of expressing a desire to grant women an equal "place" in either the organization or society. Both Marín and Campomanes suggested that, rather than being admitted to the general organization, female members should comprise a distinct body. Marín suggested the formation of a "separate class" of women and proposed that they be termed *asociadas* (female associates) to distinguish them from male members.⁶⁴ According to Marín, these *asociadas* should be selected "attending to the circumstances, talents, and qualities that esteem them, or being spouses, mothers, daughters, or sisters of members or of those who could be members."⁶⁵ Campomanes also suggested that female membership would be distinct, by indicating "their attendance at the meetings is neither the issue nor opportune."⁶⁶ Neither Marín nor Campomanes envisioned women as participating in the general assemblies of the organization alongside male members.

The Society's censor, José de Guevara Vasconcelos, also aimed to restrict women's attendance at the organization's meetings. When the Society admitted Quintina Guzmán and Benavente, Guevara immediately suggested that both be informed that their admission did not entitle them to attend meetings. Guevara proposed potential parameters for female membership that would allow women admission as a separate group. As a distinct body, Guevara explained, the women would hold their own meetings in the house of the group's president or the longest-standing female member and would have their own secretary to direct their activities and communicate these activities to the general Society.[67] Guevara's plan marginalized female members not only by placing them in a separate body but also by precluding their physical presence at the organization's headquarters. He worked to relegate women to the domestic realm instead by proposing their meetings be held in the women's homes.

Other members rebuked Guevara, arguing that the statutes allowed for women's full participation in the Society. This fundamental disagreement led the Society to establish a special commission to further consider the issue.[68] Jovellanos provided the strongest statement of support for female attendance at the organization's meetings. He contended that the Society could not admit women and then deny them access to the *juntas*:

> To open with one hand the doors of this room to the ladies and with the other to impede their entrance would be certainly a very repugnant action. How can we believe that they would be unaware of the sort of snub involved in that exclusion? "By chance," they will say, "it only involves ennobling the list of male members with the names of a few people whose company they despise or feel is dangerous? By chance is it denied to our sex the zeal and virtue of patriotism? By chance are we incompatible with courtesy and prudence? Has corruption become so widespread in our days that a woman cannot find herself alone among men who is not an object of distraction and embarrassment?"[69]

Jovellanos mocked earlier explanations for women's exclusion from meetings and suggested that women would question the veracity of their membership if they were denied access to the organization's assemblies. In this way, Jovellanos clearly asserted women's right to both be admitted to and to attend the meetings.

Yet, while Jovellanos argued that women must be allowed to participate in the meetings, his treatise suggests that he did not consider this a serious possibility. Rather, he questions whether women would actually attend the organization's meetings if permitted: "The ladies will never come to our meetings. Prudence will keep them perpetually away from them. How will this delicate virtue permit itself to come and present itself in a gathering of men of such diverse conditions and states? To mix in our discussions and readings, to confuse its weak voice in the din of our disputes and debates?"[70] In remarking that women's delicate nature would be out of place amid the impassioned debates of the *socios*, Jovellanos expressed his own views on female weakness. Here, he also relied upon his earlier formulations about women's natural limitations when it came to participating in industry and their desire to restrict themselves to activities that maintained decency. Further, in discounting the idea of creating a separate body for female members, Jovellanos questioned women's ability to be effective leaders. Ultimately, he did not offer a compelling solution. While he did not want women to participate alongside male members, neither did he endorse their incorporation into a separate body. Rather, he presented the vague suggestion that female members would work individually in support of "the common good."

Another point of debate was whether the Society should compel female members to pay annual dues as its male members did. While Marín argued that obligatory dues would deter women from joining the organization, Campomanes maintained that female members should be required to pay annual dues of 2 doubloons (approximately 150 *reales*). Luis de Imbille jumped into the debate some months later in hopes of resolving this deadlock. He anticipated that, with no annual contribution, too many women would apply to join. In making this argument, Imbille revealed the hidden class discourse imbedded in this debate over membership fees. However, he also worried that a forced contribution would make prospective female members think they were wanted in the ranks of the Society only for monetary reasons:

> And will the proposition of paying two doubloons annually be a good means of attracting them to accept the invitation to leave the appetizing rest in which they can enjoy their leisure and the diversions of frivolous pastimes that enthrall them, for approaching a lathe or a loom, to be burdened by a cushion for making lace or embroidery, and finally, to toil away the longest part of the day? This method does not seem very certain; it would be more effective to flatter their vanity, because the [female] sex conquers easily its most ingrained inclinations when it has the hope of receiving applause.[71]

Imbille argues that the Society had to encourage the participation of women—whom he describes as vain creatures predisposed to idle pastimes—by playing on their vanity, not discourage them by making demands on their pocketbooks. In addition, he worries that if they felt that they were being included only because of the money, they would not only refuse to participate themselves but also would discourage men from participating. Imbille's concern over women's vindictiveness and the havoc they might create if not admitted presents a suggestive example of the way in which negative views of female nature persisted among even the most enlightened intellectuals.[72]

In an attempt to resolve the conflict over dues, Imbille designed a plan for female admission that looked more like a reward system than one aimed at the true incorporation of women into the organization. Imbille suggested that the Society use a three-tier system to admit women. The first level of membership would be the *bienhechoras* (benefactresses), women who contributed a minimum of 120 *reales* per year to support some activity of the Society, be it renting a room for one of the *escuelas patrióticas* (patriotic schools) or providing a dowry for a poor student. The second level of membership, *meritorias* (women of merit), would be reserved for "useful citizens" whose efforts in industry or in the promotion of a strong work ethic in their homes were deemed worthy of distinction. Unlike the *bienhechoras*, the *meritorias* would not be expected to contribute an annual stipend. The last level of membership would be for women who had been awarded pecuniary prizes and would include teachers in the Economic Society's schools who deserved recognition.[73] In this system, women would not become real members. Rather, they would be awarded for virtuous behavior or monetary donations that the Economic Society deemed worthy.

That proponents of female admission were not arguing for women's active participation in the organization became even more pronounced in the discussion about what women would actually accomplish as Society members. Rather than focusing on the activities in which women could participate, the discourse centered on what women would not be required to do. Marín carefully emphasizes that the tasks expected of these *asociadas* would not entail "employ[ing] themselves in occupations inappropriate to their sex." In fact, he assures his peers that the women would be under no obligation to the Society:

> I do not intend to ridicule or extravagantly inconvenience the Ladies, giving them tasks foreign to their rest and repose, such as attending the Assemblies, or having posts or functions in the Society that would constitute even the smallest obligation or responsibility; nor even less do I pretend that for neither title nor cause should anything be demanded of them; on the contrary, I would be of the opinion that they be left alone with entire and absolute liberty to consent or not in respect to contributing annually with something of their fortunes, or those of their fathers or husbands of this Society, and to applying or not their concerns to any one of the goals of our institute.[74]

In the end, the picture Marín painted indicates that female members of the Society would not take an active role. He argued that they must not be forced to attend meetings, partake in Society projects, or pay dues. This description of female inactivity contrasts starkly with discussions on the importance of eradicating female idleness, suggesting that, while elite women were to encourage plebeian women to be industrious, they were not meant to be industrious themselves. Further, Marín's chivalric impulse to not cause the ladies discomfort is echoed in his contention that the presence of female members would encourage the male members of the Society to work harder for Spain's future. If *socias* were admitted, Marín explains, the *socios* would strive to make themselves esteemed in the eyes of their female companions. It was this male activity, not female action, that mattered in Marín's view.

Campomanes was also careful to assure his colleagues that he was not proposing that women act contrary to the nature of their sex: "It is not the intention of this Society to form a body of Amazon women who bear arms, nor to revive the times of Antonia García, of the virgin of Orleans, or of the abundant tales of knights-errant dedicated to the fanciful exploits of their Dulcineas."[75] By employing these images, Campomanes assures his colleagues that he is not suggesting women act like men. The image of the Amazon women in particular must have been a compelling one. Campomanes and his fellow Society members were undoubtedly familiar with Feijoo's reference to these "mujeres guerreras" in his *Defense of Women*. In contrast to Campomanes, who assured his audience that he did not want to create a troop of Amazon women, Feijoo aimed to dispel stereotypes about the Amazons and referred to them in his text as evidence of women's potential strength. According to Feijoo's treatise:

> What we can concede is that much fable has been mixed up in the history of the Amazon women, such as that they killed all of their male children, that they lived totally separate from the other sex, and that they only searched for men to mate once per year. Of the same character are their encounters with Hercules and Teseo, the aid of the fierce Pentesilea to the afflicted Troy, and perhaps also the visit of their queen Talestris to Alexander; but it cannot be denied without temerity, against the belief of so many ancient writers, that there was a formidable body of bellicose women in Asia, who were given the name Amazons.[76]

Feijoo celebrated the strength of these women, their ability to defend themselves "with great honor to their sex and equal opprobrium of our own."[77] In contrast, Campomanes assures his audience that he has no intention to make women act contrary to the dictates of their sex, like Amazon women. Thus, his discussion reveals his preconceived notions about what constituted appropriate female behavior. While Campomanes invoked arguments about allowing women to develop their natural abilities, he also maintained certain assumptions that worked to restrict women's activities. He expected women's main contribution in the Society to be the funding and direction of female education. He did not intend for them to be full members like the men of the Society.

Clearly, the proponents of female admission felt that women could be useful members of the Society. By helping to eradicate female idleness and encourage productivity among working women, elite women could contribute to Spain's regeneration. The vision of women as idle and wasteful creatures had become a compelling symbol of the decadence of old regime society and culture. By attacking this image, proponents of female admission promised to advance Spain toward a more enlightened future. They suggested that women's incorporation into the Society would be a positive move for the organization, the women, and the country. However, their concrete discussions of how women would be involved in the organization suggested the ambivalence of male intellectuals to fully sanction women's participation in the Society. Moreover, the men suggested a status-based division according to which the ladies were to encourage plebeian women to be industrious workers, but they were not to be industrious themselves. In this way, abstract ideas about women's equality and natural potential led to concrete suggestions that relegated all women to a circumscribed role in the nation.

Francisco Cabarrús, the only clear opponent to female admission whose voice is recorded in the official component of this debate, also assigned women a limited role in the nation.[78] As part of the committee that formed as a result of Guevara's insistence that women not attend general Society meetings, Cabarrús presented his views alongside those of Jovellanos on February 18, 1786.[79] In stark contrast to Jovellanos, Cabarrús argued that women should not be admitted to the Society.[80] Cabarrús's vehement opposition to women's admission is a bit surprising, considering the degree to which he embraced the modernizing force of Enlightenment thought in other ways.[81] It was Cabarrús, after all, who engineered some of the most significant reforms in eighteenth-century Spain, particularly in the realm of banking and finance, where he played a crucial role in the creation of a national bank. Apparently, his reforming spirit did not extend to women's proposed presence in the Economic Society. Cabarrús implored his fellow *socios* to "let us close the door forever to all of their sex and let us not allow the virtues of one example to hide the evils of a general rule."[82] It was not an argument he made lightly, but one—if the impassioned petition at the beginning of his speech can be believed—he made with great emotion.

While Cabarrús did not believe that women should be members of the Society, still he saw them as having a socially important role. In his argument, he focuses on the historical exclusion of women from deliberating bodies like the Society. He eagerly points out that even the few great women in Europe's past, such as Isabel of Castile, did not give women authority or decision-making powers, and he decries Feijoo's attempt to revive the republic of Amazon women, calling it nothing but a poet's myth. In short, he evokes the exclusion of women as an historical precedent, asking, "Do we think to overturn with impunity the order, as old as the world itself, that has always and everywhere excluded them from public deliberations?"[83] Yet Cabarrús does not simply point to history as its own justification but argues that there was a clear rationale for the exclusion: women's participation in such bodies distracted them from their natural duties as wives and mothers:

> I have seen various times, and with what veneration, with what enthusiasm, a lady who, after distributing all of the hours of her day between religion and nature, was surrounded in the evening by her mother, her brothers, her husband, and her children, still young, suckling one of them by herself: in her visage reigned an innocent happiness, award and companion of the virtue, the peace, the union, the respect and the love of those that accompanied her; they offered tremendous recompense to her for the frivolous and insipid pastimes that she had scorned. Yet do we propose to this and the rest of the ladies of her kind that they abandon this true dignity for the pleasure of coming to our assemblies?[84]

Cabarrús paints a picture of tranquil family life and argues that the admission of women into the Society would destroy it. He contends that women's familial responsibilities were their true patriotic duties: "How do we expect those to be friends of the country who are not friends of their homes? And good citizens those who scorn the obligations of mother and wife?"[85] Participation in the Society would detract from the vital contribution women made to the nation from their homes. Thus, for Cabarrús, there was a clear conflict between women's appropriate role and the role they would take on as Economic Society members.

Behind Cabarrús's discussion is a very negative portrayal of women that has led many scholars to speak of the strong, misogynistic tone that characterizes his text. In fact, Cabarrús expresses a fundamental mistrust of female nature; he paints women as petulant, frivolous, capricious, unruly, and manipulative. He claims that their admission to the Society would set a dangerous precedent, as he explains that they would first prove themselves useless, then harmful, then completely disruptive to Society business. As a result of this negative portrayal of women's nature, there seems to be a contradiction in Cabarrús's treatise. On the one hand, he suggests women have an important role to play in the domestic sphere; and on the other, he paints women in such a negative light that it is difficult to believe he considers them able to accomplish anything at all. Rather than being a contradiction, however, Cabarrús's negative portrayal of women is linked to his disdain for women's public activities. His descriptions of women in the domestic realm, as suggested above, emphasize their natural virtue, modesty, and chastity. It is only when he considers their public presence that he emphasizes their natural vices. Women's nature, Cabarrús explains, is well suited for domesticity, not politics.[86] His closing remarks illustrate his belief that women out of control, or out of the home, present a serious danger. According to Cabarrús, the debate over women's admission offers an opportunity "to present to the public an idea of what is required of any modern public policy, that is, to curtail the influence of their sex and to better our own."[87] Cabarrús went beyond arguing that women should not be admitted to the Economic Society; he portrayed public women as a threat to the progress and order of the nation.

While Cabarrús's exclusion of women is undeniable, his arguments about women's nature are not so different from those of his contemporaries who chose to incorporate women into the organization. In addition, his rationale for that exclusion—his desire for women to play a vital role in the domestic sphere—did assign women an important social role. Espousing a kind of Rousseauian doctrine, Cabarrús argued that women could contribute to the nation through their dedication to their role as wives and mothers. Cabarrús, often referred to by scholars as the "Rousseau Español," was certainly no liberator of women. But neither were his colleagues who supported female admission. Neither Cabarrús nor these other *socios* conceived of women as active participants in the public component of the project for Spain's regeneration.

SPEAKING FOR THEMSELVES

Cabarrús's strong objections to women's admission and the resolute manner in which he expressed these views in his text provoked forceful responses from two women: Josefa Amar y Borbón and Madame Levacher.[88] Amar y Borbón's text suggests that she read Jovellanos's and Cabarrús's position statements in *Memorial Literario* and deemed it necessary to contribute her views.[89] Similarly, having read Cabarrús's views in the *Mercure de France*, Madame Levacher de Valincourt penned her response, addressing it specifically to Cabarrús.[90] The participation of these two women, the only non-members to enter the debate, suggests that women contributed to shaping gender discourse in Enlightenment Spain. In her treatise, Amar y Borbón highlights the importance of female participation in the debate. As she explains, women must "defend their cause, because their silence on this occasion would confirm the common perception that women do not bother with or have any interest in serious business."[91] Here Amar y Borbón also alludes to her own participation in the Royal Aragonese Economic Society, of which she had been a member since October 1782, to make her point. Although, as she indicates, ultimately "our sentence is in their hands," she felt that her participation in the debate was at least symbolically important. By becoming involved in the debate over admission, Amar y Borbón and Levacher showed that women were interested in and capable of participating in serious activities.

Further, Amar y Borbón's and Levacher's contributions evidence women's presence in public discourse. Not only did they express their views on the question of female admission, but these views became public when both women's treatises were printed in the periodical press. *Memorial Literario*, the same periodical that featured Jovellanos's and Cabarrús's pieces, published Amar y Borbón's "Discurso en defensa del talento de las mugeres, y de su aptitud para el gobierno, y otros cargos en que se emplean los hombres" in August 1786. Levacher's text was printed in Madrid's *Espíritu de los Mejores Diarios Literarios que Se Publican en Europa* in December 1787.[92] Through both the content of their articles and their presence in the public stage of this debate, Amar y Borbón and Levacher argued that women were entitled to fully participate as equal members in Spain's political discussions and were capable of doing so.

The fact that two women could come to have a voice in the debate merits consideration. While there is little evidence to explain Levacher's contribution, Amar y Borbón's status as a member of the Royal Aragonese Economic Society helped to legitimize both her right to participate in the debate and the views she presented in her treatise.[93] During her active years in the Society, between October 1782 and June 1786, Amar y Borbón indeed proved her merit.[94] She fulfilled a number of important tasks that the Society assigned to her, including writing a critique of a poor Castilian translation of the Italian Francisco Griselini's agricultural treatise, preparing her own translation of Griselini's work, and running spinning schools along with other prominent women in Zaragoza. The members of the Madrid circle would have seen Amar y Borbón's views as more credible because of her membership in the Aragonese Society.

The fact that Amar y Borbón's treatise was accompanied by a letter from the Aragonese censor, Juan Antonio Hernández de Larrea, made it even more impressive. Constance Sullivan has stressed the importance of this letter in understanding the treatise's reception. Addressed to Amar y Borbón, Hernández de Larrea's statement supports her contentions. After reiterating some of Amar y Borbón's main points and adding a few more examples of illustrious women, Hernández de Larrea concludes:

> I would be delighted if the knowledgeable paper that you have written were published and became widely read; it would convince the reticent and disdainful, and it would demonstrate that since a lady has known how to come to the defense of her sex with such glory, has so well-stated the prerogatives that we should concede to her equals, this in itself would show that they have the incontestable right equally with men to have a seat in and a vote in the debates and councils of the Economic Society. Women without instruction, without talents, and without zeal for the nation cannot hope to aspire to this civic glory, but likewise men whose hearts lack those virtues should be banned; and thus we will all be on the same level, without any distinction whatsoever.[95]

The letter, which was also printed directly after Amar y Borbón's treatise in the August edition of the *Memorial Literario,* added a certain legitimacy to her text. Clearly, her association with the Aragonese organization was an important endorsement for her arguments.

Amar y Borbón also worked to legitimize her views by referencing in her own treatise the arguments of male contributors to the debate. Toward the end of her treatise, she refers to Jovellanos's defense of women's admission. She reiterates some of his main arguments and thanks him for his support. By making this reference to Jovellanos, she links her text and her arguments to the thoughts of a well-respected figure in the Madrid organization. Similarly, she applauds the abilities of the two women who had already been admitted to the Society. In doing so, Amar y Borbón reminds the reader that male members of the Madrid organization had already established a precedent for female membership. Both of these references helped to further legitimize her text in support of women's admission.

While Amar y Borbón tried to ally herself with Jovellanos in order to lend greater credibility to her arguments for women's admission, both she and Levacher trivialized Cabarrús's objections to female admission. In a brief summary of his arguments against women's admission, Amar y Borbón indicates that "the commendable *socio* who opposes the admission of women" worried that allowing one woman would open up the floodgates, that the female sex was too petulant, capricious, and frivolous, and that women's attendance would disrupt the meetings. Amar y Borbón dismisses all these objections as foolish. In fact, she ridicules the men of the Society in general for still pondering this question of female membership. She mocks the Society for its reluctance to admit women: "By chance could those who call themselves Friends of the Country push them out? Are they [women] perhaps a bunch of spies scattered around the realm who publicize information to outsiders of the work being done in order to benefit them? Or are the issues that the Economic Societies discuss so mysterious and intricate that they can only be understood by men?"[96] With her sarcasm, Amar y Borbón further criticizes the objections raised during the debate.

Levacher focused her critique expressly on Cabarrús. She begins by arguing that his strong remarks against women could be explained only by personal resentment. According to Levacher:

> How could you have been so cruel to my poor and weak sex, when perhaps it has done you neither good nor bad? What do I say? The vehemence with which you speak against women does not appear to indicate that you are an unfortunate victim of vicissitudes, that among the virtues the heavens dispensed to you was not the power of persuading women, and that in the delirium of your pain you wished to cause the whole of nature to revolt against its most beautiful part? What pretension! What mistake![97]

Levacher suggests that the root of Cabarrús's diatribe against the admission of women and his misogynistic views was his victimization by a woman, an argument that Feijoo had made in the *Defense* as well.

In making this claim, Levacher suggests that Cabarrús's arguments were based not on reason but on passion. Sally Ann Kitts notes that this is the beginning of the contrast that Levacher set up and developed throughout her text between her own ideas—the product of natural reason—and Cabarrús's contentions, which Levacher implies are the product of passion compounded by a sense of superiority. One of the techniques that Levacher uses to develop this dichotomy is to describe herself in overly modest terms; she refers to her "little intelligence" and says, "I am not knowledgeable." Kitts suggests that this modesty was part of Levacher's desire to portray herself as rational and coolheaded in contrast to a blindly passionate Cabarrús. According to Kitts, "Her extreme modesty and understatement also appear calculated to work in her favor and give the impression of clarity and logical expression compared with Cabarrús's arrogant claims of male superiority and vituperative phrases, some of the most vehement of which she reproduces, giving further support to her argument contrasting passion and reason."[98] As Kitts suggests, while Levacher presented her own modest views, she also portrayed Cabarrús's arrogance. For example, Levacher points to Cabarrús's description of his essay as a "discourse in which is examined [women's admission]" as indicative of his haughtiness. Levacher argues that his text did not constitute an inquiry into a question but rather presented his firm conclusions: "The word 'examine' is indicative of the problem, since the decisive way that you employ is clear, unequivocal, could not be said with more force: *In a word, I do not see any activity at all, not even one, for which women would be necessary, or even useful to the Society*. What heroism, not to say childishness, it is to cover one's self with the veil of modesty, only to have the pleasure of tearing it apart."[99] Thus, Levacher suggests that Cabarrús presented his treatise with a false modesty. He was not open to a reasoned debate; instead, he presented his own extreme views in lieu of a serious examination of the question.

By presenting herself as the reasoned participant in the debate, Levacher pointed to women's capacity to engage in rational debate and, thus, to be useful and active members of the organization. In this way, she highlighted what she and Amar y Borbón considered to be the central issue in the debate: women's natural capabilities. Both women recognized that the debate over female admission to the Society constituted an extension of the earlier debate on the natural limits of women's talents and capacities. That some intellectuals still seemed to believe that natural inequalities existed between men and women angered female intellectuals like Amar y Borbón, who considered women's equality a given. In her paper addressed to the Economic Society, she expressed her disbelief that intellectuals were still unconvinced of women's equality sixty years after Feijoo's *Defense of Women*, even as they parroted its language. Nevertheless, she devoted the first half of her text to substantiating her assertion of women's equality.

Amar y Borbón employed various strategies in arguing for women's intellectual equality. First, she examined one of the key arguments that had been used to bolster male superiority: the case of Eve. Amar y Borbón argues that Eve was not a sign of women's weakness, but of women's natural equality and intellectual curiosity. Amar y Borbón contends that the fact that God created Eve after Adam did not prove Adam's superiority: "It is true that man was created first, and was created alone, but little time passed before it was known that he could not live without a companion: the root cause for marriage and the root also of a perfect society."[100] In addition to claiming this equality from the start, Amar y Borbón reconsiders the traditional view of Eve's role in the expulsion from paradise. Although she does admit that Eve ate first from the forbidden tree and does chastise her action, Amar y Borbón also sees this as a sign of Eve's curiosity and thus indicative of her mental talents: "Detestable curiosity for sure; but curiosity is usually a sign of talent because without it nobody takes the necessary steps toward learning."[101] Further, although God told Eve that Adam should rule over her, the Aragonese writer muses, this did not constitute a natural hierarchy between men and women in terms of ability. Rather, this was simply a way of organizing labor and the family. According to Amar y Borbón, "Thus, women could be subjects to men in certain cases, but without losing by this the equality of intelligence they have to them."[102] Thus, Eve exemplified not women's inferiority but their equal footing with men.

Amar y Borbón also examined the lives of female forebears for evidence of women's abilities. She indicates that if there were fewer examples of great females than of great males this was simply the result of women being denied adequate education. Despite this disclaimer, she proceeds to cite an impressive list of women from all times and places who had proven the natural abilities of women in fields ranging from the abstract sciences to literature. She points to erudite women and to female figures who had excelled in public office, including the great Israelite judge Deborah and Spain's own Queen Isabel, as clear examples of women's capacity to excel.

Next Amar y Borbón aimed to dispel another widely held belief: that certain characteristics were inherent in each sex. She explains, "Value is regularly assigned to qualities particular to and common in men; as with everything there are exceptions such as beauty in men; we see beautiful men and ugly women, brave women and cowardly men, which serves to verify that there are no qualities that are not common to both sexes."[103] Amar y Borbón maintains that a person's attributes and character were predicated not on his or her sex but on his or her upbringing. Like Feijoo, she states that it was up to society to cultivate in women those qualities it valued.

As Amar y Borbón explains, women's inferiority was not the result of natural inequalities but rather of social conditions. For her, women's plight was clear: they were denied a proper education and then blamed for their deficiencies. Thus, she argues, women were made scapegoats for all of society's ills: "If heroes lack in valor, if ignorance reigns in the common behavior of the people, if customs become corrupted, if luxury and consumption ruin families, for all of these evils, it is shouted, women are to blame."[104] She points to the contradictions in this system that aimed to maintain male superiority. Women kept in ignorance began to see themselves as incapable of anything more, and thus they did not cultivate skills to help themselves escape this state: "Women know that they cannot aspire to any employment or public recompense, that their ideas do not extend beyond the walls of the house or the convent. If this is not enough to suffocate the greatest talent in the world, I do not know what other obstacles can be found."[105] Further, she admonishes men who kept women ignorant, who in one moment praised their beauty and simplicity and in the next criticized their intellectual inferiority.

Amar y Borbón suggests that opening up the Society's doors to women would send them the right message by encouraging them to become useful citizens. In this way, she appeals to the proponents of female admission by evoking the social utility in admitting women.[106] By rewarding meritorious women with membership, the Society would encourage the female population to aspire to greater heights. She writes, "Establish prizes and incentives for industrious and hard-working women, one being to admit them to the Society, and then they will naturally endeavor to deserve them. As long as this is not done and they remain putrid or isolated members of the social body, what achievements can they accomplish?"[107] Here, she echoes arguments made by Marín, Campomanes, and Jovellanos about how admitting women into the Society would help curb female idleness.[108]

Levacher makes it clear that, while women's participation in the Society would help encourage female productivity, it would not hinder women's ability to be good mothers or to meet their other domestic responsibilities, as Cabarrús had warned would happen. Toward the end of her text, Levacher discusses her seven-year-old daughter and her education. She explains that, in trying to develop her daughter's intellect as much as possible, she had her studying subjects as diverse as geography, history, botany, and drawing. This allowed the French author to suggest her own ideas on the importance of a solid education for women. Here, Levacher also shows her own extensive knowledge of writers and thinkers from Virgil to Milton. Kitts explains the importance of juxtaposing Levacher's own education with her role as a mother: "The introduction of her daughter into the text has an emotional impact on the reader, serving to show the maternal side of Levacher's character and exemplify that she can be a good mother and an educated, intellectually-active woman at the same time."[109] On a deeper level than even Kitts suggests, Levacher here also proposes that the participation of women in intellectual pursuits could help improve their maternal abilities. In Levacher's example, her own education enables her to better direct her daughter's education and thus prepare her for the future. Levacher refutes Cabarrús's claim that women's involvement in the Economic Society would distract them from their duties in the household.

In addressing the concrete issues related to incorporating women into the organization, the female proponents of women's membership suggest that female members should be on equal footing with their male counterparts. Accordingly, Amar y Borbón addresses the question of women's presence at the Society's *juntas*. She dismisses as absurd the notion that women and men could not meet together. After all, she argues, men and women often have to be together. She points out sardonically that their complete separation would lead to no less than the destruction of the human species. Thus, she argues forcefully for women's attendance at the Society's meetings:

> While there is some risk, this danger should not be feared more than what is present in all other occasions in which men and women gather, which does not serve to ban women in absolute, because it is necessary to come together sometimes, and because the flaw of one individual should not and could not destroy the common good. Then if women can be useful in some way to the Society, there is no reason to segregate them from it because of a remote inconvenience which does not impede other similar gatherings.[110]

Amar y Borbón similarly contends that, alongside men, female members could make key contributions to the Society. After all, the Society was not dealing with abstract concepts but with concrete issues that any observant and intelligent person could assess. In fact, she adds, women were more familiar than men with some aspects of the Society's business. In particular, she points to women's knowledge of female-dominated labors such as spinning and embroidery. By admitting women and combining men's and women's talents and knowledge, Amar y Borbón suggests, the Society would be a more effective institution.

In arguing for female admission to the Society, both Levacher and Amar y Borbón focused on women's natural equality to men. They defended women's natural capacities and argued that society's inattention to educating women explained any existing inequalities between the sexes. While the two women reiterated the arguments of male proponents that female participation would be useful to both the organization and society at large, their analysis centered on women's fitness to engage on a par with men in the life of the Society. In the treatises of the male participants in the debate, the woman question was secondary to what male authors considered to be greater questions about the nation and its future. In contrast, for Amar y Borbón and Levacher, the question of women's development and rights played a central role in the discussion. They were interested in asserting women's capacity and not simply the utility of putting them to work.

CREATION OF THE JUNTA DE DAMAS

On March 23, 1787, the Society informed the king of its desire to admit women as a separate class and asked for his thoughts on the subject: "Since it has been deemed desirable to inspire in the other sex, which has so much influence on fashion and dress, patriotic ideas, the Society has admitted in the category of associates the Marquise of Peñafiel and Doña María Isidra de

Guzmán y la Zerda [sic], daughter of the Marquises of Montealegre; and although it has resolved to admit others and to form an entire class, which will convene in regular councils, it has delayed until notifying Your Majesty and [is] waiting your sovereign resolution."[111] Although the records of the Society do not document a response, the king's later actions indicate that he supported the idea. On August 26, 1787, the Society voted to create a *junta de damas,* or women's council. Charles III agreed with the Society's decision in a decree issued the following day:

> The King understands that the admission of *Socias* of merit, and of honor, who in regular and separate councils will consider the best ways to promote virtue, productivity, and the industry of their sex, will be very advantageous to the Court, and choosing those women who because of their circumstances will be most deserving of this honorable distinction, will proceed and discuss together the ways to promote good education, improve customs by their example, and their writings, to introduce the love of labor, to curb luxury that if not checked will destroy the fortunes of individuals and prevent many marriages with damage to the State, and to substitute in their adornments national products for foreign ones; and by his simple whim His Majesty is pleased that, since so many ladies have already honored in days of old his Monarchy with the talent that characterizes Spanish women, they will follow these glorious examples, and from their councils will result as many or more advantages than those already seen, with extreme happiness of his Royal fatherly spirit produced through the Economic Councils of his Realm.[112]

The king's support for women's admission to the Society was important, as the contemporary Juan Sempere y Guarinos notes: "In Spain, until the reign of Charles III, there were no associations of women authorized by the Sovereign, with the exception of monasteries, congregations, confraternities and other councils directed solely to the exercise of piety."[113] Thus, the *junta de damas'* birth was an unprecedented and momentous event.

The creation of the women's council brought the twelve-year debate over female admission to a close—though it did not at all settle the larger questions the dispute had raised. While the acceptance of women into the ranks of the Madrid Economic Society signaled an awareness of women's potential contribution to the nation, their relegation to a separate group indicated the reluctance of male intellectuals to fully sanction women's presence in the organization. As the texts of the debate reveal, male proponents of female membership did not champion women's equality. When confronted directly with the question of women's attendance at Society meetings or participation in council debates, even advocates of female admission proposed limits to women's membership. Rather than concentrating on women's capacity to be active citizens in the developing nation, supporters of women's admission focused on the greater utility of incorporating a select group of women into the institution. These elite women would encourage the larger female population to be good citizens, not by inviting all women to take on a public role, but by urging them to alter their conduct in the private arena of work. Similarly, Cabarrús, the sole opponent to female admission recorded in the debate, suggested that women could be useful to the nation through their role as wives and mothers. He explained the value of enclosing women in the domestic sphere, thus excluding them from the public world of political discourse altogether. Whether they favored or opposed female admission, male intellectuals did not endorse the total presence of women in the public arena.

The two female participants in the debate, however, did emphasize women's capacity to be influential actors on a par with men. By invoking arguments about women's natural equality and intellectual capabilities, Amar y Borbón and Levacher centered their treatises squarely on the question of women's liberties. Further, their very participation in the debate, as well as the publication of their texts in the periodical press, demonstrates that the woman question was more than theoretical. In the midst of these debates over women's right to enter a key Enlightenment institution, women were in fact already taking a place in the realm of rational critical debate, as exemplified by the involvement of Amar y Borbón and Levacher in the discussion of what constituted a weighty issue for contemporary Spaniards. In short, the quarrel over female admission reveals that women's emergence into the world of public debate was both a significant and a contested social transformation of the era. The questions this issue raised would remain open ones, continuing to influence both discourse and action among both sexes in Spain's reformist elite.

PART II

Enacting Citizenship

4   Negotiating a Female Public
Writers and Reformers

As one of their first orders of business, the women of the *junta de damas* elected Josefa Amar y Borbón to be a member of their new council in recognition of her role in promoting the admission of women to the Economic Society.¹ In her November 1787 "Oración gratulatoria" (Congratulatory Address), a text thanking the royal institution for her membership, Amar y Borbón took the Society to task for creating a separate council for women.² To Amar y Borbón, women's auxiliary status signified the reluctance of male intellectuals to fully recognize the efforts and motivations of women like herself—to take women's sincere concern with the nation's future seriously. From the very first paragraph of her "Oración," the Aragonese writer blends her own patriotic sentiments with ridicule for the rationale cited for forming a separate female council:

> If your benevolence had not facilitated my entry into this illustrious assembly, with the estimable distinction of admitting me as a member of honor and merit, I think I would have dared to approach the door; not to interrupt its sessions, not to criticize or reprimand the establishment, not to investigate its secrets, and much less to satisfy a vain or useless curiosity. I would have come, yes, to celebrate with a truly patriotic heart, this new testimony to the love of the king for all of his subjects, irrespective of sex or rank.³

There is no mistaking Amar y Borbón's satirical tone. She derides male contributors to the debate over female admission who persistently portrayed women as potential interruptions, possible spies, vain busybodies—anything but patriotic citizens. In turn, she mocks the king's assertion that Spain is a country "irrespective of sex," since the separate council clearly constituted such a distinction. In her conclusion, she directs her anger toward the nation: "And you, my nation, my illustrious Spain! What will you do now? Will you look with indifference and perhaps with contempt at the women who dedicate themselves, in the same way as men do, to procure your happiness?"[4] Once again, she discredits those who do not give full value to women's service. Toning down her anger, she ventures that Spain will come to appreciate the efforts of the *junta de damas:* "Spain has always recognized the merit of those who have worked for her. Now, then, more than ever, she will appreciate the services of the women's council; she will praise its zeal, its intelligence, and its diligence; and she will take care to perpetuate in her annals the names of its illustrious founders, as a new and glorious epoch in her history."[5] For Amar y Borbón, this must have been more of a hope than a certain prediction.

Amar y Borbón's "Oración" reveals the contradiction that resulted from women's admission to the Madrid branch of the Economic Society in 1787. Although female membership constituted a victory for Spanish women, both the protracted dispute that produced that victory and the women's segregation in an auxiliary council illustrate that, in the 1770s and 1780s, prevailing views on women's place in the nation cast Spain's female citizens in supporting roles. Even some of Spain's most progressive reformers, like Gaspar Melchor de Jovellanos, adopted the stance that women's contributions to the nation's reform should be tailored to their sex.

Women experimented with different tacks in negotiating their role in the nation's reform in light of the increasingly circumscribed notion of female citizenship that men like Jovellanos espoused. In some cases, women's actions and arguments seem gender-blind, implicitly relying on appeals to universality and their own right to be treated fairly according to established policies. Such is the case with a number of women writers who petitioned for licenses to publish their work. These petitions, as well as women's defense of their writings in the face of censorial opposition, suggest that women both valued public exposure and felt entitled to it. At the same time, many women's writings reflect a clear awareness of the novelty of the writer's position as a female author and are directed to an equally novel female reading public. That numerous women writers saw themselves as participating in a female literary circle is apparent in their introductions, translator's notes, and choice of subject matter.

Carving out a specifically female space for action became a clear, even explicit, objective of the *junta de damas*. Women gained admission to the Economic Society less because of their own defense of their abilities and more as a result of male arguments about women's particular utility—their special provenance in addressing so-called female issues. Nevertheless, as members of the *junta de damas*, they capitalized on this argument to create a space that enabled them to exercise agency, a space where they could be active participants in the project of Enlightenment reform. In debates over the formulation of their statutes and in discussions with the general council of the Economic Society about the appropriate relationship between the two bodies, women fought to control their organization's functions. While the women's council did not win every battle with the men of the Economic Society, it did succeed in creating an organization with a striking degree of power and autonomy. Ultimately, the women's council turned segregation to its advantage by pointing to its separation from the Economic Society as being indicative of its unique position in the organization. In other words, the members of the women's council specifically drew on their status as women in order to negotiate a powerful place for themselves in the nation's reform.

At first glance, the stories of female authors petitioning for publication and female reformers arguing for their rightful role within the organization of the Economic Society may seem disconnected. After all, female authors promoted their own individual right to publish, while members of the *junta de damas* strove to establish their collective rights within a particular organization. Yet the world of publishing and the world of the Economic Society were not so far apart. Not only was the public nature of women's activities a key issue in both of these realms of Enlightenment discourse, but also the arguments women marshaled to defend their public presence in these two arenas were often identical. Not only did women emphasize over and over again the larger social utility of their activities, but also female authors and councilwomen invoked their equal status and their special female qualities in order to claim their right to contribute to public discourse.[6]

FEMALE AUTHORS AND THE SEARCH FOR A PUBLIC VOICE

Women writers' petitions for licenses to publish their works implied their desire for a public audience. That women saw an advantage to participating in public discourse in an era marked by the idea that reasoning, writing, and education would lead to social progress is not surprising. As Dena Goodman and Elizabeth C. Goldsmith explain, "Publishing and writing for a public were the acts by which a political culture was formed and a public sphere was constituted. By engaging in these discursive practices, individuals became agents in this new sphere of politics and power. Women as well as men participated; they were both its subjects and its objects."[7] However, women faced different obstacles in the path to publication. The stigma attached to female authorship could be severe. Since publication involved a measure of transgression, given the social expectations concerning women's modesty, submission, and anonymity, "going public" could be a perilous prospect for female writers.

In the face of the potential risk, women bravely submitted their works to royal censors, who evaluated them for publication licenses. Incomplete records do not permit a calculation of the total number of women who submitted their works to the censors. However, the number that did go into print suggests publication was a growing priority for the female author. Of the 173 women writers I identified as being active between 1700 and 1808, at least 92 of them, or about 53 percent, published a minimum of one work.[8] When the numbers are examined by decade, the increasing desire of women to publish becomes even more apparent. The growth in the number of women publishing their first text skyrocketed after 1780. In fact, in the 1780s and 1790s alone, more female authors published their first texts than had in the previous eighty years.[9] Also noteworthy is the decline in women publishing religious tracts. During the period 1721–1730, 71 percent of the works by female authors were on explicitly religious topics, compared to less than 12 percent in the period 1791–1800.[10] While women continued to publish books celebrating the lives of pious women or proffering advice on the proper comportment of the Christian woman, the increasingly secular character of their subject matter suggests a shift in their motivations to publish.[11]

In their petitions, female authors intimated the value they placed on circulating their works to a larger public. A number of women made clear the connection between publication and a public audience. The Marquise of la Espeja's request to publish her translation of Etienne Bonnot de Condillac's *La langue des calculs* (The Language of Calculus), for example, described her motives in terms of acquiring a public audience. According to the petition, Espeja's motivation arose from her judgment that the work "would be very useful to the public."[12] Similarly, when Magdalena Hernández de Morejón petitioned the censor for publication of her "Elogio a Bonaparte" (Tribute to Bonaparte), she proclaimed her hope "that it would achieve public light."[13] Women repeatedly declared their expectation that their work would be read and circulated among the growing reading public of eighteenth-century Spanish society. Their desire to bring their works "to public light" thus persuaded them to seek censorial approval for publication despite the risks.

The censorial process constituted just one step on the path from manuscript to publication. In order to be lawfully printed in Spain, a book required two licenses. The initial license required a censor to thoroughly review the submitted manuscript. Early in the century, the magistrate of the printing commission, under the direction of the Council of Castile, asked authors to choose their own censors. However, the biased reports these censors produced caused a shift in policy, first to requesting authors to propose three candidates from whom the censor would be chosen, and finally, by midcentury, to mandating the use of a regular group of censors paid for their work. When evaluating a text, a censor had two tasks. First, he had to review works for unacceptable material, such as slurs against the church or severe critiques of the monarchy. Second, he had to judge whether the work was worthy of publication. A poor evaluation did not spell doom for the author. Censors could allow authors to revise and resubmit, and authors could appeal a censor's decision. Once the printing commission approved a manuscript, it fell to the printer to print a copy of the work and send it to the corrector general for final review. The printing commission charged the corrector general with, in addition to the normal censorial tasks, insuring that the printer had met paper and print quality guidelines. If the work passed this final inspection, the commission set a price for the text and awarded it the second license, allowing the text's publication and sale. The book-trade reform law of March 23, 1763, eased this process somewhat by eliminating the office of corrector general, abolishing price-fixing, and removing hefty licensing fees.[14]

Women were full participants in licensing procedures. The reports of censors who evaluated women's work often reflect a gender-blind analysis of the text at hand. Just as with male author's texts, censors reviewed women's works according to the established criteria. For example, when Juan Bautista de Ezpeleta evaluated Espeja's translation of Condillac, he considered both the usefulness of the work and the merit of the translation:

> Its publication could be of widespread utility for all those who dedicate themselves to this line of study, since the author treats the material in it with the greatest precision and clarity, and the translator has rendered it into a pure and genuine Castilian, in which those that lack knowledge of the French language or do not possess the abilities required, can enjoy the writings of its knowledgeable author. For this reason, as well as because it has nothing against the faith, good customs, and royal prerogatives of His Majesty, it can be granted the license that is solicited.[15]

Thus, Ezpeleta suggested the work be approved for publication as it was an effective translation of a beneficial text. The response of the distinguished writer Pedro Estala, the censor who deemed María Luzuriaga's *Viage al interior de la China y Tartaria* (Voyage to the Interior of China and Tartary) fit for publication, followed a similar pattern. In his letters to the council praising her manuscript, Estala points to both the merits of the original work by Sir George Staunton and the quality of Luzuriaga's translation. In Estala's view, Luzuriaga provided Spanish readers with valuable data on China: "The work is extremely useful for the important information it contains on navigation, geography, commerce, natural history, and other areas of the sciences and the arts."[16] He also praises the quality of her translation: "The translation is done with much skill and precision."[17] When Luzuriaga submitted the second volume of Staunton's book, Estala proclaimed it "the most appreciable work that has been published on the empire of China" and commended Luzuriaga's translation for being "done with much knowledge, with precision, clarity, and the purity of the Castilian language."[18] Original compositions by female authors also received censorial approval. For example, when Margarita Hickey y Pellizoni requested permission to publish a poem on July 24, 1779, Nicolas Fernández de Moratín responded with this praise: "The *Dialogue* in verse that was sent to me for my censure does not contain anything against our Sacred Faith, and definitely has more merit than other works on the same topic."[19] Hickey's text was granted a license for publication on August 7, 1779. These examples suggest that male censors were willing to see women as skilled writers making valuable contributions to Spain's Republic of Letters.

Not all censors' evaluations, however, were gender-blind. Even in their praise of female-authored works, some male censors' comments divulge their awareness that the petitioner was a woman. In most cases, a censor took into account the applicant's sex in subtle ways, such as with comments about a work's genre or audience. An unusually overt mention of an author's sex is found in comments by the Archbishop Inquisitor General Don Manuel Quintano y Bonifaz on the Marquise of Tolosa's 1793 translation of Pierre Lalemant's *La mort des justes* (The Death of the Righteous). In response to Tolosa's request for both a license for publication and permission to dedicate the work to the queen, Quintano y Bonifaz sums up his high opinion of the work in this way:

> The solid piety of the author, who has also written other ascetic works, has deemed that this work circulate with esteem among those who know to appreciate similar writings: but keeping myself to the evaluation of the translation, I must confess that the language is pure, without the mix of strange voices that commonly disfigures translations, and that the method of expressing the ideas of the original is not at all servile, but rather largely energetic and appropriate to the character of our language. All of these circumstances, the fact that the Marquise of Tolosa is so esteemed among People of her Sex and Class, that the work contains such useful lessons, and above all the keen discernment

of the Queen Our Lady, who will know to celebrate the merit of the work, persuades me that it would be characteristic of her generosity, without being unworthy of her grandeur, to accept this dedication.[20]

While Quintano y Bonifaz's decision to recommend that Tolosa's petition be granted was in part based on the technique of her translation and the text's content, his comments also suggest that her position as a pious and respected woman was important. It is not that Quintano y Bonifaz wanted to reward Tolosa for her status and comportment. Rather, for this censor, Tolosa's virtue was as important as her skill in the evaluation of her work for publication. Lucky for Tolosa she had both. While Tolosa's case suggests the kinds of barriers that female authors faced, it also presents yet another example of a woman who successfully petitioned for the publication of her work, thus making it accessible to a public audience.

In some cases, censors placed seemingly insurmountable obstacles before authors, particularly in explaining why petitions were denied. For their part, female authors did not simply submit their works and then humbly accept whatever decision the censor made, to the repeated frustration of censors who disliked having their opinions challenged. Women were persistent and forceful advocates for their own work. They insisted on timely responses and frequently defended their work in light of what they considered to be unfair criticism by the censors. The often heated exchanges between male censors and the female authors they were thwarting attests to the weight women gave to the publication of their works and the lengths they would go to attain a public audience.

María de las Mercedes Gómez de Castro Aragón's bid for publication illustrates how determined a female author could be to get her work published. In 1797, Gómez de Castro petitioned for the publication of a work titled "Pintura del talento y caracter de las mugeres" (Portrait of the Talent and Character of Women). One of the first assessors of the work was Leandro Fernández de Moratín. On June 27, 1797, Moratín sent his report to the commission: "Not having noted in it anything against the royal prerogative of His Majesty and good customs, I am of the opinion that you should grant the license for its publication that is requested."[21] Thus, Moratín supported the publication of Gómez de Castro's work, but only on the narrow criteria of concordance with the church and monarchy.

Unsatisfied by Moratín's concise reply, the commission forwarded Gómez de Castro's work to a second censor on July 5, this time selecting Vicar Joseph Perez García for the task. In its repeated insistence on utility as a condition of publication, the council's charge to Perez García seems as if it were crafted to produce a negative review of the work. On August 9, 1797,

Perez García directed a letter to Bartolomé Muñoz de Torres in which he gave his evaluation of the manuscript as the commission had requested. In contrast to Moratín's support, Perez García was adamantly against the publication of Gómez de Castro's work, arguing that the plaintiff's submission was a lousy rip-off of a French work:

> The manuscript that you sent to me entitled Portrait of the Talent and Character of Women, that Doña María de las Mercedes Gómez Castro y Ballesteros seeks to send to press, *is precisely a copy* poorly done, or rather a truncated and diminished fragment, of the famous work with the title of Essay on the Character, Customs, and Talents of Women, written and published in French by the celebrated Monsieur Tomas in the year 1772, and which subsequently in the year 1773 was translated and published in Madrid in the workshop of Miguel Escribano by a Benedictine Monk with the assumed name of Dn. Alonso Puioz de Piña, whose editions in both languages have circulated widely in Spain; and there still exist many copies of them.[22]

Because of its alleged plagiarism, Perez García refers to the work as a "literary deception." In addition to leveling this serious charge, he also criticizes the prologue for being poorly organized. Thus, Perez García concludes, "This manuscript is so shapeless, so illegible, so poorly edited and ordered, that it is not necessary to enter into another examination of its merit, or the subject of the work. *It can be resolved that certainly, for the poor* state which it is in, for the respect that is owed to the public, and even for the honor of its very editor, the publication of the manuscript should be impeded and the license that is being petitioned denied." Perez García did not see how the printing council could grant a plagiarized work—and a poorly plagiarized one at that—a license for publication.

Although some of Perez García's arguments against the publication of this work center on the question of plagiarism and the poor organization of Gómez de Castro's text, the contents of the letter also suggest that his views were shaped by the sex of the author and the nature of the work's subject matter. Early on, he makes clear that his evaluation of the work is not divorced from the author's sex: "And although it is true that with respect to her sex one should perhaps excuse this defect and treat the entire work with the indulgence and favor that her sex deserves, nevertheless the poor layout of the manuscript is an unshakable hindrance which leaves no room for grace or deference on this point." The tone of Perez García's observation about the indulgent attitude censors should adopt in evaluating women's works smacks of condescension and suggests that his view of female writers differs from the even approach evaluators like Moratín adopted.

Perez García goes on to opine that the body of the work had no function other than to "speak exaggeratedly about women, and to refer to their place in a pile of events and histories." This criticism of the book's purpose more than hints at his disdain for a text devoted to a discussion of women's achievements. This contention becomes even clearer in the second section of his letter. Here, he discusses some negative views of Thomas's work, the French text that he claims Gómez de Castro has copied. Although Perez García concedes that some find Thomas's work a brilliant achievement, he focuses more on the criticisms of the work, quoting at length from a 1779 study of French literature by the Abbot Sabathien. According to Perez García,

> As a survey of critical judgments on the principal work shows, it is true that many celebrate it and esteem it for the swift brilliance of its style and for the grandeur of its thoughts that abound: but it is also true that others, even from the author's own country, strongly criticize it, such as the Abbot Sabathien, who in volume 4 of his Three Centuries of French Literature, edition of 1779, in the article on Monsieur Thomas, where after a terrible critique of the work of another author he says in an essay on page 135 that *the combination of observations of a grave sort and sublime thoughts is an insipid combination, lacking connection, full of stupidities and vain judgments, and that this work is made, according to general belief, with the goal of attracting women to a philosophical game which is not most agreeable for them.*[23]

With this quote from Sabathien, Perez García systematically denies both the value and purpose of female authors, subjects, and readers. The fact that Perez García closes his letter with this discussion raises questions about the legitimacy of his criticism of Gómez de Castro's work.

Gómez de Castro herself had concerns about the denial of her petition. In an August 19, 1797, letter, she indicates that she had been notified of this denial and requests the censor's report so that she could address his concerns. On September 5, 1797, she wrote the council another letter, in which she rebuts Perez García's claims. She starts by refuting his assertion that her work is a copy of an earlier French work by Thomas:

> With the greatest respect, *I expound that the Censor speaks* with equivocation in stating that my work is simply a copy or a truncated and diminished fragment of the famous work entitled Essay on the Character and Customs and Talents of Women, written by Monsieur Thomas in the year 1702 [sic] and subsequently translated and published in Madrid in the workshop of Miguel Escribano by a Benedictine monk. *Since only included* from this work are a few stories of Princesses and Greek and Roman women and an explication of which of the two sexes is more disposed toward friendship, which it also cites, and that of the various prac-

tices and customs of women in various realms, such as how they scorned death and what happened to them in these realms: Nothing more than the aforementioned content is from the work of Monsieur Thomas.[24]

The author explains that she had combed a number of texts, including the Bible, in order to find stories of virtuous women. In addition, she questions the right of the censor to turn down a work just because he considered it a poor translation. After all, she argues, censors were supposed to assess whether there was anything in the work that spoke against the Catholic faith, and nothing of this sort was cited. She argues that it would be relatively easy to correct some of the aspects of the organization of her prologue that had concerned the censor. Thus, she states that she should be allowed to print the work.

After being asked to evaluate Gómez de Castro's second request, Perez García wrote another note to Muñoz, dated October 13, 1797. In this correspondence, Perez García appears to accede to her argument, agreeing that the work did not speak against the Catholic faith or the king and even suggesting it might have merit for a female audience:

> The text, although little worked, does not appear to have any dogma against the Faith of the Church, nor offenses against the good customs, nor maxims or propositions against the royal prerogative of His Majesty, nor any sort of doctrine that would be against or dangerous to the tranquility and good order of the state; *and without doubt,* this work, more developed and better ordered, could be more useful to the other sex than books of gallantry and love which are the principal occupation of women in the present day, for at the least they would learn many sentiments and truths for the proper direction of their conduct and actions.[25]

This represents a significant departure from his previous fears about embroiling women in an inappropriate "philosophical game." At the same time, Perez García's newfound justification for the work's utility contains a jab at the female sex. Pointing to women's frivolous occupations allowed Perez García both to save face in light of Gómez de Castro's challenge and to call into question the value and appropriateness of that challenge. He goes on to remind the author of her need to complete some revisions, particularly the need to reorganize the text and clean it up a bit. On October 25, 1797, the council informed Gómez de Castro that it was granting permission to print the work. On December 2, Gómez de Castro indicated that she had finished revising her text and was submitting it for final review.[26]

This time Muñoz charged Manuel de Avila with the task of evaluating Gómez de Castro's text. In his January reply, Avila argues that, although it could be improved, there was no strong reason to deny the work's publication. According to Avila:

> *Having already been expounded in the* two previous censures, the judgment that I believe corresponds directly to the manuscript entitled Portrait of the Talent and Character of Women, I have nothing to add to the new copy that has been presented and that I have read, other than that if you and the council see it as appropriate, and are inclined toward the wishes of the Editor, you can favor her aspirations; because although it is certain that the work can be improved and make itself more worthy of the destiny it thinks to have, it is also true that it contains nothing against the religion, nor the state, and that it does not fail to promote some good maxims and truths that could be useful and serve for the instruction and good conduct of Women.[27]

While Avila recognized some of the shortcomings of Gómez de Castro's text identified by the previous censor, he also recognized the validity of her argument about the absence of any content against the Christian faith. Thus, he suggested that the council go ahead and approve her request for publication. However, despite Avila's lukewarm recommendation, or perhaps because of it, the council decided against the work's publication. Their decision reflects their impatience with the drawn-out debate: "Let no more discussion of this matter be admitted."[28]

Although the council wanted to put the issue to rest, Gómez de Castro wrote one more time to get in the last word. In a January 18, 1798, letter, she requested that the council return her manuscript as well as copies of the censors' letters since it would not grant a license for the publication of her work. In the opening of this brief letter, Gómez de Castro makes an interesting literary allusion: "Doña María de las Mercedes Gómez de Castro Aragón y Ballesteros, with the highest respect to you all, explains that she is aware that you have not authorized for publication a manuscript entitled Portrait of the Talent and Character of Women that she presented before you, soliciting a license and permission, in order to satisfy Mecenas [sic] who had taken her under his protection."[29] With this reference to Maecenas, a Roman knight of Etruscan descent who was an important patron of letters for such writers as Virgil, Horace, and Propertius, Gómez de Castro indirectly equates herself to these great classical authors. Further, the reference to her patron allows her to inform the council that, while it may not support her work, she has a patron who does. While Gómez de Castro's determined effort did not produce the desired result, her persistent challenges reveal her willingness to defend both her work and her right to participate in the public world of letters.

A similar battle occurred over the publication of Teresa González's almanac *Estado del cielo para el año de 1777* (State of the Heavens for the Year 1777). In this case, in spite of an attached petition by Antonio Allen García in support of the publication, Benito Bails's December 14, 1776, letter to the council criticizes the author for making frivolous predictions about the future: "I am of the feeling that you should mandate the author to make changes by cutting everything that has to do with Astrology and by abstaining from prognosticating at her whim the good and bad fortunes of men. I believe strongly that such an illustrious tribunal as yourselves would not want to credit any writer for such vulgar and harmful superstition much more far-fetched than it appears."[30] The record is unclear, but it seems that González's work was not granted a license for publication in light of Bails's criticism. When González submitted another edition of her almanac for 1778, Benito Bails was once again the censor who assessed her submission. According to his report of July 27, 1777:

> I have read by your commission *Estado del cielo para el año de 1778*, written by Doña Teresa González, to which I have no objections whatsoever in regard to the astronomical section. It only appears to me that the author owes some work to curing herself of the root sickness of being the soothsayer, as from the cover of the work it already promises *an astrological judgment in regard to the happenings of the elements and the harvest of crops,* and in the rest of the days of the year prescribes or prohibits bloody purges, etc.—with the same intrepidity of the works two times previously sent for my censure.[31]

Once again, Bails criticized González's work and deemed it unfit for publication. In charging González with "being a soothsayer," Bails went beyond simply a critique of the book and imperiled the author herself. Bails's comment transformed the female petitioner from talented author to superstitious quack.

These two rejections, both based on evaluations by Bails, spurred González to action. González penned a rather curt letter to the council when her 1778 work was not approved. First, she expresses her confusion over the concerns about her work. She explains that her 1773 work had been approved for publication and argues that the later versions conformed to the same model.[32] Thus, she protests the inconsistency of the council's assessment of works for publication. As for Bails's complaints about her prognostications, González forcefully claims:

> The work of the supplicant, as she herself will demonstrate, does not contain anything prophetic; on the contrary it is all strictly limited to the basics of Astrology, that is, that which councils, Popes, Doctors of

the Church, sound Philosophers, and knowledgeable Critics permit and authorize, because they realize the reason and experience on which these types of predictions rest and the usefulness they can serve for Agriculture, Medicine, and Navigation. Among the many authorities that the supplicant could cite in her favor, she will only include the most recommendable, and conclusive, for demonstrating without repetition the Justice of her petition.[33]

With this powerful assertion, González undercuts Bails's critique that her predictions were based on "superstition" and "whim" and instead emphasizes the logic of her method. She proceeds to quote a number of authorities to support the acceptance of the type of work she wanted to publish. For example, she quotes rule 9 of the Index of Prohibited Books compiled by the Council of Trent, which stated that the church "permits Astrologers *those judgments, that are written and created in order to help Navigation, Agriculture, and Medicine, and those that concern knowledge of the events and the general happenings of the world.*" She also cites other church-related sources such as a papal bull from Sixtus V, the writings of St. Thomas Aquinas, and the work of the mathematician Padre Tosca. All these authorities supported her contention that this type of writing was both acceptable and useful.

Further, González refers to a passage in the *Diccionario de la Lengua Castellana* that defended astrology. According to González, "But the greatest example is that, even in the Dictionary of the Castilian Language composed by the Spanish Academy, the word Astrology is affirmatively declared and defined as *that which only employs itself in the knowledge of celestial influences by observations of natural occurrences, such as the crescent shape of certain moons, and other similar occurrences; [it] has the name natural Astrology and is licit to use.*" González's final assertion references the profusion of almanacs and newspapers circulating in Spain that contained astrological predictions. Here, she was on solid ground. Apart from publishing numerous periodicals that contained such forecasts, Spain's printers turned out four or five *pronósticos* each year.[34] González indicates that these sorts of compositions had in fact served as a stimulus for the creation of her own work.

Thus, she asks that her almanac be considered for publication by a less biased censor:

With which she humbly asks of you and supplicates that you find it worthy to grant, if you deem it appropriate, in order to vindicate the offense that has been done to the author by her contemptible labeling as soothsayer; mandating that the work be reviewed anew by a dispassionate and impartial censor, just as Saint Augustine wanted for his writings; and not finding an impediment in all of it, that with the brevity that the passage of time demands for a work essentially periodic, if the supplicant succeeds by your justification, the petitioned license, and with it receives your merit.

With this not-so-humble plea for reconsideration, González ventures a harsh critique of the past censor: her request for a "dispassionate and impartial censor" implicitly labels Bails a subjective and biased reader. By suggesting Bails's conclusions, including his "contemptible labeling as soothsayer," were the product of emotion, not reason, González also underscores her own reasoned approach in both her appeal and her original work's predictions. At the same time, her reference to Saint Augustine coupled her with a great writer and thinker of the past, not unlike the way Gómez de Castro's reference to Maecenas paired her with Virgil. As a result of González's forceful arguments, she received a license to print her 1778 book on November 14, 1777.[35] Like other female writers, she felt entitled to argue her case in an instance when the censor seemed to judge her work unfairly. Unlike Gómez de Castro, González won.

The prolific writer María Rosa Gálvez, too, butted heads with the censors. When the council prohibited the publication of her comedy *La familia á la moda* (The Family in Fashion), Gálvez wrote to defend her work. In a February 26, 1805, letter, Gálvez indicates that she was most disturbed by the council's classification of her play as *"immoral and of the school of corruption and licentiousness."* She explains, "If the license had simply been denied, perhaps the author would have tolerated this event in order to avoid a drawn-out and bothersome dispute, but the reason that the accompanying note explains, about it being in some way denigrating, clearly denotes that the comedy has not been well understood. As a testament to the truth the composition itself suffices, whose purpose and objective is, as it should be, to ridicule certain vices."[36] Thus, Gálvez claims it was unjust to make these objections to her work without proof: "Neither is it just that the author be defrauded of the prize of her work nor that her compositions be censured as immoral, without presenting reasons." By pointing to the censor's errors in previous cases, she continues to push the issue of the incorrect conclusions that the censor had drawn from reading her work:

> The supplicant has, in her comedy entitled *Un loco hace ciento* [One Lunatic Makes One Hundred], evidence that the censors of the Vicar are not always just, since it was condemned by the said Tribunal, and later, examined by your illustrious predecessor, it was approved and it has been staged and published with general acclaim, and thus she dares to

hope that your judgment will serve to have the said Comedy reviewed by censors of known impartiality and intelligence, and if the result of their reports is, as the author believes, favorable to her composition, then in addition you will be ready to make the rightful amends.

When Gálvez indicated that she wanted to have the work looked at by "censors of known impartiality and intelligence," she was in effect labeling as biased and stupid those who had already examined and criticized her work. Apparently, the new censors who evaluated Gálvez's work agreed. A margin note indicates that Gálvez was awarded a license for publication on March 17.

These examples show that women claimed their place in print by defending the merits of their work and implicitly arguing for their right to be judged equally and fairly by the council. However, this was not always the tack that women writers took. In some cases, female authors utilized their position as women to their advantage. Such is the case with Gálvez's defense of her comedy *Un loco hace ciento*. When the council deemed Gálvez's comedy dangerous because it criticized France, Gálvez wrote to the head of the council to complain. She argued that her work did not have any content in conflict with Christian morality and requested that the council reconsider the previous decision. In articulating her position, Gálvez attempts to utilize her standing as a female playwright to her advantage:

> In this case, and with the peculiarity of this production being the work of a Spanish lady, whose individual circumstances the exponent believes makes her worthy of some favor, much more since she has already presented and had completely approved an original tragedy, and she hopes to continue her work, and that of her sex, she will not fail to contribute to the luster of the Spanish theater. In this case, then, she asks for you to determine that the best way of judging if the reprobation of the said comedy is or is not warranted, is that it be viewed and examined by other individuals who will give it a scrupulous, but impartial, censure.[37]

Gálvez appeals to the council to recognize her unique position as a woman writer as well as draws on her credentials as an already established playwright. By claiming that her work simultaneously advanced the cause of women and of Spanish theater, she taps into a strongly held belief among Spain's reformers: that the status of Spain's women was directly related to the status of the nation. That this was an effective strategy is evidenced by Gálvez's success. The work received a license for publication.[38]

Gálvez also utilized her position as a female author in requests for monetary support for the publication of her works. For example, when the council licensed Gálvez's 1803 *Obras poéticas* (Poetic Works) under the advice of censors Santos Díaz González, Juan Bautista de Ezpeleta, and Bartolomé

Muñoz de Torres, Gálvez decided to seek financial assistance from the king in order to underwrite the cost of publishing her work. In her letter, Gálvez expresses the importance of her work, again emphasizing her position as a female writer:

> In this state, she has found it impossible to bring the aforementioned works to light for lack of funds to cover the printing costs and, as a consequence, has been defrauded of the compensation that her applications still merit. To this could be added the desire to make public a work of which no other woman, in any nation, has equaled, since the most celebrated French women have only been limited to translating, and while some have given to light a dramatic composition, none have presented a collection of original tragedies like the exponent.[39]

By casting the publication of this manuscript as an accomplishment that would allow Spanish women to surpass their French counterparts, Gálvez lends greater force to her request that the king order the royal press to publish it.

In the plan that Gálvez outlines, the royal press would have the sole right to sell the work as its publisher. While the initial profits would go to the royal press in order to recoup the publishing costs, Gálvez indicates, she should reap the rest of the book's earnings. Her reasoning is two-pronged: "Therefore, she humbly requests that you find it suitable as an example of your renowned clemency, so that some compositions that have cost the supplicant infinite pains will not fall into oblivion." Gálvez states that by aiding her the king would demonstrate his charity, and she also makes clear her desire to have her work known. The king agreed to her plan, and in 1804 *Obras poéticas* was published. The three volumes contained a significant amount of Gálvez's writings: various poetry, three comedies *(El egoísta, Los figurones literarios,* and a translation of the French play *Bión),* two one-act plays *(Saúl* and *Safo),* and five tragedies *(Florinda, Blanca de Rossi, Amnón, Zinda,* and *La delirante).*[40]

Gálvez wrote the king again on September 19, 1804, in order to thank him and send him two copies of the published compilation. Again, in her letter, she refers to her importance as a female writer, indicating of her *Obras poéticas* "that these represent what are scarce examples by her sex, not only in Spain, but in all of Europe."[41] After emphasizing the importance of the work, Gálvez respectfully requests that the king forfeit the cost of publication and give her the complete earnings of the works. After all, she argues, the publication costs would not exceed 1,800 *reales.* Besides, if he did not agree to waive this fee, Gálvez argues, she would continue to be plagued by financial difficulties and would not be able to make a living off of her work.

If she had to let the royal printer keep the publishing costs, Gálvez writes, "then the Exponent will remain submerged in the same indigence as before receiving your first favor, as regards her inability to live on the product of her work." Gálvez's bold petition was again successful. The king granted her the entire proceeds from the publication of her work.[42]

Gálvez couched other requests as well in terms of her unique position as a female writer. In May 1801, she wrote a letter to the council charged with supervising the capitol's theaters about her five-act tragedy *Ali-Bek*. Having already secured the necessary licenses for the work to be performed and printed, Gálvez sought a special arrangement from the council. As she explains in the letter, the normal compensation awarded to writers was 3 percent of the profit for all performances of a play for a period of ten years. She herself had received this form of remuneration for other dramatic works that she had written. However, in this case, as a result of financial difficulties that she attributes to "loss of income, as a result of the latest unfortunate epidemic in Cádiz," Gálvez was requesting a flat, onetime fee of twenty-five doubloons. In making this request, Gálvez emphasizes her unique position as a female writer: "Dare I hope that you, with the interest that you take in improving the Theaters, of which we have already seen sufficient proofs, will not refuse to concede your protection to a woman, the first among Spanish women to have dedicated herself to this branch of Literature."[43] Once again, Gálvez attempts to utilize her position as a female writer in a field dominated by men to get what she needed. A margin note on the first page of her letter indicates that she succeeded: "Madrid June 4, 1801—As it is requested."

Gálvez's appeal based on her sex constituted more than an effective strategy. Many female authors described their importance as writers in terms of their place as women. Women writers recognized that the publicity of female-authored texts was crucial to the development of both female education and female literary pursuits. Through publication an author became known, not only because of the publication of her text itself, but also because literary periodicals frequently printed reviews of and commentaries on new publications. This sort of publicity could be good for women in general. That individual women's literary achievements could pave the way for other women's intellectual pursuits is exemplified by the case of Margarita Hickey. When *Memorial Literario* announced the publication of Hickey's *Poesías sagradas y profundas* (Sacred and Profound Poems), the writer placed Hickey's talents in the larger context of the notable achievements of women: "We see more every day that if they have had a literary education, and even without one, many whose strong desire has brought them to letters and has driven them methodically to books, have demonstrated by their works that they are not inferior in capacity to men."[44] The author referred to an article published in the periodical in June 1785, in which the magazine spoke of a number of Spanish women who had proven their abilities.[45] Now, the author wished to place Hickey among this group: "Many who have lived and whom we knew remained silent awaited, for reasons of modesty, an opportunity to present itself for them to reveal their merit. Among them are Doña Margarita Hikey [sic] y Pellizoni, author of the present work, which is the best testament to her instruction and talent for poetry." With its article, the *Memorial Literario* turned the announcement of the recent publication of Hickey's text into an elegy to women's accomplishments in general.

Many women authors considered themselves to be participants in a female literary world and imagined their works as both directed toward women and inspiring women to take up pen and paper. In an introductory note to her translation of Michel-Ange Marin's *Virginie, ou, La vierge chrétienne* (Virginia, or, the Christian Virgin), Cayetana Aguirre y Rosales addresses her work to unmarried Spanish women: "To the single ladies of Spain: The desire to be useful to my peers, and the importance of this work, made me think to translate it to our language."[46] Rita Caveda y Solares makes a similar appeal to women in her introduction to a collection of letters translated from an unidentified English book: "Ladies: I present to you this small volume, that for its beautiful morals and solid maxims on education belongs properly to our sex. Hopeful that someone might take advantage of these precious documents, which is the repayment that I desire, the only aim with which I present this work."[47]

Perhaps one of the most forceful examples of women's appeals is Inés Joyes y Blake's "Apologia de las mujeres" (Vindication of Women), a short piece she appended to her 1798 translation of Samuel Johnson's *The History of Rasselas, Prince of Abissinia*. The last line of Joyes y Blake's "Apologia" exemplifies the text's rousing call for women to develop their talents and band together to achieve social change: "I would like, from the top of a mountain from where all women could hear me, to give them this counsel: Hear me, women, I would say, never believe that your souls are not the equal of those of the sex that wants to tyrannize you: use the light that the Creator gave you; through you, if you want it, could come about the reform of manners which, without you, will never come about. Respect yourselves and they will respect you. Love one another."[48] With her "Apologia," Joyes y Blake endeavored to show women how they could work together to improve their lives, even in the midst of a society that itself tried to limit their conduct and relegate them to a position of lesser importance. Further,

Joyes y Blake dedicated her translation to the Count-Duchess of Benavente. With her advanced learning, her own *tertulia*, and her ascension to the presidency of the *junta de damas* of the Economic Society, Benavente was a contemporary example of a woman who had forged her own place in the public sphere. Joyes y Blake's dedication of her work to Benavente testifies to both the inspiration a fellow woman could provide and the sense of community among women in Spain's Republic of Letters.[49] Like many women who published their works, Joyes y Blake hoped that her writings and her example would encourage others and thus serve her sex.

The fact that women writers felt free to defend their own works with such vehemence reveals both the value they placed on publication and the confidence they had in their right to put forth their ideas. In case after case, female authors were quick to question the merits of censors' arguments and defend their works. They also identified themselves as serious writers, placing themselves in the company of such great authors as Virgil and Augustine. Yet what stands out in these petitions is the variety of arguments women made in support of their rights. At times, they framed their cases in terms of the merit of their works and their right to be evaluated fairly and equally based on established guidelines. At other times, they tapped into the prominent notion that the status of Spain's women indicated the nation's progress on its path to modernization and Europeanization.[50] While encouraging censors to consider the larger benefits of supporting women's writings can be seen as calling for different standards for women's work, female authors did not see these two strategies as contradictory. Rather, their flexibility served the common goal of carving out a space for women's voices in public discourse. In other words, it was the ends, not the means, that female petitioners contemplated.

EQUALITY AND AUTONOMY: THE *JUNTA DE DAMAS* PREPARES FOR ACTION

Creating a sphere of female action was also on the minds of the ten women who gathered on October 5, 1787, at the Casas Consistoriales (Town Hall) at 4:30 P.M. for the first meeting of the *junta de damas*.[51] After reading the royal decree that helped to end a drawn out debate and establish the women's organization as a part of the Economic Society, the women listed the members of their new council. This group of sixteen women included María Isidra Quintina Guzmán y la Cerda and the Countess of Benavente, who had already been elected to the Society in 1786, as well as an additional fourteen women that the Society had admitted to the new *junta de damas* on September 22, 1787. After considering the membership roster, the women got right to work. They held an election and decided upon the Countess of Montijo to be the group's first secretary. To various women present, they assigned duties in the administration of the *escuelas patrióticas* (patriotic schools), spinning schools run by the Economic Society that were now to be under the direction of the *junta de damas*. They established a regular meeting time: Fridays at 4:30 P.M. in the winter and 5:30 P.M. in the summer. And, of course, they admitted Amar y Borbón.

Undoubtedly other members of the *junta de damas* shared Amar y Borbón's disappointment, expressed in her "Oración gratulatoria," in their segregation from the general Society. No doubt they, too, fumed over arguments that belittled their commitment to the nation and its reform. However, with the terms of their admission now established, the members of the women's council tabled their anger and instead focused their energy on negotiating a position of power for themselves. That this would require significant effort became clear early on as the *junta de comisión* worked out guidelines for female participation. This initially all-male committee, devised to help ease the creation of the female congress, met more or less weekly from September 12, 1787, through October 22, 1788. At its first meeting, in addition to nominating potential *socias* and naming the Countess of Benavente to serve as the group's first president, the commission grappled with the question of the *junta de damas'* place in the overall organization.[52]

In its discussion, the commission emphasized the dependent nature of the female council with respect to the Economic Society at large. In an official report to the Society ten days later, the commission likened the *junta de damas* to the councils of agriculture, industry, and arts and crafts.[53] The report's comparison implied that the *junta de damas* was a commission established to deal with a specific issue: in this case, women and their involvement in the economy. It also signified a relationship of dependence, one in which the women's council could debate issues but ultimately had to rely on the agreement and funding of the Economic Society to act.

In June 1788, the king's chief minister, the Count of Floridablanca, presented the members of the women's council with a perfect opportunity to quash the *junta de comisión's* declaration of their dependence when he forwarded their president a copy of M.O.'s proposal for a female national dress. As discussed in chapter 3, this proposal outlined a plan to have Spain's women adopt patriotic attire in an effort to spur Spanish industry and curb luxury spending. Floridablanca considered the dress code a promising venture for the new council, so he sent the proposal along with a letter asking its members to sponsor a prize competition for the design of a national dress for women.[54] It was clear from Floridablanca's letter that he supported the idea. He was not asking the members of the women's council to evaluate the proposal; he was asking them to implement it. While the women's council was no doubt anxious to show that women could be important contributors to the project of Spain's regeneration, its members did not swallow the rhetoric of female patriotism that M.O. presented. Instead, the Countess of Montijo spoke for the group in dismissing the idea in a very firm letter addressed to Floridablanca.[55]

Montijo's letter, which recorded "what the council really thought of this new project," contained numerous objections to the treatise, including disdain for its bias against the lower classes, doubts about its promise to revolutionize Spanish industry, and admonitions that education, not restrictive legislation, would effect change.[56] In short, the women's council curtly refused Floridablanca's request. The letter that the Countess of Montijo penned in rejection of the adoption of a female national dress exemplified the *socias'* desire to stake out their own position rather than simply follow the dictates of others. As the scholar Paula de Demerson explains, "The Countess of Montijo saved Spanish women from seeing themselves converted into an army in skirts, into a monotonous and insipid herd, and she revealed at the same time that the women's council intended to conserve its spirit of independence, its liberty of judgment, and that it was not a blind instrument of the state."[57] This episode, which happened so early in the life of the *junta de damas*, set an important precedent for the independence and dynamism that would characterize the group's activities. The women's council made clear that it would not merely be an instrument for attaining others' goals. Floridablanca seems to have dropped the issue in light of the *damas'* definitive reply. No further discussion of the dress code proposal appears in the Economic Society records.

But gaining both power and independence was more difficult than this early victory suggests. Like many female authors who battled the censors, the women of the Economic Society employed various and seemingly contradictory strategies in their effort to forge their own place in the nation's reform. On the one hand, *socias* emphasized their integration in the Economic Society at large, touting themselves as serious reformers whose commitment to and rights in the royal institution mirrored those of male affiliates. On the other hand, the *damas* drew on their unique status as women whose very membership in a separate council confirmed, in their eyes, a certain level of independence. The debates over revising the *socias'* statutes, as well as the day-to-day interaction between the female council and the general membership of the Economic Society, reveal that the women of the *junta de damas* at once argued for integration and independence. In doing so, the female council crafted a relatively autonomous organization whose link with the Economic Society provided its members with the status and resources they needed to effect real change.

The *junta de damas'* efforts to formulate new statutes for the organization's governance demonstrate the members' strategy of inclusion. They felt it was important to get their voice and vote in the Society institutionalized, and they used the composition of their statutes to gain rights that male members of the organization already enjoyed. The *junta de comisión* had drafted preliminary statutes for the women's council based largely on the general statutes of the Economic Society itself, and it distributed them to *socias* in July 1788.[58] Transforming these provisional guidelines into a permanent governing code took a surprising six years, though not because of the *junta de damas'* lack of persistence.[59] Particularly from 1791 on, the group's minutes reflect both frustration with the difficulty of gaining male cooperation in the process and a heightened sense of urgency for the need to complete the document.

In the end, the persistence and maneuvering of the women's council garnered it significant power in shaping its governing document. When the *junta de damas* appealed to the general council to permit the reform of the group's original statutes, the council charged a new *junta de comisión* to complete the task, a committee made up of four *socias;* the women's president, the Countess of Torrepalma; and five male members of the Society.[60] The inefficiency of this committee resulted in protracted negotiations that reopened old questions and tested the *socias'* patience. One point of debate between the two bodies exemplifies both the annoying delays the *socias* consistently endured and the eventual victories they would enjoy. The problem at hand was how to reconcile women's participation in the election of the general council's director and other important officials with a provision in the Economic Society's statutes allowing only the forty longest-standing members of the Society a vote in its elections.[61] After deliberation, the new *junta de comisión* decided to consult the king to see if this article could be changed, so that all members, regardless of their sex, would be eligible to vote as long as they had attended at least twelve meetings of their respective councils per year. Not surprisingly, the rest of the women's council backed this proposal enthusiastically. A number of the *socias* resolved to attend the *junta general* the next day "with the goal of putting forward verbally the reasons and reflections that could support it, and to contribute to its approbation."[62]

Then came the delay. Six months later, enthusiasm turned to frustration as the women's council lamented the king's failure to respond to the Society's query regarding elections.[63] Recognizing the importance of this issue, the women's council again sent a delegation of *socias* to the general council meeting in order to call attention to the pending request.[64] Finally, on February 3, 1792, Floridablanca sent a letter to the Economic Society indicating the king's approval of the proposed change, though he was likely unaware of the *junta de damas*' renewed push. Although it had taken eight months, the women's council had achieved its goal. Its members would now have a voice in the Economic Society's elections.[65] While the women's council was undoubtedly pleased with this outcome, its tolerance for such delays shrank.

In September 1793, to relieve their frustration, the councilwomen resolved to propose a plan they hoped would, once and for all, allow them to complete their statutes. In a gutsy move, the women requested that approval by the male members of the *junta de comisión* be waived. They reminded the council that these men's frequent absences from the city had been an ongoing problem inhibiting progress on the statutes. Dismissing the idea of formulating a new commission as time-consuming, the *junta de damas* proposed to finish revising the statutes on its own: "It would prolong matters to name another new commission; it seems to the [women's] council that it could pass over this formality, and reading the statutes and examining them in the council, moving, cutting, and adding as the ladies consider suitable and, this done, pass them on to the Society so that it can see them, putting forward the corrections offered to satisfy the [general] council of the reasons it had for them."[66] In effect, this proposal would enable the *socias* to debate and consider revisions without the input of male members of the organization. Perhaps worn down by the councilwomen's repeated petitions over the past few years, the Society agreed to the *damas*' revised plan at the October 12 *junta general*.

By February of the following year, just four months later, the women's council had completed its statute revisions. The *junta de damas* appointed a prestigious commission to present the new regulations to the general council but encouraged all other members of the women's council to attend. Perhaps bracing for a fight, the women's council dispatched this delegation along with the written document "so that it could respond to the objections posed by the Royal Society."[67] Although the women crafted the document themselves, they still had to win approval from the general council of the Society and the king. The delegation came prepared to persuade the Society and to defend their statutes.[68]

At the *socias*' April 4 meeting, the committee declared victory and announced that the Society had approved the statutes. As the minutes of the *junta de damas* record: "Realized the conclusion of the statute revisions in the Society."[69] The choice of the word *revisión* makes this difficult to interpret, since it can both mean "to revise" and "to review." Thus, it is not clear whether the committee was reporting that the revision was complete, suggesting that the male members of the Society might have altered the *damas'* initial proposal, or whether the Society ratified the statutes without changes after a quick review. The fact that no discussion appears in the women's council records about conflicts raised in this process does suggest that there was little or no disagreement about the text that the women presented. The councilwomen had been quick to defend themselves in the past when they felt their rights were being trampled. After pushing so hard to have their statutes completed, they would have been unwilling to sit back and allow the Society to alter them seriously without a fight.

Having convinced the Economic Society, the women's council now had to get final approval for the new statutes from the king; the *socias* charged the Countess of Trúllas (formerly Torrepalma) and the Marquise of Ariza with the task.[70] The council's representatives had no difficulty in getting the king's rubber-stamp approval. In ratifying the statutes in their entirety, he made a direct reference to the women's role in composing the document. According to the king's formal acceptance of the statutes: "The king has seen fit to approve the statutes that the women's council of members of honor and merit of the Royal Economic Society of Madrid has formed for its government and management."[71] The recognition of the women's authorship of their own governing document was an important symbol of the legitimacy of their participation in the organization.

The new statutes of 1794 contained key differences from the provisional document of 1788.[77] A number of the statutes reflect the *damas'* desire to prove their seriousness about the role they could play in bringing the Enlightenment agenda of the Economic Society to fruition. Perhaps dismayed that relegation to a women's auxiliary implicitly devalued their possible contribution to Spain's regeneration, as Amar y Borbón had intimated in her "Oración gratulatoria," the councilwomen shaped the statutes to reflect their earnest intentions. In doing so, the *junta de damas* portrayed its members as dedicated and skilled, not unlike the Society's male affiliates. An outline of the necessary qualifications for prospective *socias*, a feature absent from the 1788 guidelines, constituted a first step in conveying the group's seriousness. In order to be elected as a member, a woman had to have a "good education and deportment, with instruction related to the goals of the organization." The women's council wanted serious members who could add to its work. This is why it did not admit Antonia de Bordonaba, a seven-year-old who solicited membership in 1797.[73]

In addition, the new statutes mandated that all members of the women's council contribute 160 *reales de vellón* per year toward the organization's projects. This placed them a bit above the *socios*, whose contribution was set at 120 *reales de vellón* per year. While the preliminary statutes had deemed this contribution voluntary for women, the 1794 statutes made it obligatory. Here, the women took their stand on an issue raised as an integral part of the debate over their admission two decades earlier. By embracing a mandatory financial contribution to the Society, the women's council proved that its members were not self-serving ladies who had joined for their own glorification. Rather, they were fully integrated members, ready to contribute on a par with men. While some of these statute alterations reflect the elitism that characterized the group, for the *damas* these revisions formed part of creating an assembly of active, dedicated members able to effect change.

The new statutes also secured more rights for the women of the Society. Attaining their right to attend meetings of the general council was among their most significant gains. According to the 1788 provisional guidelines, the female council's members could attend their own meetings but not those of the general Society. Article 6 of the final statutes removed this limitation. Now female members "could attend the sessions of the [women's] council, and those of the Society, as they wished."[74] This was an important victory for the *damas* and another indication of their drive for inclusion in the larger organization. The women had firsthand experience with how being denied access to meetings could limit their ability to participate in the life of the Society. A prime example is a 1791 incident in which the Society failed to notify the women's council of the upcoming election of new officers of the general Society. Learning of the election of Floridablanca as the new director and the reelection of the Marquis of Castrillo as the subdirector by memorandum after the fact, the women's council confronted the Society.[75] The Society countered that it had not advised any of its members or councils of the election. The women pointed out that this was an unsatisfactory explanation, since the rest of the members attended or could attend the council's gatherings at will, while the members of the women's council could attend only "when some reason demanded it." Thus, they resolved to discuss this issue further in the statutes committee.[76] Undoubtedly, this episode played a key role in the women's decision to push for inclusion in all of the Society's general meetings.

The women's council also gave itself the ability to expand its membership. Title 1 of the new statutes conferred the right to have an indeterminate number of members on the women's council. This differed from the 1788 statutes, which limited the number of main members to fifty women.[77] This was a necessary change if the group was going to grow at all. As the membership roster of the women's council in table 5 shows, by 1794 the council had already admitted fifty-one women to its ranks. This change in the preliminary statutes gave the organization room to grow, providing the possibility for a larger membership pool to help accomplish the increasingly wide range of activities the group would undertake.

In articulating their new rights, the *damas* emphasized their integration in and commonality with the larger Society. As male members did, *socias* intended to pay dues, attend general council meetings, and vote in Society elections. Emphasizing their incorporation into the general organization constituted an important aspect of gaining rights within the Society. To this end, the women's council left untouched major sections of the 1788 provisional statutes, which the *junta de comisión* had largely excerpted from the Economic Society's own governing document.[78] These sections suggest the desire of the *junta de damas* to integrate itself into the organization, to follow the same procedures and processes as male members. For instance, the women's council adopted a governing structure virtually identical to that of the general Society, empowering the same officers with the same duties.[79] *Socias* were careful to add the office of censor, absent in the 1788 text, in their revisions. The addition of the censor, whose main task was to ensure the observance of the statutes and agreements of the women's council, underscored the value that *socias* placed on the written codification of their membership in the royal organization. Title 2 of the 1794 statutes left unchanged a provisional statute that, in specifying the nature of the female council's meetings, mirrored the general Society's regulations. From the principle of majority voting to the open seating policy, the women's council embraced the democratic principles under which the Society functioned. The same democratic principles are embodied in title 3, which outlines the election of officers. The description of this process, also used by the general Society, was left unchanged in the statute revisions. The *damas'* acceptance of these sections of the provisional statutes "as is" not only suggests their desire to incorporate themselves into the male organization through similar procedural practices but also reflects their commitment to the more democratic principles of Enlightenment.

In the formation of their new statutes, the *damas* emphasized their integration in the larger organization, both to cast themselves as serious contributors and to claim key rights in the Society at large. But the statute

TABLE 5. *Members of the Women's Council, 1786–1811*

1786	January 24	Countess of Benavente
		María Isidra Quintina Guzmán y la Cerda
1787	September 22	Felipa la Roza
		Countess of Fernán Núñez
		Duchess of Almodóvar
		Countess of Montijo
		Marquise of Palacios
		María del Rosario Cepeda
		Marquise of Villa López
		Countess of Benalúa
		Countess of Santa Eufemia
		Marquise of Torrecilla
		Countess of Carpio
		Marquise of Ayerbe
		Teresa Losada y Portocarrero
		María Ana de Pontejos
	October 5	Josefa Amar y Borbón
		Marquise of Montealegre
		Princess of Asturias, María Luisa de Borbón
		Infanta María Victoria de Borbón
		Infanta María Josepha de Borbón
	October 26	Joaquina Domínguez de Aguayo
		María Rafaela de San Christóbal
	November 9	Countess of O'Reylli
		María del Rosario Jácome y Ricardos
	December 7	Countess of Torrepalma
	December 14	María Josefa de Cañas
		María Josefa de los Dolores Veytía
		Doña María Guerrero
1788	January 18	Marquise of Someruelos
	February 8	Marquise of Llano
	June 27	Viscountess of Palazuelos
	July 4	Marquise of Altamira
	August 8	Marquise of Fuerte-Híjar
	September 19	María Betencourt y Molina
1789	April 24	Mademoiselle le Masson le Golft
	May 22	Marquise of Bermudo
	November 13	Marquise of la Espeja
	November 27	Marquise of Sonora

(continued)

TABLE 5. *(continued)*

1790	February 5	Andrea de Varo Gil
	March 19	Ana Caraza y Ofarril
	September 24	María Josepha Burriel
	October 1	Marquise of Canillejas
	December 3	María Gertrudis de Velasco y Escobedo
1791	January 7	María de Roxas y Velarde
	January 21	Francisca Raón y Mariño
	June 3	Baroness of San Miguel de Perá
1793	November 15	Countess of Villalobos
		María Josepha Panes y Mangino
	December 20	Countess of Torrejón
1795	October 9	Countess of Castro Terreño
	October 30	Countess of Nieulant
1796	February 19	Josefa Díez de la Cortina y Morales
1797	December 22	Catalina Seix y Páez
1798	December 21	Francisca Cepeda de Ugarte
1799–1800	Date not known*	Ana Tully
		Isabel Parreño
		Countess of Hust
		Marquise of Portago
1799	January 18	Marquise of Villafranca
		Countess of Trastámara
	May 24	Beatriz Montiel de Vaca
	June 7	Marquise of Zilleruelo
	October 19	Countess of Aranda
1800	January 24	María Josepha Ester de Moreno
	August 2	Juana de Armendaríz
1801	September 4	Rosa O'Reilly
	September 18	Mariana Fariña de Ayala
1803	January 21	María Loreto Figueroa y Montalvo
1804	January 20	Countess of Casaflórez
	May 4	Countess of Villamonte
	July 20	Marquise of Peñafiel
	November 30	Countess of Miranda
1805	October 11	Marquise of Camarasa
		Marquise of Santa Cruz

(continued)

TABLE 5. *(continued)*

1807	February 27	Duchess of Frías y Uceda
	June 26	María de las Mercedes Porres de Sotelo
	September 18	Countess of San Román
	September 25	Marquise of San Bartolomé
1811	January 14	Petra Pedregal de Herbas
	May 27	Duchess of Mahón
	June 10	Countess of Fuentenueva
	June 17	Duchess of Santa Fé
	September 16	María de las Mercedes Santa Cruz de Merlín

*Date unknown because of the loss of the *Libro de actas de la junta de damas*, 1799–1800.
SOURCE: Compiled from the *Libros de actas de la junta de damas*, covering the years 1786–1798 and 1801–1811, SEM Archivo, Libros A/56; SEM Archivo, Legajos 93-4, 95-12, 102-3, 107-17, 117-18, 131-8, 151-15, 161-18, 164 7, 168-4, 172-5, 178-9, 192-3, 203 9, which include thank-you notes from admitted *socias* and other membership lists; *Memorias de la Sociedad Económica*, vol. 4 (Madrid: Don Antonio de Sancha, 1787), 364–76; and Paula de Demerson, *Catálogo de las socias de honor y mérito de la junta de damas matritense (1787–1811)*, Tirada Aparte de los Anales del Instituto de Estudios Madrileños, 7 (Madrid: Raycar, S.A., 1966).

debates also reflect the *damas'* desire for independence, particularly in setting their own agenda. Mindful of the 1788 dress code fiasco, the *junta de damas* set out some clear objectives for its membership in the 1794 statutes. A subtle change in the wording of the group's directive indicates the female council's desire to expand its mandate. In its 1794 bylaws, the organization clearly articulates its goals: "Its mandate is to establish and to instill good education, to better customs by its enlightenment and its example, to introduce love for work and to foster industry."[80] Unlike this call for the *socias* to "foster industry," the wording of the provisional statutes had focused more on their role as consumers. According to the 1788 statutes, the female members were to "curb luxury as well as to substitute national styles for foreign ones." This alteration, undoubtedly linked to the earlier debates over the dress code, expanded the *socias'* ability to affect industry.

In addition, the new statutes established the female council's commitment to women's education. The *junta de comisión* had originally proposed that female education should constitute a primary concern of the women's council. Accordingly, it turned over some of the Society's educational endeavors to the *damas*, namely the *escuelas patrióticas* and the *escuela de bordados* (embroidery school).[81] The women's organization embraced these responsibilities and worked to make female education one of its main priorities. The *damas* separated out information on the schools that were under their direction and concentrated this information in its own section of the statutes. While much of the basic material included in this section appeared in various places within the 1788 provisional statutes, the codification of the educational project of the *junta de damas* in a separate proviso highlighted this issue's importance to the female council.[82] In addition, the *damas* added provisions for educational committees to study the topic of female education. Title 8 of the new statutes set up and empowered two permanent committees on women's education not mentioned in 1788. These commissions, one pertaining to the moral education of women and the other to their physical education, drew on the energies of all the group's members—all *socias* had to serve on one of the two bodies. Like the female authors, the *damas* recognized themselves as women and felt a need to focus their energies on aiding their sex.

The statute debates are not the only evidence of the female council's simultaneous appeals for integration and independence. The protracted dispute over the relationship between the *junta de damas* and the general council of the Society also shows how the *socias* skillfully employed both strategies to their advantage. Early in its life, as its members strived to gain a strong foothold in the organization, the *junta de damas* tended to emphasize its incorporation into the larger Society. Take, for example, the events following the November 1792 request of the *junta general* to schedule a discussion with the *junta de damas* on the relationship between the two councils.[83] The female members gladly received a four-man delegation from the Society at their November 23 meeting, which opened with the Count of Villalobos's statement of the commission's charge: "The Society, desirous of conserving the greatest harmony and union with the ladies' council, wishes to satisfy it if it has any complaints and to maintain the perfect union so necessary and useful to the general good."[84] The women's council responded that it also desired "the greatest harmony and union." Taking advantage of the opportunity that the *socios*' presence afforded them, the *damas* proceeded to propose several policies they deemed vital to preserving this harmony. For example, the *damas* petitioned for the right of *socias* to attend reelections and requested that in various circumstances the Society postpone decision making so that the *junta de damas* could participate in deliberations. These proposals reflected the desire of the women's council to voice its own views on Society matters, for its members to have the same input male members enjoyed.

On December 7, 1792, the four *socios* once again attended the meeting of the women's council in order to announce that the Society had accepted the women's proposals.[85] The efforts of the women's council led to immediate results. For example, on February 14, 1792, the Society requested the opinion of the *junta de damas* in regard to a proposal to alter the Escuela de San Andrés, one of the *escuelas patrióticas*.[86] A memorandum suggested that the women's council attend the *junta general* the following Saturday in order to express its opinion, and the records of the women's council indicate that *socios* and *socias* debated the proposed change at the Society's meeting.[87] Women were also invited to and attended the February 16 meeting for electoral purposes. Thus, by emphasizing its need to be included in the larger organization, the women's council ensured its own input in the business of the Society.

Some *socios* resisted this push for integration. The affirmation in the April 1794 statutes of the right of members of the women's council to attend the meetings of the *junta general*, for example, angered a number of male members. These *socios* argued that if women could attend the Society's meetings, then men should be allowed to attend those of the women's council. At the July 26, 1794, meeting of the *junta general*, Simon de Codes formally motioned that men be permitted to attend meetings of the *junta de damas*: "Be it agreed that as the Ladies because of their new statutes can freely attend the *juntas ordinarias* of this royal body, of its classes and commissions, individuals can equally attend the *juntas ordinarias* and *particulares* of the Ladies themselves."[88] The director suggested that they resolve the issue at the next meeting on August 2, and he ordered a memorandum be sent announcing the meeting and its agenda so that the women's council could attend.

Although the women's council received the Society's directive, its members did not feel the issue merited discussion. Rather, they sent their own memorandum in which they argued that this issue had been resolved two years earlier.[89] They reminded the *junta general* that the Society had already approved a proposition made by the women's council in November 1792, which stated that members of the *junta general* could attend the women's council when they had business to discuss without sending notice of their intentions beforehand.[90] The *junta de damas* felt that this covered the issue of men's attendance at their meetings, and it did not see fit to send anyone to the next day's *junta general*. The women's council indicated it would be happy to attend the following *junta general* if the Society deemed it necessary.

This missive did not satisfy the Society, which called for a *junta extraordinaria* for Wednesday, August 13, at 5 P.M., to discuss whether men should be allowed to attend the *junta de damas*.[91] The debate, which is not fully recorded, centered on the utility of men attending the women's gatherings.

In the course of this discussion, the *junta* reopened an older debate on the Society's decision to incorporate women into a separate body from the beginning. The *junta* concluded the discussion by asserting that the success of the women's work thus far suggested the effectiveness of the chosen organizational structure. In the end, the Society rejected the idea of a male presence at the *socias'* meetings: "By unanimous vote of all the gentlemen present the Society declared, *there is absolutely no utility in gentlemen attending the meetings of the Ladies.*" The emphasis suggests men did not consider attending the *socias'* gatherings time well spent.

This still did not solve the tension between the two groups. On September 5, 1794, four *socios* (Andres Zurana, Francisco Gerónimo Cifuentes, Ventura de Arguellada, and Domingo de Andrade) attended the women's council to discuss the Society's displeasure with a few of the recent actions of the *junta de damas*. Zurana informed the women's council that the Society felt the *socias* were overstepping their bounds. The Society did not like the August 9 memorandum from the women's council to the Society regarding the attendance of men at the *junta de damas*. It believed that the women had assumed too much autonomy by sending the memorandum rather than attending the *junta general* as directed. Zurana also brought up a few incidents related to the Society's intention to monitor the actions of the women's council, particularly its elections.[92] Zurana pointed to the Society's regulations, which stated that the *socias* must pass the *actas* (minutes) of their meetings to the Society for confirmation. According to Zurana, "From all this, it is inferred that the council cannot proceed without approval of the Society, and by this same principle the council cannot present itself to His Majesty or his tribunals, without agreement of the Society except in certain cases." Zurana lamented the numerous incidents in which the women's council had ignored these regulations, causing discord between the two *juntas*. Zurana's commentary points to the gap between the *damas'* demand for rights and their open resistance to the Economic Society policies that they found oppressive and inconvenient. Zurana recalled the initial creation of the *junta de damas* by referring to the debate over women's admission as well as the notion that it was created to be equal to the councils of agriculture, industry, and arts and crafts. In other words, the commission viewed the *junta de damas* as "absolutely dependent on the Society, because this Royal Body had admitted [women] as members, had overcome the difficulties that this offered it, had solicited and obtained from His Majesty the admission and formation of the council, had named the first President itself."[93] For the male commission, the problem was the failure of the *junta de damas* to recognize its subordinate position in the larger body.

In response to Zurana's reminder about the dependence of the *junta de damas,* the women's council shifted strategies and argued vehemently for its independence. First, the women expressed what they saw as their relationship to the *junta general.* Rather than emphasizing their integration and participation in the larger organization, they emphasized their separate status, much as authors like Gálvez emphasized their unique place as female writers. According to the *damas:* "In its opinion the [women's] council is a separate body united to the Society to help it in the tasks that are most analogous to it, which means neither dependence nor superiority, since there cannot be these between two united things." By focusing on its segregation from the Society, the women's council pointed to its unique status as a reason for its autonomy. In addition, the *socias* indicated that, while they did not mind having their *actas* approved in most cases, this would not work for elections. They argued that such approval would not be "unsuitable except in elections because that is a dependency too outstanding that humbles without purpose." Here, the *socias* revealed that their concern went beyond carving out a space for independent action. They were determined not to be humbled, but rather to be respected as their participation in the esteemed Society warranted. Further, they argued that an absolute injunction against approaching the king directly was out of the question, because "there are occasions in which it would be detrimental to the general good and the objectives of their institution." The commission agreed to present the views of the *socias* to the Society, confirming the good will of the women's council in its desire to both get along and fulfill its obligations.

Unresolved as to how to deal with the *damas'* response, the Society established another commission, made up of the *socias* Trúllas, Fuerte-Híjar, Teresa Losada, and the Marquise of Valdeolmos and *socios* Miguel de Manuel, Simon de Viegas, Andres Zurana, and Francisco Gerónimo Cifuentes.[94] Starting on October 20, the committee met to address the issues raised by the *junta de damas.* The official report of the committee, dated March 31 and signed by all members except Cifuentes, contained the group's findings. The report explained that the committee had determined not to discuss the relationship between the women's council and the general Society at a theoretical level, but rather to focus on concrete matters at hand. As such, the report detailed the committee's second resolution, its agreement with the *socias'* original contention that it was not useful to limit their ability to appeal to the king directly. This preserved an important avenue for the *damas* to have their voices heard.

Finally, the commission focused on the issue of whether the women's council must have its elections approved by the Society, and whether the women had to wait for this approval before the new officers could take their posts and the king could be notified of the results.[95] After extensive discussion of how the statutes left this issue unresolved, the committee suggested a solution: "In this case, the most noble, the most honorable to the Society, and the women's council, and that which would ensure the most solid reputation of prudence in our activities would be, the committee judges, to return this matter to the previous state, before all the disputes, that is, to go back to the time when the council of ladies notified the Society of its having elections; and to give the minutes a simple confirmation, in the ordinary way, without making any other agreement, or declaration."[96] This approval, which was essentially a rubber stamp, need not happen before the *junta de damas* requested the king's approval. In fact, the committee suggested that having the king wait for the Society's approval could be construed as showing a lack of respect for the monarchy.

But there was tension even within the commission itself. In addition to the committee's official report, the *junta general* received two other reports: one by Francisco Gerónimo Cifuentes, dated March 19, and one by the four *socias*, dated April 14. In his report, Cifuentes took a harder stand, emphasizing that the women's council must gain approval for each and every one of its actions. Unwilling to sign the commission's official report, Cifuentes argued that the women's council was completely subordinate to the Society. He pointed to the fact that the women's council had to have its members confirmed by the Society as being indicative of this subordination: "With what better clarity can one wish to establish the intimate relationship between this council and the Society from this point forward? If in order to deliberate on this most decisive issue, that being the admission of its members, it needs another additional approval, how can one believe that in the rest of its activities it should not receive from the same hand the ultimate legitimation of its decisions?"[97] Recalling the language of the original *junta de comisión*, Cifuentes argued that the *junta de damas* was like the other three councils of the organization and should be required to follow similar practices in relation to the Society as a whole.

Unlike Cifuentes, the *socias* on the committee supported the position outlined in the official report. However, as they explained in their own statement, they felt the need to further clarify their views on the relationship between the general and the women's councils, particularly in light of Cifuentes's report. The *socias* explained the origins of their organization in a way that substantiated their vision of the *junta de damas* as a united but not dependent entity:

The petition to admit Ladies and the manner by which this was deemed best came from the Society; and while the king agreed in part with the Society's propositions, he differed very much in the manner, since instead of agreeing with what the Royal Body proposed, he created a council that he mandated would be joined to it, but he prescribed that it would have separate councils and he outlined its obligations: He entrusted the care of its establishment to the Royal Society, which added, in attention to its own policies, the title of *socias* to all of the ladies who should belong to the said council.[98]

Thus, the *socias* used their segregation as evidence of their independence. As for the issue of having their acts approved by the Society, the report indicated that the *socias* themselves added this to their statutes as a "sign of their desire to be a united part of that Body." Nevertheless, the women's council argued, "it was not its intention to give this Article all of the scope that the Royal Society has wanted to give it since: yes, the council wanted the affirmation of this Royal Body, in order to assure itself of the success of its operations, but it was never its intention to enslave its ideas."[99] The report also mocked the suggestion that the Society needed to approve women's council elections before new officers could fill their posts. The *socias* argued that it was the members of that same *junta* who were most qualified to select the candidate best suited for the job. Perhaps the Society might offer reasons why a certain woman would be a good officer, but it could never eliminate the officer selected by the women's council through an official election. Clearly, the women's council saw its relationship with the Society as a much looser affiliation than did Cifuentes.

In concluding, the women confirmed the position taken in the general report that supported the rights of the female council to approach the king directly. The women stated that their position was the best way to keep the peace and preserve the intention of the monarchy in creating the women's council. Their document reflected their spirit of independence. Even though the committee's report was fairly advantageous in preserving their autonomy, the councilwomen's report shows that they were not completely satisfied with it. Further, they were not content to allow Cifuentes to present his diatribe without refuting his views. The *socias* wanted to, and did, make clear to the Society that they were not subordinate to it.

In 1807, after nearly two decades of the *junta de damas'* work, the Economic Society was still trying to clarify the role of women in the organization. When the *junta de damas* referred to itself as a *cuerpo*, or "body," in the minutes to its January 23, 1807, meeting, the Society bridled and once again called for discussion of the relationship of the women's council to the Economic Society at large. In the eyes of male Society members, the female council crossed the line by referring to itself as a "body." *Socios* considered the *junta de damas* an appendage to the body of the general Society, not a body in and of itself. The women's council responded with surprise and most likely a roll of the eyes. Its members argued that they had been using the term *cuerpo* to describe their council practically since its inception. Further, the women's council pointed to the dictionary definition of *cuerpo* to prove the accuracy of its chosen label:

> According to the Dictionary of our language, it means a group of people in whatever Republic or Community; and since it adds that this group of people has a head, members, offices for the dispatch of business, its own statutes and laws, daily representation authorized by direct and serious commissions from a higher authority for the handling of funds [and] the solicitation and discussion of its rights, it appears that the council in using it alternatively to women's council, or ladies' council, does not usurp the title of any other establishment.[100]

In short, the women's council did not understand the fuss and suggested that the Society's complaint simply revived a tired issue.

Unsatisfied with this response, the Society had its censor formulate a statement of the relationship between the two groups. After reviewing the minutes of the January 23 and February 6 meetings of the *junta de damas*, as well as other documents related to the admission of women into the Society, the censor wrote on March 6, 1807 (read in the March 7 *junta general*): "It cannot be denied that the council of ladies of honor and merit is an integral part of the Society, and to confirm this one must only cite the title of the statutes of the council itself, which say thus, 'statutes of the council of *socias* of honor and merit of the Royal Economic Society of Madrid.' It is not then a council joined to this royal body, as it was announced publicly, and as the ladies insinuate in their answer, it is part of the general body of the Society."[101] Here, the censor put forth the *socios'* view that the *junta de damas* constituted a limb of the Economic Society, not its own body. This report, which emphasized the integration of the councilwomen into the general Society, was sent to the *junta de damas* in care of María del Rosario Cepeda y Mayo on March 12; there is no recorded response from the women. While the Society might have seen this as an assertion of its control over the women's organization, its efforts at regulating the activities of the *socias* seem to have been unsuccessful. There were no apparent changes in the behavior of the *socias* after this incident. In fact, when the *junta de damas* decided to close some of the vocational schools under its administration because of financial problems in 1811, the Society objected that the *socias* had made the decision without consulting the *junta general*. Despite the initial complaints of the male members, the decision of the *damas* stood firm. To the *socios'* displeasure, the women's council achieved a significant degree of independence.

Not surprisingly, the committee that formed to select the first members of the Madrid women's council and to draft its provisional charter emphasized the dependence of the female membership on the larger organization. In the formation of its statutes and in its early acts, the women's council challenged this dependence. The strategies the women's council used to forge a place for its members varied. When it suited them, the women of the *junta de damas* emphasized their integration in and commonality with the larger Society. For example, they appealed to the larger body for equal treatment when they claimed the right to vote in the Society's elections and the right to attend meetings of the general council. Once it had established these rights, however, the women's council focused on its separation from the organization as a sign of its independence. While the Economic Society's decision to relegate its female members to a separate organization disappointed many of Spain's prominent women, once this decision was made they endeavored to use their separation to their advantage. By emphasizing its segregation, the women's council pointed to its unique status as a reason for its independence. In doing so, the *junta de damas* formed a sphere where its members could take up issues they saw as central to Spain's future and the future of its female citizens.

Pointing to the unique abilities of women to contribute to Spain's public discourse was not a strategy confined to the women of Madrid's Economic Society. Female authors also showed their ability to negotiate their place in the nation's world of letters by appealing to their exceptional status as women. That women made identical arguments in two seemingly disparate arenas is important. By the 1770s, the idea was well entrenched that women's social utility was not defined by what women could accomplish as active citizens but rather by how their presence in public life served as a symbol of Spain's move toward modernization. As women saw this limited idea of their participation in the public realm of Enlightenment discourse take root, they sought to marshal to their advantage arguments about the unique abilities of the female sex. Whether in the meeting room of the Casas Consistoriales or on the page of a censorial petition, women skillfully navigated the shifting gender discourse on citizenship so clearly brought to light in the debate over female admission to the Society.

5 Public Works

Female Citizens as Mothers and Workers

Carving out a space for their active participation in Spain's eighteenth-century reform was of serious concern to many Spanish women. As the Economic Society *socias* who empowered the *junta de damas* for action demonstrate, women claimed universal rights and female privilege simultaneously. By conjoining these two seemingly contradictory positions, women succeeded in creating a space where they could contribute to shaping the nation's future. Once women had established this space, many of them endeavored to tackle problems whose solutions they believed would help women. After all, the notion that the status of Spain's female population reflected the status of the nation constituted more than simply an effective argument that women employed to their advantage. For many of Spain's women, it represented a deeply held belief. Thus, not surprisingly, many women devoted their energy to tackling the difficult question of how to improve the lot of Spain's female inhabitants.

The best example of this steadfast dedication to so-called women's issues, and thus the focus of this chapter, is the work of the *junta de damas*. The tireless energy with which the *junta de damas* tackled its agenda has amazed the few historians who have examined its records. In her portrait of the Countess of Montijo, one of the group's busiest members, Paula de Demerson observes that, in light of the many obligations elite women shouldered, the level of their participation in the *junta de damas* is remarkable.[1] The time commitment required of the group's members was enough to scare off women more interested in leisure than reform. First, the council expected its *socias* to be present at weekly meetings. Records confirm members complied with steady attendance. Take, for example, the year 1788, when the group consisted of twenty-three members, only nineteen of whom resided in Madrid. Of the year's forty-four sessions, twenty-four meetings had ten to twelve *socias* present and only twelve meetings had less than six present. But attendance at Society meetings did not represent the bulk of a member's responsibilities. *Socias* took on multiple, time-consuming tasks, from working on committees to balancing finances. Some became guardians of Economic Society institutions, thereby providing hands-on management that included performing periodic inspections, writing comprehensive reports, keeping accounts, recruiting and hiring staff, and, of course, planning for the future. No less demanding were the tasks assigned to special commissions or the constant duties of the group's president, censor, and secretary. Indeed, *socias'* consistent attendance at weekly meetings and ready welcome of extensive assignments reveal the serious intent with which the members of the *junta de damas* undertook their agenda aimed at bettering the lives of Spain's women.

There were two main components of the *junta de damas'* Enlightenment project for women. The first centered on female education. The members of the women's council avowed the need to educate Spain's female population, specifically to prepare them for their role as mothers. The women's council emphasized that children were the nation's future citizens and, as a result, women's role in educating them constituted their main task as citizens. The *junta de damas* labored to create civic mothers by educating and encouraging them, emphasizing the special role women had to play in the nation's future. In turn, *socias* saw themselves as mothers of the nation and accordingly extended their mothering duties to the nation. The second element of the *socias'* Enlightenment project for women was their focus on economic activity. From providing women with vocational training to evaluating technological innovations, the members of the women's council aimed to advance Spanish industry by making women productive laborers. As with the debate over female admission, there was a hidden class gulf between these two components of their agenda. The members of the women's council suggested that elite women support the nation by concentrating on their domestic responsibilities, but they encouraged plebeian women to exhibit their patriotism by becoming productive laborers in the nation's industries.

EDUCATING FEMALE CITIZENS

While the belief that women had an intellectual capacity equal to that of men had become widely held among Spain's Enlightenment elite by the middle of the eighteenth century, the purpose of female education remained a contentious issue. Education could be an end in itself, or it could simply prepare women for their position as wives and mothers. The *junta de damas* justified much of its platform for female education, particularly education of elite women, based on the latter reasoning. In engaging in this discussion, Spain's *socias* were knowingly participating in a larger European debate, as many of them had read texts such as Madame d'Épinay's *Les conversations d'Emilie*, published in Spanish translation in 1797, or were aware of the arguments expressed in Mary Wollstonecraft's *A Vindication of the Rights of Women*, which enjoyed a lengthy review announcing its translation into French in 1792.² Yet these debates also had particular Spanish roots, as the varied texts on the woman question mentioned in chapter 1 suggest. In their writings and their day-to-day activities, *socias* firmly tied female education to women's role as mothers. Through their influence on their children, members of the *junta de damas* argued, mothers enjoyed tremendous influence over the future of the nation.

One way the women's council articulated its position on this issue was by publishing reports produced by educational committees.³ As noted in chapter 4, the *junta de damas* wrote into its statutes a provision for creating two commissions to study female education. The council's records give an idea of the various subjects, related to both the moral and physical education of women, that these commissions considered. A list of topics that the Countess of Trúllas, the president of the *junta de damas* at the time, proposed on February 20, 1795, demonstrates that the scope of the committees was wide ranging (see table 6). *Socias* considered everything from what subjects women should study and how much they should learn about government to how long they should nurse their babies and what clothes infants should wear.⁴

The extant reports from these committees, written as responses to questions like those Trúllas posed, reveal the *socias'* underlying concern with motherhood, a subject that enters into practically all the commissioned writings even when the designated topic does not seem to encompass it. The value the members of the *junta de damas* placed on women's role as mothers cannot be overstated. Josefa Amar y Borbón, who compiled many of her thoughts on female education in her 1790 book *Discurso sobre la educación física y moral de las mujeres*, took up this issue in a treatise she submitted to the council, "Reglas generales de moderación de costumbres a las jóvenes que se hallan en edad de recivir estado" (General rules on the moderation of the customs of young girls when they are at the age of reception).⁵ At the December 18, 1795, *junta de damas*, Montijo presented this text, in which Amar y Borbón discussed the role that parents should play in helping young women select their future stations. Amar y Borbón considered the two options that were the only acceptable choices available to women at the time: marriage and the convent. Amar y Borbón warned parents to be forthcoming in describing these two options to their daughters. Of marriage, she explained, "But if they prefer the state of Matrimony, as this has within it more obligations, in respect to the husband, to the children, to the servants, and to the government of the House, it therefore requires more instruction before embracing it, because rarely does it happen that one does well what one is ignorant of."[6] In particular, Amar y Borbón stressed the value of married women's role as mothers: "The care and rearing of sons and daughters is an obligation so essential that wives should know it from the moment they contract marriage, and it is necessary to persuade them that it is a natural obligation of that state."[7] Amar y Borbón considered married women's responsibilities to their children to be crucial and demanded that women be instructed so they would fulfill their duties well.[8]

Part of preparing women for this tremendously important role involved teaching girls to avoid the excesses of luxury. A good mother, in Amar y Borbón's eyes, instilled virtue in her children and, in particular, sought to steer them away from the temptations of idleness and luxury. This was especially important for young girls, she argued, who must be prepared for their future role as heads of household economies. Embracing industriousness, she noted, would enable women to take up their domestic role with enthusiasm: "Diligence and a love of work softens the seclusion of the home, and for lack of these qualities many see it as a jail; taking into account this view young girls should be taught to abhor idleness."[9] In the Marquise of Ariza's report on the importance of female education for the family economy, she echoed Amar y Borbón's concern that women who valued idleness and luxury would be ill suited for their role in the household. In her treatise, read at the November 13, 1795, meeting of the *junta de damas* by the Countess of Montijo, Ariza focused on the pragmatic nature of a woman's education.[10] She argued that simply learning fact after fact would not prepare a girl to run the household economy; rather, she maintained, the point of a good education was to teach women how to think. Ariza described the educated woman as a prudent decision maker, which in domestic terms, she translated into skill as a household consumer. As did Amar y Borbón, Ariza warned about the ill effects of luxury, the need to prevent wives from making "superfluous expenditures that ruin the house and destroy the family." These warnings emphasized both the importance and the dangers of women's consumption. Upper-class women needed preparation to assume their role as household managers, and a key aspect of this preparation involved educating them on the follies of luxury.

TABLE 6. *Topics on Women's Education Presented by the Countess of Trúllas for Discussion by the* Junta de Damas *in 1795*

Problems for the Commission on Moral Education

---

1. How important is religion to the education of women?
2. At what age and in what way is it advisable to present women with the primary ideas on religion?
3. Women being entrusted with the early education of men, what methods should they employ with boys to begin to provide them with knowledge of our sacred religion?
4. How important to politics and the good outcome of affairs of state is it [the education of women]?
5. How important to the domestic economy is it [the education of women]?
6. General rules of domestic economy on issues pertaining to women.
7. General rules that are most advisable for reducing household expenses.
8. What lessons should be given to women?
9. What amount of knowledge should be given [to women] in education on the civil constitution and public affairs?
10. Instructions particular to young girls to guard them against the most common risks in the selection of a person designated for matrimony.
11. Rules most suitable for liberating women from the harms of luxury and fashion, without wanting for decency or making them the object of ridiculous reproach.
12. General rules on the moderation of the customs of young girls when they are at the age of reception.

(continued)

But lessons alone would not produce savvy managers, so Ariza also emphasized the importance of practical experience. She proposed that, after girls received instruction, they be entrusted with governing a part of the household. According to Ariza, "From this method it results that, accustomed to governing the household, women could more easily take over in the management of their estates, or haciendas, when the occupations or absences of their husbands demanded it, and how much this education will contribute so that when they reach the state of widowhood they will fulfill perfectly their duties as Mothers, and tutors of their children."[11] In touting the value of providing women with hands-on experience in managing household expenditures, Ariza pointed to the many situations that would lead women to play an extensive role in managing domestic accounts. At the

TABLE 6. *(continued)*

Problems for the Commission on [the] Physical Education [of Children]

1. Should children be given food other than milk?
2. If so, what would be most appropriate?
3. How long is suitable for nursing?
4. How should they be worked enough to be healthy but not too much so that they turn out imperfect?
5. Is it healthier to dress children in less clothing than more, and should they have their heads covered or uncovered?
6. Is it more suitable to accustom them to the crib or have them sleep in bed?
7. What methods should be used to facilitate swaddling and prevent the damage that occurs during it?
8. What foods are most appropriate, so that they grow up robust?
9. At what age should you begin to give them solid foods, which ones, and in what quantity?
10. Should girls wear corsets, and if they should, until when should they go without them?
11. What dress is appropriate so that they acquire strength, agility, and grace in their movements?
12. What exercise is most suitable in infancy?

same time, part of Ariza's suggestion stems from her desire to make women skilled managers who would command the respect of their families and provide strong role models for their children. Ariza explains, "The well-educated woman who knows the true interests of her husband and family will become more worthy of their esteem and love: she teaches her children by her example, and these imprints from the education of a good Mother will serve them as a reminder that will last their entire lives." Ariza emphasized the lifelong influence mothers had on their children and argued for education that would prepare women for this domestic role.

Educating future mothers also entailed teaching them how to rear healthy children. The Marquise of Sonora's discussion of the twelve issues that Trúllas proposed regarding physical education took up this crucial aspect of female education.[12] Considered at the January 22, 1796, meeting of the *junta de damas*, Sonora's text focused on infant care techniques and included not only her own valuable observations but also knowledge from contemporary medical texts.[13] Sonora considered various issues related to early child rearing, from eating and exercise to how to deal with certain ailments. Clearly, for the *socias* of the *junta de damas*, the education of women in preparation for their role as mothers was a central issue.

However, the *socias* went beyond simply stressing women's place in the household and their role as educators of their children. They also pointed to the larger significance of this to the Spanish nation. Such was the case with an essay the Marquise of Fuerte-Híjar presented to the *junta de damas* at a November 27, 1795, meeting. Like Amar y Borbón and Ariza, Fuerte-Híjar considered female consumption patterns to be of great importance to the family and, by extension, the nation. Thus, she started her presentation on topic eleven, "Rules most suitable for liberating women from the harms of luxury and fashion, without wanting for decency, or making them the object of ridiculous reproach," by suggesting the *socias* themselves reject luxury in order to serve as good role models for the nation's women.[14] At the same time, she emphasized the need to make clear the import of this issue. To simply force people to curtail luxury purchases without explaining why, Fuerte-Híjar argued, would only cause resentment. Rather, the women's council must make clear the need for the policy "and the benefit that it would bring to the public cause; by stopping this monster that devours fortunes and virtues, that knows no other merit than ostentation of riches and their waste." Thus, for Fuerte-Híjar, education was key to achieving the desired goal: "This Lady finds only one means, that is good education that cultivates judgment." She described how people came to value opulence over more important qualities such as virtue and argued that through education this development could be reversed. Teachings about the follies of luxury, if "inculcated in the spirits of young women [and] fortified by examples of famous women, could produce moderation in our dress."[15] As with the other portrayals of women's education, here Fuerte-Híjar focused on the formative role of women. In this case, her argument extends the role of women as educators; they are not simply educating their immediate families, but they are educators to the nation. In line with Enlightenment ideas, Fuerte-Híjar indicated that this educational effort led by women, not restrictions and laws, should transform social values.

The tenuous link Fuerte-Híjar made between female education and national reform in her response to topic eleven would have appeared less tenuous to her fellow *socias*, who had listened just a few weeks earlier, at their November 6, 1795, meeting, to her more overt statement on how mothers shaped the nation's citizenry. On this earlier date, Fuerte-Híjar chose to respond to topic four, concerning how female education related to a nation's politics and its affairs of state. After insisting that the education of women was key to a nation's success, Fuerte-Híjar laid out an argument on the importance of women as educators of their children: "Until they grow up, men will always receive the seeds of virtue, or vice, at the hands of their mothers, and since in any given situation women greatly influence the ideas and the behavior of men, their education is of no little importance to the State, inspiring in them from childhood good maxims of religion, of true honor, and Patriotism."[16] No doubt Fuerte-Híjar assumed that women played a key role in their capacity as educators of Spain's citizenry. At the same time, however, her text opens up a dilemma. In arguing that women played a key role in preparing future citizens, she seems to gender citizenship as male. After all, she identifies the influence of mothers on the ideas and conduct of "men" as the core of women's contribution to the nation. Rather than rejecting female citizenship, however, Fuerte-Híjar's text resolves the tension between women's domestic and civic responsibilities by establishing two different models of citizenship, one for women and one for men. In this gendered model, women's citizenship derived in large part from their maternal role as caretakers and educators.

The Countess of Montijo articulated the basis for this bifurcated view of citizenship in her analysis of how much women should learn about government, specifically "the civil constitution and public affairs."[17] In making her argument about women's social role, she focused on what she considered to be fundamental differences between men and women. Montijo argued, as Jovellanos had done during the debate over women's admission to the Economic Society, that these natural differences should determine men's and women's places in society. She explained that men's physical makeup shaped their social functions: "In the same way that man was created as strong and robust to ward off danger and to resist all of the elements, he was made able and destined for all arts and arduous tasks." She derived from the female body a more domestic role for women: "On the contrary, to woman was assigned the domestic governance, to prepare in Infancy the minds and hearts of children for virtue instructed in the principles of religion, to elevate their souls, and to direct them toward good. According to these laws of nature, women are excluded from political functions and public employments; it does not seem to me that they could be taught knowledge of the constitution and civil affairs without risking inverting the order that has been outlined." Montijo argued that women were not built for politics, rather, their main function as determined by their nature was to shape and educate their children. The censor who evaluated Montijo's text for publication expressed surprise that a woman so interested herself in pursuing her own education would relegate women to this role. Of Montijo's tract, the censor wrote: "The censor has not been able to stop admiring this brief treatise from a person who for her constant dedication and love of study should be the exception of the very doctrine that she proposes."[18]

Despite the apparent irony, Montijo was not suggesting that women abandon educational activities. Rather, for Montijo, women's education would have more significance if it recognized these fundamental differences in men's and women's roles and focused women's energies on fulfilling what she saw as their natural role. Through this natural role, women could reach their true potential and make a significant contribution as citizens. According to Montijo, "One can see that the more women attempt to make themselves like men, the less power they have. That those who have done the most good for their Country have done it through the path that nature has laid for them; a woman is worth more as a woman, and less as a man, and every time that she wants to make known her rights she has the advantage." In making this argument, Montijo rejected universalism and instead relied on arguments about women's unique nature to empower them. After all, the extension of women's natural virtues into the sphere of politics would benefit the nation. Montijo explained, "The man enlightened by familiar and peaceful discussions in the bosom of his family will bring to the Society and to the State useful ideas that will have been communicated by a virtuous woman." Rather than minimizing women's power, Montijo and other *socias* pointed to women's natural virtue and maternal instincts in order to assert the importance of women's contribution to Spain's future.

In 1796, the Economic Society requested that the *junta de damas* submit some of its members' works to the censor for publication. In its April 7, 1796, letter to the Countess of Montijo, the Society underscored the *socias*' belief that women could educate the nation: "In the meeting celebrated by our Royal Economic Society on Saturday the 2nd of this month, we discussed the utility that could result in the enlightenment of the public upon the publication of the essays and treatises written by the Ladies; and wishing that it be executed with the most brevity possible, it was agreed to request a license from the Council presenting a list of those works in the usual form."[19] In response, the *junta de damas* submitted seven works composed by its members that covered many of the topics Trúllas had proposed the previous year. The fact that all these texts related to the commissions on female education indicates that the women's council wanted this aspect of its work to be publicized and its views on education to be made public. *Socias* wanted a role in shaping the contemporary discourse on female education, and at this juncture they were successful.

In a March 14, 1801, letter to the Economic Society deeming the *socias*' texts worthy of publication, the censor underlined their value as instructional materials for mothers throughout Spain.[20] The publication of these tracts suggests the importance of the *junta de damas* in shaping educational debates as well as the significance the women themselves placed on this aspect of their work. Their vision of civic motherhood constituted an important articulation of the way these women conceived of female citizenship. By expounding on the need to educate women for this role, the women's council saw itself as contributing to the process of creating this female citizenry.

In addition to preparing other women for civic motherhood, the members of the *junta de damas* embraced the role themselves. They conceived of themselves as mothers to the nation, and as such, they endeavored to extend their mothering duties to all of Spain. A key example is their administration of the Inclusa, a foundling home in Madrid that dated back to 1567. Originally founded by members of the Order of St. Francis, the Inclusa came under state control in 1615 as one of the royal hospitals of Madrid. Anxious to take charge of and reform this important royal institution, the *damas* employed arguments about their nature as women that gave them special insights into running the Inclusa. The female council's appeals led to its eventual control of the institution. In early modern Europe, it was an unprecedented and extraordinary feat for women to take charge of such an extensive and vital royal institution.[21]

The Countess of Montijo first proposed at the group's July 11, 1789, meeting that the women's council take over the administration of the Inclusa.[22] Montijo's petition to her fellow *socias* began by lamenting the institution's poor state. With wet nurses caring for two to four babies at a time, Montijo explained, many of the infants were malnourished.[23] This, compounded by rampant illness, led to high mortality rates. Montijo did not exaggerate her claims. The state of the Inclusa worsened during the course of the eighteenth century, partly because of a significant increase in the number of foundlings left at the institution. Whereas the institution admitted 500 foundlings in 1700, in 1789 the annual number had more than doubled, to 1194. Indeed, the number of foundlings admitted reached its height in the years around Montijo's request.[24] At the same time, the amount of charity given to help support the Inclusa declined, partially because of a significant reduction in funds from one of its major sources. Much of the Inclusa's income derived from parishes that donated money in exchange for the institution's service in taking care of abandoned children. This system broke down as more individuals took babies straight to the Inclusa themselves, without using the parish as an intermediary.[25] Whereas, in 1700, 250 of the infants, or 50 percent, admitted came with alms, in 1800 only 39, or .032 percent, did. The increasing admittance rate and inadequate funds combined to create substantial and rising mortality rates, which increased dramatically from 53.8 percent in the second decade of the eighteenth century to become a steady 70 percent in the second half of the century.[26] Annual death totals, recorded only after 1787, further illustrate the high death rate at the institution.[27] In short, the chances that an infant left at the Inclusa in the late eighteenth century would live were abysmal.

Considering its deplorable state, Montijo insisted that the Inclusa should have been one of the first priorities of the Economic Society. However, she continued, men were not equipped by nature with the same sentiments that women had, such as "compassion, natural affection, and a liking for children." Montijo explained, "While men use their knowledge and cultivated talents governing the Republic, they divide and fulfill the important tasks among them; we are left with the sweet care of those innocent creatures, whose hearts, formed by us from the beginning, will someday be the tools of public happiness."[28] Here, Montijo evokes a very gendered argument to explain why the women's council should be in charge of the foundling home. As men concerned themselves with governing the state, women must do their own part to help the common good. Since women's nature equips them with certain maternal qualities, the care of abandoned infants was clearly an appropriate realm in which to fulfill their duty to the *patria*.

Spurred by Montijo's speech, the women's council officially requested this commission in October 1792. The *socias* sent letters to the Economic Society and the king requesting that the women's council be placed in charge of the foundling home in Madrid. In support of its petition, the council attached a report drawn from Montijo's July 1789 presentation detailing the poor state of the Inclusa and the reasons why the *socias* in particular were so well suited for its administration. In their report, the *damas* played on the desires of the new monarch to improve Spain's standing in Europe: "Thus the [Women's] Council that promises to carry out this mission, which, serving as an example to the Nation and to Europe, will justify even more the noble and wise designs that the August Founder had in establishing it, hopes for the compassion of Your Majesty." On December 18, 1792, Montijo received a letter from the Society indicating that its members had read the women's request "with pleasure."[29] However, the *damas* ultimately received a negative reply to their request, which they noted at their July 19, 1793, meeting.

In 1796, they again petitioned the king. In this case, the ability to go directly to the king—a right the women's council had fought to preserve in debates with the general Society—proved essential in achieving the *socias'* goal. In the appeal to the king, the Countess of Montijo painted the loss of the foundlings as a loss for the nation. After explaining the high death rates at the Inclusa, Montijo suggested, "It will surely be one of the most worthy and most sweet tasks that the paternal heart of Your Majesty will put in our charge, that by providing the means to achieve such a great good; this will follow the natural order."[30] Here again, Montijo returned to the argument that, since women's nature equipped them with maternal instincts, they were best suited for the job. Using the same language as in her 1789 petition, Montijo pointed to the natural propensity of women to care for infants, as well as their patience and tenderness toward them. She asked that these natural characteristics be put to use to help the foundlings: "It is hoped that those to whom the perversity of customs, misery, and inhuman barbarity have deprived the sweet solace of their own mothers will be touched by the effects of these natural inclinations." Montijo continued: "Their cries and painful shouts suffice to move the compassionate spirit of Your Majesty; and when we have in sight that pitiful spectacle, do not doubt, Your Majesty, that it will have an almost irresistible force to move us to procure their relief, and that there will not be one who will not feel in herself vividly the tender violence of the impulses of maternal love."[31] Montijo's dramatic invocation of women's maternal drive helped the cause. On October 10, the king responded by asking the *socias* to submit a plan for the Inclusa's reform.[32] At its October 25 meeting, the women's council chose Montijo to craft such a plan.

At the council's November 18 meeting, Montijo outlined the five planks of her ambitious plan. First, she proposed to overhaul the selection process for wet nurses and, by extension, everything having to do with the feeding, cleaning, and care of the infants. Second, she recommended that the Inclusa be moved from its current location in the heart of the growing city of Madrid to a more healthful site. Third, she suggested that the women's council manage the Inclusa's assets as it saw fit. Fourth, she assured the king that the women's council would present him with annual reports detailing the number of infants admitted, the number that died, the costs, and other pertinent information so that he could judge for himself whether the *socias'* work improved the institution. Finally, she noted that, upon taking over the Inclusa, the women's council would compile a report of the institution's status. In submitting the council's admittedly vague plan to the king, Montijo explained the obstacle to outlining the needed reforms: "It is impossible to figure [the changes] without knowledge of the extent of the abuses that have occurred in this house up to now as a result of self-interest, preoccupation, and ignorance. Only the result is clear: that is, the death of the Children; but the causes unfortunately are quite hidden, and consequently it is not easy to indicate all of the remedies other than the most general ones until a complete and informed inspection discovers them."[33]

On September 13, 1799, the king finally gave the *junta de damas* complete control over the Inclusa, and on October 2 the group officially assumed management of the institution.[34] The women's council took its responsibility seriously and set out to revamp the institution. As Joan Sherwood has argued, the takeover of the Inclusa by the *junta de damas* signaled a major shift in the history of the foundling home: from a site of patriarchal charity to a modern bureaucratic institution.[35] Guiding this transformation was no small task. In fact, while the *junta de damas* continued to perform its other functions, the minutes of its meetings suggest that the supervision of the Inclusa became its primary duty.

With the Countess of Montijo at the helm as *curadora* (guardian) of the Inclusa, the *socias* implemented substantial reforms. They immediately hired a second doctor and a second surgeon—their first step in increasing the institution's staff, which they doubled between 1799 and 1805—separated sick infants from healthy ones, and provided new furnishings. The women's council considered Santiago García's *Breve instrucción sobre el modo de conservar los niños expósitos* (Brief Guide on the Way to Care for Foundlings) a guiding doctrine, and they made changes based on the book's suggestions. For example, they opened the windows to bring in fresh air, and they swept the rooms and disinfected them with vinegar daily.[36] One of the biggest changes was the Inclusa's relocation to a new building on the Calle del Soldado in 1801, which as Sherwood explains, "removed [the Inclusa] from the noise and dust of the traffic of the Puerta del Sol."[37] No less radical was the female council's decision, in the early nineteenth century, to experiment with the substitution of artificial feeding for wet nurses.[38]

Not surprisingly, many of the changes the women's council implemented also meant an increase in expenditures. The construction of the new building alone resulted in a mortgage of 121,000 *reales*. With funding shortages confronting them at every turn, the *socias* responded with innovative fund-raising strategies. For example, by creating a system in which contributors to the Inclusa had their names and donations printed in the city's daily newspaper, *Diario de Madrid*, the women's council successfully exploited the pride and reputation of wealthy Spaniards.[39] In addition, the women's council dispatched assertive volunteers to take up collections at Saturday mass. Who could say no to the Countess of Montijo? Through these methods, the *junta de damas* helped to accommodate increasing expenditures at the Inclusa.

The women's council enthusiastically reformed an institution that was in desperate need of alteration. The task was a major one, and it dominated the council's activities from 1799 onward. Keeping accounts, hiring doctors, supervising repairs, evaluating new theories on child rearing, approving petitions for adoptions, fund-raising—the jobs were endless and time-consuming.[40] Despite the *socias'* efforts, mortality rates at the Inclusa remained high. Sherwood's research demonstrates that the early nineteenth century saw no great improvements: "In the disastrous year of bad harvests of 1804, mortality rates were the highest in the 300 years of the hospital's history. Finally, in another famine year, 1812–13, the fortunes of the Inclusa reached their nadir. Of all the infants admitted, each and every one died. In 1844 the mortality rate was still 85 per cent."[41]

These failures did not indicate that the *damas'* solutions were inadequate. Rather, the consistently high mortality rates underscored the insurmountable nature of the problem at hand. As Sherwood explains, "It was not until the development of aseptic techniques at the end of the nineteenth century that bringing together large numbers of infants was not likely to be a serious risk to their health and well-being."[42] In addition, Sherwood identifies wars, bad weather, and the financial difficulties of both church and state in the first half of the nineteenth century as barriers to any significant improvements. The grim statistics aside, however, the *junta de damas'* administration of the Inclusa constituted a significant chapter in Spain's history, both for its contribution to altering the very character of the nation's public health and welfare institutions and because it represented the first time that women were placed at the helm of such an important state institution.

The *socias'* administration of the Inclusa also extended their role as civic mothers over Spanish society in general. The members of the women's council became surrogate mothers in charge of shepherding Madrid's abandoned foundlings into adulthood, if possible. That Spain's male citizens were not fit for this task seemed obvious to the women of the *junta de damas*, who argued that the natural virtues of womanhood—motherhood among them—led them to take on the challenges of the Inclusa. Their argument in claiming their new role bolstered a discourse of difference. Unlike Locke's blank slates, men and women here figured as beings whose biological makeup predetermined their social roles. However, the *socias* did not see this differentiation as limiting; rather, they viewed it as empowering, and it may have been their only option considering how debates on female citizenship had evolved since the 1770s. That difference assured them a unique and essential place in the nation, a foothold from which they could make concrete contributions to the future of Spain—and in particular to the future of Spain's citizens.

162 / Enacting Citizenship

THE *DAMAS* FOCUS ON INDUSTRY

Its project of social motherhood led the women's council to another realm of Enlightenment reform: Spain's economic regeneration. Here the socias assumed administration of some of the Economic Society's educational projects focused on incorporating women into domestic industry. As discussed in chapter 3, Society members such as Marín, Campomanes, and Jovellanos viewed female labor as an essential ingredient in Spain's economic recovery. To wit, the Society designed a number of schools to help foster female industrial output by furnishing young girls with vocational training in appropriate industries. Among these schools were the *escuelas patrióticas* (patriotic schools), institutions whose very name reflects the strong link the members of the Economic Society envisioned between female labor and female citizenship. Just as elite women's education would ready them to benefit the nation as civic mothers, plebeian women's education in industry would enable them to be patriotic citizens through their labor. The *junta de damas* fully embraced this class-based notion of citizenship and applied itself to a project its members believed would simultaneously help Spain's poorer women and foster the nation's economic growth.

The Economic Society's various educational institutions for female industrial training all had one common goal: the incorporation of women into Spain's struggling industries. Instituted in 1776, the *escuelas patrióticas* became the first of the Society's public schools focused on industrial education.[43] The four *escuelas patrióticas* in Madrid—San Ginés, San Sebastián, San Martín, and San Andrés—concentrated on teaching women and girls basic spinning and weaving skills using various materials, including linen, canvas, wool, and cotton. The Economic Society also founded a number of schools aimed at educating girls in more advanced artisanal skills. Among these were a lace-making and an embroidery school. That the curricula of all these schools centered on textile production reflects both the feminization of the needle trades in the eighteenth century and the desire of the Economic Society to train women in industries "appropriate to their sex."[44] Instruction in textile work allowed for the incorporation of women into industries that would both help improve Spain's economy and constitute appropriate work for the women involved.

The statutes of the schools themselves echoed the Society's concerns about improving Spain's industry, particularly in relation to the larger international market. Section 15 of the embroidery school's statutes, for example, encouraged the school's teacher to instruct the students particularly in "the stitches that are most necessary because there are few people in

Spain who know how to do them." Along the same lines, statute 20 encouraged the teacher to make embroidered clothing "in the same style as those that come from abroad," and statute 19 indicated that the teacher should use only Spanish-made cloth for the school's embroidery projects.[45] These three dictates evidence eighteenth-century Spanish economists' concerns about the increased consumption of foreign, particularly French, manufactures over domestic products. The statutes of the Society's lace-making school reveal similar concerns. According to the school's statutes, the Society created the institution "with the goal of introducing and encouraging work in all genres of thread lace, giving an honest occupation to the women and girls of this Court, and avoiding the consumption of foreign products."[46] Clearly, as in the case of the embroidery school, the motive behind the lace-making school's creation was the desire to promote Spanish industry and in turn give Spain a stronger footing in foreign markets.

The *junta de damas'* support of this goal can be seen in the considerable role its members played in the administration and the daily operations of all these educational institutions. Their supervision entailed placing teachers, setting salaries, providing materials and facilities, administering prize competitions (including awarding dowries to students of the patriotic schools), charting each school's progress, keeping accounts, and solving the problems that inevitably arose. The *junta de damas* not only embraced these projects, it improved them. Unlike in the case of the perpetually troubled Inclusa, when the women's council took over the government of these public schools, it often turned failing projects into successes.

When the *damas* assumed control of the *escuelas patrióticas* in 1787, the schools were in a poor state.[47] Plagued by an inconsistent number of students from year to year, uneven production levels, poor quality instruction, and erratic inspections for the first decade after their creation in 1776, the schools were failing. Not pleased with the schools' financial state, the Economic Society was considering closing them down.[48] However, when the women's council took over partial direction of the schools in 1787, as the historian Olegario Negrín Fajardo explains, "the march of the schools became regular and they began to see the fruits of their labor."[49] As early as their third meeting after formation as the *junta de damas*, the council members had become aware that the Economic Society planned to pull funding from the schools and had already begun to discuss how to reform the *escuelas patrióticas*.[50] They called for reports on the status of each institution as well as inventories of their materials, marking the beginning of their greater vigilance in overseeing the schools. In addition, the *damas* made some immediate changes in the administration of the schools, such as terminating

Felipe Beltrán, the teacher and director of the school of San Ginés, whom they saw as a barrier to the institution's success and the reason for its poor financial state. They also assigned *ayudantas,* or teacher's assistants, to each school, a practice employed previously with some success at San Martín. By adding the provision that the *ayudanta* be chosen from the best students, the women's council encouraged students to work hard by providing an enticing reward for those who excelled. *Ayudantas,* after all, often received favorable treatment when the damas apportioned prizes, handed out dowries, or filled vacant teaching posts.

The *junta de damas* also discussed long-range changes such as making improvements in the type of skills each school should teach. This occurred in the case of San Andrés in 1792, when the Marquise of Ariza suggested that the school no longer focus on instruction in making wool cloths but rather on making lace and weaving linens. Also in 1792, the *damas* added basic reading and writing instruction to the schools' curricula. The reforms that the *junta de damas* implemented in its first decade as administrator of the *escuelas patrióticas* led to a considerable increase in attendance, as well as higher quality education for those enrolled.[51]

Negrín Fajardo praises the performance of the *junta de damas* in the years after 1797 as well. In 1797, the Society gave the women's council complete charge of the schools' finances. This came at a particularly troublesome time, since the early nineteenth century presented financial difficulties for the Economic Society as a whole. Negrín Fajardo, however, extols the continued dedication of the members of the *junta de damas* and their ability to keep the schools running in such austere times. He points to the schools' status reports that document their continued success as a result of the *socias'* efforts. For example, a report on the state of the schools at the end of 1806 recorded: "In spite of the fact that the four patriotic schools have suffered the effects of public calamities, they have made advances. The biggest testimony to the progress of the teaching in the four initial patriotic schools, as well as in the Royal school of embroidery, is offered by the results of the practical examinations for the acquisition of their respective prizes, which took place on the 31st of January of this year; the audience applauded in elegy and admiration of the numerous and brilliant works that were awarded prizes."[52] Indeed, the women's council was instrumental in keeping the *escuelas patrióticas* afloat. It was not until 1811 that it was finally forced to close the schools for lack of funds.

The life of the Economic Society's embroidery school also illustrates the success of the women's council in getting the Society's educational projects on track.[53] When the women took over the embroidery school officially in

1787, it was still stalled in the start-up phase.⁵⁴ Although the Economic Society had attempted to open an embroidery school as early as 1782, their failure to negotiate a contract favorable to the proposed teacher, Josefa Joaquina Ruiz y Careaga, led to her decision to run a school on her own. After Ruiz y Careaga's death in 1785, the Society decided to try again to open an embroidery school under its direction, and it received royal approval on June 9, 1786, for the establishment of a school under the tutelage of Margarita Diez. However, as with Ruiz y Careaga, the Society had problems coming to an agreement with Diez. The Society still had not finalized its plans for the school when the *junta general* became apprised of Diez's death on April 5, 1788.

The death of Diez not only marked the beginning of the *junta de damas*' significant involvement in the school but also signaled the first time that the Economic Society's embroidery school as originally conceived really got under way.⁵⁵ Indeed, the school finally seemed to take off under the direction of the women's council. With the death of Diez, the *socias* immediately began the search for a new teacher to fill the vacant post. At its April 25 meeting, the *junta de damas* discussed the need for a new embroidery teacher, lamenting that there was only one application for the position, from a Vicente Duménes. Rather than select Duménes, the women decided to place an ad in the *Diario de Madrid* soliciting more applications. Pleased with the response, the women discussed the six applicants at their November 21 meeting.⁵⁶

After deliberation, the women's council selected Josef Nieto for the job. Nieto proposed that he would run the school with the help of his wife, Isabel Pérez, and his daughter María Rada, a former student of Ruiz y Careaga's. Nieto would teach drawing and direct the workshop, his wife would teach white embroidery and quilting, and his daughter would teach all types of embroidery with silks and precious metals.⁵⁷ Undoubtedly acting in Nieto's favor was the fact that, as he stated in his petition, his wife knew how to "do white embroidery and quilting in the same style as in France," having been a student of the Frenchwoman Madame Flaman.⁵⁸ The *junta de damas* agreed to appoint Nieto, pending his family's examination on January 28, 1789, by a committee of six *socias*. Nieto, Pérez, and Rada completed the exam successfully, and the women's council finalized Nieto's appointment at its meeting on January 30. At that meeting, the *socias* elected Phelipa de la Rosa and the Marquise of Someruelos as *curadoras* for the embroidery school and named Juan Agustín García as the school's catechism instructor.⁵⁹

Before embroidery instruction began under Nieto and his family, the terms of their contract still remained to be determined.⁶⁰ As negotiated, the arrangement between Nieto and the *junta de damas* obligated him to teach twenty-four girls during a four-year period.[61] Rada was to teach sixteen of the girls, and Pérez was to teach the remaining eight. Rada's students were not to be under twelve years of age, and Pérez's were to be no younger than nine or ten. In exchange for his teaching, the Economic Society agreed to pay Nieto nine *reales* per day and provide a location for the school. Nieto had to provide the students with all their materials, but this meant that he could keep whatever profit he made from their work. In addition, for each student who was found to be "perfectly taught" at the end of her four-year period of instruction, Nieto would receive a bonus of two hundred *reales*. Although he was supposed to encourage Christian behavior in his students, Nieto did not have the responsibility of instructing the students in church doctrine. Rather, the contract indicated that the *junta* would appoint a church official for the school in order to instruct the girls in Christian doctrine.

The arrangement between Nieto and the *junta de damas* made it clear who was in charge. Not only did the women's council spell out precisely how it expected Nieto to run the school, but the contract also expressed in general terms Nieto's subservience to the *damas*. As the contract explains, "The teacher is subordinate to the women in all that corresponds to the good government and direction [of the school]." Unlike in the earlier case of Ruiz y Careaga, the women's council made sure that it was the Economic Society, not the hired teacher, who was going to run the school. The general council of the Economic Society formalized the contract with Nieto on June 2, 1789. For the first time, the Economic Society was at the helm of the embroidery school it had decided seven years earlier to found.

By the summer of 1789, the school was in full swing under Nieto and the women's council. On July 10, he petitioned the women's council to be able to advertise for more students, now that the school was established in its new location. On October 16, the school was renamed the Real Escuela de Bordados al Cuidado de la Sociedad Económica de Esta Corte (the Royal Embroidery School under the Care of the Economic Society of this Court). This new, rather cumbersome name symbolized the new direction of the school under the close supervision of the women's council. It also marked the beginning of a highly successful period in the life of the school. The support of the royal family suggests the degree to which the school flourished under Nieto and the *damas*. The king and queen, who sent a number of their garments to be embroidered by Nieto's students, were always pleased with the results.[62] In fact, when the queen donated six thousand *reales* to be divided among the students of various artisanal schools under the direction of the Economic Society in August 1793, she made sure that the students of the embroidery school received the largest portion of the stipend.[63]

The women's council itself displayed satisfaction with the school by awarding healthy bonuses to Nieto, Pérez, and Rada year after year. On January 20, 1792, for example, the *curadoras* of the school informed the women's council that they had presented Rada with a bonus for her "application and extraordinary work in the instruction of the students."[64] The women's council also voted to give the embroidery instructors another 640 *reales* on February 22, 1793, twice what was awarded to the teachers at other schools on February 2 of that same year.[65] Nieto's contract was renewed more than once, and records indicate that he was still at the school in 1810. Although the school survived Napoleon's invasion of Spain in 1808, funding issues increasingly plagued the Economic Society as a whole. The last few entries we have on the school in 1811 indicate its shrinking financial base.[66] It was the work of the women's council that both got the school off the ground and kept it running.

For women of the lower classes, this kind of artisanal training offered numerous advantages. On a practical level, it provided them with a vocational training opportunity that could lead to economic advancement. The contract that the *socias* signed with the embroidery teacher Josef Nieto in 1789 suggests some of the concrete benefits that girls stood to gain from attending the embroidery school. At the most basic level, girls received free drawing and embroidery instruction from Nieto, Pérez, and Rada.[67] In addition, the Society obligated Nieto to provide rewards to the most dedicated and improving students. The contract outlines the reward as one *real* daily during the second year of a student's instruction, two the third year, and four the fourth year. If after four years of instruction a girl wanted to remain in Nieto's workshop, he must consider her to be a skilled laborer and pay her accordingly for her work. The fact that Nieto was not to admit or dismiss any students without the approval of the *curadoras* also provided the girls with a degree of security that they might not have been able to find in other workshops.

Further, every six months (usually in June and December), the women's council sponsored prize competitions with the aim of encouraging the students in their work. Often, the prizes took the form of a cash bonus. For example, at the March 22, 1793, meeting of the women's council, the Marquise of Valdeolmos announced that Petrona Manzanares, Balbina García, and Manuela Fadejas—three girls who had embroidered a waistcoat for the king—had each been awarded a bonus of eighty *reales*.[68] In addition to furnishing these cash bonuses, the women's council also awarded students with a certificate upon completion of the four-year program. For example, at the December 23, 1803, meeting of the *junta de damas*, the current *curadora* of the school, María Josepha Panes y Mangino, informed the council that Ana María Sul, Margarita Ulorix, and Josepha López had all completed the requirements for certification.[69] Considering that students made a point of petitioning to receive these when they had accidentally been overlooked, the certificates must have provided some use in substantiating one's skills.

The lace-making school offered similar benefits. Not only did students acquire instruction in a variety of lace-making techniques, but the school also provided them with all the materials they needed for their training. In addition, as with the embroidery school, the students of the lace-making school were given prizes to reward their progress.[70] At the end of each year, as outlined in article 4 of the school's statutes, the Society awarded fifteen prizes to the most deserving students. With five first prizes at 120 *reales*, five second prizes at 100 *reales*, and five third prizes at 80 *reales*, the Economic Society allotted 1,500 *reales* for the annual competition. The students were to begin work on July 1 on pieces they wished to submit to the prize competition, thus allowing enough time for each student to complete an adequate sample for the judges to examine. The students could also earn bonuses for making certain types of lace. According to article 6, students who made *punto de Garbeta* and *punto sencillo de Flandes* were to be rewarded one-third of the value of the lace they produced, and students who performed "the rest of the labors including *punto doble de Flandes*" were to receive one-half of the value. At the prize competition in December 1785, the Society presented 120 *reales* each to Crisanta Cudero, Marta Roman, and Gabriela Rodríguez, who made *punto doble de Flandes*, 100 *reales* each to Josepha Lainz and María Tirado, who made *Red de Flandes*, and 80 *reales* to Felipa Pon, who made *Punto de Garbeta*. The rest of the students were each awarded 40 *reales* for their continued work.[71] As at the embroidery school, the teacher was forbidden to admit or dismiss students without the permission of the school's directors, giving the students a significant degree of security.

The embroidery and lace-making schools also opened up further employment opportunities for women as teachers. The Economic Society received applications for teaching positions from a number of women over the years. Those who petitioned for employment included Margarita Diez, Vicenta Gutiérrez, Jacinta Palacios, María Briteño, Theresa Farel, Crisanta Cudero, Agustina Castilla y Calvo, and María Correas, among others. The Economic Society employed a number of these women to instruct students at its artisanal schools. While it is debatable to what degree the embroidery and lace-making schools helped to improve Spanish industry as a whole, they did provide both their students and their teachers with a respectable way to earn a living.

The nonmonetary benefits that working-class women obtained from the Economic Society's artisanal schools are practically impossible to ascertain. However, it is important to consider that these schools provided young women not only with economic opportunities but also with artistic ones. Feminist art historians have demonstrated that the more scholars understand the ways in which gender shapes artistic production, the more they realize how much of the art women have created has gone unnoticed because of its relegation to the world of crafts.[72] The devaluation of women's artwork is in part the result of the long-prevailing belief that women's creations were not products of artistic genius. As Merry Wiesner explains, "The work which women artists, writers, and scientists did produce was often judged to be the result not of genius, but of nimble fingers, diligence in observation, skill at following the example of a male teacher, or bee-like industriousness, in others words, 'craft,' not 'art' or 'science.'"[73] Indeed, a woman's creation was seen as simply the result of hard work but not artistry.

Embroidery in particular is a prime example of an art form that over time was devalued to the status of craft. Wiesner agrees, "The best example of loss of status in an art form is embroidery, which in the Middle Ages was practiced by both women and men often organized into male-directed craft guilds and paid on a scale equivalent to painting, but which throughout the early modern period became increasingly identified as feminine."[74] Thus, as women came to produce more of the embroidery and lace work, the artistic worth of these objects declined. This was certainly true in Spain. In the sixteenth and seventeenth centuries, embroidery was a male domain whose practitioners rated high esteem for their artistic talent. Even King Philip II and his successor Philip III were skilled embroiderers. By the eighteenth century, embroidery came to be lumped in with other textile production, and women increasingly were trained in the field.[75] As historians of women and work have shown, the increased feminization of a task often meant "deskilling" and lower wages. Embroidery and lace making no longer were seen as art but as crafts, and contemporaries saw the training of women in these fields as a question of industry.

That the Economic Society saw the embroidery and lace-making schools as creating workers and not artists is clear in how it initially integrated the institutions into its governing structure. The Society split its pedagogical projects into two distinct categories: industrial and popular. The mandate of the industrial schools, placed under the council of industry, consisted of training girls and young women in the production of textile manufactures. The popular schools, under the council of arts and trades, on the other hand, focused on training male students in the production of artistic objects with the ultimate goal of securing them a formal apprenticeship.[76] By entrusting the embroidery and lace-making schools to the council of industry and not the council of arts and trades, the Economic Society clearly relegated them to the lower status of craft and gendered that definition.

However, that definition provided an opening for working-class women. The new ideas on women's economic role that the Society touted not only helped women gain access to steady employment but also furnished them with artistic training. We may never know if these women considered themselves artists. Did the lace-making teacher Theresa Farel believe she was training young artists? Did the fifty students under Nieto, Rada, and Pérez's instruction in 1796 consider the creative aspects of their work? While they might have appreciated the outlet for creativity or found pride in their accomplishments, in all likelihood none of these women considered themselves artists. With real material needs to consider, women chose embroidery or lace making because these constituted viable employment options. Nevertheless, via the artisanal schools the *damas* administered, working-class women contributed to Spain's cultural life.

By overseeing these various schools, the women's council participated in both the educational and the economic mission of the Economic Society. However, its involvement in Spain's industrial development was not limited to educational projects. The women's council also encouraged the participation of women in industry through its administration of the Montepío de hilazas (literally, an assistance fund for yarn), a program that furnished women with raw materials they could use to manufacture textile goods. The idea behind the Montepío de hilazas, established in 1778, was to provide young women who had been trained in the *escuelas patrióticas* with immediate and steady work. Afraid that these potential laborers would fail to maintain their skills if there was a significant lag between their schooling and their employment, the creators of the Montepío designed the program to give the graduates a solid start. As it grew, the Montepío also aimed to incorporate the mothers and sisters of these new laborers into Spain's textile industry.

The women's council voted to accept the task of directing the Montepío on March 30, 1790, in response to a request from the *junta general* dated two days earlier.[77] As was its practice when undertaking a new venture, the council immediately selected six *socias* to make an inventory of the Montepío's holdings and scheduled a mid-April *junta extraordinaria* to discuss the state of the program. Ultimately, Fuerte-Híjar and Josefa de Rojas were put in charge of directing the new project, which was, simply put, a mammoth task. Gathering enough raw materials to serve the needs of the Montepío's workers, who numbered as many as three hundred by 1796, in itself presented a challenge. The historian Paloma Fernández-Quintanilla marvels at the prospect of coordinating the delivery of sufficient supplies: "Providing raw materials constituted by itself a complete world of activities that began in their acquisition from the places of origin—the mountains of León and Burgos, for linens and woolens; the Valencian region, for silks, etc.—the transport to Madrid, their preparation in laundries and fulling mills on the banks of our modest Manzanares, their preparation and storage, through to the warehouse and their further distribution."⁷⁸ Selling the products also involved tremendous effort. The *socias'* minutes record their negotiations with prospective buyers. Here again, the scale should not be overlooked. At the council's October 7, 1791, meeting, for example, Fuerte-Híjar estimated that the Montepío had sold 50,008 handkerchiefs since the *socias* had taken direction of the institution nineteen months earlier—enough handkerchiefs to supply approximately one-quarter of Madrid's residents.⁷⁹

In the day-to-day operations of the Montepío, the *junta de damas* drew on its experience gained in administering the Society's schools. For example, the group adopted for its new venture a governing structure identical to that found in the schools, as well as used the same system for reporting the status of the Montepío to the women's council. The *damas* also adopted familiar mechanisms to encourage workers at the Montepío, such as sponsoring prize competitions with monetary awards for exceptional producers. How worthwhile the *damas'* efforts turned out to be is difficult to determine, in part because there are insufficient extant records available to fully analyze the *junta de damas'* administration of the Montepío. An 1803 report that the Count-Duchess of Benavente presented to her fellow councilwomen suggests the women's organization enjoyed a degree of success. Benavente's accounting showed the Montepío in the black, proving at least that the *socias* had achieved a degree of financial viability for the program.⁸⁰ The Montepío constituted yet one more way in which the *junta de damas* worked to encourage the involvement of women in Spain's industry.⁸¹

CREATING NETWORKS

The educational and industrial projects of the *junta de damas* enabled its members to make their mark on eighteenth-century Spain. As associates of a prestigious, royal-sponsored institution, the *damas* adopted an agenda tailored to what they considered to be the chief concerns of the nation's women. Their dedication and hard work made the *socias'* names synonymous with the programs they set forth. This reputation went well beyond the walls of Madrid, extending into surrounding cities and provinces and occasionally even neighboring countries. Building on both the strength of their names and the fame of the women's council, the members of the *junta de damas* came to occupy the center of a growing network of people and institutions focused on the status of Spanish women and the health of Spain's industry. As the heart of this network, the female council achieved even greater involvement in shaping the nation's ongoing reform.

The successful industrial projects the *socias* took on made them a crucial point of contact for questions about domestic industry. In fact, because of its high level of involvement in women's artisanal training, the *junta de damas* gained a reputation as a clearinghouse for information about these endeavors. As a result, the *damas* received correspondence from teachers throughout Europe seeking employment. For example, on October 26, 1792, the women's council discussed a note from Carlota Lille, a resident of Paris who was looking for a position "in some school, or institute such as those that the council has under its direction, for the instruction of drawing, painting, and miniatures." In response to Lille's request, the women's council noted that, "although persuaded of the utility that this teaching could bring, they could not admit her, because of the scarcity of funds."[82] The women's council also considered requests for its assistance in identifying teachers to fill positions in other Spanish cities. For example, at its February 13, 1789, meeting, Rita López de Porras read a dispatch from the governor of Cádiz asking the *damas* to locate a skilled embroidery instructor for a school in his city. In this case, the *junta de damas* did not know of any candidates and thus simply passed along the request to the *junta general*.[83] At its March 13 meeting, the women's council decided to follow up on a suggestion made by the *junta general* to place an ad in the *Diario de Madrid* and post notices advertising the position of embroidery instructor that was open in Cádiz. On April 17, the women's council received applications from María Padilla and María Josepha Litz, who both wanted to teach there. The council made plans to test the two girls for possible placement. Indicative of the number of such requests sent to the *damas,* on the same day that the council received Padilla's and Litz's applications, it also took delivery of a letter from Judas Joseph Zebriada y Zerezeda, a priest in the city of Calahorra, who was starting two schools for poor girls and needed to find teachers. His letter asked the *damas* to provide him with names of anyone qualified and interested in the positions. Thus, the *junta de damas* created a network that helped to facilitate the instruction and learning of artisanal skills for women both in and out of Madrid.

The female council's reputation increased its members' direct involvement in industry. Just as the group became a hub for women's industrial education, its members also became chief consultants in industrial innovation. When the Economic Society received proposals for new manufacturing methods that promised to revolutionize Spanish industry, particularly in what were increasingly seen as the female industries related to textile production, it passed them on to the *junta de damas* for consideration. For example, on April 8, 1791, the Society sent the *damas* a memorandum from two men identified simply as Mr. Salamanca and Mr. López, who had built a machine that allowed three people to spin at the same time. The machine was based on a design suggested by Miguel Gerónimo Suarez. The *junta de damas* agreed that the Countess of Superunda would take three skilled girls with her and evaluate the merits of the new invention. At the next week's meeting, Superunda presented her findings. Since the bobbin was broken in the second spinner's place, Superunda had been able to see the machine operate with only two spinners. She indicated that the machine, not constructed according to the original design, had a significant flaw in the way that the wheel rotated. As a result, the spinner at station three was slowed down, even when the two girls exchanged places. The addition of the third spinner was certain to make the problem even more pronounced. Superunda also felt that the force needed to run the machine was excessive.[84] Thus, she concluded that the machine would not be useful in any of the Society's educational institutions.

In addition to examining new manufacturing methods, the women's council also inspected cloth samples from various locations in Spain in order to evaluate their quality. On April 30, 1790, for example, *socias* considered some linen samples sent from Zamora by Andrés Fernandez Diez. The women's council found the cloth, woven by poor young women, to be of good quality, and "determined to ask about the cut of the linen, where it was from, and how high its value was for each pound of material."[85] As with the inspection of new inventions, this practice aimed to help improve the production of Spanish goods in female-dominated industries. The women's council received a steady stream of petitions to examine everything from a machine that promised to revolutionize the spinning of silk thread to a treatise on training women to be tailors. Clearly, many in the nation's industries looked to the *junta de damas* as a source of authority in such matters.

Through this network of workers and inventors, the *junta de damas* did shape industry beyond Madrid. But in order to truly influence the nation, the *socias* determined to enlist the help of elite women throughout Spain. Montijo and her compatriots had successfully created a space where they could participate in the nation's reform, and they wished to extend that space to elite women living outside of the capital. Consequently, the women's council encouraged the formation of female auxiliary councils in Economic Societies located in other key urban centers.

The role that the Madrid *socias* played in incorporating women in other Economic Societies is clearest in the case of Valladolid.[86] The Marquise of Fuerte-Híjar suggested the formation of a women's council in Valladolid in 1793. An article in the *Diario de Madrid* reports:

> The Señora Marquesa de Fuerte-Híjar has proposed and promoted in Valladolid a Council of Ladies joined to the Economic Society of that town. No doubt: The Señora Marquesa de Fuerte-Híjar, wishing to establish in Valladolid an association of Ladies, has done a benefit to the Nation, not only for the good that it brings to the young women of that land, but also because it offers the ladies of that area some occupation that, in addition to filling all of the duties that are prescribed by God and Humanity, allows them to act in a way that is so agreeable to our Monarchs.[87]

Fuerte-Híjar's suggestion that women be incorporated into the Valladolid organization followed a request from the Viscountess of Valoría for assistance in finding a teacher for a school in Valladolid.[88] The *damas* in Valladolid apparently heeded Fuerte-Híjar's advice and formed their own body. On September 27, 1793, the Madrid women's council considered a letter from the Duke of Alcudía, in which he enclosed a copy of the statutes created by the Valladolid Society "for the establishment of an Association of Ladies." After having Montijo read the statutes aloud to the *junta* and hearing the opinions of the Marquise of Fuerte-Híjar—"as the most informed on this matter"—the women's council decided to send a positive response concerning the document. According to the minutes, "The Council voted to respond to His Excellency that not having found in them anything deserving of criticism, it seems that by observing them the Association of Ladies of Valladolid could progress in its establishment and serve as a stimulus in the advancement of women, resulting from all of this much benefit to that city."[89] The fact that the women's council in Madrid was consulted in the formulation of statutes for a similar body in Valladolid suggests its influence on the creation of other women's councils in Spain.[90] The *damas'* desire to see the "advancement of women" beyond Madrid motivated them to help organize women's participation in other Economic Societies.

Similarly, the activities in Madrid spurred the involvement of women in Osuna. In this case, the presence of two key Madrid *socias* on the Osuna Economic Society's roster suggests the extensive reach of the capitol city's *junta de damas*. Among the three women who were made honorary members of the Real Sociedad Económica de Amigos del País de Osuna were the Count-Duchess of Benavente, admitted in 1787, and María Isidra Quintina Guzmán y la Cerda, admitted in 1798. The Countess of Beaufort (Francisca Leopolda Beaufort y Toledo) joined these two *socias* with her membership in 1803.[91] The records of the *junta de damas* do not speak to any activities these women took up in Osuna. However, their membership alone evidences the spread of women's participation beyond Madrid.

The link between the Madrid organization and the participation of women in Economic Societies other than those located in Valladolid and Osuna is not as clear. Women were members of the Society in Avila, and in fact their admission was quickly approved there with no real debate. As Jorge Demerson explains in his study of Avila's Economic Society, "It observed 'that it would be advisable to admit as *socias* a few ladies who wished to contribute on their own to the goals of the institution of the Society.' "[92] Similarly, the Society in Granada admitted a number of women. María Luisa Astrauli, Luisa del Pulgar (Countess of la Ximera), María de la Soledad Cerviño y Pontejos, María de la Concepción Cerviño y Pontejos, Catalina Martín y Abril, and María de los Dolores Miranda all appear in the category of *socios de mérito* on a list of members of the Real Sociedad Económica de Granada dated February 13, 1798.[93] In addition, Jean Sarrailh points to the participation in Lugo of María Reguera de Mondragón, "who took the floor several times to discuss popular education."[94]

The Society in Aragon had a brief but intriguing debate over what to do with its female members. In addition to Josefa Amar y Borbón, four other women were accepted to the Aragonese Economic Society in this era. However, the *socios* of the Aragonesa specifically rejected the notion of creating a women's council.[95] On August 27, 1787, Floridablanca wrote a letter encouraging the Aragonese Society to create a *junta de damas*. To follow up, the Marquis of Ayerbe informed his fellow members in December of the activities and practices of Madrid's *junta de damas*, which he was particularly knowledgeable about since his wife was herself a member.[96] Then, at the February 15, 1788, meeting of the Society, the Marquis of Ayerbe submitted a plan for the creation of such a women's council in Aragon. Ayerbe's plan was never adopted, and in fact Juan Hernández de Larrea presented a report in April 1791 titled "Informe sobre la inconveniencia de formar una junta de damas en la Sociedad" (Treatise on the Inconvenience of Forming a

Women's Council of the Society).[97] Although the Aragonese Society was prepared to accept a very accomplished woman such as Amar y Borbón, it was not ready to open its doors completely to female members. In any case it would be doubtful that Amar y Borbón, given her arguments in the Madrid controversy, would have been receptive to the idea even if it had meant the expansion of female membership. Either way, Aragon would not be swayed by the active example of the *junta de damas* in Madrid. Despite this disappointment, the latter successfully helped incorporate women into a number of Economic Societies throughout Spain, in part through direct intervention and in part through the example of what female members could accomplish.

Clearly, the members of the *junta de damas* had established their credibility and had exploited the opportunity offered by admission, proving that those who had argued on their behalf were right to claim that women had an important contribution to make in Spain's regeneration. The council furthered debates on female education and worked to publicize its views by disseminating the findings of its educational commissions to a wider public. The women's council did more than tout the importance of civic motherhood; its members practiced it. As an extension of their belief in the importance of preparing mothers to mold future citizens, the women of the *junta de damas* conceived of themselves as mothers of the nation. As such, they aimed to cultivate these prospective citizens, as their administration of the Inclusa exemplifies.

Further, by directing programs aimed at providing training for female workers and taking an active interest in technological developments, especially in industries using female labor, its members extended the organization's role beyond education. Through its administration of the Society's numerous vocational schools for women, the *junta de damas* hoped to employ plebeian women in the project of Spain's regeneration. The great success of this project lies in the number of working-class women who gained access to both artistic training and employment as a result of the *socias'* ingenuity and hard work. These new industrial laborers enjoyed the fruits of the *junta de damas'* efforts to address the place of women in the nation's economy. In addition, the women's council encouraged and facilitated artisanal training, industrial development, and female membership in Economic Societies outside of Madrid, thereby helping to forge an extended network focused on issues the *socias* deemed vital to women's lives.

The fact that women focused their efforts on issues pertinent to women exemplified their desire to bring the needs and value of Spain's female citizens to the forefront of Enlightenment debates. In the female sphere of action that they had worked to create, the *socias* of the *junta de damas* forged an Enlightenment project for women. By employing gendered arguments promoting their special insight into these problems, they continued to negotiate a space in which they could participate in a meaningful way in the nation's reform. Yet the *socias'* labors also reinforced a vision of female citizenship grounded in both gender and class-based distinctions. In the female council's design, elite women became civic mothers while plebeian women became patriotic workers. The *junta de damas* encouraged the idea of women as citizens, but in practice its members assumed certain limits to how women might exercise that role. For all the value they held for the nation, women became citizens as mothers and workers, never simply as Spaniards.

6   Between Reason and Passion

Citizenship in Translation

In response to the circumscribed version of female citizenship that male intellectuals advocated, an increasing number of eighteenth-century Spanish women articulated a theory of citizenship that distinguished between the sexes. Both female authors and councilwomen emphasized their unique qualities as women in order to establish their place in Spain's reform movement. Asserting their innate virtues and maternal instinct, women claimed a significant and powerful role for female citizens. Yet this role entailed specific, class-based forms as women became either civic mothers or industrial workers. Ultimately, this strategy ghettoized female participation in politics and the state. Near the turn of the century, at least a few women began to imagine a new paradigm, one that united characteristics traditionally deemed male or female in such a way as to make both indispensable to the model citizen.

One arena where women's voices began to be heard was in translations.[1] As suggested in chapter 4, publication posed a risk for women since it challenged dominant beliefs on appropriate feminine comportment. The literary scholar Tina Krontiris has pointed out that translation long comprised one method women employed in order to mitigate the risks of publication. According to Krontiris, translation was perceived as "a less active and hence less masculine literary activity than original composition."[2] However, translating was not as passive an occupation as it might appear. The original text provided women with a shield behind which they could—and did—express themselves. To begin with, the simple act of rendering the text into another language constitutes an authorial act. As the literary theorist Françoise Massardier-Kenney explains, "Since translation is also a legitimizing process for a writer—a writer takes on the authority implied in being an author in so far as he or she becomes translated—a translator can become an active textual producer in the very process of choosing who will be translated."³ In addition, translators often provided their own textual exegesis in the form of translator's introductions, footnotes, or other editorial mechanisms. Translations thus interpreted, not merely transmitted, an original work. Furthermore, many translators did not remain faithful to the original. Through subtle, or even overt, transformations in the text, translators often imbued a work with a slightly new or altogether distinct meaning.⁴ In sum, translating provided women with a less risky, yet still effective, way of transmitting their views into print and, by extension, into the arena of public debate.

One woman who took advantage of translation as a forum was María Romero Masegosa y Cancelada, who published the first Spanish translation of Madame de Graffigny's *Lettres d'une péruvienne* (1747) in 1792.⁵ Romero's text is worth looking at in depth because it demonstrates the degree to which female intellectuals strived to understand and define their presence in the public sphere. Graffigny's tale provided a compelling template for Romero.⁶ Engrossed by Graffigny's captivating plot and riveted by her text's critical appraisal of European society and culture, particularly its denunciation of aristocratic excess and patriarchal rule, Romero set out to translate the work to her own national context. The continuities and deviations between Graffigny's work and Romero's translation suggest the extent to which Romero shared Graffigny's views.⁷ Romero's embrace of Graffigny's gender critique indicates that, despite their different national heritages, Romero and Graffigny shared fundamental concerns about the condition of women, including the inadequacy of female education and women's loss of status in marriage. Indeed, by extending Graffigny's critique of French women to Spanish society, Romero suggests that women have to embrace, or be allowed to embrace, new attitudes and practices in order to contribute to Spain's future.

That Romero was concerned with leading Spain toward a glorious future is clear in her treatment of Spain's imperial history. This issue is important because, while Graffigny's original story relied on casting the Spanish conquistadors as villains, Romero's translation completely undermines this political message. Graffigny's story relies on the Black Legend, a version of Spain's history rooted in the writings of sixteenth-century Dutch and English Protestants, which depicted Spain as a nation cloaked in the darkness of Catholicism, a darkness that led to the unjust treatment of indigenous populations in the conquest of the Americas and prevented Spain's development as a true European power.⁸ Romero develops her own interpretation of Spain's presence in the New World, one that works to eradicate the Black Legend and enhance the country's religious piety. In fact, Romero suggests that a profound transformation in Spaniards' religious values must constitute a central part of the equation for the nation's reform. As Romero rewrites Graffigny's tale, she creates a new heroine that is at once rational and passionate, reasoned and faithful. Romero eschews the notion that reason alone can bring about Spain's regeneration and instead posits a new model in which passion—a traditionally feminine quality—plays a key role. Romero's text demonstrates how at least one Spanish woman reconciled the false dichotomy between reason and passion and how this reconciliation contained the potential for women's greater political participation. However, by defining this participation in terms contrary to the Enlightenment ideal of the rational citizen, this conception of female citizenship ultimately excluded women altogether.

FINDING A VOICE

Translation provided a number of Spanish women with a viable route to publication, one that helped them to receive serious recognition for their work but mitigated the risks of public exposure. That female translators' works achieved acceptance is suggested in part by the amount of attention they received in the periodical press. The publication of most extant translations by female authors was announced in one or more of the literary magazines that circulated among Spain's literati, accompanied by a short summary of the work and occasionally a brief critique of the text. For example, the *Diario de Madrid* published this description to announce the publication of María Antonia de Río y Arnedo's translation of Jean-François Saint-Lambert's briefly titled *Sara Th . . .* : "This short work, valued for its simplicity, presents a model of how to carry out the obligations of a mother of a family, an example of the happiness that the execution of these tasks produces, and an agreeable portrait of the delights of country life; in order to formulate a firm idea of the merit of this novel, it suffices to say that it is one of those that is mentioned in the excellent and celebrated poem *The Seasons.*"[9] In addition to this sort of summary praising the content of a work, reviews of translations often contained a comment on the effectiveness of the translation. For example, in the "Translated Books" section of Madrid's *Memorial Literario* of April 1794, the paper wrote of María Antonia Fernanda de Tordesillas Cepeda y Sada's *Instrucción de una señora cristiana para vivir en el mundo santamente*, "The translation came out well and is worthy of the public."[10] Of course, these were not always glowing reviews. A reviewer for *Memorial Literario* had a less than complimentary opinion of María Rosa Gálvez's translation *Catalina, ó la bella labradora* in 1802. After providing a summary in which he describes the mix of comedic and dramatic elements in the play, the reviewer criticizes Gálvez's style of translation: "This drama is translated from French, but it is not translated into Castilian; rather, it has remained in a hybrid language that is in style among the crowd of bad translators."[11] Here, it is not the nature of the review that is most important, but the fact that women's translations were considered worthy of discussion by the journal's editors. These notices also frequently mentioned the bookseller carrying the work and its price, so that interested readers could purchase the publication and read it for themselves. For example, the announcement of the publication of Josefa de Alvarado Lezo Pacheco y Solís's translation *Compendio de la filosofía moral* informed potential readers that the book was available at Fernández's Bookstore for twelve *reales* in parchment and eighteen in full binding.[12] What is clear, then, is that women's translations were accepted as readable and often valuable texts by male censors, male editors, male reviewers, male publishers, and male booksellers, who themselves formed part of Spain's Enlightenment society.

This acceptance, however, did not erase all the barriers, external and internal, that women faced on the road to publication. The difficult struggle for self-expression that women writers faced in the early modern period constitutes a central theme of Graffigny's *Lettres d'une péruvienne*, explaining in part Romero's choice of the work for translation. The *Lettres* recounts the tale of Zilia, an Incan princess whom the Spanish seize during their conquest of Peru on the very day she is to marry her royal suitor, Aza. Written as an epistolary novel, the work contains Zilia's letters to Aza, in which she chronicles her bewildering journey from Peru to Paris, a journey that curiously seems to transport the sixteenth-century princess to eighteenth-century France. Zilia's letters, composed with *quipus*, knotted cords whose patterns constituted an Incan system for keeping records and sending messages, describe the violent destruction of her Incan city at the hands of the Spanish, her treacherous ocean passage to Europe, and the naval battle in which the French overtake her Spanish captors and apprehend her. Zilia's narrative acquaints Aza with her newfound ally, Déterville, the French naval captain whose adoration for her leads to her residence in Paris. Zilia, however, takes Déterville's romantic inclinations for simple friendship, and her heart remains true to Aza. Zilia's visits to Parisian gatherings, her budding friendship with Déterville's sister Céline, and her stint in a nearby convent provide the backdrop for her reflections on contemporary French society. Toward the end of the novel, the honorable Déterville locates Aza in Spain, and Zilia is heartbroken to learn that he is engaged to another woman. Rather than accept Déterville's proposal of marriage, Zilia retreats to a country estate purchased with looted Incan treasures.

Throughout her travails, Zilia's writing allows her to survive the traumatic events of her life. Graffigny continually reminds the reader of the importance of Zilia's ability to record her experience, vividly describing Zilia's anguish when her French captors seize her *quipus*, her constant worry over the diminishing supply of her cords, and her exhilaration when, six months after her *quipus* are exhausted, she learns French well enough to put pen to paper.[13] As Judith Curtis has explained, *Lettres* "is very much about the process of equipping the heroine with a language and a pen that will together enable her to explore and describe her world."[14] Graffigny develops this theme from the very beginning of her work. Zilia's letters, in fact, become Graffigny's own tool for self-expression when, in her foreword, Graffigny lets her own work masquerade as another's by suggesting that her role has been merely to edit Zilia's letters for publication.[15] To a certain extent, Graffigny's use of an imaginary editor simply epitomizes the popular penchant for muddling reality and fantasy in readers' minds, as exemplified in other contemporary best-sellers such as Jean-Jacques Rousseau's *Julie, ou La nouvelle Héloïse* (1761) and James Macpherson's *The Works of Ossian* (1765). Nevertheless, the device also muffles her own voice by having Zilia, rather than Graffigny herself, articulate her social critique.

The text's treatment of the subject of the female writer undoubtedly appealed to Romero, who, in her translator's note to *Cartas de una peruana*, reveals her own struggle for self-expression in light of the perilous position of the female writer. While Romero portrays herself as a kind of amateur intellectual who puts forth her work with trepidation, this depiction seems to mask the confident individual who emerges and encourages women to learn from her example. Romero describes how, with the advice of her brother, she pulled herself out of "that state of near stupidity" in which she was submerged and began to read meaningful works, learn French, and translate the volume in hand.[16] By explaining that her brother created her as a scholar—that he is the original author of her intellectual pursuits—Romero shields her entry into the Republic of Letters and makes him the instigator. It is interesting to note that, among the frivolous works she read, Romero lists those of Zayas. Perhaps Romero did not want to suffer the same fate as Clara Jara de Soto.

However, while Romero is cautious in describing her beginnings as a writer, her desire to emphasize her own talents and hard work eventually comes through. Her modest tone disappears when she recounts the project at hand: "I dedicated myself to translating this text, which I achieved ... through hard work, since with managing my household, as well as the many other tasks that fall to me (for which the town in which I live is a trustworthy witness), I could not devote myself freely to its study."[17] In turn, she hopes that her own passage into the realm of Enlightenment discourse will push other women toward the door: "I give to the public the product of my work in order to encourage other women that dare to share the results of theirs."[18]

Romero's use of the verb "to dare" suggests the potential risks female authors faced in "going public." Her account of her own journey serves to critique the social barriers to women's intellectual pursuits, to decry the difficulties she herself faces as she strives to find her own voice. Just as Zilia's letters enable Graffigny to voice her views on French society, Romero finds in Graffigny's text an avenue to meaningful self expression. While translating allows Romero to portray herself as the reluctant novice, the text she publishes speaks more to her other persona—the hardworking crusader whose bold views present a vision of a new Spanish woman who will help lead the nation toward a new era.

THE FOLLIES OF IGNORANCE

The new woman that Romero envisioned emerges from a close reading of her translation of Graffigny's *Lettres d'une péruvienne*. One of the hallmarks of Graffigny's text is its attention to the condition of women in eighteenth-century society, undoubtedly another reason Romero was compelled to translate this work. Graffigny's story employs a standard literary device, placing her critique of French women in the mouth of a "primitive" outsider, as in Montesquieu's *Lettres persanes*. Through Zilia's observations, Graffigny laments the status of women whose lack of education and limited choices have destined them to lead unfulfilling lives of folly, idleness, and overconsumption. At the same time, Graffigny posits an alternative in the character of Zilia: the educated woman whose intellectual pursuits and autonomy offer her, literally, a new life. Romero builds on the gender critique embedded in Graffigny's work. In polemical footnotes at key junctures in the text and in her opening translator's note, Romero broadens Graffigny's commentary on the position of women to encompass Spanish women as well.[19] In addition, by presenting her views in her own voice, not filtered through Zilia as in the original, Romero enables herself to comment even more strongly than Graffigny on the state of women in European society.

One of the key concerns that Romero and Graffigny share is the poor state of female education. After all, while convent schools or private tutors did provide surprisingly good educations for some of Spain's female elite, Spanish women, like their French counterparts, remained at the mercy of male relatives who may or may not have been concerned with their intellectual training.[20] Graffigny's heroine identifies one of the signs of women's insufficient education when she remarks on French women's poor command of their own language. "They do not even know the proper usage of their native language," she marvels. "Rarely do they speak it correctly, and I have noticed not without great surprise that I am now more expert than they in that regard."[21] In a footnote, Romero extends Graffigny's criticism to Spanish society: "They do not teach any of us women Castilian, and although you cannot deny that there are among us some very affluent women who are articulate, it is no less true that most of us speak quite poorly."[22] Romero's footnote not only identifies the same weakness among Spain's women but also reminds the reader who is to blame for women's poor speech by referencing those unnamed souls who neglect female education.[23] More important, Romero's remarks come from her own lips, not Zilia's, as in Graffigny's version. By avoiding the filter of Zilia the "primitive" outsider, Romero lends even greater force to her observations.

Romero's voice again rings out loud and clear as she critiques the role men play in keeping women ignorant. Romero wholeheartedly concurs when Graffigny's Zilia, echoing the Lockean notion of the tabula rasa, argues that women cannot be expected to possess some natural knowledge but rather must be educated by society. Romero's words, not Zilia's, provide a direct analysis of why men neglect women's education:

> "Listen here," they will say, "to what will happen: women already want to get cheeky with us when they know anything more than how to read: we will not be able to put up with them and their babbling if we open the door to their studies." Gentlemen, this is a fearful terror, born from laziness: Keeping us women ignorant, you men do not need to know more than you already do, and if we advance a bit you will need to study more soundly and tighten the stirrups.[24]

Here, Romero boldly chastises men who fear educated women, labeling these men emotional and lazy, qualities more often associated with the female sex. In addition, Romero gets at the crux of the issue—men's anxiety about retaining control over "cheeky" women. With her admonition that men may have to "tighten the stirrups," Romero likens the male-female relationship to one between rider and beast, a startling image of domination.

In addition to rebuking Spanish men for preventing women from learning, Romero's text also addresses the larger societal implications of women's lowly status. Vanity and profligacy are just two of the social ills that the author believes will be eradicated through female education. Here again, Graffigny provides Romero with a solid springboard, since her original text takes up these issues. For example, in letter 28, echoing age-old debates on luxury, Graffigny's heroine remarks on French society's penchant toward overconsumption: "The men and women wear finery so splendid and so covered with useless decoration."[25] While Graffigny's outsider comments on both men's and women's attire, eighteenth-century readers would have certainly understood from contemporary debates on luxury that women were thought to be the key culprits in overspending. The gendered character of this critique becomes clear in Romero's footnote: "Zilia also speaks in another section of the vast time that they waste at the dressing table. I very much desire that our dress, which is not only costly but also bothersome, be simplified; such that from here on out it will serve but for our comfort and protection."[26] Even more forcefully than does Graffigny, Romero ties female idleness and luxury directly to women's lack of education. Her translator's note explains, "We women regularly use all our energy in the adornment of our bodies, leaving (so to speak) idle and abandoned the rational spirit with which we honor the Supreme Being, and which distinguishes us from beasts."[27] Here again, Romero underscores the distinction between irrational beasts and rational women while also pointing to the need to cultivate that innate reason in the female sex.

The notion that women should be included in the nation's reform was espoused by a number of Spain's philosophes, but some of Romero's gender critique took her beyond the mainstream of Spanish Enlightenment thought. Many called for improved female education and touted the positive influence educated women could have as workers, as consumers, and as mothers of Spain's future citizens.[28] However, few followed Graffigny, as Romero did, in rejecting women's expected stations as wife and mother. It is primarily through the story's ending that Graffigny provides her radical attack against women's traditional social roles. When Graffigny's Zilia receives reports that Aza has been unfaithful, she is devastated. For many readers, the convenient removal of Aza eliminated any impediment to the welcome union of Zilia and Déterville. However, Graffigny provides no suggestion at the end of the work of an impending matrimony, no hint that Zilia will abandon her newfound freedom in exchange for domestic bliss with Déterville. As Elizabeth J. MacArthur argues in a study of Graffigny's *Lettres d'une péruvienne* and Madame de Charrière's 1785 *Lettres écrites de*

Lausanne, such a wide-open ending bucked convention and undoubtedly contributed to the author's intended message. MacArthur explains, "The fact that these inconclusive plots are accompanied by feminist commentary on society suggests that the failure to close might represent a protest against the 'closures' generally imposed on women."[29] Romero's decision to keep Graffigny's ending intact provides compelling evidence of the Spanish author's agreement with Graffigny's assessment of women's limited options.

The strength of this argument lies in understanding that a number of contemporary readers, unsatisfied with Graffigny's ending and in particular with Zilia's single status, turned writers and fashioned alternative endings to Graffigny's story. In fact, there are five known sequels to Graffigny's work, including Romero's 1792 one-letter addition discussed below. The first anonymous sequel appeared in French and consisted of seven letters from Déterville, his sister Céline, and Zilia. These letters suggested a potential transformation in Zilia's relationship with Déterville, setting up a probable marriage between the two (after Zilia's presumed conversion to Catholicism) and thus the romantic, happy ending some might have preferred. The second addition to Graffigny's text came in 1749, when Hugary de Lamarche-Courmont published his own thirty-five-letter work in French. Written from the perspective of Aza, Lamarche-Courmont's version explains the lovers' separation as a misunderstanding and in the end reunites the two with plans of marriage.[30] The sequel by the anonymous writer and Lamarche-Courmont's additions were often published anonymously together with Graffigny's original thirty-eight-letter edition of 1747, leading readers to conclude that she had authored them as well. After all, marriage—to either Déterville or Aza—seemed a more suitable outcome.[31]

This error led Graffigny to publish a new edition of her text in 1752 to which she affixed three additional letters making clear Zilia's choice of autonomy over marriage. In Graffigny's later text—the edition on which Romero's translation is based—the story ends with Zilia's response to Déterville's last plea for her heart. Despite Aza's recent nuptials to another woman, Zilia chooses not to engage in a passionate relationship with Déterville. She explains, "It is in vain that you would flatter yourself to think that you can make my heart take on new chains."[32] Rather, Zilia resolves to maintain self-possession and live a life of introspection. These letters confirmed Graffigny's intention with her original work, presumably closing the door to sequels that attempted to cage Zilia in marriage either to Aza or to Déterville. However, this new edition did not stop other writers from pondering Zilia's fate. Both R. Roberts's 1774 English sequel and Madame Morel de Vindé's 1797 version persisted in partnering Zilia with Déterville.[33]

Romero also saw fit to rewrite Graffigny's ending, as I discuss below. However, she does not marry her off as many contemporaries who changed the ending did. Rather, in keeping with her attention to the question of women's place in society, Romero leaves intact Graffigny's criticism of women's limited options. Additional commentary throughout the text confirms Romero's agreement with the French author's critique of marriage. For example, in letter 34, when Graffigny's Zilia laments wives' economic subjection to their husbands, Romero adds a witty footnote ridiculing men who make their families live like paupers while they, for sheer avarice, hoard nearly all their earnings.[34]

Not all readers of Romero's text agreed with her decision to preserve Graffigny's unresolved ending. An anonymous annotation to the copy of *Cartas de una peruana* housed in the National Library in Madrid makes clear one Spanish reader's desire to see Zilia and Déterville married. Penned in at the very end of the story is an almost illegible note in eighteenth-century script: "Zilia at long last you married your friend, good I say I am very happy, yes, very happy. Zilia [and] Déterville, Céline and her husband, Aza and his wife lived happily ever after. The Author Romero."[35] In order to make this ending the extension of Romero's text, the anonymous reader scribbled over Romero's last sentence, changing the word *friendship* to read *passion*. Just as readers reacted to Graffigny's unusual and meaningful ending, so this Spanish reader objected to Romero's essential conservation of Graffigny's plot, and by extension, the critique of marriage it contained.

In her critique of the current state of Spanish women, Romero points toward a new type of woman: one not saddled with the burdens of ignorance and inferiority. While much of Romero's gender critique entailed seconding Graffigny's own observations and extending them to the Spanish case, Romero's notes allowed her to voice her own views directly, something that even Graffigny did not do. For Romero, the key was to differentiate women from innately irrational beasts while at the same time emphasizing the need to cultivate women's ability to reason. Romero wanted to send a clear message to Spain's men: only through education could women begin to aid, rather than harm, their nation.

THE FOLLIES OF HYPOCRISY

Romero's desire to improve the state of Spain's women must be considered in conjunction with another key agenda of her text: its attempt to repair Spain's miserable reputation. Considering this goal, Graffigny's text seems an odd choice for Romero, since the French author's condemnation of the

Spanish conquest as an act of barbarity motivated by a lust for gold drives her narrative. After all, if not for the Spaniards' cruelty, Zilia and Aza could have stayed together in their "primitive" utopia. In addition, Graffigny's choice to cast Zilia as an idealized Incan princess, rather than a contemporary eighteenth-century Peruvian, heightens the contrast between virtuous Indians and vicious Spaniards. As Julia V. Douthwaite explains, eighteenth-century Europeans entertained disparate notions of Peru past and present: "A paradoxical juxtaposition of primitive and civilized, ancient Peru appears a most un-savage model of lawful, orderly *(policé)* society. But modern-day Peruvians are portrayed very differently by eighteenth-century travelers, who speak of a lazy, secretive and superstitious people."[36] Graffigny's stylized view of the Incas was heavily shaped by Garcilaso de la Vega's 1616 *Los comentarios reales de los Incas*. However, as Douthwaite argues, Graffigny even recasts Garcilaso's account of the Incas, editing out mention of less fulsome characteristics such as their warrior culture, their territorial ambitions, and their social rigidity. Against this rosy portrait of the Peruvians, Graffigny evokes the Black Legend, depicting the conquest as the brutal invasion of an amiable and appealing population at the hands of vile Spanish soldiers.

While Romero also exalts much of Zilia's Incan culture, she completely objects to Graffigny's vision of the Spanish conquest. From the very beginning, Romero aims to correct Graffigny's portrayal of the Spanish conquerors as barbarians, by cleaning up the work's historical introduction, a component Graffigny added to the 1752 edition. One of Romero's main concerns is to expunge references to the Spaniards as barbarians whose greed led them to the Americas. In the third paragraph of the introduction, for example, Graffigny describes the Peruvians as a happy and cultured people until "avarice, coming from the heart of a world whose very existence they never suspected, cast upon their lands tyrants whose barbarity became the shame of humanity and the crime of their century."[37] Romero cuts the second half of this sentence and launches straight into the next paragraph, which details the conditions that made Peru ripe for conquest.[38] When translating Graffigny's commentary on how the Peruvians mistook the Spaniards for gods, Romero excises another unflattering description of the Spaniards, "whose rage even the most lavish offerings and humiliating homages could not assuage."[39] Similarly, while Romero admits that the Indian belief that the Spaniards were immortals "gives a sense of the ingenuousness of those peoples," she does not add, as Graffigny does, "and of how easy the Spaniards found it to seduce them."[40] Romero proceeds to eliminate the lengthy diatribe on Spain's victimization of Peru that follows. By cutting phrases, or even whole paragraphs from Graffigny's historical introduction, Romero rewrites the conquest.

Romero sticks to this project in the body of the work. In her first letter to Aza, Zilia bemoans her capture by writing, "I am submerged in an abyss of darkness, and my days resemble the most frightening of nights."[41] Here, Romero adds a lengthy footnote in which she sympathizes with the Incan princess's feelings of loss and fear. After all, she writes, Zilia's own country had just been turned upside down. In particular, she validates Zilia's distress over the destruction of Incan temples, explaining, "Although they were idolatrous, they were in the opinion of those people as sacred as any other."[42] Romero's compassion, however, does not signify her belief in Spain's culpability. She points out that even Spanish conquistadors were themselves the victims of violence in the Americas. By way of example, she names Francisco Pizarro, the conqueror and first viceroy of Peru, who was murdered by followers of his rival, Diego de Almagro, in 1541, noting that Pizarro was a figure whom even French historians often eulogized. Thus, Romero concludes that Spaniards cannot be blamed for the violent excesses of a few men: "Those acts, in which neither the Spanish government, nor the majority of Castilians, played any part whatsoever, foreigners employ to denigrate our conduct in those countries, wishing without doubt that they were angels, when they themselves were in their own way human, very human."[43] Here, Romero points to the participation of other European powers in the conquest. While she admits that no Europeans were "angels," she decries attempts to tarnish the names of national heroes like Pizarro and insists Spain's presence in the Americas cannot be characterized on the basis of the disgraceful acts of a minority.

In the remainder of her translation, Romero continues to omit the derogatory characterizations of Spaniards included in Graffigny's version. Through simple word changes, she tries to downplay the barbarity of the Spanish conquerors that Graffigny highlights. For example, Romero frequently eliminates harsh adjectives used to describe the Spaniards. When Zilia laments her captivity in letter 2, Romero alters the language from "those ferocious people, that you call Spaniards" to "those people you call Spaniards."[44] A few sentences down the page, she replaces "those barbarians" with "those people." Although Romero does use the term "savage Spaniards" in letter 4, she quickly appends a footnote to explain that "the Indians called Europeans savages as we called them; with that we are even."[45]

Romero's need to excise the objectionable commentary on Spaniards reflects her own fashioning of the conquest. She rejects the portrayal of the conquest as an undertaking in which Spanish barbarians exploited the new world merely for profit. Instead, she implies that moral objectives, namely the desire to spread Christianity, underscored Spain's presence in the Americas. In addition, she points to other positive aspects of Spain's explorations in the New World. For example, she applauds their discovery of the Americas as a scientific accomplishment. When Graffigny's text describes the "vast spaces [that] separated the cities of the Sun from our world," Romero interjects that "the Spaniards overcame those obstacles."[46] For Romero, the conquest can only be recorded as a splendid moment in her nation's history.

Romero is not the only writer to use her alteration of Graffigny's text as a vehicle for nationalist sentiment. In R. Roberts's version, for example, he puts praise for England in the mouth of Déterville. When Roberts's Déterville travels to England, he reports back to Zilia, "Yet I cannot help telling you, though a Frenchman, that the English manners are more suitable to my taste than those of my own nation.... The country, in general, is well cultivated; and those parts which are not, have a romantic wildness, which is beautiful in the highest degree."[47] Roberts has Déterville go on to describe "well built" London with its "magnificent" buildings and "well furnished" theaters, and to revel in the country's remarkable literary achievements. Déterville explains, "Their poetry, in particular, has a sublimity which the French tongue will not admit of."[48] In contrast to his praise of all things English, when Déterville journeys to Rome he scarcely notices his surroundings. His letters explain that he is too consumed with his love for Zilia to notice the city's features.

However, Romero's translation is much more than a simple apologia for the Spanish conquest or an attempt to make the work more palatable to a Spanish audience. In fact, a key aspect of her refashioning of the story of Spanish conquest is her resurrection of the Catholic faith. Her translator's note at the beginning of the work suggests that sincere religious devotion motivated her to alter Graffigny's novel. According to Romero, "The original contains some expressions lacking respect for our sacred Religion, so although they were spoken by the mouth of a pagan, this is not a sufficient reason to leave them to offend the delicate, Catholic sensibilities of the Spanish nation; and certainly it repulsed me to print those expressions contrary to our sacred beliefs."[49] As this statement indicates, she did not wish to perpetuate what she considered to be unnecessary and unfounded criticisms of Spain and Catholicism. Of course, there is always the possibility that her religious profession is not the product of true belief, but rather the result of self-censorship. Indeed, Graffigny's *Lettres d'une péruvienne*, banned by Rome in 1765, also received the scorn of Spanish Inquisitors who, in a 1796 edict, complained that the book attacked the Catholic faith under the guise of showing the virtues of Zilia.[50] However, this interpretation neglects the strong religious critique imbedded in Romero's translation.

Along these lines, perhaps the most significant alteration Romero makes to Graffigny's novel is the addition of an entire letter at the end of the work. Rather than simply end with Zilia's declaration of autonomy, as Graffigny does, Romero adds a letter to Déterville and Céline in which Zilia describes her conversion to Christianity. In this additional letter, Romero's Zilia details her long debates with a local priest, the books she reads in her garden, and her slow but certain conversion to Christian beliefs. Relating her discussions with the priest, Zilia exclaims, "Oh, with such wisdom he knew how to inspire in me religious sentiments! He asked me about and listened to the tenets of my old religion with such sweet complacency, already supporting some, already reprimanding others, and offering the Catholic tenets with such simple and familiar reasoning, and in such an insinuating and persuasive tone, that without resisting I became interested in and adopted his opinions."[51] Significantly, Romero portrays Zilia's conversion as the product of reason and thought, not passion and fear.[52] Romero ends the text with an allusion to the afterlife, to Zilia's ultimate happiness. It is an indication that Zilia's strong ties to Aza and her Incan heritage have been replaced by what Romero sees as the ultimate friendship, her relationship to God: "These will be my supplications until my last breath in which paying to nature the inevitable tribute, I close my eyes to the light of day amidst the sweetness of Divine love and in the arms of the most pure and indelible friendship."[53] Zilia's realization of the "true" faith and the reader's assurance of her probable salvation represent, in Romero's eyes, Zilia's enlightenment.

But what does conversion mean for Zilia as a woman? Does her embrace of Christianity somehow limit her autonomy, supplying the type of ending that Graffigny purposely avoided? One could argue that Romero's conversion of Zilia allows the author's nationalist project to trump her gender critique. However, Romero does all she can to maintain the view of marriage inherent in Graffigny's ending. Romero does not convert Zilia to Christianity and *then* marry her off, as at least three other contemporary sequels do. Nor does she choose to relocate Zilia in a convent, which would assuredly have been a more standard course for an unmarried Christian woman. Thus, while Romero's revised ending clearly takes on a new meaning in terms of the work's religious critique, it does not alter the commentary on marriage and women's limited options.

At the same time, Zilia's conversion outside the confines of the convent contributes to the larger religious project that Romero advances in her translation. While Romero does not critique the church per se, she *does* posit a type of religious revolution. Her key concern is the cleavage between religious ideology and actual behavior. In this sense, Zilia's religious life outside a convent reinforces Romero's stance that it is spirituality, and not external institutions, that lies at the heart of true religious conviction. For example, when in letter 24 Déterville's mother bequeaths all her wealth to her eldest son, leaving Déterville and Céline to fend for themselves, Romero's footnote asks with misgivings, "Is it possible that such final acts are the work of a human being who has been educated in the principles of the Catholic faith?"[54] Similarly, in letter 27, when Zilia joyfully informs Aza that she has recovered four trunks containing religious objects from their beloved Peru, Romero comments on Zilia's worship of these golden statues and the gods they represent: "Take as genuine the great respect with which the Infidels talk about the objects of their worship; they pronounce with extraordinary veneration the names of their false deities and they observe a prolix and scrupulous punctuality in the performance of their duties."[55] Romero laments their adulation of false idols, but she adds that Catholics could learn something from Zilia's sincere devotion:

> But what anguish! How differently we behave ourselves, those of us who luckily call ourselves Catholics! The Temples are entered with as much sprightliness as a public theater—our impenitent and ungodly attitude shows our irreligion, offering only an image of unruliness and negligence of customs—and at times they become a place for scandalous and sacrilegious reunions. The environs are a theater for the diversions of blasphemous youth, drunks, and gamblers, who pronounce obscene words to the whole world while the parents of such children watch with indifference, and finally where, to the horror of true Catholics, the corners of the venerable Churches become sewers or depositories of human waste. Should we put up with this? Is this acceptable? . . . Where have we arrived?[56]

In juxtaposing such irreverent behavior with Zilia's worship of her Incan relics, Romero questions the sincerity of European religious life. While Romero fully rejects the content of Zilia's religious beliefs, she is impressed by the Incan princess's passionate display of her religious faith. In Romero's supplementary letter, Zilia's embrace of Christianity, arrived at through the exercise of Enlightenment reason, redirects her profound devotion toward the "true" church, thus making her a model believer in Romero's eyes.

This religious critique considered, it is still possible to see Zilia's conversion to Christianity as merely an indication of Romero's desire to fully assimilate the Incan heroine to European ways. In this argument, Zilia's newfound cosmology would imply a certain change in her outsider status. In closing her last letter, Romero's Zilia informs Déterville and Céline, "At last, I am one with you, my beloved protectors: I am ready to initiate myself in the society of Christianity with the Sacred baptismal waters."[57] Zilia's adoption of Christianity works as a kind of assimilation. No longer the independent, autonomous outsider, Zilia is now "one" with her friends, a member of their "society."

There are two main problems with this interpretation. First, Zilia has already fallen victim to the process of assimilation in Graffigny's own text. For example, Graffigny's Zilia gratefully dons European attire in letter 12, pleased that she will no longer stand out so conspicuously. In addition, she no longer communicates in her native language via her Incan *quipus*, but in French with pen and paper instead. Further, Graffigny's own ending implies Zilia's adoption of a more European lifestyle. Her retreat to a landed estate purchased through the transformation of her sacred Incan objects into European currency suggests Zilia's own abandonment of her Incan ways.[58] Romero did not need to change Graffigny's text to force Zilia's assimilation; Zilia had already lost key aspects of her culture in the original plot. If anything, Zilia's humble way of addressing her "beloved protectors" in Romero's ending preserves a comfortable hierarchy between the Indian princess and her European friends.

Second, Romero seems attentive to the importance of defending some of Zilia's cultural uniqueness. Ironically, at the same time that she defends the Spanish conquest of other societies, Romero argues for the need to encourage a greater awareness of cultural difference. For example, in letter 11, Romero chastises the French women in Graffigny's tale who ridicule Zilia for her Incan attire. Romero writes in a footnote, "This is without doubt the result of our poor education; indeed, we should inspire in children from infancy the idea that men dressed in one way are as rational as those dressed in another, and it is simply an accident of circumstances related necessarily to the chance of being born here or there."[59] In letter 13, Romero again seizes on Zilia's mistreatment, this time in the household of Déterville's mother, to comment in a footnote on the abuse of foreign visitors:

> There are some people who treat foreigners unjustly and even inhumanely just because they are foreigners. Do these foreigners cease to be like us, or like all creatures made of the same supreme material as all men? And fully considering the subject, do not their faults deserve our compassion more than our hatred? It is the worst prejudice to wish

misery on an Italian because he is not my countryman. . . . Is the weight of being far from his land, in an unknown country, without parents, relatives, friends, or connections that can serve for support and shelter against misfortune not enough for a foreigner, without us adding the heavy burden of our cruelty and maltreatment?[60]

Romero's rhetorical questions condemn the inhospitable reception that Zilia receives as a result of her cultural differences.[61]

Instead, Zilia's religious conversion must be considered in the context of Romero's appraisal of the disparity between religious ideals and actual behavior. Zilia's conversion serves as the culmination of Romero's critique of the thin veneer of European religiosity. Significantly, Zilia does not simply adopt a European perspective on her faith, accepting Christian doctrine in theory but not in practice. In this sense, her conversion does not signify her assimilation to European customs. Rather, Zilia's newfound religious sentiment is more profound than that reigning in Europe. It combines the doctrinal teachings of Christianity with the passion of Zilia's primitive beliefs and the rationality of Enlightenment principles. Zilia is not full of empty pronouncements of faith but rather exemplifies true devotion. Thus, through Zilia's conversion, Romero completes the critique of European Christianity that Graffigny begins, providing in the character of Zilia a model for true religious conviction.

Of course, there is no denying that Zilia's conversion also plays into Romero's revised vision of the conquest. After all, it is not merely Zilia's adoption of Christianity that Romero desires but also the conversion of all the Incas to the "true" religion. Romero's Zilia implores her fellow Peruvians to follow in her footsteps: "Oh lucky Peruvians! You already have in your hemisphere the germ of the truth: cultivate it and you will enjoy an invaluable fruit. Suffer with patience the weaknesses of some of our conquistadors, because they are men, because so much good can never come without a price, and because justice demands it."[62] Here, Romero allows Zilia to voice a minor critique of the behavior of Spanish conquistadors, echoing her earlier admonition that humans are sometimes prone to commit errors. A couple of pages down, she lists her hopes for the future: "Sustain Aza on the path to salvation with the beliefs he has embraced, animate and strengthen the courage of the Spaniards in the task which at their own cost they have undertaken, and inspire in my beloved compatriots the docility to embrace the religion I adore."[63] Romero's use of the word *docility* might suggest her desire to assimilate peaceful Indians to European customs. However, it is essential to keep in mind Romero's ultimate goal: the inspiration of a new kind of religious faith among Europeans. Thus, the compatriots that Zilia prompts to open their hearts to the true faith are not Indians at all, but rather stand-ins for the European audience that Romero hopes will learn from Zilia's conversion.

Zilia's Peruvian identity undergoes a profound shift in Romero's translation. In Graffigny's novel, Zilia's status as a Peruvian critiques the Spaniards for the barbarity of the conquest. By casting Zilia as an Incan princess, a member of a society that Graffigny's contemporaries idealized, rather than as an eighteenth-century Peruvian with all the negative qualities this implied, Graffigny breaths life into the Black Legend. In her vision of the conquest, the Spaniards appear as greedy marauders intent on destroying a peaceful and intelligent society for material gain. Romero rejects Graffigny's historical portrait. By adding footnotes, slightly altering the text's wording, and expunging phrases altogether, Romero rewrites the conquest. In her novel, the conquest becomes a valued national project aimed at spreading Christian doctrine among a spiritual, but unknowingly idolatrous, people. However, the message she sends with Zilia's conversion is less about Peru and more about her hopes for a religious reformation in Europe itself, one that would replace false expressions of belief with true piety.

Romero's text exemplifies how translation could be a powerful tool for women to publicize their views without the potential danger inherent in original authorship. By using the original as a template instead of the final word, Romero found room to express her own ideas through the text itself, something not uncommon among eighteenth-century translators. While she makes her arguments from the margins, literally, her forceful footnotes and provocative changes place her own views at center stage. In part, Romero's arguments are an extension of Graffigny's own. When Graffigny condemns women's idleness, vanity, and overconsumption, Romero responds with her own censure of female folly. When Graffigny critiques women's lack of education, Romero chastises men for preventing female learning. When Graffigny laments women's limited choices, Romero concurs by embracing the assessment of female enclosure. However, by voicing her own views rather than placing them in the mouth of Zilia, Romero gives new force to the gender critique inherent in Graffigny's plot.

The notion that Spain's religiosity impeded its progress is a powerful trope that Romero herself addresses in the form of the Black Legend. In this version of the past, Spaniards become barbarians and savages who raped and pillaged virtuous and complex civilizations in the name of God and gold. Unable to overcome its religious fervor, Spain remains the nation of Christianity, that dark force that would forever inhibit its Enlightenment. In contrast to this historical narrative, Romero's translation argues that

Christianity is not the dark force: ignorance and hypocrisy are. When Zilia is won over to Christianity through reasoned debate, when she embraces faith after becoming convinced of its veracity, Romero rejects the traditional dichotomy of light and dark. For Romero, there is nothing problematic about arguing, on the one hand, for the need to cultivate women's reason and, on the other, for instilling passion in the country's religious devotees.

In fact, this combination of reason and passion is key to Romero's re-creation of Graffigny's Peruvian princess. The rational Zilia of Graffigny's narrative becomes at once rational and passionate in Romero's version. An educated woman, Zilia employs reasoned inquiry to evaluate and eventually adopt Christian beliefs, but, in Romero's eyes, it is her passionate embrace of her new religion that sets her above the typical European. This fusion of reason and passion is what, for Romero, makes Zilia a truly enlightened woman. Romero complicates the normal opposition of reason and passion, enlightenment and religion, and in doing so places religion and passion at the heart of the rational sphere of public debate. In essence, Romero's text valorizes traditionally feminine qualities, enabling impassioned women to enter the realm of rational discourse on a par with men.

On the face of it, this formulation seemed to broaden women's path to politicization. After all, this argument, which combined in women the passionate and the rational, simply constituted the logical extension of the *junta de damas'* praise of women's emotive, maternal nature in its members' articulation of female citizenship. However, by designating women's passion as a central feature of their involvement in civil society, Romero's ideal distanced women from the Enlightenment model of the critical, rational citizen. The trajectory of this discourse, from reason to rational passion, shows how women's claim to citizenship increasingly moved away from the very ideology that had sponsored their emergence into the citizenry in the first place. In the end, Romero's formulation proved tenable only within the covers of her remarkable book. In the social, political, public realm of nineteenth-century Spain, passion and reason, women and men came to understand themselves as parts of separate, and indeed unequal, worlds.[64]

Conclusion

The story of emerging female citizens in the eighteenth century does not have as happy an ending as one might have hoped. Given the tremendous energy, intellectual force, and social influence Spanish women had in Enlightenment discourse and activities, it is perhaps surprising, even disappointing, that they were not able to sustain this momentum. In the first half of the nineteenth century, particularly after 1815, women lost many of the gains they had made during the previous one hundred years. Spain's nineteenth-century *tertulias* were dominated by male intellectuals, and the Madrid-based *junta de damas* did not play the prominent role that it had played only years earlier. The next few decades did not witness the same flowering of women's writing and artistic production, and many female authors restricted their publications to female-appropriate genres such as poetry. This new century spawned the clear articulation of a separate spheres ideology, where women, now the angels in the home, lost much of the ground they had gained the century before.

Rather than constituting an abrupt shift, however, the angel-of-the-house paradigm that dominated women's lives in the nineteenth century was rooted in the gendered discourse that came to define women's public role in Enlightenment Spain. The debate over women's admission to the Economic Society in Madrid shows just how quickly Spanish intellectuals moved away from the language of universal rights in defining women's place in the country's regeneration. The push for women's incorporation into this royal-sponsored institution stemmed from an increased belief in women's natural equality and capabilities—a shift in public opinion amply demonstrated by the debate over Feijoo's *Defense of Women* and the increasing female participation in the *tertulia* and the Royal Academy of Fine Arts of San Fernando. However, as male intellectuals advocated women's presence in the ranks of the Economic Society, they outlined relatively passive roles for female citizens, where social standing largely dictated the nature of women's participation. *Socios'* arguments referenced the particular utility of women, not women's ability to participate on an equal level with male citizens, and thus removed the debate from the language of liberal ideology altogether.

In order to negotiate a place for themselves in the nation's reform movement, women reacting to this circumscribed version of female citizenship often relied on arguments about the particular merits of women, rather than liberal theory's emphasis on universality and natural rights. Faced with both the need to justify their participation in the world of Enlightenment reform and the desire to carve out a sphere of real activity for themselves, women resorted to a number of seemingly contradictory arguments. At times, they invoked their equal status and equal rights, while at other times they relied on arguments grounded in their special status as women. This was true in the case of female authors who sought the publication of their works, and it was true in the statute debates of the Economic Society, in which *socias* argued simultaneously for their full incorporation into and independence from the rest of the Society. For the *socias*, utilizing arguments for separation became a powerful tool for avoiding dependence and turned the Society's assumption of their subsidiary, and thus inferior, status on its head.

Similarly, María Romero Masegosa y Cancelada's thoughtful rendition of Graffigny's *Lettres d'une péruvienne* bespoke how women, both rational and passionate, could play a key role in the nation's growth. In Romero's eyes, Enlightenment intellectuals erroneously valued reason over passion and, in doing so, neglected the power of these two forces combined. The reconciliation of reason and passion, as represented both in Romero's translation and in the *damas'* claim for the emotive power of maternal citizenship, evidenced the flexibility of liberal discourse as Spanish women put it into practice. By articulating these various claims, women gained the right to participate actively in the reform of the nation. The wealth of texts published by women during this era and the *junta de damas'* active reform agenda evidence how successful women were in negotiating their place in the nation's regeneration.

What, then, is the significance of this story—both the great rise in women's visibility in the eighteenth century and their seeming retreat from civic life in the nineteenth? This book has shown that the process that facilitated women's entrance into—and ushered them out of—the social center of modern Spain is complex and cannot simply be blamed on the inadequacies of liberal theory. Arguments about women's place in the nation did not occur in a vacuum, but rather formed a part of broader political discussions on nationhood, modernity, and progress. As these larger discussions unfolded, they revealed that men and women did not see appeals to universal rights as theoretically incompatible with a gender-specific civil society. Calls for female action, rather than unchanging and unadulterated appeals to equality, arose from and confronted shifting political realities and conceptions. The Spanish case shows that political ideologies are not static but acquire their meaning in the daily negotiation between discourse and lived experience.

That Spanish women did not succeed in making this flexible version of citizenship work was not their fault. Gender, passion, integration, class, and equality are issues that still trouble the workings of democracy in the modern era. That Spanish women shifted tactics and pointed to their unique status as women is understandable; it was probably the only strategy they could have successfully employed, considering the limited citizenship role men had begun to assign to them. Spain's *ilustradas* could not have foreseen that their strategies would lead to a version of the liberal state that gendered the citizenry male—one that maintained a powerful sway during most of the nineteenth and twentieth centuries and casts long shadows over our own time. The eighteenth century was no female paradise, but the combined effect of women like Josefa Amar y Borbón, the Count-Duchess of Benavente, and Ana María Mengs cannot be ignored. Against the tremendous odds of patriarchy, women seized an opportune moment and forged an active role for themselves in the nation. Women occupied a significant space in the civic realm in Enlightenment Spain, and remnants of their activity, discourse, and strategies would remain for new waves of emerging female citizens to revive and revise.

Notes

INTRODUCTION

1. The relationship between Goya and the Duchess of Alba so intrigued surrealist filmmaker Luis Buñuel that in 1927 he composed a screenplay surrounding the affair titled *Goya*. See Pedro Christian García Buñuel, ed., *Guión y synopsis cinematográfica de Luis Buñuel* (Teruel: Instituto de Estudios Turolenses, 1992). Buñuel's film never came to the screen; Henry Koster's 1959 film *The Naked Maja* did. It featured Ava Gardner and Anthony Franciosa as the artistically entwined pair. Carlos Blanco Soler, Antonio Piga Pascual, and Manuel Pérez Petinto discuss the details of Alba's exhumation in *La duquesa de Alba y su tiempo* (Madrid: Ediciones y Publicaciones Españolas, S.A., 1949).

2. On Francisco de Goya's portrayal of women, see the exhibition catalogue for a show at the National Gallery of Art: Janis A. Tomlinson, ed., *Goya: Images of Women* (New Haven: Yale University Press, 2002). Also see Rebecca Haidt, "*Los besos de amor* and *La maja desnuda:* The Fascination of the Senses in the Ilustración," *Revista de Estudios Hispánicos* 29 (1995): 477–503; and Susan Waldmann, *Goya and the Duchess of Alba* (Munich: Prestel-Verlag, 1998). For more on the Duchess of Alba's life, see Carmen Barberá, *La duquesa de Alba* (Barcelona: Editorial Planeta, S.A., 1995); and Joaquín Ezquerra del Bayo, *La Duquesa de Alba y Goya: Estudio biográfico y artístico* (Madrid: Aguilar, 1959).

3. Among the now hallmark studies are Dena Goodman, *The Republic of Letters: A Cultural History of the French Enlightenment* (Ithaca: Cornell University Press, 1994); and Linda K. Kerber, *Women of the Republic: Intellect and Ideology in Revolutionary America* (Chapel Hill: University of North Carolina Press, 1980).

4. Jean Sarrailh's *L'Espagne éclairée de la seconde moitié du XVIIIe siècle* (Paris: C. Klincksieck, 1954) and Richard Herr's *The Eighteenth-Century Revolution in Spain* (Princeton: Princeton University Press, 1958) remain key points of departure for contemporary scholars of Spain's Enlightenment. More recent studies include Joaquín Álvarez Barrientos and José Checa Beltrán, eds., *El siglo que llaman ilustrado: Homenaje a Francisco Aguilar Piñal* (Madrid: Consejo

Superior de Investigaciones Científicas, 1996); Joaquín Álvarez Barrientos, François Lopez, and Inmaculada Urzainqui, *La república de las letras en la España del siglo XVIII* (Madrid: Consejo Superior de Investigaciones Científicas, 1995); Francisco Sánchez-Blanco Parody, *El absolutismo y las luces en el reinado de Carlos III* (Madrid: Marcial Pons, 2002); Francisco Sánchez-Blanco Parody, *La Ilustración en España*, ed. Akal Hipecu, Historia del pensamiento y la cultura no. 29 (Madrid: Ediciones Akal, S.A, 1997); and Francisco Sánchez-Blanco Parody, *La mentalidad ilustrada* (Madrid: Taurus Ediciones, S.A., 1999).

5. For excellent examples of these differing models of studying women, see Bonnie S. Anderson and Judith P. Zinsser, *A History of Their Own: Women in Europe from Prehistory to the Present* (New York: Harper and Row, 1988); and Joan Wallach Scott, *Gender and the Politics of History*, Gender and Culture Series (New York: Columbia University, 1988).

6. Jürgen Habermas, *The Structural Transformation of the Public Sphere: An Inquiry into a Category of Bourgeois Society*, trans. Thomas Burger and Frederick Lawrence (Cambridge: MIT Press, 1989). Page references are to the 1998 MIT Press paperback edition.

7. Mary P. Ryan, "Gender and Public Access: Women's Politics in Nineteenth-Century America," in *Habermas and the Public Sphere*, ed. Craig Calhoun (Cambridge: Cambridge University Press, 1992), 261.

8. Among the most important works to critique Habermas from a gendered perspective are Catherine Hall, "Private Persons versus Public Someones: Class, Gender, and Politics in England, 1780–1850," in *White, Male, and Middle Class: Explorations in Feminism and History* (New York: Routledge, 1992), 151–171; Joan B. Landes, *Women and the Public Sphere in the Age of the French Revolution* (Ithaca: Cornell University Press, 1988); Glenna Matthews, *The Rise of Public Woman: Woman's Power and Woman's Place in the United States, 1630–1970* (New York: Oxford University Press, 1992); Johanna Meehan, ed., *Feminists Read Habermas: Gendering the Subject of Discourse* (New York: Routledge, 1995); Carole Pateman, "Feminist Critiques of the Public/Private Dichotomy," in *The Disorder of Women: Democracy, Feminism, and Political Theory* (Cambridge, U.K.: Polity Press, 1989), 118–140; the forum on the public sphere with Daniel Gordon, David A. Bell, and Sarah Maza in *French Historical Studies* 17, no. 4 (Fall 1992): 882–953; and Bonnie G. Smith, *Ladies of the Leisure Class: The Bourgeoises of Northern France in the Nineteenth Century* (Princeton: Princeton University Press, 1981).

9. Joan B. Landes, "The Public and the Private Sphere: A Feminist Reconsideration," in *Feminists Read Habermas: Gendering the Subject of Discourse*, ed. Johanna Meehan (New York: Routledge, 1995), 91–116; and Landes, *Women and the Public Sphere in the Age of the French Revolution*.

10. Lynn Hunt, *The Family Romance of the French Revolution* (Berkeley: University of California Press, 1993), 203.

11. French historians have begun to examine how women's continued presence in public life post-1789 complicates this picture. See, for example, Carla Hesse, *The Other Enlightenment: How French Women Became Modern*

(Princeton: Princeton University Press, 2003); and Steven D. Kale, *French Salons: High Society and Political Sociability from the Old Regime to the Revolution of 1848* (Baltimore: Johns Hopkins University Press, 2004).

12. See, for example, Nicholas Henshall, *The Myth of Absolutism: Change and Continuity in Early Modern European Monarchy* (New York: Longman, 1992); and Helen Nader, *Liberty in Absolutist Spain: The Habsburg Sale of Towns, 1516–1700* (Baltimore: Johns Hopkins University Press, 1990).

13. Peter Gay, *The Enlightenment: An Interpretation*, 2 vols. (New York: Knopf, 1966–1969).

14. Some key works include Anthony J. La Vopa and Lawrence E. Klein, eds., *Enlightenment in Europe, 1650–1850* (San Marino, CA: Huntington Library, 1988); J. G. A. Pocock, *Barbarism and Religion*, vols. 1 and 2 (Cambridge: Cambridge University Press, 1999); Knud Haakonssen, ed., *Enlightenment and Religion: Rational Dissent in Eighteenth-Century Britain* (New York: Cambridge University Press, 1996); James E. Bradley and Dale K. Van Kley, eds., *Religion and Politics in Enlightenment Europe* (Notre Dame, IN: University of Notre Dame Press, 2001), David Sorkin, "From Context to Comparison: The German Haskalah and Reform Catholicism," *Tel Aviver Jahrbuch für Deutsche Geschichte* (Israel) 20 (1991): 23–58; and David Sorkin, "Reform Catholicism and Religious Enlightenment," *Austrian History Yearbook* 30 (1999): 187–219.

15. On the importance of retaining some sense of the cosmopolitan nature of the Enlightenment, see John Robertson, "The Enlightenment above National Context: Political Economy in Eighteenth-Century Scotland and Naples," *Historical Journal* 40, no. 3 (1997): 667–97.

16. Carmen Martín Gaite's *Usos amorosos del dieciocho en España*, 5th ed. (Barcelona: Editorial Anagrama, 1994)—translated by María G. Tomsich as *Love Customs in Eighteenth-Century Spain* (Berkeley: University of California Press, 1991)—was one of the initial explorations into the world of the eighteenth-century Spanish woman. Other pioneers include Paula de Demerson, *La Condesa de Montijo, una mujer al servicio de las luces* (Madrid: Fundación Universitaria Española, 1976), whose work has recovered much on women in the Economic Societies, and Paloma Fernández-Quintanilla, *La mujer ilustrada en la España del siglo XVIII* (Madrid: Ministerio de Cultura, 1981), who pinpointed a number of avenues for further archival work. Fernández-Quintanilla published a series of articles largely based on research from this book. See "Una española ilustrada: Doña María Isidra Quintina de Guzmán y de la Cerda," *Tiempo de Historia* 5, no. 60 (November 1979): 96–105; "La junta de damas de honor y mérito," *Historia 16* 5, no. 54 (October 1980): 65–73; "Los salones de las 'damas ilustradas' madrileñas en el siglo XVIII," *Tiempo de Historia* 5, no. 52 (March 1979): 44–53; and "Un traje nacional femenino. Floridablanca quiso uniformar a las españolas," *Historia 16* 3, no. 30 (October 1978): 115–21.

17. See, for example, David R. Ringrose, *Spain, Europe, and the "Spanish Miracle," 1700–1900* (Cambridge: Cambridge University Press, 1996); and Adrian Shubert, *A Social History of Modern Spain*, A Social History of Europe Series (London: Routledge, 1992). Much of this historiography is indebted to

similar work on industrialization, such as Maxine Berg, *The Age of Manufactures, 1700–1820* (London: Fontana Press, 1985); and Myron Guttman, *Toward the Modern Economy: Early Industry in Europe, 1500–1800* (New York: Knopf, 1988); and on political modernization, such as David Blackbourn and Geoff Eley, *The Peculiarities of German History: Bourgeois Society and Politics in Nineteenth-Century Germany* (Oxford: Oxford University Press, 1984).

18. Sally Ann Kitts, *The Debate on the Nature, Role, and Influence of Woman in Eighteenth-Century Spain* (Lewiston: Edwin Mellen Press, 1995).

19. Emilio Palacios Fernández's *La mujer y las letras en la España del siglo XVIII* (Madrid: Ediciones del Laberinto, S.L., 2002) provides a nice synthesis of much of this work. See chapters 2, 4, and 6 of my text for additional bibliography.

20. Josefa Amar y Borbón was one of the most important women writers of her day. Of the more recent work done on Amar y Borbón, the best is by Constance A. Sullivan. See "Constructing Her Own Tradition: Ideological Selectivity in Josefa Amar y Borbón's Representation of Female Models," in *Recovering Spain's Feminist Tradition*, ed. Lisa Vollendorf (New York: Modern Language Association, 1991), 142–59; "Josefa Amar y Borbón and the Royal Aragonese Economic Society," *Dieciocho: Hispanic Enlightenment* 15, nos. 1–2 (1992): 95–148, which also includes a number of transcribed documents concerning Amar y Borbón's life and writings; "Josefa Amar y Borbón (1749–1833)," in *Spanish Women Writers: A Bio-Bibliographical Source Book*, ed. Linda Gould Levine, Ellen Engelson Marson, and Gloria Feiman Waldman (Westport, CT: Greenwood Press, 1993), 32–43, which includes a brief survey of Amar y Borbón's life and writings as well as an excellent analysis of Amar y Borbón's treatment by scholars; and "The Quiet Feminism of Josefa Amar y Borbón's 1790 Book on the Education of Women," *Indiana Journal of Hispanic Literatures* 2, no. 1 (1993): 49–73.

21. Mónica Bolufer Peruga, *Mujeres e ilustración: La construcción de la femininidad en la Ilustración española* (Valencia: Artes Gráficas, S.A., 1998).

22. See Linda K. Kerber, *No Constitutional Right to Be Ladies: Women and the Obligations of Citizenship* (New York: Hill and Wang, 1998).

23. One instructive example is scholarship on women's consumer riots, which shows women to be essential political actors beyond the realm of official politics. See, for example, Pamela Beth Radcliff, "Citizens and Housewives: The Problem of Female Citizenship in Spain's Transition to Democracy," *Journal of Social History* 36, no. 1 (2002): 77–100; and Pamela Beth Radcliff, "Women's Politics: Consumer Riots in Twentieth-Century Spain," in *Constructing Spanish Womanhood: Female Identity in Modern Spain*, ed. Victoria Lorée Enders and Pamela Beth Radcliff (Albany: State University of New York Press, 1999), 301–23.

24. Mónica Bolufer Peruga and Isabel Morant Deusa, "On Women's Reason, Education, and Love: Women and Men of the Enlightenment in Spain and France," *Gender and History* 10, no. 2 (August 1998): 187.

25. Count of Floridablanca to Domingo de Iriarte, Oct. 20, 1791, quoted in Herr, *Eighteenth-Century Revolution*, 317.

26. Herr, *Eighteenth-Century Revolution*, 297.
27. Ibid., 336.
28. For a lengthier discussion of this, see ibid., chapter 13.

1. THE WOMAN QUESTION

1. Benito Jerónimo Feijoo y Montenegro, *Defensa de la mujer*, ed. Victoria Sau (Barcelona: Icaria, 1997), 15. Unless otherwise indicated, all translations are mine.

2. For example, scholars have tied at least thirty-seven works to derogatory comments Feijoo made about the medical profession. See Agustín Millares Carlo, "Apéndice," in Benito Jerónimo Feijoo y Montenegro, *Teatro crítico universal*, vol. 1, *Clásicos castellanos*, vol. 48 (Madrid: Espasa-Calpe, S.A., 1941), 55–78, cited in Herr, *Eighteenth-Century Revolution*, 39. For a more recent edition of *Teatro crítico universal*, see Feijoo, *Teatro crítico universal*, 7th ed., ed. Angel Raimundo Fernández González (Madrid: Cátedra, 2002).

3. Elizabeth Franklin Lewis, "Feminine Discourse and Subjectivity in the Works of Josefa Amar y Borbón, María Gertrudis Hore, and María Rosa Gálvez" (Ph.D. diss., University of Virginia, 1993), 29. As a result, there is quite an extensive bibliography on Feijoo's work in general. See, for example, Ignacio Elizalde Armendariz, "Feijóo, representante del enciclopedismo español," in *II simposio sobre el Padre Feijóo y su siglo*, ed. Cátedra Feijoo, vol. 1 (Oviedo: Centro de Estudios del Siglo XVIII, 1981), 321–45, which considers Feijoo in the context of the French encyclopedists and explains which writers most influenced his work. For more on Feijoo's views on women and the debate they sparked, see Bolufer Peruga, *Mujeres e ilustración*, 29–59; Edward V. Coughlin, "The Polemic of Feijóo's 'Defensa de las mujeres,'" *Dieciocho: Hispanic Enlightenment* 9, nos. 1–2 (1986): 74–85; Kitts, *The Debate on the Nature*, especially 13–50; Palacios Fernández, *La mujer y las letras*, 22–28; and Paloma de Villota, "El siglo de la Ilustración y la capacidad intelectual de la mujer," in *Mujeres y hombres en la formación del pensamiento occidental*, vol. 2, ed. Virginia Maquieira D'Angelo (Madrid: Ediciones de la Universidad Autónoma de Madrid, 1989), 185–96.

4. Herr, *Eighteenth-Century Revolution*, 40.

5. English translations during Feijoo's lifetime include *An Essay on Woman; or, Physiological and Historical Defense of the Fair Sex* (London: W. Bingley, 1765); *An Essay on the Learning, Genius, and Abilities of the Fair Sex* . . . (London: D. Steel, 1774); and *Three Essays or Discourses on the Following Subjects, a Defense or Vindication of the Women* . . . (London: T. Becket, 1778). For more bibliographic information, see Palacios Fernández, *La mujer y las letras*, 25.

6. Gisela Bock, *Women in European History*, trans. Allison Brown (Oxford: Blackwell Publishers, 2002), 4.

7. Jacob Ornstein, "Misogyny and Pro-Feminism in Early Castilian Literature," *Modern Language Quarterly* 3 (1942): 226. For a broader discussion of early feminist claims, see Constance Jordan, *Renaissance Feminism: Literary Texts and Political Models* (Ithaca: Cornell University Press, 1990).

8. Ornstein, "Misogyny and Pro-Feminism," 226.

9. Ornstein argues that few anti-female texts existed: "The scarcity of anti-feminist documents contrasts with the luxuriant development of pro-feminist literature. It can be maintained that a certain urging of Spanish gallantry forbids the calumny of a sex to whom only respect and veneration are due, and which demands an instantaneous defense when these obligations are violated" (ibid., 233).

10. My analysis of Isabel relies heavily on the work of Elizabeth A. Lehfeldt, including "Ruling Sexuality: The Political Legitimacy of Isabel of Castile," *Renaissance Quarterly* 53 (2000): 31–56; and "The Gender of Shared Sovereignty: Texts and the Royal Marriage of Isabella and Ferdinand," in *Women, Texts, and Authority in the Early Modern Spanish World*, ed. Marta V. Vicente and Luis R. Corteguera (Aldershot: Ashgate, 2004), 37–55. Also critical to understanding how fifteenth-century writers reacted to the problematic question of female rule, either as supporters or as critics of Isabel's reign, is Barbara F. Weissberger's outstanding volume *Isabel Rules: Constructing Queenship, Wielding Power* (Minneapolis: University of Minnesota Press, 2004). Also see her "'Deceitful Sects': The Debate about Women in the Age of Isabel the Catholic," in *Gender in Debate from the Early Middle Ages to the Renaissance*, ed. Thelma Fenster and Clare A. Lees (New York: Palgrave, 2002), 207–35, for discussion of how the presence of a female monarch shaped fifteenth- and sixteenth-century gender debates.

For additional studies of Isabel's life and reign, see Tarsicio de Azcona, *Isabel la Católica: Estudio crítico de su vida y su reinado* (Madrid: Biblioteca de Autores Cristianos, 1993); David A. Boruchoff, ed., *Isabel la Católica, Queen of Castile: Critical Essays* (New York: Palgrave Macmillan, 2003), especially Elizabeth Teresa Howe's "Zenobia or Penelope? Isabel la Católica as Literary Archetype," 91–102; Peggy K. Liss, *Isabel the Queen: Life and Times* (New York: Oxford University Press, 1992); and Marvin Lunenfeld, "Isabella I of Castile and the Company of Women in Power," *Historical Reflections* 2, no. 4 (1977): 207–29.

11. On Juana, see Bethany Aram, "Juana 'the Mad's' Signature: The Problem of Invoking Royal Authority, 1505–1507," *Sixteenth-Century Journal* 29, no. 2 (1998): 331–58.

12. For more on Enrique, including attacks on his sexuality, see Barbara Weissberger, "'A tierra, puto!': Alfonso de Palencia's Discourse of Effeminacy," in *Queer Iberia: Crossing Cultures, Crossing Sexualities*, ed. Gregory Hutcheson and Josiah Blackmore (Durham, N.C.: Duke University Press, 1999), 291–324; and Weissberger, *Isabel Rules*, chapter 3.

13. Lehfeldt, "The Gender of Shared Sovereignty," 39. Also see Weissberger, *Isabel Rules*, chapter 3.

14. Lehfeldt, "The Gender of Shared Sovereignty," 42. For Weissberger's analysis of *Jardín*, see *Isabel Rules*, 29–44.

15. Julio Puyol, ed., *Crónica incompleta de los Reyes Católicos (1469–1476)* (Madrid: Tipografía de Archivos, 1934), 239.

16. Lehfeldt, "The Gender of Shared Sovereignty," 49–50.

17. Lehfeldt, "Ruling Sexuality," 50–51.
18. Mary Elizabeth Perry, *Gender and Disorder in Early Modern Seville* (Princeton: Princeton University Press, 1990). On Cádiz, see Paloma Fernández Pérez, "Mujeres y burguesía en el Cádiz del siglo XVIII," in *La burguesía española en la edad moderna*, ed. L. M. Enciso, vol. 1 (Valladolid: Universidad de Valladolid, 1996), 281–98; and Paloma Fernández Pérez, *El rostro familiar de la metrópoli: Redes de parentesco y lazos mercantiles en Cádiz, 1700–1812* (Madrid: Siglo XXI de España Editores, 1997).
19. Andres Navagero, *Viaje a España*, trans. José María Alonso Gamo (Valencia: Editorial Castalia, 1951), 57, quoted in Perry, *Gender and Disorder*, 14.
20. Perry, *Gender and Disorder*, 9.
21. Rainer H. Goetz, "The Problematics of Gender/Genre in *Vida i sucesos de la monja alférez*," in *Women in the Discourse of Early Modern Spain*, ed. Joan F. Cammarata (Gainesville: University Press of Florida, 2003), 91–107; Mary Elizabeth Perry, "From Convent to Battlefield," in *Queer Iberia: Crossing Cultures, Crossing Sexualities*, ed. Gregory Hutcheson and Josiah Blackmore (Durham, NC: Duke University Press, 1999), 394–419. Also see Catalina de Erauso, *Memoir of a Basque Lieutenant Nun Transvestite in the New World*, trans. Michele Stepto and Gabriel Stepto (Boston: Beacon Press, 1996); and Sherry Velasco, *The Lieutenant Nun: Transgenderism, Lesbian Desire, and Catalina de Erauso* (Austin: University of Texas, 2000). For a broader look, see Susan Migden Socolow, *The Women of Colonial Latin America* (Cambridge: Cambridge University Press, 2000).
22. See Electa Arenal, "The Convent as Catalyst for Autonomy: Two Hispanic Nuns of the Seventeenth Century," in *Women in Hispanic Literature: Icons and Fallen Idols*, ed. Beth Miller (Berkeley: University of California Press, 1983), 147–83; Elizabeth A. Lehfeldt, *Religious Women in Golden Age Spain: The Permeable Cloister*, Women and Gender in the Early Modern World Series (Aldershot: Ashgate, 2005); and Lisa Vollendorf, *Reclaiming the Body: María de Zayas's Early Modern Feminism* (Oxford: Oxford University Press, 2001), 131–39. On colonial Latin America, see Kathryn Burns, *Colonial Habits: Convents and the Spiritual Economy of Cuzco, Peru* (Durham, NC: Duke University Press, 1999).
23. See Lehfeldt, *Religious Women*, chapter 2, for discussion of convent estate management, and chapter 3 for nuns' legal actions.
24. See Lehfeldt, *Religious Women*, chapter 1; Elizabeth A. Lehfeldt, "Spatial Discipline and Its Limits: Nuns and the Built Environment in Early Modern Spain," in *Gender, Architecture, and Power in Early Modern Europe*, ed. Helen M. Hills (Aldershot: Ashgate, 2003), 131–49; and María Pilar Manero Sorolla, "On the Margins of the Mendozas: Luisa de la Cerda and María de San José (Salazar)," in *Power and Gender in Renaissance Spain: Eight Women of the Mendoza Family, 1450–1650*, ed. Helen Nader (Urbana: University of Illinois Press, 2004), 113–31. For more on widows in Spain, see Jodi Bilinkoff, "Elite Widows and Religious Expression in Early Modern Spain: The View from Avila," in *Widowhood in Medieval and Early Modern Europe*, ed. Sandra Cav-

allo and Lyndan Warner (London: Longman, 1999), 181–92; and Stephanie L. Fink De Backer, "Widows at the Nexus of Family and Community in Early Modern Castile" (Ph.D. diss., University of Arizona, 2003).

25. See Jodi Bilinkoff, *The Avila of Santa Teresa: Religious Reform in a Sixteenth-Century City* (Ithaca: Cornell University Press, 1989); Gilian T. W. Ahlgren, *Teresa of Avila and the Politics of Sanctity* (Ithaca: Cornell University Press, 1996); Alison Weber, *Teresa of Avila and the Rhetoric of Femininity* (Princeton: Princeton University Press, 1990); and Alison Weber, "The Three Lives of the *Vida:* The Uses of Convent Autobiography," in *Women, Texts, and Authority in the Early Modern Spanish World,* ed. Marta V. Vicente and Luis R. Corteguera (Aldershot: Ashgate, 2004), 105–25. For a broader discussion of female visionaries as political actors, see Luis R. Corteguera, "The Making of a Visionary Woman: The Life of Beatriz Ana Ruiz, 1666–1735," in *Women, Texts, and Authority in the Early Modern Spanish World,* ed. Marta V. Vicente and Luis R. Corteguera (Aldershot: Ashgate, 2004), 165–82.

26. See Elizabeth A. Lehfeldt, "Discipline, Vocation, and Patronage: Spanish Religious Women in a Tridentine Microclimate," *Sixteenth-Century Journal* 30, no. 4 (1999): 1009–30; and Lehfeldt, *Religious Women,* chapters 4–6.

27. Magdalena S. Sánchez, *The Empress, the Queen, and the Nun: Women and Power at the Court of Philip III of Spain* (Baltimore: Johns Hopkins University Press, 1998). Also see Magdalena S. Sánchez, "Melancholy and Female Illness: Habsburg Women and Politics at the Court of Philip III," *Journal of Women's History* 8, no. 2 (Summer 1996): 81–102.

28. For a concise discussion of women and inheritance practices in Castile, see Lehfeldt, *Religious Women,* chapter 2. In the introduction to her volume *Power and Gender in Renaissance Spain: Eight Women of the Mendoza Family* (Urbana: University of Illinois Press, 2004), editor Helen Nader argues that noble women's involvement in helping families maintain, consolidate, and increase their influence both locally and nationally was accepted and even expected. That women's power was sanctioned in this way has led Nader to argue that matriarchy existed alongside patriarchy in early modern Spain. Whether the degree of autonomy women exercised in elite society should be labeled matriarchal is debatable; however, her point that women's activism does not always challenge patriarchy but can actually serve to reinforce it is important. See the wonderful essays in *Power and Gender* for examples of elite women's influence.

29. María Isabel Barbeito Carneiro, "Feminist Attitudes and Expression in Golden Age Spain: From Teresa de Jesús to María de Guevara," in *Recovering Spain's Feminist Tradition,* ed. Lisa Vollendorf (New York: Modern Language Association of America, 2001), 48–68. On *beatas,* also see Mary Elizabeth Perry, "*Beatas* and the Inquisition in Early Modern Seville," in *Inquisition and Society in Early Modern Europe,* ed. Stephen Haliczer (London: Croom Helm, 1987), 147–68. On another form of female religious organization, see Susan Eileen Dinan, "Confraternities as a Venue for Female Activism during the Catholic Reformation," in *Confraternities and Catholic Reform in Italy, France,*

and Spain, ed. John Patrick Donnelly and Michael W. Maher, Sixteenth-Century Essays and Studies, vol. 44 (Kirksville, MO: Thomas Jefferson University Press, 1999), 191–213.

30. Renée Levine Melammed, *Heretics or Daughters of Israel?: The Crypto-Jewish Women of Castile* (New York: Oxford University Press, 1999). Also see Mary E. Giles, ed., *Women in the Inquisition: Spain and the New World* (Baltimore: Johns Hopkins University Press, 1999), part 1; and Gretchen D. Starr-LeBeau, "Writing (for) Her Life: *Judeo-Conversas* in Early Modern Spain," in *Women, Texts, and Authority in the Early Modern Spanish World*, ed. Marta V. Vicente and Luis R. Corteguera (Aldershot: Ashgate, 2004), 57–72. On women as guardians of Islamic tradition, see Ronald E. Surtz, "Morisco Women, Written Texts, and the Valencia Inquisition," *Sixteenth-Century Journal* 32, no. 2 (2001): 421–33.

31. For compilations of this recent scholarship, see Giles, *Women in the Inquisition*; Marta V. Vicente and Luis R. Corteguera, eds., *Women, Texts, and Authority in the Early Modern Spanish World* (Aldershot: Ashgate, 2004); and Lisa Vollendorf, ed., *Recovering Spain's Feminist Tradition* (New York: Modern Language Association of America, 2001)

32. Miguel de Cervantes, *Don Quixote*, book 1, chapter 33, quoted in Georgina Dopico Black, *Perfect Wives, Other Women: Adultery and Inquisition in Early Modern Spain* (Durham, NC: Duke University Press, 2001), 2.

33. *La formación de la mujer cristiana*, the Castilian translation of *De institutione feminae christianae* prepared by Juan Justiniano, was printed in Valencia in 1528; Alcalá in 1529; Sevilla in 1535; Zamora in 1539; Zaragoza in 1539, 1545, and 1555; and Valladolid in 1584. In addition to being published in these eight Spanish editions, the work was also translated into and printed in French, Italian, German, and English during the sixteenth century. Like Vives's work, León's text also benefited from a number of editions, published in Salamanca in 1583, 1586, 1587, 1595, and 1603, and in Madrid in 1632. Antonio Palau y Dulcet and Agustín Palau Baquero, *Manual del librero hispanoamericano*, vol. 27 (Barcelona: Librería Palau, 1976), 420–24. For an interesting case study that shows the continuing influence of these texts in the eighteenth century, see Kelly Donahue-Wallace, "*La casada imperfecta:* A Woman, a Print, and the Inquisition," *Mexican Studies* 18, no. 2 (2002): 231–50.

34. Juan Luis Vives, *The Education of a Christian Woman: A Sixteenth-Century Manual*, ed. and trans. Charles Fantazzi (Chicago: University of Chicago Press, 2000), 72.

35. Fray Luis de León, *La perfecta casada*, with a prologue by José López Navarro (Madrid: Ediciones Rialp, S.A., 1968), 45.

36. Vives, *Education of a Christian Woman*, 186.

37. León, *La perfecta casada*, 139.

38. Ibid., 147.

39. Vives, *Education of a Christian Woman*, 254.

40. Jose López Navarro, prologue to *La perfecta casada*, by Fray Luis de León (Madrid: Ediciones Rialp, S.A. 1968), 14.

41. León, *La perfecta casada*, 85.
42. Vives, *Education of a Christian Woman*, 110.
43. Ibid., 195. Also see Juan Luis Vives, *De los deberes del marido*, in *La mujer cristiana: De los deberes del marido y Pedagogía pueril*, ed. and trans. Lorenzo Riber (Madrid: M. Aguilar, 1944).
44. María Carmen García-Nieto París, ed., *Ordenamiento jurídico y realidad social de las mujeres, siglos XVI a XX: Actas de las cuartas jornadas de investigación interdisciplinaria* (Madrid: Universidad Autónoma de Madrid, 1986), 49.
45. Though Zayas was the most outspoken, she was by no means alone. Scholars are still uncovering seventeenth-century texts by and about women. See, for example, Teresa Langle de Paz, "Beyond the Canon: New Documents on the Feminist Debate in Early Modern Spain," *Hispanic Review* 70, no. 3 (2002): 393–420, which analyzes an anonymous 1699 defense of women that Langle de Paz suggests demonstrates "an uninterrupted feminist tradition in Early Modern Spain" (395).
46. Amy Katz Kaminsky gives details about some of sixteenth-century Spain's educated female elite in her introduction to *Water Lilies: An Anthology of Spanish Women Writers from the Fifteenth through the Nineteenth Century* (Minneapolis: University of Minnesota Press, 1996), 1–14.
47. Lisa Vollendorf, "'No Doubt It Will Amaze You': María de Zayas's Early Modern Feminism," in *Recovering Spain's Feminist Tradition*, ed. Lisa Vollendorf (New York: Modern Language Association of America, 2001), 105.
48. Stephen Gaselee, "The Spanish Books in the Library of Samuel Pepys," *Supplement to the Bibliographical Society's Transactions* 2 (1921): 1–49.
49. María de Zayas y Sotomayor, *The Enchantments of Love*, trans. H. Patsy Boyer (Berkeley: University of California Press, 1990), 1, quoted in Vollendorf, *Reclaiming the Body*, 64.
50. Ibid., 65.
51. María de Zayas y Sotomayor, *The Disenchantments of Love*, trans. H. Patsy Boyer (Binghamton, NY: State University of New York Press, 1997), 37–38, quoted in Vollendorf, *Reclaiming the Body*, 85.
52. Zayas, *Disenchantments*, 244, quoted in Vollendorf, "No Doubt It Will Amaze You," 110.
53. Zayas, *Disenchantments*, 108, quoted in Vollendorf, "No Doubt It Will Amaze You," 112.
54. Ibid., 116.
55. Ibid.
56. Archivo Histórico Nacional, Madrid, Spain, Consejos Legajo 5556 (1).
57. May 4, 1790, letter in ibid.
58. Feijoo's *Defense of Women* is not the only text in which he expresses his views on women. Among his other interesting writings are "Uso más honesto de la arte obstetricia," in which he argues for women's training as obstetricians, and "Carta de un religioso a una hermana suya, exhortándola a que prefiriese el estado de religiosa al de casada," in which he explains some of the advantages for

women who become nuns rather than wives. For more specifics on his other texts, see Kitts, *Debate on the Nature,* 26–29.

59. Richard Herr points out that Feijoo's essays cited more than two hundred French texts and sixty-four other foreign works. For more on Feijoo's sources, see G. Delpy, *L'Espagne et l'esprit européen: L'oeuvre de Feijoo (1725–1760)* (Paris: Librairie Hachette, 1936).

60. B. G. Feijoo, *Teatro crítico universal,* vol. 5, no. 5, quoted in Herr, *Eighteenth-Century Revolution,* 37.

61. Feijoo, *Defensa de la mujer,* 18–19.

62. Thomas Laqueur, *Making Sex: Body and Gender from the Greeks to Freud* (Cambridge: Harvard University Press, 1990).

63. Feijoo, *Defensa de la mujer,* 20.

64. Ibid., 16–17.

65. Ibid., 17.

66. Ibid., 18.

67. Ibid.

68. Ibid., 18.

69. Ibid., 29–30.

70. Ibid., 38.

71. Ibid., 39.

72. Ibid., 40.

73. Ibid., 56.

74. Ibid., 57.

75. Ibid., 59–73. Feijoo drew his examples mainly from Spain, Italy, France, and Germany, causing one contemporary English translator to add his own section on great women from the British Isles. For a broader analysis of the use of catalogues of women in eighteenth-century Spanish texts, see Mónica Bolufer Peruga, "Galerías de 'mujeres ilustres' o el sinuoso camino de la excepción a la norma cotidiana (ss. XV–XVIII)," *Hispania* 60, no. 204 (2000): 181–224.

76. Feijoo, *Defensa de la mujer,* 61.

77. Ibid., 77.

78. In Kitts, *Debate on the Nature,* chapter 2 examines a number of the responses to Feijoo's *Defense of Women.* Also see Bolufer Peruga, *Mujeres e ilustración,* chapter 1.

79. Manco de Olivares's pamphlet was dated December 1, 1726. See Kitts, *Debate on the Nature,* 33–34.

80. Laurencio Manco de Olivares, *Contradefensa crítica a favor de los hombres: Que en justas quejas manifiesta . . . contra la nueva defensa de las mujeres que escribió el M.R.P. Maestro F. Benito Jerónimo Feijoo en su Teatro crítico,* 1726, quoted in Kitts, *Debate on the Nature,* 33.

81. Salvador José Mañer, *Crisol crítico-theológico, histórico, político physico, y mathemático en que se quilatan las materias, y puntos que se le han impugnado al Theatro Crítico y pretendido defender en la demostración crítica el M.R.P. Lector Fr. Martín Sarmiento* (Madrid: Bernardo Peralta, 1734), quoted in Bolufer Peruga, *Mujeres e ilustración,* 40.

82. Jaime Ardanaz y Centellas, *Tertulia histórica y apologética o examen crítico, donde se averigua en el crisol de monumentos antiguos y escritores de mayor autoridad, lo que contra Fray Jerónimo Savanarola escribe el Rmo. P. Maestro Fray Benito Jerónimo Feijoo en el tomo primero del Teatro crítico universal* (n.p., 1727).

83. Bolufer Peruga, *Mujeres e ilustración*, 55.

84. Kitts, *Debate on the Nature*, 42.

85. Juan Antonio Santareli, *Estrado crítico en defensa de las mugeres contra el Theatro crítico universal de errores comunes*, 1727, quoted in Kitts, *Debate on the Nature*, 44.

86. Ricardo Basco Flancas, *Apoyo a la defensa de las mugeres, que escrivió el R. Mo P. Fr. Benito Feyjó y crisis de la contra-defensa crítica que a favor de los hombres, y contra las mugeres, dió a luz temerariamente Don Laurencio Manco de Olivares, en dictamen que da de ella a una señora* (Madrid: Viuda de Blas de Villanueva, 1727), 3.

87. Ibid., 7.

88. Ibid., 33.

89. Martín Martínez, *Carta defensiva que sobre el primer tomo del Theatro crítico universal . . . le escribió su más aficionado amigo* (Madrid: Imprenta Real, 1726), quoted in Bolufer Peruga, *Mujeres e ilustración*, 46.

90. Miguel Juan Martínez y Salafranca, *Desagravios de la muger ofendida: Contra las injustas quexas de la Contradefensa crítica de D. Laurencio Manco de Olivares* (Madrid: Pedro Díaz, 1727).

91. See Kitts, *Debate on the Nature*, 39.

92. Benito Jerónimo Feijoo, *Ilustración apologética al primer y segundo tomo del Teatro-crítico donde se notan más de cuatrocientos descuidos al autor del Anti-teatro y de los setenta, que éste imputa al autor del Teatro crítico, se rebajan los sesenta y nueve y medio* (Madrid: Miguel Escribano, 1773), quoted in Kitts, *Debate on the Nature*, 46.

93. Catherine Jaffe, "Subject Pleasure: Writing the Woman Reader in Eighteenth-Century Spain," *Dieciocho: Hispanic Enlightenment* 22, no. 1 (Spring 1999): 38.

94. Juan Sempere y Guarinos, *Ensayo de una biblioteca española de los mejores escritores del reynado de Carlos III*, vol. 3 (Madrid, 1786), 24, as translated by Herr in *Eighteenth-Century Revolution*, 40–41.

2. ADMITTED EQUALS

1. Nigel Glendinning, *A Literary History of Spain: The Eighteenth Century* (New York: Barnes and Noble, 1972), 15. For a study of images of female readers in particular, see Jaffe, "Subject Pleasure," 35–59.

2. On the French salons, see Goodman, *The Republic of Letters;* Kale, *French Salons;* Landes, *Women and the Public Sphere;* and Carolyn Lougee's classic study *"Le Paradis des Femmes": Women, Salons, and Social Stratification in Seventeenth-Century France* (Princeton: Princeton University Press, 1976). For

England, see Deborah Heller, "Bluestocking *Salons* and the Public Sphere," *Eighteenth-Century Life* 22, no. 2 (1998): 59–82. For the German case, see Deborah Hertz, *Jewish High Society in Old Regime Berlin* (New Haven: Yale University Press, 1988). Chapter 2 of Goodman's *The Republic of Letters* provides an excellent analysis of the various twentieth-century historiographical approaches to the study of the *salonnière*, including a discussion of Daniel Mornet's *La vie parisienne au XVIIIe siècle: Leçons faites à l'école des hautes études sociales* (Paris: F. Alcan, 1914); of Kingsley Martin's *French Liberal Thought in the Eighteenth Century: A Study of Political Ideas from Bayle to Condorcet* (New York: Harper and Row, 1963); and of Alan Kors's *D'Holbach's Coterie: An Enlightenment in Paris* (Princeton: Princeton University Press, 1963).

Of course, there continue to be some doubters who call into question the centrality of salon women. Jolanta T. Pekacz's *Conservative Tradition in Pre-Revolutionary France: Parisian Salon Women* (New York: Peter Lang, 1999), for example, argues that *salonnières* were not indispensable hosts, but rather mere recipients of male attendees' ideas who often became the mouthpieces of conservative ideals. Pekacz, however, relies on many of the tropes of those whom Goodman solidly refutes, as well as erroneously confuses the content of women's salons with the role of salon women. Also see Ulrike Weckel, "A Lost Paradise of a Female Culture? Some Critical Questions Regarding the Scholarship on Late Eighteenth- and Early Nineteenth-Century German Salons," trans. Pamela E. Selwyn, *German History* 18, no. 3 (2000): 310–36.

3. While interpretations like Goodman's have helped reshape the view of women's role in various European cities' salons, they have yet to make a significant mark on historical writing on Spain. In part, this is due to the paucity of sources available for a study of the Spanish case. Some scholars of women's history who have begun to argue for the significance of women in Spain's *tertulias* include Fernández-Quintanilla, *La mujer ilustrada;* Fernández-Quintanilla, "Los salones de las 'damas ilustradas'"; Margarita Ortega López, "El siglo XVIII," in *Las mujeres de Madrid como agentes de cambio social,* ed. Margarita Ortega López (Madrid: Instituto Universitario de Estudios de la Mujer, Universidad Autónoma de Madrid, 1995), 3–55; Africa Martínez Medina, *Espacios privados de la mujer en el siglo XVIII* (Madrid: Horas y Horas, 1995), 58–68; and Palacios Fernández, *La mujer y las letras,* 95–115.

4. While this chapter focuses on the four *tertulias* hosted by Sarría, Benavente, Fuerte-Híjar, and Montijo, this does not mean these were the only female-organized gatherings in Madrid. These were the only *tertulias* of a serious nature for which I was able to uncover sufficient documentation; however, there may have been many more. In his journal, William Beckford describes his visit during December 1787 to one of Madame Badaan's biweekly gatherings, where approximately forty to fifty women met to discuss a wide variety of issues. Beckford recounts the lively conversation he had during this meeting, noting in particular a discussion on the poetry of the Persian writer Hafiz and the Turkish author Mesihi. *The Journal of William Beckford in Portugal and Spain, 1787–1788,* ed. Alexander Boyd (London: Rupert Hart-Davis, 1954),

301–2. Unfortunately, I have found no reference to this *tertulia* outside of Beckford's account.

In *Espacios privados*, 19, 62–64, Martínez Medina indicates that the Duchess of Berwick hosted a regular *tertulia* for diplomatic figures at court, and that Cecilia Vanvitelli, the wife of Sabatini, hosted her own *tertulia* at her residence on the Calle de la Reja or, after her move in 1790, on the Plaza de los Afligidos. Various Italian artists such as Anton Raphaël Mengs, Juan Tami, and Felice Gazola were among those rumored to attend Vanvitelli's gatherings. Martínez Medina also mentions the possibility of gatherings hosted by the Duchess of Abrantes, the Countess of Jaruco, and the Marquise of Merlin (118).

The Viscount of San Alberto references the *tertulia* of the Marquise of Branciforte for foreign diplomats and Spanish intellectuals, and Vicente Orti y Brull's biography of the Duchess of Villahermosa, entitled *Doña María Manuela Pignatelli de Aragón y Gonzaga, Duquesa de Villahermosa*, credits her with a *tertulia* as well (vol. 1, *Los Duques de Villahermosa* [Madrid: Viuda é Hijos de M. Tello, 1896]). In other words, the scope of these *tertulias* may have been more extensive than what is suggested by the documentation I have found to date.

5. Martín Gaite, *Love Customs*, 42.

6. Ibid. Here Martín Gaite relies heavily on the writings of José Clavijo y Fajardo, who was highly critical of women, to make her assertions.

7. Manuel Serrano y Sanz, *Apuntes para una biblioteca de escritoras españolas desde el año 1401 al 1833*, vol. 1 (Madrid: Impresores de la Real Casa, 1903), 22.

8. Margarita Nelken, *Las escritoras españolas* (Barcelona: Editorial Labor, S.A., 1930), 172.

9. Joseph R. Jones, "María Rosa de Gálvez: Notes for a Biography," *Dieciocho: Hispanic Enlightenment* 18, no. 2 (Fall 1995), 174. For more on Gálvez's life, see Julia Bordiga Grinstein, "La rosa trágica de Málaga: Vida y obra de María Rosa de Gálvez," *Anejos de Dieciocho* 3 (2003), especially chapter 1.

10. Sullivan, "Josefa Amar y Borbón (1749–1833)," 32.

11. Ibid., 32–33.

12. Cepeda y Mayo's exam was recorded in Don Manuel Espinosa de los Monteros, *Relación de los exercicios literarios, que la Señora Doña María del Rosario Cepeda y Mayo, hija de D. Francisco de Cepeda y Guerrero . . . y de la Señora Doña Isabel Mayo, actuó los días 19, 22, y 24 de Septiembre del presente año . . .* (Cádiz: Impresor Real de Marina, 1768). Also see Pedro Álvarez de Miranda, "¿Una niña en la Academia? El caso de María del Rosario Cepeda y su orgulloso padre," *Boletín de la Real Academia Española* 82 (January–June 2002): 39–45.

13. For consideration of how the expansion of women's educational opportunities in the eighteenth century had roots in earlier centuries, see Lisa Vollendorf, *The Lives of Women: A New History of Inquisitional Spain* (Nashville: Vanderbilt University Press, 2005), 171–86.

14. See Paula de Demerson, *María Francisca de Sales Portocarrero (Condesa*

del Montijo): Una figura de la Ilustración (Madrid: Editora Nacional, 1975), chapter 2; Gloria A. Franco Rubio, "Educación femenina y prosopografía: Las alumnas del Colegio de las Salesas Reales en el siglo XVIII," *Cuadernos de Historia Moderna* 19 (1997): 171–81. For a good comparative perspective on the vast intellectual life that thrived within convent walls, also see Charlotte Woodford, "Women as Historians: The Case of Early Modern German Convents," *German Life and Letters* 52, no. 3 (1999): 271–80.

15. Orti y Brull, *Doña María Manuela Pignatelli*, 110–13.
16. Demerson, *María Francisca de Sales Portocarrero*, chapter 2.
17. Serrano y Sanz, *Apuntes para una biblioteca*, vol. 1, 268.
18. The Countess of Fernán-Nuñez, for example, resided in Paris for a short while. January 15, 1790, minutes of the *junta de damas* indicate that Fernán-Nuñez sent her annual dues to the organization from Paris where she was temporarily staying. *Libro de actas de la junta de damas*, 1790–1791, Archivo de la Real Sociedad Económica Matritense de Amigos del País (hereafter SEM Archivo), Libro A/56–2.
19. Orti y Brull, *Doña María Manuela Pignatelli*, 132–33.
20. For a discussion of the dating of Lemos's salon, see María Dolores Tortosa Linde, *La Academia del Buen Gusto de Madrid (1749–1751)* (Granada: Universidad de Granada, Departamento de Filología Española, 1988), 23–28.
21. The *Actas de la Academia del Buen Gusto*, albeit incomplete, still exist and are housed at the Biblioteca Nacional in Madrid, ms. 18.476. The twenty-six folders contain incomplete member attendance lists, partial lists of works discussed, and some manuscripts of various literary works. This is the largest source base available for any eighteenth-century *tertulia*. See Tortosa Linde, *La Academia del Buen Gusto*, which provides a brief history of the *academia* as well as a partial transcription of what is found in the acts. For previous studies of the *academia*, see Leopoldo Augusto de Cueto, *Poetas líricos del siglo XVIII*, Biblioteca de autores españoles desde la formación del lenguaje hasta nuestros días, no. 61 (Madrid: Ediciones Atlas, 1952), lxxxvi–xcii; and José Miguel Caso González, *De ilustración y de ilustrados* (Oviedo: Instituto Feijóo de Estudios del Siglo XVIII, 1988), 53–100.
22. The principal members of Sarría's *tertulia* are listed in the manuscript records of the academia along with the nickname that each member had: Antonio Nasarre y Ferriz, el Amuso; the Count of Torrepalma (1706–1767), el Difícil; Agustín de Montiano y Luyando (1697–1764), el Humilde; José Villarroel, el Zángano; José Antonio Porcel y Salablanca (1715–1794), el Aventurero, Ignacio de Luzán Claramunt de Suelves y Gurrea (1702–1754), el Peregrino; Luis José Velázquez de Velasco (1722–1772), el Marítimo, Duke of Bejar, el Sátiro; and Count of Saldueña, el Justo Desconfiado. Besides the nine principal members listed above, there were four other members who are only known by their nicknames (El Remiso, El Ícaro, El Aburrido, and El Incógnito) and who have not been identified. Tortosa Linde, *La Academia del Buen Gusto*, 35.

Relying on a document by Luzán, Cueto in *Poetas líricos del siglo XVIII* indicates that it is also possible that the Duke of Medina-Sidonia, the Duke of

Arcos, Francisco Scotti Fernandez de Córdoba, the Marquis of Casasola, the Marquis of Montehermoso, the Marquesa of la Olmeda, Alonso Santos de León, and Francisco de Zamora participated (lxxxix–xc). Four of these may be the members who are listed in the academia's records simply by nickname. While Caso González in *De ilustración y de ilustrados* believes, as Cueto suggests, that the academia meetings were most likely attended by more than the core group, he does not consider this group because of the meager proof of their participation (55–56).

23. For example, this is how Sempere y Guarinos refers to it in *Ensayo de una biblioteca española de los mejores escritores del reynado de Carlos III*, vol. 6, 140.

24. For a precise listing of the works discussed at the salon's meetings, see Tortosa Linde's transcription in *La Academia del Buen Gusto*, 73–123. For the actual works themselves, consult ms. 18.476 at the National Library in Madrid.

25. Caso González, *De ilustración y de ilustrados*, 81.

26. In his "El teatro de Nicasio Alvarez de Cienfuegos y las ideas de la Ilustración," Pablo Carrascosa Miguel indicates that Cienfuegos presented his *Zorayda* at Fuerte-Híjar's *tertulia*. Carrascosa Miguel's paper from the title conference held in Madrid on November 27–30, 1999, is published in *Repercusiones de la Revolución francesa en España* (Madrid: Hispagraphis, S.A., 1990), 645–75. Also see Palacios Fernández, *La mujer y las letras*, 112–13.

27. Fuerte-Híjar's writings are only beginning to be studied. See the work of Alberto Acereda, including *La Marquesa de Fuerte-Híjar: Una dramaturga de la Ilustración: Estudio y edición de* La sabia indiscreta (Cádiz: Universidad de Cádiz, 2000); "Una comedia inédita de la Ilustración española: *La sabia indirecta* de la Marquesa de Fuerte-Híjar," *Dieciocho: Hispanic Enlightenment* 20, no. 2 (Fall 1997): 231–62; and "Una figura relegada de la Ilustración: La Marquesa de Fuerte-Híjar y su *Elogio de la Reina* (1798)," *Cuadernos de Investigación Filológica* 23–24 (1997–1998): 195–212.

28. October 8, 1803, diary entry in Lady Holland, *The Spanish Journal of Elizabeth Lady Holland*, ed. Earl of Ilchester (London: Longmans, Green, and Company, 1910), 102–3. In a later section of her journal, Lady Holland writes that Montijo "was much connected with and is still extremely attached to Jovellanos, whose cause she has maintained with great ardor and firmness during his cruel persecution" (193).

29. Herr, *Eighteenth-Century Revolution*, 407.

30. Demerson, *María Francisca de Sales Portocarrero*, 115.

31. The regular male members of the Countess of Montijo's *tertulia* included Antonio Palafox, the Bishop of Cuenca; Juan Antonio Rodrigálvarez; Baltasar Calvo; Antonio Guerrero; Antonio Posada; José Yeregui; Antonio Tavira, the Bishop of Salamanca; Antonio Cuesta; Jerónimo Cuesta; Pedro de Silva; Padre Félix Amat; Joaquín Lorenzo Villanueva; Manuel Rosell; Estanislao de Lugo; Joaquín Ibarra; Ignacio López de Ayala; Juan Meléndez Valdés; and Gaspar Melchor de Jovellanos. Demerson, *María Francisca de Sales Portocarrero*, 311–12.

32. Fernández-Quintanilla, *La mujer ilustrada,* 39.

33. This incident involved Montijo's son, the Count of Teba. Teba wrote "Discurso sobre la autoridad de los ricos hombres y cómo la fueron perdiendo hasta llegar al punto de opresión en que se hallan hoy" and planned to present it to the Academy of History. Beforehand, Teba sent a copy of the treatise anonymously to the royal family. It took all of Montijo's power to prevent her son's exile. According to Fernández-Quintanilla, many people thought Montijo herself had composed the treatise. See Fernández-Quintanilla, *La mujer ilustrada,* 40.

34. Condesa de Yebes, *La condesa-duquesa de Benavente: Una vida en unas cartas* (Madrid: Espasa-Calpe, S.A., 1955), 70.

35. The acquisition of this palace in 1783 was part of a larger trend among Spanish nobility to move to the outskirts of Madrid, thus creating a certain distance between themselves and the monarch. Fernández-Quintanilla, *La mujer ilustrada,* 36.

36. Holland, *The Spanish Journal,* 195.

37. Among the paintings Goya completed for Benavente's home at La Alameda are *El asalto al coche, El columpio, La cucaña, La caída del burro, La conducción de una piedra en una obra, La procesión, La Pradera de San Isidro, Las cuatro estaciones, La merienda, La gallina ciega, La era,* and *Los caprichos.* Yebes, *La condesa-duquesa de Benavente,* 41–42; and Martínez Medina, *Espacios privados,* 65. For an analysis of Goya's portraits of Benavente, see Andrew Schulz, "Goya's Portraits of the Duchess of Osuna: Fashioning Identity in Enlightenment Spain," in *Women, Art, and the Politics of Identity in Eighteenth-Century Europe,* ed. Melissa Hyde and Jennifer Milam (Aldershot: Ashgate, 2003), 263–83.

38. Lady Holland explains of the Duke: "He obtained permission during his favor at Court to import from foreign countrys [sic] what books he chose for his own library, notwithstanding they were prohibited by the Inquisition, and he took advantage of this to collect a very good and extensive library, chiefly of classics, history, voyages, and books of science, which he intended for the use of the public; but this intention he was not permitted by the Governt. [sic] to carry into effect." Holland, *The Spanish Journal,* 196. A letter from the Count-Duchess of Benavente to the inquisitor general dated May 23, 1807, illustrates her interest in the library; she asks the inquisitor to ensure the delivery of eight volumes of a twenty-three-volume set of engravings that had been detained because they contained nude figures. While her husband originally ordered the work, the duchess's specific defense of it suggests she is well acquainted with it. Archivo Histórico Nacional (hereafter AHN), Sección Nobleza, Osuna Cartas 417/33.

39. Yebes, *La condesa-duquesa de Benavente,* 88.

40. Concerning discussions with musicians and composers, see ibid., 105–10, chapter 10. Concerning queries from writers, see, for example, AHN, Sección Nobleza, Osuna Cartas 417/5, 417/7, 417/10, 417/14, 417/23, and 417/28. Concerning dialogue about scientific innovations: Yebes indicates that Benavente

was the recipient of numerous gifts such as watches or a book on surgery because of her reputation for having an interest in science. She also kept a telescope in her salon. Yebes, *La condesa-duquesa de Benavente*, 54–55.

41. Yebes, *La condesa-duquesa de Benavente*, 189–91.
42. Holland, *The Spanish Journal*, 195.
43. This poem is attributed in the *Actas de la Academia del Buen Gusto* to "El Incógnito," who is one of the heretofore unidentified members of the salon. It was read at the February 19, 1750, reunion.
44. *Actas de la Academia del Buen Gusto*, carpeta 3. I am indebted to Lisa Vollendorf for her help in translating this poem.
45. *Actas de la Academia del Buen Gusto*, carpeta 3.
46. R. Merritt Cox, *Tomás de Iriarte*, Twayne's World Authors Series, 228 (New York: Twayne Publishers, 1972), 35–59.
47. Ibid., 58–59.
48. Villarroel alludes to the participation of Arcos in his book *Poesías sagradas y profanas* when he writes that his work is "written by command of their Excellencies the Duchess of Arcos and the Marquise of Sarría." Quoted in Tortosa Linde, *La Academia del Buen Gusto*, 50. Juan Sempere y Guarinos also indicates that Arcos was a member of the salon in *Ensayo de una biblioteca española*, vol. 6, 140. For more on the attendance of women, see Cueto, *Poetas líricos del siglo XVIII*, xvi–xvii; and Tortosa Linde, *La Academia del Buen Gusto*, 49–55.
49. Tortosa Linde shows that the discussion of some of Castrillo's romances would have been pertinent to the discussion of other works presented to the academy. It is not clear if Castrillo herself read these works at the meetings or if she was only known to the salon members through her friend José Villarroel, who may have brought her works to the group. Tortosa Linde, *La Academia del Buen Gusto*, 54–55.
50. Serrano y Sanz, *Apuntes para una biblioteca*, vol. 2, 25–26. This poem, entitled *La nunca bastantemente celebrada musa de mi señora la Marquesa de Castrillo había empezado un poema heróico, cuya materia eran las glorias de Salamanca, su patria, y antes de concluirlo murió*, was read at the April 23, 1750, reunion of Sarría's salon.
51. For an excellent discussion of women's admittance to the French Academy, see Mary D. Sheriff, *The Exceptional Woman: Elisabeth Vigée-Lebrun and the Cultural Politics of Art* (Chicago: University of Chicago Press, 1996), 73–104.
52. One of the more complete listings of female academicians can be found in Germaine Greer, *The Obstacle Race: The Fortunes of Women Painters and Their Work* (New York: Farrar, Straus, and Giroux, 1979), chapter 15, 292–309. Still, Greer emphasizes the limitations of academy membership for women.
53. José Parada y Santín, *Las pintoras españolas* (Madrid: Imprenta del Asilo de Huérfanos del S.C. de Jesús, 1902), 53.
54. Ibid., 54.
55. Estrella de Diego, *La mujer y la pintura del XIX español (Cuatrocientas*

olvidadas y algunas más) (Madrid: Ediciones Cátedra, S.A., 1987). Even Margarita Ortega López, who, in a brief survey of women in eighteenth-century Madrid, portrays women as fairly active seems to undermine the importance of early female academicians. Although Ortega López couches their participation in positive terms, she cannot help adding that the achievements of these academicians were limited. According to Ortega López in "El siglo XVIII," "The presence of 11 female academicians of Fine Arts in the Academy of San Fernando in Madrid in the last third of the century, or the reading of a speech from the first female academician of language, Isidra Quintina Guzmán, were prominent and well-known acts among Madrid society, though their protagonists were not of outstanding quality" (42).

Often scholars who minimize women's participation in the academy underestimate their numbers. Such is the case with Ortega López's work. And the same is true of Antonina Rodrigo in *Mujeres de España (Las silenciadas)*, who counts twelve academics of honor and six of merit in the eighteenth century ([Barcelona: Plaza and Janes, S.A., 1979], 228).

56. Diego, *La mujer y la pintura*, 53. As Carl Goldstein explains in *Teaching Art: Academies and Schools from Vasari to Albers* (Cambridge: Cambridge University Press, 1996), "During the 1700s academies became the principal centers of art instruction, so that to entertain the notion of becoming an artist was to prepare for entry into an academy" (49).

57. For more complete studies of the Academy of San Fernando, see Claude Bédat, *L'académie des beaux-arts de Madrid: 1744–1808* (Toulouse: Association des Publications de l'Université de Toulouse, 1973); and Andrés Úbeda de los Cobos, *Pintura, mentalidad, e ideología en la Real Academia de Bellas Artes de San Fernando: 1741–1800* (Madrid: Universidad Complutense de Madrid, 1988). For more general studies, also see Francisco Aguilar Piñal, "Las academias del siglo XVIII como centros de investigación," in *I Borbone di Napoli e i Borbone di Spagna*, ed. Mario Di Pinto, vol. 2 (Napoli: Guida Editori, 1985), 391–404; and Nikolaus Pevsner, *Academies of Art: Past and Present* (Cambridge: Cambridge University Press, 1940).

58. Jonathan Brown, "Academies of Painting in Seventeenth-Century Spain," in *Academies of Art: Between Renaissance and Romanticism*, ed. Anton W. A. Boschloo, 177–85 (The Hague: SDU Uitgeverij, 1989).

59. Bédat, *L'académie des beaux-arts*, 3.

60. Archivo de la Real Academia de Bellas Artes de San Fernando (hereafter RABA), Legajo 3–34/1. Bédat discusses these statutes in *L'académie des beaux-arts*, chapter 2.

61. Bédat, *L'académie des beaux-arts*, 162.

62. These numbers were compiled from a study of the *Libros de académicos* (honor, RABA, Legajo 3/14; mérito, RABA, Legajo 3/18; and supernumerario, RABA, Legajo 3/19). My figures vary a bit from those of Bédat, who indicates that there were 176 *académicos de honor*, 180 *académicos de mérito*, and 45 *supernumerarios*. Bédat, *L'académie des beaux-arts*, 161–63.

63. Juan Agustín Ceán Bermúdez, *Diccionario histórico de los más ilustres*

profesores de las Bellas Artes en España, vol. 2 (1800; reprint, Madrid: Reales Academias de Bellas Artes de San Fernando y de la Historia, 1965), 305–6.

64. RABA, Legajo 40–4/1.

65. RABA, Legajo 3/84.

66. *Distribución de los premios concedidos por el Rey Nuestro Señor á los discípulos de las nobles artes, hecha por la Real Academia de San Fernando en la junta general de 12 de julio de 1769* (Madrid: Imprenta de la Viuda de Eliseo Sanchez, 1769), 15.

67. RABA, Legajo 40–4/1.

68. Ibid.

69. Ibid.

70. Ibid.

71. The Academy admitted fifteen women as academics of honor. Of these fifteen women, nine received joint titles as academics of honor and merit, and two received joint titles as academics of honor and honorary directors. Thus, only four women were appointed solely as academics of honor.

72. *Distribución de los premios concedidos por el Rey Nuestro Señor á los discípulos de las nobles artes, hecha por la Real Academia de San Fernando en la junta general de 3 de agosto de 1766* (Madrid: Imprenta de la Viuda de Eliseo Sanchez, 1766), 28–29. Her appointment is also recorded in the academy's records; see RABA, Legajo 70–5/5. Jerónimo Herrera Navarro also lists Huéscar in his *Catálogo de autores teatrales del siglo XVIII* (Madrid: Fundación Universitaria Española, 1993), 424. Although Herrera Navarro does not point to any specific existing works that Huéscar wrote, he draws from J. A. Alvarez y Baena when he writes: "She was a studious lady and an aficionado of literature and painting. She did various translations of tragedies and other works from the French." Alvarez y Baena, *Hijos de Madrid, ilustres en santidad, dignidades, armas, ciencias, y artes: Diccionario histórico por el orden alfabético de sus nombres*, 4 vols. (Madrid: B. Cano, 1789–1791).

73. Bédat, *L'académie des beaux-arts*, 139.

74. Santa Cruz presented works at the *juntas ordinarias* on December 1, 1782, August 29, 1790, August 5, 1798, and July 25, 1805, as well as at the academy's public exhibitions of 1798, 1799, 1800, 1802, and 1805. The less active Listenois exhibited at the *juntas ordinarias* of July 6, 1788, and June 1, 1794, as well as the public exhibition of 1794.

75. *Juntas ordinarias, generales y públicas desde el año 1770 hasta 1775*, RABA, Legajo 3/83, *junta ordinaria*, April 2, 1773, 193–94.

76. *Juntas ordinarias, generales y públicas desde el año 1770 hasta 1775*, RABA, Legajo 3/83, *junta ordinaria*, June 21, 1771, 125.

77. Linda Nochlin, "Why Have There Been No Great Women Artists?" in *Women, Art, and Power and Other Essays* (New York: Harper and Row, 1988), 160.

78. Goldstein, *Teaching Art*, 55; and Nochlin, "Why Have There Been No Great Women Artists?" 160–61.

79. Nochlin, "Why Have There Been No Great Women Artists?" 159.

80. Mireia Freixa, "Las mujeres artistas desde la Revolución francesa al fin del siglo," in *Historia del arte y mujeres,* ed. Teresa Sauret (Málaga: Universidad de Málaga, 1996), 71–89.

81. An instructive discussion of women artists and the problematics of genre in the sixteenth century is Mary D. Gerrard, "Here's Looking at Me: Sofonisba Anguissola and the Problem of the Woman Artist," *Renaissance Quarterly* 47, no. 1 (1994): 74–101.

82. Goldstein, *Teaching Art,* 118.

83. María del Carmen Saíz, *Cabezas de las obras del Rafael de Urbino grabadas por María del Carmen Saíz, académica de mérito de la Real de S. Fernando* (n.p., 1816). While there is no indication of the publisher, the book records that it could be purchased on Calle Cava Baxa next to la Posada de las Castillas.

84. RABA, Legajo 55-2/1.

85. Ibid. An 1817 sheet indicating the procedures to be followed in holding public exhibitions contains instructions for submissions. According to Rule #6, the academy announced these exhibitions to the public in the *Diario de Madrid,* indicating that prospective exhibitors could submit work to be judged by professors of the academy for possible exhibition. RABA, Legajo 55-2/1.

86. *Juntas ordinarias, generales y públicas desde el año 1786 hasta 1794,* RABA, Legajo 3/85, 134–36.

87. *Juntas ordinarias, generales y públicas desde el año 1786 hasta 1794,* RABA, Legajo 3/85, *junta ordinaria,* October 5, 1794, 301.

88. Greer also notes the involvement of nonmembers in the French salons. For example, in 1791, a jury of forty artists (twenty academicians and twenty nonmembers) selected the paintings for the salon of that year. The resulting exhibition featured 794 paintings by 258 artists. Of these artists, 190 were nonmembers; 21 were women. Greer, *The Obstacle Race,* 297.

89. Ceán Bermúdez, *Diccionario histórico.* Concerning Ana Meléndez, see vol. 3, 114; María Prieto, vol. 4, 124–25; Barbara María de Hueva, vol. 2, 305–6; and the Duchess of Huéscar, vol. 4, 379–80.

90. RABA, Legajo 40-4/1. In addition to other works cited in this chapter, see the following for more information on Ana María Mengs: Ángel María Barcía y Pavón, *Catálogo de la colección de dibujos originales de la Biblioteca Nacional* (Madrid: Tipográficos de la Revista de Archivos, Bibliotecas, y Museos, 1906), #9665–6; Ceán Bermúdez, *Diccionario histórico,* vol. 2, 119–20; Joaquín de Entrambasaguas y Peña, "Tres notas para la historia del arte," *Revista de la Biblioteca, Archivo, y Museo del Ayuntamiento de Madrid* 6, no. 22 (1929): 215–20; Matilde López Serrano, *Presencia femenina en las artes del libro español* (Madrid: Fundación Universitaria Española, 1976), 27–29; Pilar de Miguel Egea, "Breve semblanza de Ana María Mengs," in *IV Jornadas de Arte: El arte en tiempo de Carlos III,* ed. Departamento de Historia del Arte Diego Velázquez, Centro de Estudios Históricos, Consejo Superior de Investigaciones Científicas (Madrid: Editorial Alpuesto, S.A., 1989), 387–93; José Luis Morales y Marín, *Pintura en España, 1750–1808* (Madrid: Ediciones Cátedra, S.A.,

1994), 290–91; Pelayo Quintero Atauri, "Ana Mengs," *Boletín de la Sociedad Española de Excursiones* 15 (1907): 13–15; Pelayo Quintero Atauri, *Mujeres ilustres: Apuntes biográficos sobre las pintoras Teresa Nicolau Parody y Ana María Mengs* (Madrid: Ibérica, 1907); and Leo R. Schidlof, *La miniature en Europe aux 16e, 17e, 18e et 19e siècles*, vol. 2 (Austria: Akademische Druck—u. Verlagsanstalt, 1964), 566.

91. Ceán Bermúdez, *Diccionario histórico*, vol. 3, 119–20.

92. Ministerio de Cultura, *Antonio Rafael Mengs, 1728–1779* (Madrid: Museo del Prado, 1980), 24; and Miguel Egea, "Breve semblanza de Ana María Mengs," 393.

93. *Distribución de los premios concedidos por el Rey Nuestro Señor á los discípulos de las nobles artes, hecha por la Real Academia de San Fernando en la junta pública de 20 de agosto de 1793* (Madrid: Imprenta de la Viuda de Ibarra, 1793), 32–33.

94. Greer, *The Obstacle Race*, 12.

95. Quintero Atauri, *Mujeres ilustres*, 14. There is no clear evidence of how much Teresa Concordia Marón participated in Ana María Mengs's artistic education. As Greer explains, "Usually the recorded master of a painter from an art dynasty is a father, regardless of his mother's role in his earliest motivation and training, but there are cases where a woman has been specifically named as the teacher of her sons and daughters." In Mengs's case, the mother's position as an artist has essentially been overlooked, probably due to the significant artistic reputation of the father. For more on mothers as art teachers, see Greer, *The Obstacle Race*, 26–27.

96. Greer, *The Obstacle Race*, 13.

97. Ceán Bermúdez, *Diccionario histórico*, vol. 4, 124–25, informs us of her work in *grabado al agua fuerte*.

98. Greer discusses the loss of many female artists' oeuvres due to the little value assigned to their work or the fact that their better works are often attributed to men who painted in similar styles. See chapter 7 of *The Obstacle Race*, 132–50.

99. *Donaciones a la Academia, 1786–1830*, RABA, Legajo 15–1/1. This work is also listed in an inventory of the academy's holdings. *Inventario: Noticia de las pinturas que posee la Real Academia de Bellas Artes de San Fernando, 1796–1805*, RABA, Legajo CF-1/2, item #43.

100. This work was first shown to the academy members in the August 3, 1794, *junta ordinaria*.

101. *Inventario: Noticia de las pinturas que posee la Real Academia de Bellas Artes de San Fernando, 1796–1805*, RABA, Legajo CF-1/2.

102. *Inventario: Noticia de las pinturas que posee la Real Academia de Bellas Artes de San Fernando, 1817*, RABA Legajo CF-2/17.

103. Ironically, all these works were relegated to the academy's warehouse in the mid-1990s. Although the museum used to have a room dedicated to the work of eighteenth-century female academicians, in a reorganization of the

museum, the result of "a new director and a new criteria," this room was dismantled and the works placed in storage.

104. Parada y Santín's *Las pintoras españolas* quotes from the acts of the academy: "'The 27th of April of 1804, Doña Micaela Ferrer, named academic of merit on the 13th of April 1777, passed away in this city. She proved herself not unworthy of this title through her continued application to painting and drawing, her ability to which she owed her maintenance, living alone and without ever distancing herself from all of the duties that make a woman worthy" (60–61).

105. Ibid., 62.

106. Ibid., 63.

3. ON EQUAL TERMS?

1. In a memorandum that he composed on October 21, 1775, and delivered to the general council of the Economic Society one week later, Marín argued that women should be admitted to the fledgling organization. Manuel José Marín, Memorandum on the admission of women to the Economic Society, to the director and members of the Sociedad Económica de Amigos del País in Madrid, Spain, October 21, 1775, SEM Archivo, Legajo 3/2, 7. Also transcribed in Olegario Negrín Fajardo, *Ilustración y educación: La Sociedad Económica Matritense* (Madrid: Editora Nacional, 1984), 133–43.

2. Perhaps the most complete examination of the debate is found in Kitts, *Debate on the Nature*, 139–72. Also see Bolufer Peruga and Morant Deusa, "On Women's Reason, Education, and Love," especially 197–205; Demerson, *María Francisca de Sales Portocarrero*, 127–37; Lucienne Domergue, *Jovellanos á la société économique des amis du pays de Madrid (1778–1795)* (Toulouse: France-Ibérie, 1971), 233–66; Fernández-Quintanilla, *La mujer ilustrada*, 55–77; Elizabeth Franklin Lewis, "Feijoo, Josefa Amar y Borbón, and the Feminist Debate in Eighteenth-Century Spain," *Dieciocho: Hispanic Enlightenment* 12, no. 2 (1989): 188–201; Elizabeth Franklin Lewis, *Women Writers in the Spanish Enlightenment: The Pursuit of Happiness*, Women and Gender in the Early Modern World Series (Aldershot: Ashgate, 2004), 26–38; Negrín Fajardo, *Ilustración y educación*, 33–38 and 131–83, which contains a number of the treatises on women's admission transcribed; Olegario Negrín Fajardo, *La educación popular en la España de la segunda mitad del siglo XVIII: Las actividades educativas de la Sociedad Económica Matritense de Amigos del País* (Madrid: Universidad Nacional de Educación a Distancia, 1987), 118–30; Palacios Fernández, *La mujer y las letras*, 62–76; and Villota, "El siglo de la Ilustración," especially 194–96. For more on the *junta de damas* in general, also see Paula de Demerson, *Catálogo de las socias de honor y mérito de la junta de damas matritense (1787–1811)*, Tirada Aparte de los Anales del Instituto de Estudios Madrileños, 7 (Madrid: Raycar, S.A., 1966); Fernández-Quintanilla, "La junta de damas," 65–73; Fernández-Quintanilla, *La mujer ilustrada*, 79–113, 125–34;

and Jean Sarrailh, *La España ilustrada de la segunda mitad del siglo XVIII*, trans. Antonio Alatorre (Madrid: Fondo de Cultura Económica, 1992), 257–59.

3. There is a large body of literature on the Economic Societies. For more on the Madrid Economic Society, see Francisco Aguilar Piñal, *La Real Sociedad Económica Matritense de Amigos del País* (Madrid: Artes Gráficas Municipales, 1972); José Luis García Brocara, *La Real Sociedad Económica Matritense de Amigos del País* (Madrid: Publicación de la Real Sociedad, 1991); and Negrín Fajardo, *Ilustración y educación*. There are also a number of monographs on Economic Societies outside of Madrid. Most of these give a brief overview of the Societies' creation and a description of their subsequent activities. See, for example, Francisco Almela y Vives, *La Real Sociedad Económica de Amigos del País de Valencia* (Valencia: Artes Gráficas Soler, S.A., 1967); Juan Luis Castellano Castellano, *Luces y reformismo: Las Sociedades Económicas de Amigos del País del reino de Granada en el siglo XVIII* (Granada: Imprenta Provincial, 1984); Rufino Cano González and R. Clara Revuelta Guerrero, *Escuelas y talleres de la Sociedad Económica de Amigos del País de Valladolid (1783–1820)* (Valladolid: Secretariado de Publicaciones e Intercambio Editorial, Universidad de Valladolid, 2002); Jorge Demerson, *La Real Sociedad Económica de Amigos del País de Avila (1786–1857)* (Avila: Imprenta de "El Diario de Avila," 1968); Jorge Demerson, *La Real Sociedad Económica de Valladolid (1784–1808): Notas para su historia*, Universidad de Valladolid, Departamento de Historia Moderna, Estudios y Documentos, 28 (Valladolid: Gráficas Andrés Martín, 1969); José Francisco Forniés Casals, *La Real Sociedad Económica Aragonesa de Amigos del País en el periodo de la Ilustración (1776–1808): Sus relaciones con el artesanado y la industria* (Madrid: Confederación Española de Cajas de Ahorros, 1978); Asunción López Martinez, *La Sociedad Económica de Amigos del País de Málaga* (Málaga: Grafima, Servicio de Publicaciones, Diputación Provincial de Málaga, 1987); and Enrique Soria Medina, *La Sociedad Económica de Amigos del País de Osuna* (Seville: Gráficas del Sur, 1975).

For more on the Economic Societies in general, see Gonzalo Anes Álvarez, "Coyuntura económica e 'ilustración': Las Sociedades de Amigos del País," in *Economía e Ilustración en la España del siglo XVIII* (Barcelona: Ediciones Ariel, 1969), 11–41; Ramón Carande, "El despotismo ilustrado de los 'Amigos del País,'" in *Siete estudios de historia de España* (Barcelona: Ediciones Ariel, 1969), 143–81; Jorge Demerson and Paula de Demerson, *La decadencia de las Reales Sociedades Económicas de Amigos del País* (Oviedo: Centro de Estudios del Siglo XVIII, Universidad de Oviedo, 1978); Herr, *Eighteenth-Century Revolution*, 154–63; Sarrailh, *La España ilustrada*, 230–89; Robert Jones Shafer, *The Economic Societies in the Spanish World (1763–1821)* (Syracuse, NY: Syracuse University Press, 1958); and Donald R. Street, "The Economic Societies: Springboard to the Spanish Enlightenment," *Journal of European Economic History* 16, no. 3 (Winter 1987): 569–85. Paula de Demerson, Francisco Aguilar Piñal, and Jorge Demerson's *Las Sociedades Económicas de Amigos del País en el siglo XVIII* (San Sebastian: Gráficas Izarra, 1974) is a bit outdated as an archive guide because of a reorganization of the Madrid Economic Society's archive, but it still contains some valuable information, including a useful bibliography.

4. Herr, *Eighteenth-Century Revolution*, 156. In "Coyuntura económica e 'ilustración,'" Anes Álvarez lists ninety-five Economic Societies formed between 1765 and 1808 (26–30).

5. The Madrid Economic Society held its first official meeting on September 16, 1775, at the Casas Consistoriales in the Plaza de la Villa.

6. Pedro Rodríguez Campomanes, *Discurso sobre el fomento de la industria popular* (Madrid: Don Antonio de Sancha, 1774), 10.

7. Campomanes estimated the population of the Spanish peninsula and surrounding islands at 11 million and calculated that half were women. From the total 5,500,000 women, he subtracted 1,500,000, who were either too young (under seven), too old, too sick, or unable to work for some other reason. Thus, he arrived at 4 million women "fit to employ themselves honestly in such industries and to aid the sustenance of their respective families." *Discurso sobre el fomento de la industria popular*, 47.

8. Antonio de la Quadra, "Memoria sobre que se dé ocupasion á las mugeres, que se suponen ociosas en Madrid, leída en la junta general de 14 de octubre de 1775," in *Memorias de la Sociedad Económica*, vol. 2 (Madrid: Don Antonio de Sancha, 1780), 14–19.

9. Ibid., 15–16.

10. Campomanes, *Discurso sobre el fomento de la industria popular*, 49.

11. Pedro Rodríguez Campomanes, *Discurso sobre la educación popular de los artesanos y su fomento*, ed. Francisco Aguilar Piñal (Madrid: Editora Nacional, 1978), 208.

12. Ibid., 209.

13. For a discussion of other discourses that consider Spanish women through the lens of the nation's Muslim past or with comparisons to the Orient, see Bolufer Peruga, *Mujeres e ilustración*, 89–97.

14. Concerned with women's limited participation in the nation's economy, Charles III promulgated a royal decree on January 12, 1779, mandating that women must in no way be prevented from working in occupations appropriate to their sex. According to the decree, "It is mandated that with no pretext shall the teaching of women and girls be impeded nor hindered, by the Guilds of this Kingdom nor any other persons, in those labors and trades that are appropriate to their sex." AHN, *Real Cédula*, no. 491; quoted in Paloma Pernil Alarcón, "Carlos III y la formación profesional de la mujer," in *Actas del Congreso Internacional sobre "Carlos III y la Ilustración,"* ed. Pablo Fernández Albaladejo, vol. 3, *Educación y pensamiento* (Madrid: Ministerio de Cultura, 1989), 446. Charles's decree illustrates a view completely in line with that of Campomanes. By training women in manufacturing, the decree explained, women's idle hands would be put to work, freeing up men to work in areas such as agriculture and military service.

Charles followed up his 1779 decree with two others aimed at making women useful workers. First, in a May 11, 1783, decree, Charles called for free schools to educate Spain's girls. As Pernil Alarcón explains, this was "the first time in Spanish history that education of poor girls was proposed." AHN, *Real Cédula*, no. 621; quoted in Pernil Alarcón, 449. Second, on September 2, 1784, Charles issued a decree "by which it is declared in support of the faculty of all the women of this Kingdom to work in the manufacture of yarn, as well as in all other Arts with which they want to occupy themselves and which are compatible with the decorum and strengths of their sex." AHN, *Real Cédula*, no. 688; quoted in Ángel López Castán, *Los gremios artísticos de Madrid en el siglo XVIII y primer tercio del siglo XIX: Oficios de la madera, textil y piel* (Madrid: Ediciones de la Universidad Autónoma de Madrid, 1991), 265. If any doubt existed concerning whether women should be allowed to participate in light industry after the 1779 decree barring restrictions on women's training in trades appropriate to their sex, this decree made it clear that women could not be prohibited from laboring in those industries.

15. Gaspar Melchor de Jovellanos, "Informe dado á la junta general de comercio y moneda sobre el libre ejercicio de las artes," in *Obras publicadas e inéditas de Don Gaspar Melchor de Jovellanos*, ed. Candido Nocedal, vol. 2 (Madrid: Ediciones Atlas, 1952), 36. Jovellanos presented his speech to the Economic Society in 1785.

16. Ibid., 33.

17. Ibid., 34.

18. Ibid.

19. Quadra also championed increased training for women in industry, but spent little time arguing for it, since he felt that the calculations stood on their own "to give proof of the benefit that would result from spinning schools." "Memoria sobre que se dé ocupasion á las mugeres," 14.

20. Campomanes, *Discurso sobre la educación popular*, 210. Campomanes also used history to prove that well-educated women could often surpass men: "If you consider past experience, it affirms that genius does not distinguish the sexes; and that well-educated women do not match men in lights [knowledge] nor in aptitude, but in manual tasks, they are much more agile than men" (211).

21. Jovellanos, "Informe sobre el libre ejercicio de las artes," 33.

22. Ibid.

23. Ibid., 34.

24. Campomanes, *Discurso sobre la educación popular*, 206.

25. Pedro Rodríguez Campomanes, "Memoria sobre la admisión de señoras, presentada a la Real Sociedad Económica de Amigos del País por el Conde de Campomanes el 18 de noviembre de 1775 sobre las admisión de las señoras en ella," in Fernández-Quintanilla, *La mujer ilustrada*, 154.

26. Campomanes, *Discurso sobre la educación popular*, 215.

27. Part of my analysis of this dress code proposal appeared previously as "Fashioning the Enlightenment: The Proposal for a Female National Dress in Eighteenth-Century Spain," *Dieciocho: Hispanic Enlightenment* 23, no. 1 (Spring 2000): 76–85.

28. Various scholars have theorized about the real identity of M.O., but the

evidence is not conclusive. Their work suggests that the author was a man, and I tend to agree, although my own assertion is based more on my view of the content of the proposal and less on concrete archival evidence. Francisco Aguilar Piñal gives two possible identifications for the author. The first is José de Espinosa y Brun. In volume 3 of his *Bibliografía de autores españoles del siglo XVIII*, Aguilar Piñal indicates that Espinosa y Brun is included in AHN, Estado, 323 (10), as the one who asked for the license to publish the treatise. In volume 6, Aguilar Piñal indicates that Antonio Palau y Dulcet and Agustín Palau Claveras attribute the tract to Francisco Mariano Nifo y Cagigal ([Madrid: Consejo Superior de Investigaciones Científicas, 1984, 1991], 3:205, 6:60. In volume 11 of their *Manual del librero hispanoamericano*, the Palaus do attribute the treatise to Nifo y Cagigal but give no indication of the source for this dedication ([Barcelona: Librería Palau, 1958], 73). Demerson hypothesizes that someone connected to the military wrote the treatise, perhaps a sailor named Navarrete (*María Francisca de Sales Portocarrero*, 163–64). Martín Gaite postulates with no clear evidence that the proposal was composed by Josefa Amar y Borbón (Martín Gaite, *Usos amorosos*, 154). This attribution is highly unlikely given Amar y Borbón's views on women.

29. *Discurso sobre el luxo de las señoras y proyecto de un traje nacional* (Madrid: Imprenta Real, 1788). There is also a facsimile edition (Madrid: Mondadori España, S.A., 1987). The *Gaceta de Madrid* announced the volume was for sale in June 1788, and an excerpt of the treatise was printed in the July 1788 edition of *Memorial Literario*, 448–53. The dress code proposal has been considered only briefly by past scholars of Enlightenment Spain. Demerson and Fernández-Quintanilla have treated it as a meaningful episode in the life of the women's council. As I explain in the next chapter, I agree with their contention that the council's strong rejection of the proposal was an important step in the organization's effort to establish itself as an independent body with its own beliefs and its own agenda. Demerson, *María Francisca de Sales Portocarrero*, 155–65; Fernández-Quintanilla, *La mujer ilustrada*, 101–8; and Fernández-Quintanilla, "Un traje nacional femenino," 115–21. In Kitts's *Debate on the Nature*, she argues that the proposal was indicative of evolving notions on women's intelligence and capabilities in the second half of the eighteenth century (208–10). I disagree with this assessment. See my "Fashioning the Enlightenment."

30. See Kitts, *Debate on the Nature*, chapters 3 and 4, especially 81–83, 115–24. For more on critics of women and clothing consumption, see Rebecca Haidt, "The Name of the Clothes. *Petimetras* and the Problems of Luxury's Refinements," *Dieciocho: Hispanic Enlightenment* 23, no. 1 (Spring 2000); 71–75; and Catherine Jaffe, "From *Precieuses Ridicules* to *Preciosas Ridículas*: Ramón de la Cruz's Translation of Molière and the Problems of Cultural Adaptation," *Dieciocho: Hispanic Enlightenment* 24, no. 1 (Spring 2001): 147–76.

31. *Discurso sobre el luxo de las señoras y proyecto de un traje nacional*, 14.

32. Ibid., 19.

33. Since one *vellón real* equaled about twenty United States cents in 1792, according to James Clayburn La Force Jr., *The Development of the Spanish Tex-*

tile Industry, 1750–1800 (Berkeley: University of California Press, 1965), this would have been about $23,600,000 in 1792 United States dollars.

34. In particular, the author points to France and England as the recipients of Spain's lost wealth. Not only does she cite the national luxury industries of these two competitors as being injurious, but she also alludes to France and England's interference in Spain's trade with her colonies. Thus, M.O. argues that purchases from French and English manufacturers and traders took a considerable chunk of the nation's wealth.

35. M.O. also points out that this situation was particularly detrimental to women: "Certainly it is not us women who lose the least in this. How many women who live in misery could have married, if they had not shown off their vanity with undue restraint? And how many of those who dress today with more pomp than their station accords them will lament their madness when age makes them know they have passed their time to establish themselves with honor, and that they are already irremediably condemned to a sad loneliness and a laborious old age?" *Discurso sobre el luxo de las señoras y proyecto de un traje nacional*, 24.

36. Ibid., 25.

37. There were a variety of responses to the perceived demographic decline in eighteenth-century Spain, but several writers agreed with M.O.'s assertion that luxury was contributing to the decline in marriages. See Kitts, *Debate on the Nature,* especially 185–90 and 206–8.

38. *Discurso sobre el luxo de las señoras y proyecto de un traje nacional*, 27.

39. Ibid., 9. In addition, M.O. ended an introductory letter addressing her proposal to Floridablanca, the king's minister, in a way that not only expressed her modesty, but underlined her patriotism: "If you do not consider this of merit, you will know to overlook it and to pardon the considerable affection of a Lady for her country."

40. Ibid., 60.

41. Fernández-Quintanilla, *La mujer ilustrada*, 106.

42. In particular, the author notes that foreign laces and embroidery must not be used and suggests the incorporation of Catalan textiles in their place. Similarly, while the author suggests that women should be free to select their own headwear, she encourages the nation to make rules regarding women's handkerchiefs, mainly to avoid the use of costly English and Italian crêpes.

43. *Discurso sobre el luxo de las señoras y proyecto de un traje nacional*, 34–35.

44. The appeal to patriotism that runs throughout the treatise was especially important in terms of encouraging women to participate in a project for the nation's benefit. The author makes clear that the dress code is not aimed at limiting freedoms, but rather is a project concerned with the nation's glory: "To prohibit certain clothing for the convenience of the State is to bear resentment toward individual freedom. To prohibit them for their own utility and to give glory to the nation is to excite them to obey with enthusiasm." Ibid., 30. Here, the author is clearly making reference to the dress restrictions created by the

Italian Leopoldo de Gregorio, the Marquis of Esquilache, who was the first secretary of state and finance under Charles III.

On March 10, 1766, Esquilache ordered *madrileños* not to wear the popular style of wide-brimmed hats and full capes. Esquilache's reasoning was that these hats and capes allowed criminals to hide their faces and thus escape arrest. The city's protest against this policy culminated in a violent riot on March 23. The following day, the king accepted the crowd's demands, notably the exile of Esquilache and a repudiation of the dress policy. Clearly, the author of this volume did not want to inspire a similar reaction to the creation of a female national dress. M.O. felt this would not happen if women understood that wearing the prescribed dress was a way of supporting their country.

45. The author did not mean for her suggestions to be an exhaustive list of the possibilities for dividing women into various classes. In fact, she points out that one of the benefits of this plan is how easily a new class can be incorporated, simply by "ordering that some silver embroidery be of gold, and that a few little braids be added to the sides and a few little ribbons to the braids." Ibid., 53

54. She does, however, mean to maintain strict guidelines. She suggests that if her treatise has left the dress of any class of women unclear, the secretary of state should fill in the blanks.

Further, the striking emphasis on maintaining even the slightest gradations of class distinction becomes even more pronounced in the very last paragraph of the treatise, where she describes what women who have sons or brothers in different stations should do: "Be it established that they have to wear the dress that corresponds to the son or brother with whom they are living[;] . . . and in case they are separated from both of them, they may wear the one that corresponds to the son or brother of a higher rank. But widows will wear that which they wore with their husbands; and daughters who have fathers, that dress which corresponds to his rank or class, and not the dress corresponding to their brother's rank, even if it is higher" (57). Here the author expresses concern for the possibility that someone might choose to wear the dress of one relative who is of a slightly higher station than her other relative, and makes clear the regulations concerning this issue. The discussion of this scenario illustrates M.O.'s overwhelming concern with containment along class lines.

46. A doorkeeper was not simply someone who stood guard at the door, but was invested with controlling access to key political figures and their offices.

47. She does not recommend this for the wives of brigadiers, field marshals, squadron leaders, lieutenant generals, or generals. She indicates that their fancy clothes would be too expensive and would not correspond to the divisions as created for the others.

48. Luis de Imbille quickly followed on the heels of Marín and Campomanes cited above: "Memoria sobre la admisión de asociadas," 1776, SEM Archivo, Legajo 3/2. Also transcribed in Negrín Fajardo, *Ilustración y educación*, 147–50. Presented on February 23, 1776.

49. Kitts's *Debate on the Nature* suggests, "The proposal appears to have been shelved and the content of the articles up to 1776 suggests that a decision

could not be reached on the question of exactly which classes of women to admit, linked to the issue of financial contribution" (147). There was a brief discussion of Marín's 1775 treatise at the meeting of the general council on December 21, 1778. Having heard that the Society was considering publishing an excerpt from his earlier speech, Marín addressed the council to request that it either print the document word for word in its entirety or not at all. According to Marín, "This subject, well exposed to the public through a simple text, and not accompanied by the reasons and proofs in which it is founded, could not only seem ridiculous, but could also give me a reputation for extravagance." Marín worried that the public would see the idea as "strange sounding" and "scandalous" if not presented with the complete text of his argument. In the end, the Society did not publish Marín's treatise, and the debate over women's admission did not resurface until January 1786. SEM Archivo, Legajo 3/2.

50. Quintina Guzmán was elected as a member of the Real Academia Española in 1784, and she earned a doctorate from the University of Alcalá in 1785. In other words, she was highly qualified to participate in the organization. Benavente was also an educated and active *ilustrada* with much to contribute to the Society. See chapter 2 for a discussion of Benavente's *tertulia*. It is possible that the Duchess of Alba was offered admission at this time but refused. See Domergue, *Jovellanos á la société économique*, 252.

51. Ignacio López de Ayala, "Papel sobre si las señoras deben admitirse como individuos de las sociedades," in *Ilustración y educación: La Sociedad Económica Matritense*, ed. Olegario Negrín Fajardo (Madrid: Editora Nacional, 1984), 176–83.

52. Ibid., 176.
53. Ibid., 177.
54. Ibid., 179–80.
55. Ibid., 178.
56. Marín, Memorandum on the admission of women, 12.
57. Ibid., 4.
58. Martín Gaite, *Love Customs*, 15.
59. Marín, Memorandum on the admission of women, 14.
60. Gaspar Melchor de Jovellanos, "Memoria sobre si se debían o no admitir las señoras en la Sociedad Económica de Madrid (1785)," in Negrín Fajardo, *Ilustración y educación*, 160. Also printed in *Poesía, teatro, prosa* (Madrid: Taurus Ediciones, S.A., 1979), 165–72, and in Domergue, *Jovellanos á la société économique*, 340–43. For more on Jovellanos's views on women, see Bonifacio Chamorro, "Jovellanos y las mujeres," *Letras: Revista del Hogar* 8, no. 85 (August 1944): 1–3.

61. Campomanes wholeheartedly seconded Marín's argument: "All of us are left persuaded by one simple reading of his excellent treatise." "Memoria sobre la admisión de señoras," 155.

62. Ibid., 157.
63. Ibid.

64. Marín rejected the little-used *socia* and the inaccurate *académica* before selecting *asociadas*. Memorandum on the admission of women, 3.

65. Ibid.

66. Campomanes, "Memoria sobre la admisión de señoras," 155.

67. Guevara suggested these parameters on February 4, 1786. With this plan, Guevara hoped the Society would benefit from female membership while also maintaining proper decorum. For further analysis of Guevara's proposal, see Domergue, *Jovellanos á la société économique*, 250.

68. The committee was made up of six *socios:* Francisco Cabarrús, the Marquis of Castrillo, the Marquis of Ayerbe, Lorenzo Irisarri, the Marquis of Alcocébar, and Gaspar Melchor de Jovellanos.

69. Jovellanos, "Memoria sobre si se debían o no admitir las señoras," 158.

70. Ibid., 160.

71. Imbille, "Memoria sobre la admisión de asociadas," 7–8.

72. As Kitts explains of Imbille, "He makes no reference to possible altruistic reasons for wanting to join and rather emphasizes what he considers the risks involved in refusing them admittance, that they may well actively work against the Society and its members in an act of vengeance. This presents a negative view of women, portraying them as petty, self-interested and vindictive." *Debate on the Nature*, 146.

73. Imbille's suggestion was not so far from Campomanes's perception of how women would fit into the organization. Campomanes himself had discussed three tiers of female participation: the *damas* who would provide the financial and administrative backing for the schools, the teachers who would provide instruction, and the poor women and girls who would benefit from a basic education and vocational training. He even suggested the possibility of admitting teachers according to merit, and without requiring a contribution, as a way of praising their efforts.

74. Marín, Memorandum on the admission of women, 6.

75. Campomanes, "Memoria sobre la admisión de señoras," 143.

76. Feijoo, *Defensa de la mujer*, 56.

77. Ibid.

78. Francisco Cabarrús, "Memoria sobre la admisión y asistencia de las mujeres en la Sociedad Patriótica," in *Ilustración y educación: La Sociedad Económica Matritense*, ed. Olegario Negrín Fajardo, 150–56. Madrid: Editora Nacional, 1984), 150–56. Also printed in Domergue, *Jovellanos á la société économique*, 344–48, and in SEM Archivo, Legajo 79/7.

79. It is not clear in what order Jovellanos's and Cabarrús's papers were actually read. As both Domergue and Kitts point out, a reference in Cabarrús's paper to a speech given by Jovellanos makes it clear that Cabarrús at least intended to go first. See Cabarrús, "Memoria sobre la admisión," 151. In addition to the question of order, there is also some mystery about whether the two treatises were read at the same meeting. In fn. 33 on p. 256 of *Jovellanos á la société économique*, Domergue refers to a letter by D. Policarpo that suggests Cabar-

rús's text was read a few days later than Jovellanos's. Further, Demerson asserts that Jovellanos was not present at the meeting during which Cabarrús's speech was read, and that Jovellanos himself read Cabarrús's treatise on March 27. See *María Francisca de Sales Portocarrero*, 131–33. Negrín Fajardo also contends that Jovellanos was absent. See *La educación popular en la España*, 124.

Regardless of the order in which, or the dates on which, they were read, it is clear that contemporaries saw the two treatises as countering each other, two extreme positions on one issue. See quotations to this effect in fn. 34 of Domergue, *Jovellanos á la société économique*, 257. In fact, Domergue ponders the possibility that Cabarrús's text was an exercise in debating, a position paper written specifically to counter Jovellanos rather than a truthful assertion of Cabarrús's belief. Domergue points to the overly extreme position that Cabarrús takes, the close relationship between Jovellanos and Cabarrús—who tended to agree on these sorts of issues—and the incongruity between Cabarrús's assertions on women and his other views as an *ilustrado* as all suggestive of the notion that this paper was the result of an agreement between the two men to have Cabarrús write a statement countering Jovellanos's arguments.

Kitts responds to Domergue's assertion: "Given that no indication of this pact is made within the two texts and the lack of any concrete evidence to support it, this can only remain an interesting speculation. In response to Domergue it could be noted that such opinions as those of Cabarrús were far from unusual and that his views are by no means as extreme as some. It could also be argued that if Jovellanos' paper was designed to represent the opposite case and as such be equally as 'extreme' as that of Cabarrús, it falls far short of the mark, presenting very limited arguments either in favour of women's admittance or in defence of their abilities as a sex, and presents a weak case for their admission to the Society." *Debate on the Nature*, 149.

80. While Cabarrús did not want women admitted as members, he did not consider their monetary support problematic. In addition to arguing that women who were predisposed to do so would donate money to the Society without the incentive of admission, Cabarrús also opined that the state, not private citizens, should be the real source of financial support for the organization. See Cabarrús, "Memoria sobre la admisión de señoras," 154.

81. Bolufer Peruga and Morant Deusa emphasize the importance of understanding Cabarrús's speech in the larger context of his life: "Until now, those who have studied the thinking of this interesting character and his political activity, have not paid attention to the significance of his opposition to the admission of women to the Economic Society of Madrid. On the other hand, those who have studied that debate, when looking at the position which Cabarrús took in the affair, have not related it satisfactorily to his social and political make-up, restricting themselves to pointing out his misogyny." "On Women's Reason, Education, and Love," 201–2.

82. Cabarrús, "Memoria sobre la admisión," 151. Cabarrús started his speech with an emotionally charged explanation of why he felt he must speak out on the issue. As Kitts aptly explains, "He paints a vivid picture of himself as the sole

champion of the truth, the only man of integrity who is not prepared to sacrifice his beliefs in order to fall in line with the misguided opinions of the majority who are swayed by popular opinion and behaviour." *Debate on the Nature,* 153. In Cabarrús's view, the truth was not that the admission of women would benefit the Society because women contributed to improving Spain's future, as had been suggested by past orators. Rather, Cabarrús suggested that the admission of women, whom he characterized as manipulative and unruly, would be very damaging to the organization.

83. Cabarrús, "Memoria sobre la admisión," 152.
84. Ibid., 153.
85. Ibid.
86. The idea that women are naturally suited for the home is expressed throughout Cabarrús's text. He explains that women should "be limited to domestic duties for which they appear to be destined." At the same time, he argues that "the given exclusion of women from all public deliberations is founded, as you can see, in reasons taken from their own sex." Ibid., 152, 154.
87. Ibid., 156.
88. Besides the work by Constance A. Sullivan cited in the introduction, other interesting analyses of Amar y Borbón's writings include Robert Baum II, "The Counter-Discourse of Josepha Amar y Borbón's *Discurso,*" *Dieciocho: Hispanic Enlightenment* 17, no. 1 (1994): 7–15; Bolufer Peruga and Morant Deusa, "On Women's Reason, Education, and Love," esp. 196–201 and 207–10; Mónica Bolufer Peruga and Isabel Morant Deusa, "Josefa Amar y Borbón: Une intellectuelle espagnole dans les debats de lumières," *Clio: Histoire, Femmes, et Sociétés* 13 (2001): 69–97; Lewis, "Feijoo, Josefa Amar y Borbón, and the Feminist Debate in Eighteenth-Century Spain," which considers the influence of Feijoo on Amar y Borbón's "Discurso en defensa de las mujeres"; Lewis, *Women Writers in the Spanish Enlightenment,* chapter 2; Eva M. Kahiluoto Rudat, "La mujer ilustrada," *Letras Femeninas* 2, no. 1 (Spring 1976): 20–32; Manuel López Torrijo, "El pensamiento pedagógico ilustrado sobre la mujer en Josefa Amar y Borbón," in *Educación e ilustración en España: III coloquio de historia de la educación* (Barcelona: Publicaciones del Departamento de Educación Comparada e Historia de la Educación, Universidad de Barcelona, 1984), 114–29; Carmen Chaves McClendon, "Josefa Amar y Borbón y la educación femenina," *Letras Femeninas* 4, no. 2 (Fall 1978): 3–11; Carmen Chaves McClendon, "Josefa Amar y Borbón: Essayist," *Dieciocho: Hispanic Enlightenment* 3, no. 2 (1980): 138–61, which includes a copy of Amar y Borbón's "Discurso en defensa del talento de las mugeres"; Carmen Chaves McClendon, "Josefa Amar y Borbón: A Forgotten Figure of the Spanish Enlightenment," in *Seven Studies in Medieval English History and Other Historical Essays Presented to Harold S. Snellgrove,* ed. Richard H. Bowers (Jackson: University Press of Mississippi, 1983), 133–39; and Carmen Chaves McClendon, "Neojansenist Elements in the Work of Josepha Amar y Borbón," *Letras Femeninas* 7, no. 1 (Spring 1981): 41–48. On Amar's role in the Aragonese Economic Society, see Guillermo Pérez Sarrión, "Casual Poverty in the Spanish Enlightenment: Josefa Amar y Borbón and the

Real Sociedad Económica Aragonesa de Amigos del País," *Dieciocho: Hispanic Enlightenment* 26, no. 2 (Fall 2003): 265–93; and Villota, "El siglo de la Ilustración," 191–93.

89. Dated June 5, 1786, Amar y Borbón's treatise was sent from Zaragoza, read at the June 24 meeting of the Society, and published two months later in the August edition of *Memorial Literario*. Her appeal for women's admission was published with a brief introduction on the debate under the title "Discurso en defensa del talento de las mugeres, y de su aptitud para el gobierno, y otros cargos en que se emplean los hombres; compuesto por Doña Josepha Amar y Borbón, sócia de mérito de la Real Sociedad Aragonesa de los Amigos del País," in *Memorial Literario* (Madrid), 32 (August 1786): 399–438. This version appears edited by Carmen Chaves McClendon in *Dieciocho: Hispanic Enlightenment* 3, no. 2 (1980): 138–61, with a brief analysis of Amar y Borbón's writings, and in Negrín Fajardo, *Ilustración y educación*, 162–76. Bolufer Peruga and Morant Deusa, in "On Women's Reason, Education, and Love," indicate it was even translated into Italian in 1789 (197). Sullivan has argued that, although Amar y Borbón refers only to the position statements published in the *Memorial Literario* in her treatise, she knew about the debate earlier than their publication and may have even been in Madrid when the treatises where originally read in January and February 1786. See "Josefa Amar y Borbón and the Royal Aragonese Economic Society," 113.

90. Madame Levacher de Valincourt, "Carta al Señor Don Francisco Cabarrús, Consejero de S.M. Católica, en respuesta al discurso que pronunció en la Real Sociedad Económica de los Amigos del País, establecida en Madrid, contra la admisión de las señoras mujeres en las sociedades literarias," *Espíritu de los Mejores Diarios Literarios que Se Publican en Europa* (Madrid), 17 (December 17–29, 1787): no. 73, 675–77; no. 74, 683–85; no. 75, 691–99; no. 76, 700–701; no. 77, 708–10. I have not been able to locate much useful information on Levacher beyond this treatise. Kitts does indicate that Levacher is listed in the *Catalogue général des livres imprimés de la Bibliothèque Nationale*, vol. 96 (Paris: Imprimerie Nationale, 1929), 959, as the author of two short poems and a plan on education housed in the Bibliothèque Nationale in Paris.

91. Amar y Borbón, "Memoria sobre la admisión de señoras en la Sociedad," in *Ilustración y educación: La Sociedad Económica Matritense*, ed. Olegario Negrín Fajardo (Madrid: Editora Nacional, 1984), 170.

92. *Espíritu de los Mejores Diarios Literarios que Se Publican en Europa* was a Madrid-based periodical that covered artistic and scientific developments in other parts of the world. As the preface to the 1787 volume indicates, "This work will make known with the greatest exactitude and impartiality all of the news, curious or important, in Metaphysics, Jurisprudence, Medicine, Surgery, Chemistry, Botany, Ecclesiastical, Civil, and Natural History, Sacred and Worldly Eloquence; finally in all of the branches of the Sciences and the Arts." The contents of the *Espíritu* were quite varied. For example, among the items included in the 1787 volume were a letter from a Roman duke on Voltaire, a notice about the establishment of an antislavery group in Philadelphia, and a

treatise by the French scientist Mr. le Gentil on binoculars. The publication was printed three times a week (Mondays, Thursdays, and Saturdays) under the editor Cristóbal Cladera (1760–1812) from 1787 to 1791.

93. The Aragon organization selected Amar y Borbón as a member in October 1782, five years before the *junta de damas* was established in Madrid. In choosing to admit her, the Aragonese Economic Society did not engage in a lengthy debate on women's admission as the Madrid Society did. Rather, the discussion focused on Amar y Borbón's specific qualifications. Amar y Borbón sent a letter to the director of the Aragonese Economic Society dated October 8, 1782, in which she made the Society aware of her qualifications and offered them a copy of the first volume of her translation of Xavier Lampillas's five-volume *Ensayo histórico-apologético de la literatura española contra las opiniones preocupadas de algunos escritores modernos italianos*. According to Sullivan, "The letter is polite and astute, for it puts the Director and the members of the Economic Society on the spot with its clear implication that Amar knows the goals and methods the Society espouses, and her delicate but firm suggestion that she herself has already produced something totally coherent with those goals."

The minutes of the October 11 meeting record the receipt of Amar y Borbón's letter and book and indicate that she was voted into membership. On October 18, Miguel de Tornos delivered a letter to Amar y Borbón to inform her of her new membership, and that same day she replied to the Economic Society, expressing her enthusiasm and pride. In this case, the issue was not the admission of women, but the admission of a specific woman. Sullivan, "Josefa Amar y Borbón and the Royal Aragonese Economic Society," 95–148.

94. Sullivan points to a number of reasons why Amar y Borbón may have curtailed her participation in the activities of the Aragonesa, ranging from family issues (her husband suffered a serious stroke in 1786) to ideological ones (her recognition that the men of the Aragonese Economic Society were little concerned with furthering the education of privileged women). Sullivan, "Josefa Amar y Borbón and the Royal Aragonese Economic Society," 114–18.

95. "Carta de Don Juan Antonio Hernández de Larrea, á Doña Josepha Amar, diciendo su parecer sobre el discurso antecedente," *Memorial Literario* (Madrid), 7 (August 1786): 438. Also reproduced in Sullivan, "Josefa Amar y Borbón and the Royal Aragonese Economic Society," 131–36.

96. Amar y Borbón, "Memoria sobre la admisión de señoras en la Sociedad," 170.

97. Levacher, "Carta al Señor Don Francisco Cabarrús," 676.

98. Kitts, *Debate on the Nature*, 162–63.

99. Levacher, "Carta al Señor Don Francisco Cabarrús," 685.

100. Amar y Borbón, "Memoria sobre la admisión de señoras en la Sociedad," in Negrín Fajardo, 165.

101. Ibid.

102. Ibid.

103. Ibid., 168.

104. Ibid., 162.
105. Ibid., 164.
106. She also assuaged fears that women would flood into the Society in great numbers. Membership in the Society, she argued, would be strictly based on merit: "In this way the men who comprise the [general] council will not have the capacity to admit women except those who merit it, nor will women solicit this distinction as beauties or as *petimetras*, but rather as industrious and useful [contributors] to the country." Ibid., 171.
107. Ibid.,
108. While the class contingencies present in the male proponents' treatises are not as pronounced in Amar y Borbón's text, her reference to the utility of women's financial contribution to the organization's coffers does suggest that she may have adhered to certain class assumptions as well.
109. Kitts, *Debate on the Nature*, 163–64.
110. Amar y Borbón, "Memoria sobre la admisión de señoras en la Sociedad," 173.
111. The text for this *real orden* can be found in a number of the *legajos* [files] of the *junta de damas*. See, for example, SEM Archivo, Legajo 93/4.
112. SEM Archivo, Legajo 93/4.
113. Juan Sempere y Guarinos, *Ensayo de una biblioteca española de los mejores escritores del reynado de Carlos III*, vol. 5 (Madrid: Imprenta Real, 1789), 213–18.

4. NEGOTIATING A FEMALE PUBLIC

1. The minutes state, "We give her this sign of recognition, for the paper she published in favor of women, when they aired the issue of whether or not we should be admitted to the Society." *Libro de actas de la junta de damas, 1787–1789*, SEM Archivo, Libro A/56-1.
2. I owe this interpretation to Constance Sullivan's skillful reading of Amar y Borbón's writings. See her argument on this in "Josefa Amar y Borbón (1749–1833)," 36.
3. Josefa Amar y Borbón, "Oración gratulatoria que la Señora Doña Josefa Amar y Borbón, elegida socia de honor y mérito, dirigió a la junta de señoras de la Real Sociedad Económica de Madrid," dated November 3, 1787, *Memorial Literario* (Madrid), December 1787, 588–92.
4. Ibid., 591.
5. Ibid., 592.
6. In her *European Feminisms, 1700–1950: A Political History* (Stanford: Stanford University Press, 2000), 21–23, Karen Offen demonstrates that "individualist" arguments grounded in the innate equality that exists among humans and "relational arguments," which emphasized women's rights as women, were often intertwined.
7. Elizabeth C. Goldsmith and Dena Goodman, eds., *Going Public: Women and Publishing in Early Modern France* (Ithaca: Cornell University Press, 1995), 2.

8. It is impossible to compile a complete list of writings and translations by women from the eighteenth century. My own research has been supplemented by some excellent resources. Invaluable are Francisco Aguilar Piñal's *Bibliografía de autores españoles del siglo XVIII*, 8 vols. (Madrid: Consejo Superior de Investigaciones Científicas, 1981–1995); and Manuel Serrano y Sanz, *Apuntes para una biblioteca de escritoras españolas desde el año 1401 al 1833*, 2 vols. (Madrid: Impresores de la Real Casa, 1903), reprinted in *Biblioteca de autores españoles desde la formación del lenguaje hasta nuestros días*, vols. 268–71 (Madrid: Ediciones Atlas, 1975).

I have also found the following secondary works helpful in the search for information on women authors: Ada M. Coe, *Catálogo bibliográfico y crítico de las comedias anunciadas en los periódicos de Madrid desde 1661 hasta 1819*, Johns Hopkins Studies in Romance Literatures and Languages, extra vol. 9 (Baltimore: Johns Hopkins Press, 1935); Lucienne Domergue, "Penser les femmes, pensée des femmes dans l'Espagne des lumières," in *Femmes-philosophes en Espagne et en Amérique Latine*, ed. Lucienne Domergue (Paris: Editions du Centre National de la Recherche Scientifique, 1989), 11–25; Carolyn L. Galerstein, ed., *Women Writers of Spain* (New York: Greenwood Press, 1986); Julia Bordiga Grinstein, "Panorama de la dramaturgia femenina española en la segunda mitad del siglo XVIII y principios del siglo XIX," *Dieciocho: Hispanic Enlightenment* 25, no. 2 (Fall 2002): 195–218; Jerónimo Herrera Navarro, *Catálogo de autores teatrales del siglo XVIII* (Madrid: Fundación Universitaria Española, 1993); Luzmaría Jiménez Faro, ed., *Hasta 1900*, vol. 1, *Poetisas españolas: Antología general* (Madrid: Ediciones Torremozas, 1996); Amy Katz Kaminsky, ed., *Water Lilies: An Anthology of Spanish Women Writers from the Fifteenth through the Nineteenth Century* (Minneapolis: University of Minnesota Press, 1996); Francisco Lafarga, *Las traducciones españolas del teatro francés (1700–1835)* (Barcelona: Publicacions i Edicions de la Universitat de Barcelona, 1993); Kathleen McNerney and Cristina Enríquez de Salamanca, *Double Minorities of Spain: A Bio-Bibliographic Guide to Women Writers of the Catalan, Galician, and Basque Countries* (New York: Modern Language Association of America, 1994); Margarita Nelken, *Las escritoras españolas* (Barcelona: Editorial Labor, S.A., 1930); María del Pilar Oñate, *El feminismo en la literatura española* (Madrid: Espasa-Calpe, S.A., 1938); Palacios Fernández, *La mujer y las letras*; and Cristina Ruiz Guerrero, *Panorama de escritoras españolas*, vol. 2 (Cádiz: Universidad de Cádiz, Servicio de Publicaciones, 1997), 33–60. In using these texts, particularly Serrano y Sanz, I have made certain choices about what writers to count. I have not included, as he does, people about whom something is written but who were not clearly writers themselves. Nor have I included women who wrote in the Americas or Portugal. I have also not considered anonymous works or undated works that I could not concretely identify as being of eighteenth-century origin. Thus, the numbers below are conservative estimates.

9. According to my research, the numbers of living female authors publishing their first work in Spain, by decade, were: 1700–1710: 1; 1711–1720: 0; 1721–1730: 7; 1731–1740: 10; 1741–1750: 7; 1751–1760: 8; 1761–1770: 8;

1771–1780: 8; 1781–1790: 28; 1791–1800: 26; 1801–1808: 6 (note that the dating for 5 identified works could not be determined and thus these are not included in the tally for any decade).

10. According to my research, the numbers of religious texts that living female authors published in Spain, by decade, were: 1700–1710: 0; 1711–1720: 0; 1721–1730: 5; 1731–1740: 8; 1741–1750: 6; 1751–1760: 4; 1761–1770: 5; 1771–1780: 6; 1781–1790: 5; 1791–1800: 3; 1801–1808: 3; date unknown: 0.

11. For more on the complex nature of textual production and circulation among female religious, see Sherry M. Velasco, "Visualizing Gender on the Page in Convent Literature," in *Women, Texts, and Authority in the Early Modern Spanish World*, ed. Marta V. Vicente and Luis R. Corteguera (Aldershot: Ashgate, 2004), 127–48. Also see María José Alvarez Faedo, *A Bio-Bibliography of Eighteenth-Century Religious Women in England and Spain* (Lewiston, NY: Edwin Mellen Press, 2005).

12. Marquise of Espeja, 1804, letter reproduced in Serrano y Sanz, *Apuntes para una biblioteca de escritoras*, vol. 1, 278.

13. Magdalena Hernández de Morejón to Pedro Cevallos, May 18, 1802, letter reproduced in Serrano y Sanz, *Apuntes para una biblioteca de escritoras*, vol. 1, 500.

14. See Diana M. Thomas, "The Book Trade in Ibarra's Madrid," *The Library* 5 (1983): 335–58.

15. Juan Bautista de Ezpeleta to Bartolomé Muñoz de Torres, November 14, 1804, letter reproduced in Serrano y Sanz, *Apuntes para una biblioteca de escritoras*, vol. 1, 279. The work received a license for publication on December 1, 1804.

16. Pedro Estala to Bartolomé Muñoz de Torres, August 3, 1798; letter reproduced in Serrano y Sanz, *Apuntes para una biblioteca de escritoras*, vol. 2, 21.

17. Ibid.

18. Pedro Estala to Bartolomé Muñoz de Torres, December 16, 1798; letter reproduced in Serrano y Sanz, *Apuntes para una biblioteca de escritoras*, vol. 2, 21.

19. Nicolas Fernández de Moratín, August 1, 1779, letter reproduced in Serrano y Sanz, *Apuntes para una biblioteca de escritoras*, vol. 1, 507.

20. Manuel Quintano y Bonifaz to Duque de la Alcudía, May 28, 1793, AHN, Estado Legajo 3248.

21. Leandro Fernández de Moratín, June 27, 1797, AHN, Consejos Legajo 5562 (4).

22. Joseph Perez García to Bartolomé Muñoz de Torres, August 9, 1797, AHN, Consejos Legajo 5562 (4). In this and subsequent quotations, italics are reproduced as shown in the original text.

23. Ibid.

24. María de las Mercedes Gómez de Castro Aragón y Ballesteros, September 5, 1797, AHN, Consejos Legajo 5562 (4).

25. Joseph Perez García to Bartolomé Muñoz de Torres, October 13, 1797, AHN, Consejos Legajo 5562 (4).

26. María de las Mercedes Gómez de Castro Aragón y Ballesteros, December 2, 1797, AHN, Consejos Legajo 5562 (4).
27. Manuel de Avila to Bartolomé Muñoz de Torres, January 9, 1798, AHN, Consejos Legajo 5562 (4).
28. *Matrícula de impresiones*, AHN, Consejo de Castilla Legajo 37, quoted in Serrano y Sanz, *Apuntes para una biblioteca de escritoras*, vol. 1, 467.
29. María de las Mercedes Gómez de Castro Aragón y Ballesteros, January 18, 1798, AHN, Consejos Legajo 5562 (4).
30. Benito Bails, December 14, 1776, AHN, Consejos Legajo 5538-7.
31. Benito Bails, July 27, 1777, AHN, Consejos Legajo 5538-7.
32. Tomás Antonio Sanchez evaluated González's 1773 work, which was approved for publication on October 9, 1773.
33. Teresa González, 1777, AHN, Consejos Legajo 5538-7.
34. Francisco Aguilar Piñal, *La prensa española en el siglo XVIII: Diarios, revistas, y pronósticos* (Madrid: Consejo Superior de Investigaciones Científicas, 1978).
35. There is no indication in the AHN file of either the identity or the opinions of the second censor, who approved González's book for publication.
36. María Rosa Gálvez to Señor Governador del Consejo, February 26, 1805, letter reproduced in Serrano y Sanz, *Apuntes para una biblioteca de escritoras*, vol. 1, 451-52.
37. María Rosa Gálvez to Señor Governador del Consejo, May 28, 1801, letter reproduced in Serrano y Sanz, *Apuntes para una biblioteca de escritoras*, vol. 1, 453-54.
38. The year the work received the license was either 1810 or 1816.
39. María Rosa Gálvez, November 21, 1803, quoted in María Rosa Gálvez, "Safo," "Zinda," y "La familia a la moda," ed. and with an intro. by Fernando Doménech (Madrid: Publicaciones de la Asociación de Directores de Escena de España, 1995), 13.
40. For an analysis of how Gálvez's plays provided a gender critique of her society, see Lewis, *Women Writers in the Spanish Enlightenment*, 97-152; and Daniel S. Whitaker's work, especially "Clarissa's Sisters: The Consequences of Rape in Three Neoclassic Tragedies of María Rosa Gálvez," *Letras Peninsulares* 5, no. 2 (1992): 239-51.
41. María Rosa Gálvez, September 19, 1804, quoted in Gálvez, "Safo," 14.
42. Some scholars have argued that Gálvez's success must be attributed to her intimate relationship with the court figure Manuel Godoy. This assertion, first made by Guillén Robles in 1873, has been the dominant opinion. Daniel Whitaker, however, finds no evidence of an amorous relationship between Godoy and Gálvez and believes theirs to be more an alliance between artist and patron than between lovers. In support of this view, Fernando Doménech questions why Gálvez would have had to take so many steps to achieve her desired goal if Godoy was such a strong advocate.
43. María Rosa Gálvez to Señores de la Junta de Dirección de Teatros, May

21, 1801, letter reproduced in Serrano y Sanz, *Apuntes para una biblioteca de escritoras*, vol. 1, 450–51.

44. *Memorial Literario* (Madrid), vol. 18, 341–42; reproduced in Serrano y Sanz, *Apuntes para una biblioteca de escritoras*, vol. 1, 511.

45. The main purpose of this June 1785 article was to praise the achievements of María Isidra Quintina Guzmán y la Cerda. In doing so, the article places Guzmán y la Cerda in the context of other female achievers of eighteenth-century Spain. For example, it refers to the translating work of Catalina de Castro and the literary exercises of María del Rosario Cepeda y Mayo. See *Memorial Literario* (Madrid), June 1785, 147–77.

46. Cayetana Aguirre y Rosales, translator's note to *Virginia, o la doncella cristiana: Historia siciliana, que se propone por modelo á las señoras que aspiran a la perfección*, by Michel-Ange Marin, vol. 1 (Madrid: Repullés, 1806), n.p.

47. Rita Caveda y Solares, translator's note to *Cartas selectas de una señora á una sobrina suya, entresacadas de una obra inglesa impresa en Filadelfia, y traducidas al español por Doña Rita Caveda y Solares* (Madrid: García y Compañía, 1800), iv–v.

48. Inés Joyes y Blake, "Apología de las mujeres," appended to Samuel Johnson, *El príncipe de Abisinia: Novella*, trans. Inés Joyes y Blake (Madrid: Imprenta de Sancha, 1798), quoted in Bolufer Peruga and Morant Deusa, "On Women's Reason, Education, and Love," 207.

49. A number of female authors dedicated their works to Benavente. In fact, Teresa González's *Estado del cielo para el año de 1778* contained a dedicatory to Benavente as well.

50. For a comparative example of female authors couching their publications in terms of national advancement, see Wendy Rosslyn, "Making Their Way into Print: Poems by Eighteenth-Century Russian Women," *Slavonic and East European Review* 78, no. 3 (2000): 407–38.

51. The minutes of the women's council meetings are recorded in a series of volumes each entitled *Libro de actas de la junta de damas*. The existing volumes cover the activities of the *junta de damas* from 1787–1798 and 1801–1811. They are housed in SEM Archivo, Libros A/56–1 through A/56 10. Libro A/56–6, which covers 1798–1801, is missing. According to Libro A/56–1, the women present at this first meeting were Montijo, Santa Eufemia, Pontejos, Villalópez, Torrecilla, Ayerve, Palacios, Benalúa, Zepeda, and Losada.

52. The activities of this commission are recorded in *Libro de acuerdos de la junta de comisión, nombrada por la Real Sociedad Económica de Madrid, para tratar del reglamento de la de señoras socias de honor y mérito, 1787–1788*, SEM Archivo, Libro 55.

53. "Informe que la junta de comisión hace a la Sociedad sobre el estado de sus sesiones," September 22, 1787, in *Libro de acuerdos de la junta de comisión, nombrada por la Real Sociedad Económica de Madrid, para tratar del reglamento de la de señoras socias de honor y mérito, 1787–1788*, SEM Archivo, Libro 55.

54. Letter from Floridablanca to Montijo dated June 16, 1788, Biblioteca de

la Real Academia de la Historia, 9/5211, 181–84. There are also copies of this letter in the Biblioteca Nacional's copy of *Discurso sobre el luxo de las señoras y proyecto de un traje nacional* (Madrid: Imprenta Real, 1788) and in the SEM Archivo, Legajo 98/16. This letter was first read at the June 27 meeting of the women's council, where the group decided to take some time before responding.

55. Letter from Montijo to Floridablanca dated July 5, 1788, Biblioteca de la Real Academia de la Historia 9/5211, 181–84. There are also copies of this letter in the Biblioteca Nacional's 1788 *Discurso* and in the SEM Archivo, Legajo 98/16. The letter is reproduced in Demerson, *María Francisca de Sales Portocarrero*, 371–73 and partly reproduced in Fernández-Quintanilla, *La mujer ilustrada*, 147–49.

56. See my "Fashioning the Enlightenment," 76–85.

57. Demerson, *La Condesa de Montijo*, 18.

58. After five months of deliberation, the *junta de comisión* announced the completion of the preliminary statutes on April 30, 1788, and distributed them on July 21, 1788. "Copia de los estatutos provisionales para la junta de señoras," July 21, 1788, SEM Archivo, Legajo 93/8.

59. Sociedad Económica de Madrid, *Estatutos de la junta de socias de honor y mérito de la Real Sociedad Económica de Madrid* (Madrid: Imprenta de Sancha, 1794), SEM Archivo, 359/13, Foll 1–30. The statutes are also transcribed in Negrín Fajardo, *Ilustración y educación*, 60–72, and Demerson, *María Francisca de Sales Portocarrero*, 376–83.

60. Montijo informed the women's council of this decision at its May 13, 1791, meeting.

61. This provision was found in article 12, title 3 of the Economic Society's statutes. The information on the discussion of this issue comes from the minutes of the July 15, 1791, meeting of the *junta de damas*. At this meeting, the president of the *junta de damas*, the Countess of Torrepalma, reported on the business of the *junta de comisión* based on a report formulated by the committee the previous afternoon. SEM Archivo, Legajo 118/28.

62. *Libro de actas de la junta de damas, 1790–1791*, SEM Archivo, Libro A/56–2.

63. Discussed at the January 13, 1792, meeting of the *junta de damas*.

64. The appointed delegation consisted of the Marquise of Valdeolmos, Teresa Losada, the Marquise of Canillejas, and Montijo. In addition, the group decided that, if the Society intended to take a delegation made up of both men and women to see Floridablanca, then Torrepalma and Montijo would represent the women's council. As a result of their visit to the general council, the Marquise of Canillejas informed the *junta de damas* at its January 20 meeting, the Society agreed to send representatives from both the general and women's councils to petition Floridablanca for the king's response. In the end, this final push was unnecessary. On January 27, Torrepalma reported that she had learned through correspondence with Josefa Castello that the king's answer had already been dispatched.

65. At the March 31, 1792, meeting of the women's council, the final order

of business was to read a memorandum from the Society dated March 29. It included one hundred copies of the king's resolution to alter article 12 of title 3 of the statutes, and each *socia* was given a copy. At the November 16, 1792, meeting of the women's council, *socias* read for the first time a memorandum from the Society requesting a list of all members who had attended at least twelve meetings in the past year and thus were eligible to vote in upcoming elections.

66. September 27, 1793, *Libro de actas de la junta de damas, 1792–1794,* SEM Archivo, Libro A/56–3.

67. *Libro de actas de la junta de damas, 1792–1794,* SEM Archivo, Libro A/56–3.

68. At the February 28, 1794, *junta de damas* meeting, this committee reported that it had begun reading the Society's statutes and would continue until the task was completed.

69. *Libro de actas de la junta de damas, 1792–1794.*

70. At the April 11 meeting, the women's council read a memorandum sent by Trúllas and Ariza from Aranjuez indicating that they had submitted the statutes for approval. In their note, they indicated that the Duke of Alcudía "received them with the greatest esteem, saying that he would read them many times to learn them, but not to change them." April 11, 1794, *Libro de actas de la junta de damas, 1792–1794,* SEM Archivo, Libro A/56–3.

71. Sociedad Económica de Madrid, *Estatutos de la junta de socias de honor y mérito,* 37. This decree was included in a letter sent to the Countess of Trúllas and the Marquise of Ariza from Aranjuez on April 10, 1794, and signed by the Duke of Alcudía. The women's council read this letter at its April 25, 1794, meeting and decided to attend the next *junta general* to discuss the publication of the newly formed statutes. At the May 10, 1794, *junta general,* the Society decided to print 750 copies of the statutes (recorded in the margin to the *actas* of the May 2, 1794, *junta de damas*). The women's council recorded notice that the new statutes were ready to be picked up at its July 11 meeting and final receipt of its copies of the new statutes at its July 18 meeting. *Libro de actas de la junta de damas, 1792–1794,* SEM Archivo, Libro A/56 3.

72. Pilar Ríos Izquierdo and Ana Rueda Roncal consider some of the differences between the 1788 and 1794 statutes in "Análisis de las normas jurídicas de la junta de damas de honor y mérito," *Torre de los Lujanes* 13 (September 1989): 151–61. However, their discussion is preliminary and their argument does not go beyond stating that formal statutes are evidence of the seriousness of the women's council.

73. Montijo responded simply to her request "that the council did not have members of this type." See February 10, 1797, minutes in *Libro de actas de la junta de damas, 1797–1798,* SEM Archivo, Libro A/56–5, and Demerson, *María Francisca de Sales Portocarrero,* 148.

74. Sociedad Económica de Madrid, *Estatutos de la junta de socias de honor y mérito,* 4.

75. Torrepalma called a *junta extraordinaria* of the women's council to meet

on December 6, 1791, in order to discuss a few urgent matters. One of the most pressing issues had to do with the Society's elections.

76. *Libro de actas de la junta de damas, 1790–1791*, SEM Archivo, Libro A/56-2.

77. See title 1, section 1 of the 1788 statutes.

78. To see their similarity to the Economic Society statutes, compare to *Estatutos para la Sociedad Económica de los Amigos del País de Madrid*, in *Ilustración y educación: La Sociedad Económica Matritense*, ed. Olegario Negrín Fajardo (Madrid: Editora Nacional, 1984), 43–59.

79. Titles 4, 5, and 6 outline the responsibilities of the offices of president, censor, and secretary, respectively. While the 1788 statutes are not as precise in defining these responsibilities, there are no significant differences between them and the resulting 1794 statutes.

80. Sociedad Económica de Madrid, *Estatutos de la junta de socias de honor y mérito*, 3.

81. "Informe que la junta de comisión hace a la Sociedad sobre el estado de sus sesiones," September 22, 1787, SLM Archivo, Libro 55.

82. These schools were considered throughout titles 7 and 8 of the provisional statutes. In the 1794 statutes, title 9 concentrates solely on the schools.

83. On November 18, the Society informed the *junta de damas* that it had established a commission made up of Manuel de Ambrona, Luis Gabaldon, Juan Agustin Garcia, and the Count of Villalobos to discuss the relationship between the two *juntas*. Upon receiving this letter, Montijo communicated with Torrepalma, who informed the men that they could come to the *junta de damas* meeting when convenient. This information is included in the November 23, 1792, *actas* of the *junta de damas*. See *Libro de las actas de la junta de damas, 1792–1794*.

84. These are Villalobos's words as summarized by Montijo in the *actas* of the *junta de damas*.

85. *Libro de actas de la junta de damas, 1792–1794*.

86. February 15, 1793, *Libro de actas de la junta de damas, 1792–1794*, SEM Archivo, Libro A/56-3.

87. The *junta general* notes for February 16, 1793, state that the issue was "discussed by the Ladies and Gentlemen in attendance." Quoted in the margin of the February 8, 1793, *Libro de actas de la junta de damas, 1792–1794*, SEM Archivo, Libro A/56-3.

88. *Extracto de lo que resulta acerca de la moción que hizo el Sr. D. Simon de Codes de si convendría que los individuos de la Sociedad concurran a las juntas de las señoras como lo hacen estas á las de dicho real cuerpo*, September 20, 1801, SEM Archivo, Legajo 135/10.

89. On August 8, the women's council took note of the Society's memorandum and penned a response. *Libro de actas de la junta de damas, 1792–1794*.

90. Recorded in the December 7, 1792, *Libro de actas de la junta de damas, 1792–1794*, SEM Archivo, Libro A/56-3.

91. An August 11, 1794, memorandum was sent to Montijo to announce the

junta extraordinaria. In this letter, the Society also asked the women's council to postpone elections, which it already had scheduled for August 12. At the August 13 *junta extraordinaria,* Montijo read a letter in the name of the women's council that indicated it had canceled elections out of good will. The letter also took pot shots at the Society for its slow movement in finalizing the women's statutes. See SEM Archivo, Legajo 135/10.

92. Specifically, Zurana points to the minutes of the August 12 meeting that signaled elections would be held on August 18, as well as to the completed elections and the request for their approbation by the king before the Society's approval of the meeting, as evidence of the insubordination of the *junta de damas*.

93. Quoted from SEM Archivo, Legajo 9/36, in Negrín Fajardo, *La educación popular en la España del siglo XVIII,* 139.

94. At its October 10 meeting, the women's council recorded that the Society still had some concerns over how to settle the conflict between the two bodies and wanted to establish this commission.

95. On April 30, the Society sent the *junta de damas* an indication of the decision it had made based on various perspectives the commission had presented to the *junta general*. The women's council discussed this letter at its May 1 meeting, and it immediately sent the *actas* from the meetings of August 12 and 18 and September 19 of the previous year to the Society for approbation. The three reports of the commission are in SEM Archivo, Legajo 137/5.

96. "Informan lo que se les ofrece sobre los puntos que penden en este negocio," March 31, 1795, SEM Archivo, Legajo 137/5.

97. Untitled report by Francisco Gerónimo Cifuentes, March 19, 1795, SEM Archivo, Legajo 137/5.

98. Untitled report from Trúllas, Valdeolmos, Losada, and Panes, April 14, 1795, SEM Archivo, Legajo 137/5.

99. Ibid.

100. February 6, 1807, minutes. *Libro de actas de la junta de damas, 1805–1808,* SEM Archivo, Legajo 202/7.

101. SEM Archivo, Legajo 202/7.

5. PUBLIC WORKS

1. Demerson, *María Francisca de Sales Portocarrero,* 141–43.

2. For a lengthier discussion of the reception of French pedagogical texts in Spain, see Mónica Bolufer Peruga, "Pedagogía y moral en el siglo de las luces: Las escritoras francesas y su recepción en España," *Revista de Historia Moderna* 20 (2002): 251–92. Mary Wollstonecraft's review appeared as a serial article in four editions of *Diario de Madrid:* 250 (September 6, 1792): 1043–45; 252 (September 8, 1792): 1051–52; 282 (October 8, 1792): 1179–81; and 283 (October 9, 1792): 1183–85.

3. For more on these commissions, see chapter 9 of Demerson, *María Fran-*

cisca de Sales Portocarrero (169–81); and Negrín Fajardo, *La educación popular en la España de la segunda mitad del siglo XVIII*, 140–49.

4. *Libro de actas de la junta de damas, 1795–1796*, SEM Archivo, Libro A/56-4, February 20, 1795 meeting. The February 19, 1796, minutes contain a similar list of suggested topics for 1796.

5. Amar y Borbón also devotes part 2, chapter 13, of her book to this topic. *Discurso sobre la educación física y moral de las mujeres*, ed. María Victoria López-Cordón Cortezo (Madrid: Ediciones Cátedra, S.A., 1994).

6. Montijo's summary of Amar y Borbón's text, *Libro de actas de la junta de damas, 1795–1796*, December 18, 1795.

7. Ibid.

8. For more on Amar y Borbón's views on motherhood, see Elizabeth Franklin Lewis, "The Sensibility of Motherhood: Josefa Amar y Borbón's *Discurso sobre la educación física y moral de las mujeres*," *Eighteenth-Century Women: Studies in Their Lives, Work, and Culture* 2 (2002): 209–41.

9. Montijo's summary of Amar y Borbón's text, *Libro de actas de la junta de damas, 1795–1796*, December 18, 1795.

10. Montijo's summary of Ariza's text, *Libro de actas de la junta de damas, 1795–1796*, November 13, 1795.

11. Ibid.

12. While Sonora's thoughts were not recorded in the minutes because of their length, the main points she expressed in her discussion are summarized in a report from a censor who evaluated them for publication. *Informe sobre el mérito de las siete memoriales formadas por las señoras*, March 14, 1801. SEM Archivo, Legajo 146/11.

13. The censor describes her sources in his report: "Her own observations and those that she has read in translations of the best medical texts form the principal basis of this speech." Also see Susana María Ramírez Martín, "Proyección científica de las ideas de Tomás Romay sobre la vacuna de la viruela en la inclusa madrileña," *Asclepio* 54, no. 2 (2002): 109–28.

14. *Libro de actas de la junta de damas, 1795–1796*, November 27, 1795.

15. Ibid.

16. *Libro de actas de la junta de damas, 1795–1796*, November 6, 1795.

17. Montijo presented this at the October 9, 1795, *junta de damas*. Its content is derived from *Informe sobre el mérito de las siete memoriales formadas por las señoras*, March, 14, 1801.

18. Ibid.

19. Ibid.

20. Ibid.

21. Joan Sherwood, *Poverty in Eighteenth-Century Spain: The Women and Children of the Inclusa* (Toronto: University of Toronto Press, 1988), xiii. For more on the Inclusa, also see Paula de Demerson, *La Real Inclusa de Madrid a finales del siglo XVIII* (Madrid: Raycar, S.A., 1972); Fernández-Quintanilla, *La mujer ilustrada*, 92–96; Joan Sherwood, "El niño expósito: Cifras de mortalidad de una inclusa del siglo XVIII," *Anales del Instituto de Estudios Madrileños* 18

(1981): 299–312; and Florentina Vidal Galache, *Bordes y bastardos: Una historia de la Inclusa de Madrid* (Madrid: Compañía Literaria, 1995).

22. *Proposición de la Condesa de Montijo á la junta de señoras, sobre lo útil que será el que solicitase tomar á su cuidado la crianza de los niños expósitos de la Inclusa,* July 11, 1789, SEM Archivo, Legajo 105/6.

23. The nurses who worked at the Inclusa came from the poorest families and received very low wages for their services. For example, between 1700 and 1770, a wet nurse could expect to receive around three *reales* per day for food plus twenty-two *reales* per month in salary. This was often supplemented by allotments for oil, wine, and soap, as well as a place to sleep, shared with another wet nurse, in the Inclusa. In exchange for this salary, the wet nurse was expected to care for two to three infants. For more on the lives of the wet nurses of the Inclusa, see Sherwood, *Poverty in Eighteenth-Century Spain,* 40–41 and 51–91. For more on wet nurses in Spain, see Mónica Bolufer Peruga, "La lactancia asalariada en Valencia a finales del siglo XVIII," *Saitabi* 43 (1993): 255–68; and Carmen Sarasúa García, *Criados, nodrizas, y amos: El servicio doméstico en la formación del mercado de trabajo madrileño, 1758–1868* (Madrid: Siglo Veintiuno de España Editores, S.A., 1994).

24. According to Sherwood, the number of foundlings admitted climbed unevenly during the century: 500 in 1700; 804 in 1710; 426 in 1720; 526 in 1730; 617 in 1740; 809 in 1750; 693 in 1760; 685 in 1770; 748 in 1780; 1,194 in 1789; 849 in 1790; and 1,202 in 1800. See *Poverty in Eighteenth-Century Spain,* 23.

25. For some suggestions on why the reliance on the parish as intermediary lessened during the course of the eighteenth century, see ibid., 21.

26. Sherwood records the percentage of Inclusa children who died either at the hospital or in the care of a wet nurse as follows: 53.8 percent in the 1700s, 57 percent in the 1710s, 56 percent in the 1720s, 66.6 percent in the 1730s, 87 percent in the 1740s, 74 percent in the 1750s, 73.8 percent in the 1760s, 68 percent in the 1770s, 66 percent in the 1780s, and 72.1 percent in the 1790s. Ibid., 143.

27. Sherwood records the percent of deaths to admissions as follows: 79.75 percent in 1787, 81.5 percent in 1788, 84.0 percent in 1789, 75.6 percent in 1790, 79.4 percent in 1791, 80.0 percent in 1792, 85.8 percent in 1793, 78.4 percent in 1794, 82.8 percent in 1795, 82.1 percent in 1796, 87.6 percent in 1797, 76.4 percent in 1798, 83.1 percent in 1799, 83.9 percent in 1800, 84.5 percent in 1801, and 84.0 percent in 1802. Ibid., 146.

28. *Proposición de la Condesa de Montijo á la junta de señoras.*

29. *Libro de actas de la junta de damas, 1792–1794,* SEM Archivo, Legajo 105/6. In the *actas* of the *junta de damas* for December 25, 1792, Montijo indicated receipt of a letter dated December 18 that thanked the women for their zeal in respect to the care of the foundlings and told them to make sure to inform the Society of the result of their petition to the king. See *Libro de actas de la junta de damas, 1792–1794.*

30. "Copia de la representación hecha a S.M. por la junta de señoras de honor y mérito, sobre encargarse de la casa de expósitos de esta corte," October

4, 1796, SEM Archivo, Legajo 148/9. Also transcribed in Fernández-Quintanilla, *La mujer ilustrada*, 151–52.

31. Ibid. Explaining industriousness as a necessary by-product of mothering was not unique to the *junta de damas*. Marta V. Vicente has shown how women in Barcelona couched justification for their business enterprises in familial terms as well. See "Textual Uncertainties: The Written Legacy of Women Entrepreneurs in Eighteenth-Century Spain," in *Women, Texts, and Authority in the Early Modern Spanish World*, ed. Marta V. Vicente and Luis R. Corteguera (Aldershot: Ashgate, 2004), 183–95.

32. Recorded in the *actas* of the October 25, 1796, meeting of the women's council. *Libro de actas de la junta de damas, 1795–1796*.

33. *Libro de actas de la junta de damas, 1792–1794*, November 18, 1792.

34. Demerson, *La Real Inclusa*, 2.

35. Sherwood, *Poverty in Eighteenth-Century Spain*.

36. Ibid., 196.

37. Ibid., 195.

38. This project was adopted in 1803 after extensive discussion of its merits by the women's council, the doctors of the Inclusa, and the Royal Academy of Medicine. Sherwood details the plan: "The señoras took up the project with their usual thoroughness. For the first four months the infant was to be on a program of breast-feeding, alternating with wheat paste or *papilla* of day-old bread dissolved in goat or asses' milk. Then the infants were to be weaned. At this crucial point the doctor would have liked all the infants transferred back into the Inclusa where their diets could be monitored closely, 'because many died at this point.' . . . For the moment, a full-time goat keeper was added to the staff. The Countess del Montijo devised a kind of portable cushion whereby two infants at a time could rest under the mammae of the goat to facilitate the process." Sherwood indicates that this project was supported because of the problems of feeding large numbers of infants as well as notions that wet nurses were morally corrupt. *Poverty in Eighteenth-Century Spain*, 197–202. For more about contemporary views on breast-feeding and wet nurses, see Mónica Bolufer Peruga, "Actitudes y discursos sobre la maternidad en la España del siglo XVIII: La cuestión de la lactancia," *Historia Social* 14 (Fall 1992): 3–22.

39. Sherwood, *Poverty in Eighteenth-Century Spain*, 204.

40. Concerning petitions for adoptions, for example, at the October 9, 1801, meeting of the *junta de damas* the Marquise of Sonora presented a request from Francisca de la Cruz, who wanted to adopt a son from the Inclusa. After receiving a favorable report of the circumstances and qualities of de la Cruz, the women's council agreed to grant her request. *Libro de actas de la junta de damas, 1801–1802*, SEM Archivo, Libro A/56–7.

41. Sherwood, *Poverty in Eighteenth-Century Spain*, 205.

42. Ibid.

43. For more on the *escuelas patrióticas* beyond that contained in general

studies of the Economic Societies, see Paula de Demerson, "Les écoles patriotiques de Madrid entre 1787 et 1808," *Cahiers du monde hispanique et lusobrésilien (Caravelle)*, 13 (1969): 83–95; the work of Olegario Negrín Fajardo; and Dolores Palma García, "Las escuelas patrióticas de hilazas creadas en la villa de Madrid durante el reinado de Carlos III," *Anales del Instituto de Estudios Madrileños* 18 (1981): 443–55.

44. On the feminization of the needle trades, see Judith G. Coffin, *The Politics of Women's Work: The Paris Garment Trades, 1750–1915* (Princeton: Princeton University Press, 1996); and Miguel Capella Martinez, *La industria en Madrid: Ensayo histórico crítico de la fabricación y artesanía madrileñas*, vol. 1, *Del fuero viejo al año 1700*; vol. 2, *Siglos XVIII al XX, desde 1701 a 1912* (Madrid: Artes Gráficas y Ediciones, S.A., 1962–1963), vol. 1, 422–33, vol. 2, 361–33. The desire to train women in industries "appropriate to their sex" is expressed in regards to the embroidery school, for example, in SEM Archivo, Legajo 81/9. For another example of an Enlightenment institution focused on preparing young women for useful and appropriate work, see Teresa González's study of midwives and scientific societies, "Midwives in Early Modern Spain," in *The Art of Midwifery: Early Modern Midwives in Europe*, ed. Hilary Marland (London: Routledge, 1993), 95–114.

45. *Reglamento formado por la Real Sociedad Económica de Madrid para govierno de la escuela gratuita de bordados bajo la Real Protección de S.M.*, August 17, 1786, SEM Archivo, Legajo 83/9.

46. *Reglamento para la escuela de encaxes*, SEM Library, R.4732, 2.

47. Although the *junta de damas* began to run the schools in 1787, it did not fully take charge of the schools' finances until 1797. Negrín Fajardo, *La educación popular*, 167.

48. Ibid., 179.

49. Ibid., 168.

50. October 19, 1787 meeting. Recorded in *Libro de actas de la junta de damas, 1787–1789*.

51. Negrín Fajardo, *La educación popular*, 182.

52. Untitled report on the escuelas patrióticas, 1806, quoted in Negrín Fajardo, *La educación popular*, 183.

53. Unless otherwise noted, the information on the life of the embroidery school under the direction of the *junta de damas* is drawn from the minutes of the women's council meetings.

54. The fact that the *junta de damas* would take over the embroidery school was announced at the September 26, 1787, meeting of the commission established to determine the statutes of the women's section. *Libro de acuerdos de la junta de comisión, nombrada por la Real Sociedad Económica de Madrid, para tratar del reglamento de la de señoras socias de honor y mérito, 1787–1788*. At the October 13, 1787, general meeting, the Economic Society officially determined that the embroidery school (as well as the other *escuelas patrióticas*) would be under the direction of the women's council.

55. In "Una escuela madrileña de bordado," *Revista de la Biblioteca*,

Archivo, y Museo del Ayuntamiento de Madrid XV, no. 53 (1946), María Victoria González Mateos argues, "You can say that after the death of this woman [Diez] was when the school really began to function as such and it entered a period of real production" (71–72).

56. The women's council did record the receipt of an application from María Briteño at the November 28, 1788, meeting. However, they decided to inform Briteño that her application was late and that the position had already been filled. *Libro de actas de la junta de damas, 1787–1789.*

57. This is outlined in his November 19, 1788, application to the *junta de damas*. SEM Archivo, Legajo 94/14.

58. María Luisa Barreno, "Bordadores de cámara y situación del arte de bordar en Madrid durante la segunda mitad del siglo XVIII," *Archivo Español de Arte* 47, no. 187 (1974): 291.

59. Negrín Fajardo, *La educación popular*, 202.

60. This is clear in the women's council's report to the *junta general* on the activities of schools under the *socias'* direction on March 28, 1789. SEM Archivo, Legajo 94/5.

61. The terms of Nieto's contract are explained in a March 17, 1789, memo from the Countess of Montijo to the *junta general*. SEM Archivo, Legajo 94/14.

62. González Mateos, "Una escuela madrileña de bordado," 75.

63. San Ginés, San Sebastián, San Martín, San Andrés, the school of blond lace and the first class of white lace at the Escuela de la Real Sociedad were each given six hundred reales to divide among their students; the Embroidery School and the second class of the Adornos de la Escuela de la Real Sociedad were each given twelve hundred reales to divide among their students. This was discussed at the August 9, 1793, meeting. *Libro de actas de la junta de damas, 1792–1794.*

64. Ibid.

65. The prize amounts were confirmed after the fact at the March 22, 1793. meeting. Ibid. These kinds of prizes were given to teachers intermittently. Another example was discussed at the January 23, 1795, meeting, in which the Economic Society agreed to give teachers at various schools, including the four *escuelas patrióticas* and the embroidery school, each an ounce of gold. *Libro de actas de la junta de damas, 1795–1796.*

66. The very last record I found that refers to the embroidery school is from the May 20, 1811, minutes of the *junta de damas*, which records the new *curadora* of the school.

67. SEM Archivo, Legajo 94/14.

68. The king paid 240 *reales de vellón* for the waistcoat. *Libro de actas de la junta de damas, 1792–1794.*

69. *Libro de actas de la junta de damas, 1803–1804*, SEM Archivo, Libro A/56-8.

70. *Reglamento para la escuela de encaxes*, SEM Library, R.4732.

71. These prizes were awarded in spite of the fact that the examination committee found that the students had made much less progress than in previous years because of the continual illness of their teacher, Theresa Farel. Farel, as per

her contract, received 1,027 *reales* and 17 *maravedis* as a bonus. SEM Archivo, Legajo 77/7.

72. Rozsika Parker and Griselda Pollock, *Old Mistresses: Women, Art, and Ideology* (London: Routledge and Kegan Paul, 1981).

73. Merry Wiesner, *Women and Gender in Early Modern Europe* (Cambridge: Cambridge University Press, 1993), 148.

74. Ibid.

75. See Capella Martinez, *La industria en Madrid*, vol. 1, 422–33; vol. 2, 361–63.

76. Negrín Fajardo, *La educación popular*, 165–66.

77. *Libro de actas de la junta de damas, 1790–1791*.

78. Fernández-Quintanilla, *La mujer ilustrada*, 91.

79. *Libro de actas de la junta de damas, 1790–1791*.

80. Fernández-Quintanilla, *La mujer ilustrada*, 92.

81. For more on the Economic Society and the Montepío, see Domergue, *Jovellanos á la société économique*, 75–123.

82. *Libro de actas de la junta de damas, 1792–1794*.

83. *Libro de actas de la junta de damas, 1787–1789*.

84. *Libro de actas de la junta de damas, 1790–1791*, April 15 meeting.

85. *Libro de actas de la junta de damas, 1790–1791*.

86. For a partial discussion of women's participation in the Economic Society in Valladolid, see Demerson, *La Real Sociedad Económica de Valladolid*, 23–25.

87. *Diario de Madrid* (Madrid), November 16, 1793, 1307–8; quoted in Serrano y Sanz, *Apuntes para una biblioteca de escritoras*, vol. 2, 147.

88. At the January 13, 1792, meeting of Madrid's *junta de damas*, the Marquise of Fuerte-Híjar discussed this request. The minutes refer to the *vizcondesa* as "Presidenta de la Sociedad de Valladolid." This seems to have been a loose term; the announcement in the *Diario de Madrid* of Fuerte-Híjar's suggestion indicates that the women were not yet incorporated officially into the organization. Madrid's *junta de damas* apparently searched for a new teacher and fulfilled Valoría's request. On February 24, socias considered applications from Ana María Hannequin and Tecla Blázquez, and on March 21 the council held *oposiciones* to evaluate the two candidates. Hannequin was selected, and at the March 23 meeting, the women's council charged Fuerte-Híjar with informing the "junta de señoras de Valladolid" of its recommendation.

On March 30, the Countess of Montijo read a letter from the Marquise of Fuerte-Híjar at Aranjuez, dated March 24, in which she agreed to "advise the Sra Vizcondesa de Valoría presidenta of the [women's] council of Valladolid." On April 20, Teresa Losada read an April 15 letter from Valoría thanking the *junta de damas* and Montijo "in the name of the ladies of Valladolid" for their work in obtaining a good teacher for their city.

After the new teacher arrived in Valladolid, Valoría sent another thank-you to the Madrid women's council dated May 13 (read at the June 1 *junta de damas*) to show the pleasure "of that council of ladies" with the selection of Hannequin. SEM Archivo, Libro 1/56-3.

89. *Libro de actas de la junta de damas, 1792–1794*. The women's council noted the receipt of the statutes at its September 20 meeting but postponed any real discussion until September 27 because it had too much business at hand.

90. The group in Valladolid was probably much smaller than its counterpart in Madrid. A list of members who attended the meetings in Valladolid, composed by Jorge Demerson, includes only three women: the Marquesa de Olias *(socia honoraria)*, María de Sierra y Salcedo *(socia honoraria)*, and the Vizcondesa de Valoría, listed as "President de la Junta de Damas(?)." *La Real Sociedad Económica de Valladolid*, 35–39.

91. Listed in a chart of socios in Soria Medina, *La Sociedad Económica de Amigos del País de Osuna*, 207, 201, 193 respectively.

92. Jorge Demerson argues that, despite the liberal nature of the Society's attitude, the participation of women never became much of a reality. Their only part in the group's activities was to select prize recipients from the spinning school. He explains that, in comparison to the very active *junta de damas* in Madrid, in Avila the participation of women "was frankly insignificant." I have not investigated documents from Avila to either confirm or refute Demerson's assertion. Demerson, *La Real Sociedad Económica de Amigos del País de Avila*, 39.

93. Castellano Castellano, in *Luces y reformismo*, indicates that this classification of membership, reserved for outstanding professors and artisans who were residents of the city or lived within its jurisdiction, did not carry an obligation to pay dues. It did, however, require the member to help realize the goals of the Society, and accordingly it allowed for a vote in the *juntas* (188–89). In this work, no women appear on lists of members of the Economic Societies in Vera, Almuñécar, Baza, or Motril (389–90). When Catalina Martín y Abril sent some of her drawings to the Real Academia de Bellas Artes de San Fernando, she included her title as a member of the Real Sociedad Económica de Granada in her correspondence. See RABA Archivo, Legajo 3/86, for records for the *junta ordinaria*, October 5, 1800, 146. Richard Herr indicates women were admitted to the Basque and Aragonese Societies. See *Memorial Literario* (Madrid), April 1786, 474.

94. Sarrailh, *La España ilustrada*, 259. Evidence for this assertion comes from the two speeches published in the *Memorial Literario* under the title "Discursos leídos en la Real Sociedad Económica de Lugo, por Doña María Reguera y Mondragón," vol. 15, 99 and 226–33.

95. Sullivan, "Josefa Amar y Borbón (1749–1833)," 33. The women are listed in María Victoria López-Cordón Cortezo's introduction to her edition of Amar y Borbón's *Discurso sobre la educación física y moral de las mujeres* as María Adelaida Destreham in 1792, María Francisca de Sales Portocarrero (Countess of Montijo) in 1801, and Juana Rabasa y de Soler in 1805 ([Madrid:

Ediciones Cátedra, S.A., 1994], 33). However, they did not constitute a women's council, and as Sullivan argues, Amar y Borbón was the only woman to actively contribute to the organization before the 1980s. "Josefa Amar y Borbón and the Royal Aragonese Economic Society," 97.

96. While the Marquise of Ayerbe was not a member of Aragon's Economic Society, she did present a short piece entitled "Método para blanquear hilos" to the organization. It is listed in José Francisco Forniés Casals's *Fuentes para el estudio de la Sociedad y la Económica Aragonesas, 1776–1808: Documentos citados en las actas de la Real Sociedad Económica Aragonesa de Amigos del País* (Zaragoza: Diputación Provincial, Institución "Fernando el Católico," 1980), 118 (from *Resumen de las actas,* 156–57).

97. Forniés Casals cites these documents in *Fuentes,* 24–25.

6. BETWEEN REASON AND PASSION

1. This chapter contains material that appeared as Theresa Ann Smith, "Writing out of the Margins: Women, Translation, and the Spanish Enlightenment," *Journal of Women's History* 15, no. 1 (Spring 2003): 116–43.

2. Tina Krontiris, *Oppositional Voices: Women as Writers and Translators of Literature in the English Renaissance* (New York: Routledge, 1992), 20–21.

3. Françoise Massardier-Kenney, "Translation Theory and Practice," in *Translating Slavery: Gender and Race in French Women's Writing, 1783–1823,* ed. Doris Y. Kadish and Françoise Massardier-Kenney (Kent, OH: Kent State University Press, 1994), 1–7.

4. A number of eighteenth-century Spaniards expressed concern over translations that were too liberal. See, for example, Antonio de Capmany y Suris de Montpalau's 1776 *Arte de traducir el idioma Francés al Castellano,* ed. María del Carmen Fernández Díaz (Santiago de Compostela: Universidad de Santiago de Compostela, Servicio de Publicacións e Intercambio Científico, 1987).

5. María Romero Masegosa y Cancelada, trans., *Cartas de una peru*ana . . . *traducidas al castellano con algunas correcciones, y aumentada con notas, y una carta para su mayor complemento . . . , by Madame de Graffigny* (Valladolid: Oficina de la Viuda de Santander, é Hijos, 1792). In the January 14, 1794, issue of the *Correo Literario de Murcia,* María Josefa de Rivadeneyra accuses Romero of plagiarizing her translation of Graffigny. Romero refutes these charges in an April 4, 1794, letter to the *Correo*'s editor. In "Les *Lettres péruviennes* en Espagne," *Bulletin Hispanique* 64 bis (1962): 412–23, Marcelin Defourneaux supports Romero y Cancelada's defense and suggests that two distinct translations were written around the same time. To date, scholars have been unable to locate Rivadeneyra's translation. Also see Luis Alberto Sánchez, "Una iluminista olvidada: Las 'Cartas peruanas' de Madame de Graffigny," *Cuadernos Americanos* 16, no. 3 (1957): 185–95.

6. Since English Showalter rediscovered this text in 1964, scholars have uncovered the complexities of Graffigny's work and resituated it as a hallmark text in the study of Enlightenment critique. Despite Showalter's claim that

Graffigny's best-seller "deserves to remain forgotten," his rediscovery of the text, which he examined in his "An Eighteenth-Century Best-Seller: *Les Lettres Péruviennes*," provoked a complete reassessment of Graffigny's work (Ph.D. diss., Yale University, 1964). More recent scholarship has confirmed the popularity of Graffigny's tale and begun to situate her in the Enlightenment canon. Booksellers reprinted *Lettres d'une péruvienne* forty-six times in France in the thirty years after its initial publication in 1747, and translators rendered the story into English, Italian, Spanish, Portuguese, German, and Swedish by 1835.

On the work's popularity, see Janet Gurkin Altman, "A Woman's Place in the Enlightenment Sun: The Case of F. de Graffigny," *Romance Quarterly* 38, no. 3 (1991): 261–72; Thomas M. Kavanagh, "Reading the Moment and the Moment of Reading in Graffigny's *Lettres d'une Péruvienne*," in *Eighteenth-Century Literary History*, ed. Marshall Brown (Durham, NC: Duke University Press, 1999), 136–58; David Smith, "The Popularity of Mme de Graffigny's *Lettres d'une Péruvienne*: The Bibliographical Evidence," *Eighteenth-Century Fiction* 3, no. 1 (1990): 1–20; and David Smith, "Graffigny *Rediviva*: Editions of the *Lettres d'une Péruvienne* (1967–1993)," *Eighteenth-Century Fiction* 7, no. 1 (1994): 71–78.

Excellent works on race and gender in the text include Janet Gurkin Altman, "Graffigny's Epistemology and the Emergence of Third-World Ideology," in *Writing the Female Voice: Essays on Epistolary Literature*, ed. Elizabeth C. Goldsmith (Boston: Northeastern University Press, 1989), 172–202; Janet Gurkin Altman, "Making Room for 'Peru': Graffigny's Novel Reconsidered," in *Dilemmes du roman: Essays in Honor of Georges May*, ed. Catherine Lafarge (Saratoga: Anma Libri, 1989), 33–46; Julia V. Douthwaite, *Exotic Women: Literary Heroines and Cultural Strategies in Ancien Régime France* (Philadelphia: University of Pennsylvania Press, 1992); and Christine Roulston, "Seeing the Other in Mme de Graffigny's *Lettres d'une Péruvienne*," *Eighteenth-Century Fiction* 9, no. 3 (1997): 309–26.

7. I have compared Romero's version to the 1752 French edition reprinted in Madame de Graffigny, *Lettres d'une péruvienne*, ed. Gianni Nicoletti (Bari: Adriatica Editrice, 1967). Unless otherwise indicated, all French translations are from Françoise de Graffigny, *Letters from a Peruvian Woman*, trans. David Kornacker (New York: Modern Language Association of America, 1993), which is based on the 1752 edition.

8. On the Black Legend, see Paul Ilie, "Exomorphism: Cultural Bias and the French Image of Spain from the War of Succession to the Age of Voltaire," *Eighteenth-Century Studies* 9, no. 3 (1976): 375–89; Paul J. Hauben, "White Legend against Black: Nationalism and Enlightenment in a Spanish Context," *Americas* 34, no. 1 (1977): 1–19; and Richard L. Kagan, "Prescott's Paradigm: American Historical Scholarship and the Decline of Spain," *American Historical Review* 101, no. 2 (1996): 423–46.

9. *Diario de Madrid* (Madrid), September 26, 1795, quoted in Serrano y Sanz, *Apuntes para una biblioteca de escritoras*, vol. 2, 145.

10. *Memorial Literario* (Madrid), April 1794, 144–46. Fr. Eugenio de Zebal-

los, the censor of this text, also remarked on the skill of the translator in a letter to the council dated July 2, 1775. See Serrano y Sanz, *Apuntes para una biblioteca de escritoras,* vol. 2, 546.

11. Quoted in Serrano y Sanz, *Apuntes para una biblioteca de escritoras,* vol. 1, 454.

12. *Memorial Literario* (Madrid), November 1786, 335.

13. For more on language, see Madeleine Dobie, "'Language inconnu': Montesquieu, Graffigny, and the Writing of Exile," *Romanic Review* 87, no. 2 (1996): 209–24; Madeleine Dobie, "The Subject of Writing: Language, Epistemology, and Identity in the *Lettres d'une Péruvienne,*" *Eighteenth Century* 38, no. 2 (1997): 99–117; Diane Fourny, "Language and Reality in Françoise de Graffigny's *Lettres d'une Péruvienne,*" *Eighteenth-Century Fiction* 4, no. 2 (1992): 221–38; Nancy K. Miller, "The Knot, the Letter, and the Book: Graffigny's *Peruvian Letters,*" in *Subject to Change: Reading Feminist Writing,* ed. Nancy K. Miller (New York: Columbia University Press, 1988), 125–61; and François Rosset, "Les noeuds du langage dans les *Lettres d'une péruvienne,*" *Revue d'Histoire Littéraire de la France* 96, no. 6 (1996): 1106–27.

14. Judith Curtis, "Anticipating Zilia: Madame de Graffigny in 1744," in *Femmes savantes et femmes d'esprit: Women Intellectuals of the French Eighteenth Century,* ed. Roland Bonnel and Catherine Rubinger (New York: Peter Lang, 1994), 129–54, especially 129.

15. Scholars continue to debate the degree to which Zilia's experience parallels Graffigny's own. Biographical studies include Curtis, "Anticipating Zilia," 129–54; Christine Roulston, "No Simple Correspondence: Mme de Graffigny as 'Epistolière' and as Epistolary Novelist," *L'Esprit Créateur* 40, no. 4 (2000): 31–37; English Showalter Jr., "Graffigny at Cirey: A Fraud Exposed," *French Forum* 21, no. 1 (1996): 29–44; and English Showalter Jr., "A Woman of Letters in the French Enlightenment: Madame de Graffigny," *British Journal for Eighteenth-Century Studies* 1 (1978): 89–104.

16. Romero, *Cartas,* 13–14.

17. Ibid., 14–15.

18. Ibid., 17.

19. Graffigny's text, too, contains footnotes; however, unlike Romero's, Graffigny's notes merely supply the reader with useful information on the historical context, such as definitions of Incan terms Zilia uses. See Aurora Wolfgang, "Intertextual Conversations: The Love-Letter and the Footnote in Madame de Graffigny's *Lettres d'une Péruvienne,*" *Eighteenth-Century Fiction* 10, no. 1 (1997): 15–28.

20. Amazing examples of women who gained access to education in eighteenth-century Spain, include María Isidra Quintina Guzmán y la Cerda, who received a doctorate from the University of Alcalá in 1785 at the age of seventeen. On the validity of this degree, see Theresa Ann Smith, "New Visibility: Women and the Public Sphere in Eighteenth-Century Spain" (Ph.D. diss., University of California, San Diego, 1999), chapter 1, 51–66. Also see Margarita

Ortega López, "La educación de la mujer en la ilustración española," in *Simposium internacional sobre educación e ilustración: Dos siglos de reformas en la enseñanza* (Madrid: Ministerio de Educación y Ciencia, 1988): 193–222.

21. Graffigny, *Letters from a Peruvian Woman*, 146.
22. Romero, *Cartas*, 427.
23. This is not to say that Graffigny does not denounce society's role in making women ignorant. For example, as Graffigny's Zilia reports in letter 34, "Here it is wished, as elsewhere, that women possess merit and virtue. But nature would have had to make them thus, for the upbringing they are given is in such opposition to the goal proposed that it appears to me to be the great masterpiece of French inconsequence." Graffigny, *Letters from a Peruvian Woman*, 142. Still, Romero's reminder that women are not at fault for their poor education comes at a moment when Graffigny's emphasis is on women's ignorance, not the guilty party.
24. Romero, *Cartas*, 432–33. This footnote comes at the end of the first paragraph of Graffigny, *Letters from a Peruvian Woman*, 148.
25. Graffigny, *Letters from a Peruvian Woman*, 121.
26. Romero, *Cartas*, 351.
27. Ibid., 9.
28. The most noteworthy example of a Spanish text that develops a notion similar to Mary Wollstonecraft's Republican Motherhood is Josefa Amar y Borbón's 1790 *Discurso sobre la educación física y moral de las mujeres*.
29. Elizabeth J. MacArthur, "Devious Narratives: Refusal of Closure in Two Eighteenth-Century Epistolary Novels," *Eighteenth-Century Studies* 21, no. 1 (1987): 1–20, esp. 6.
30. In his story, Lamarche-Courmont emphasizes the shared ethnicity of Aza and Zilia and, thus, implicitly the ethnic divide that separates Zilia and Déterville.
31. These first two sequels are reprinted in Nicoletti's edition. See Graffigny, "Suite des *Lettres d'une péruvienne*," and [Hugary de Lamarche-Courmont], "Lettres d'Aza," in Graffigny, *Lettres d'une péruvienne*, 325–41 and 343–93.
32. Graffigny, *Letters from a Peruvian Woman*, 172.
33. Madame de Graffigny, *The Peruvian Letters, Translated from the French with an Additional Original Volume by R. Roberts* (London: T. Cadell, 1774); and Madame Morel de Vindé, "Suite del 1797," in *Lettres d'une péruvienne*, by Madame de Graffigny, ed. Gianni Nicoletti (Bari: Adriatica Editrice, 1967), 395–437.
34. Graffigny, *Letters from a Peruvian Woman*, 149; Romero, *Cartas*, 435–36.
35. Anonymous note on p. 518 of Romero, *Cartas*, Biblioteca Nacional, Madrid, Spain, R/37328.
36. Julia V. Douthwaite, "Relocating the Exotic Other in *Lettres d'une Péruvienne*," *Romanic Review* 82, no. 4 (1997): 456–74, esp. 461–62. On Graffigny's casting of Zilia as an Incan princess, also see Bonnie Arden Robb, "The Easy

Virtue of a Peruvian Princess," *French Studies* 46, no. 2 (1992): 144–59; and Heidi Bostic, "The Light of Reason in Graffigny's *Lettres d'une Péruvienne*," *Dalhousie French Studies* 63 (Summer 2003): 3–11.

37. Graffigny, *Letters from a Peruvian Woman*, 7.
38. Romero, *Cartas*, 22–23.
39. Graffigny, *Letters from a Peruvian Woman*, 9; Romero, *Cartas*, 26.
40. Romero, *Cartas*, 27; Graffigny, *Letters from a Peruvian Woman*, 9.
41. Graffigny, *Letters from a Peruvian Woman*, 18.
42. Romero, *Cartas*, 46.
43. Ibid.
44. Graffigny, *Lettres d'une péruvienne*, 155 (my translation); Romero, *Cartas*, 65.
45. Romero, *Cartas*, 96.
46. Graffigny, *Letters from a Peruvian Woman*, 10; Romero, *Cartas*, 27.
47. Graffigny, *The Peruvian Letters . . . with an additional original volume by R. Roberts*, 153–54.
48. Ibid., 154.
49. Romero, *Cartas*, 6.
50. Marcelin Defourneaux, *Inquisición y censura de libros en la España del siglo XVIII*, trans. J. Ignacio Tellechea Idígoras (Madrid: Taurus Ediciones, S.A., 1973), 142.
51. Romero, *Cartas*, 511–12.
52. Romero further emphasizes that Zilia's conversion is due to rational inquiry, as Zilia speaks of her new cosmology now that she has "become so convinced of these truths." Ibid., 513–14.
53. Ibid., 518.
54. Ibid., 301–2.
55. Ibid., 345–46.
56. Ibid., 346–47.
57. Ibid., 515.
58. Downing A. Thomas makes this argument in "Economy and Identity in Graffigny's *Lettres d'une Péruvienne*," *South Central Review* 10, no. 4 (1993): 55–72.
59. Romero, *Cartas*, 152.
60. Ibid., 185–86.
61. This does not mean, however, that Romero erases the subtle racial and ethnic hierarchy extant in Graffigny's text. For example, the presence of Zilia's Chinese servant places Zilia on a plane with her European consorts by underscoring the fact that she is a member of Peru's elite.
62. Romero, *Cartas*, 514.
63. Ibid., 517–18.
64. On the nineteenth century, see Susan Kirkpatrick, *Las románticas: Women Writers and Subjectivity in Spain, 1835–1850* (Berkeley: University of California Press, 1989).

Selected Bibliography

ARCHIVES

Archivo de la Real Academia de Bellas Artes de San Fernando de Madrid. Madrid, Spain.
Archivo de la Real Academia Española. Madrid, Spain.
Archivo de la Real Sociedad Económica Matritense de Amigos del País. Madrid, Spain.
Archivo Histórico Nacional. Madrid, Spain.
Archivo Histórico Nacional, Sección Nobleza. Toledo, Spain.
Biblioteca de la Real Academia de la Historia. Madrid, Spain.
Biblioteca Municipal, Colleción de manuscritos. Madrid, Spain.
Biblioteca Nacional, Colleción de manuscritos. Madrid, Spain.

PRINTED SOURCES

Acereda, Alberto. "Una comedia inédita de la Ilustración española: *La sabia indirecta* de la Marquesa de Fuerte Híjar." *Dieciocho: Hispanic Enlightenment* 20, no. 2 (Fall 1997): 231–62.
———. "Una figura relegada de la Ilustración: La Marquesa de Fuerte Híjar y su *Elogio de la Reina* (1798)." *Cuadernos de Investigación Filológica* 23–24 (1997–1998): 195–212.
———. *La Marquesa de Fuerte Híjar: Una dramaturga de la Ilustración: Estudio y edición de* La sabia indiscreta. Cádiz: Universidad de Cádiz, 2000.
Agueda Villar, Mercedes. "Mengs y la Academia de San Fernando." In *II simposio sobre el Padre Feijóo y su siglo*, ed. Catedra Feijóo, vol. 2, 445–76. Oviedo: Centro de Estudios del Siglo XVIII, 1983.
Aguilar Piñal, Francisco. "Las academias del siglo XVIII como centros de investigación." In *I Borbone di Napoli e i Borbone di Spagna*, ed. Mario Di Pinto, vol. 2, 391–444. Naples: Guida Editori, 1985.
———. *Bibliografía de autores españoles del siglo XVIII*. 8 vols. Madrid: Consejo Superior de Investigaciones Científicas, 1981–1995.

———. *Indice de las poesías publicadas en los periódicos españoles del siglo XVIII*. Cuadernos Bibliográficos, ed. José Simón Díaz, no. 43. Madrid: Consejo Superior de Investigaciones Científicas, 1981.

———. *La prensa española en el siglo XVIII: Diarios, revistas, y pronósticos*. Madrid: Consejo Superior de Investigaciones Científicas, 1978.

———. *La Real Sociedad Económica Matritense de Amigos del País*. Madrid: Artes Gráficas Municipales, 1972.

Aguilera, Emiliano M. *Pintores españoles del siglo XVIII*. Barcelona: Iberia-Joaquín Gil, Editores, S.A., 1946.

Aguirre y Rosales, Cayetana, trans. *Virginia, o la doncella cristiana: Historia siciliana, que se propone por modelo á las señoras que aspiran a la perfección*, by Michel-Ange Marin. 4 vols. Madrid: Repullés, 1806.

Agulló y Cobo, Mercedes. *Más noticias sobre pintores madrileños de los siglos XVI al XVIII*. Madrid: Ayuntamiento, Delegación de Cultura, 1981.

Ahlgren, Gilian T. W. *Teresa of Avila and the Politics of Sanctity*. Ithaca: Cornell University Press, 1996.

Alarcón, Norma, and Sylvia Kossnar. *Bibliography of Hispanic Women Writers*. Bloomington: Chicano-Riqueño Studies, 1980.

Alidiere, Emmanuelle. *Teresa Cabarrús*. Genève: Editions Ferni, 1974.

Almela y Vives, Francisco. *La Real Sociedad Económica de Amigos del País de Valencia*. Valencia: Artes Gráficas Soler, S.A., 1967.

Alonso Pimentel, María Josefa. *Discurso que la Excma. Sra. Condesa, Duquesa de Benavente, Marquesa de Peñafiel, &c. hizo a la Real Sociedad Económica de Madrid, el día de su recepción 22 de julio de 1786*. Madrid: Don Antonio de Sancha, 1786.

Alonso Seoane, María José. "Adaptaciones narrativas en el siglo XVIII español: *El amor desinteresado* de Pablo de Olavide." In *Traducción y adaptación cultural: España-Francia*, ed. María Luisa Donaire and Francisco Lafarga, 199–209. Oviedo: Universidad de Oviedo, 1991.

Altman, Janet Gurkin. "Graffigny's Epistemology and the Emergence of Third-World Ideology." In *Writing the Female Voice: Essays on Epistolary Literature*, ed. Elizabeth C. Goldsmith, 172–202. Boston: Northeastern University Press, 1989.

———. "Making Room for 'Peru': Graffigny's Novel Reconsidered." In *Dilemmes du roman: Essays in Honor of Georges May*, ed. Catherine Lafarge, 33–46. Saratoga: Anma Libri, 1989.

———. "A Woman's Place in the Enlightenment Sun: The Case of F. de Graffigny." *Romance Quarterly* 38, no. 3 (1991): 261–72.

Alvarado Lezo Pacheco y Solís, Josefa de, trans. *Compendio de la filosofia moral*, by Francesco Maria Zanotti. Madrid: Joaquin Ibarra, 1785.

———, trans. *La lengua de los cálculos*, by Etienne Bonnot de Condillac. Madrid: Impresa Ruis, 1805.

Álvarez, Fray Alonso. *Memorias de las mugeres ilustres de España*. Vol. 1. Madrid: Imprenta de Sancha, 1798.

Álvarez Barrientos, Joaquín. "El modelo femenino en la novela española del siglo XVIII." *Hispanic Review* 63, no. 1 (1995): 1–18.

———. *La novela del siglo XVIII*. Historia de la literatura española, ed. R. de la Fuente, 28. Madrid: Ediciones Júcar, 1991.

Álvarez Barrientos, Joaquín, and José Checa Beltrán, eds. *El siglo que llaman ilustrado: Homenaje a Francisco Aguilar Piñal*. Madrid: Consejo Superior de Investigaciones Científicas, 1996.

Álvarez Barrientos, Joaquín, François Lopez, and Inmaculada Urzainqui. *La república de las letras en la España del siglo XVIII*. Madrid: Consejo Superior de Investigaciones Científicas, 1995.

Álvarez de Miranda, Pedro. "¿Una niña en la Academia? El caso de María del Rosario Cepeda y su orgulloso padre." *Boletín de la Real Academia Española* 82 (January–June 2002): 39–45.

Álvarez Faedo, María José. *A Bio-Bibliography of Eighteenth-Century Religious Women in England and Spain*. Lewiston, NY: Edwin Mellen Press, 2005.

Álvarez y Baena, J. A. *Hijos de Madrid, ilustres en santidad, dignidades, armas, ciencias, y artes: Diccionario histórico por el orden alfabético de sus nombres*. 4 vols. Madrid: B. Cano, 1789–91.

Amar y Borbón, Josefa. "Discurso en defensa del talento de las mugeres, y de su aptitud para el gobierno, y otros cargos en que se emplean los hombres; compuesto por Doña Josepha Amar y Borbón, sócia de mérito de la Real Sociedad Aragonesa de los Amigos del País." *Memorial Literario* (Madrid) 32 (August 1786): 399–438.

———. *Discurso sobre la educación física y moral de las mujeres*. Ed. María Victoria López-Cordón Cortezo. Madrid: Ediciones Cátedra, S.A., 1994.

———. "Oración gratulatoria que la Señora Doña Josefa Amar y Borbón, elegida socia de honor y mérito, dirigió a la junta de señoras de la Real Sociedad Económica de Madrid." *Memorial Literario* (Madrid) (December 1787): 588–92.

———, trans. *Discurso sobre el problema de si corresponde a los párrocos y curas de las aldeas el instruir a los labradores en los buenos elementos de la economía campestre: Al qual va adjunto un plan que debe seguirse en la formación de una obra dirigida a la mencionada instrucción del Señor Francisco Griselini, miembro de las principales académias de Europa, y Secretario de la Sociedad Patriótica de Milan*. Zaragoza: Impresor de la Real Sociedad, 1784.

———, trans. *Ensayo histórico-apologético de la literatura española contra las opiniones preocupadas de algunos escritores modernos italianos*, by Xavier Lampillas. 5 vols. Zaragoza: Blas Miedes, 1782.

Anderson, Bonnie S., and Judith P. Zinsser. *A History of Their Own: Women in Europe from Prehistory to the Present*. New York: Harper and Row, 1988.

Anes Álvarez, Gonzalo. "Coyuntura económica e 'ilustración': Las Sociedades de Amigos del País." In *Economía e ilustración en la España del siglo XVIII*, 11–41. Barcelona: Ediciones Ariel, 1969.

———. *Economía e ilustración en la España del siglo XVIII*, 3rd ed. Barcelona: Editorial Ariel, 1981.

———. "Ecos de la Revolución francesa en España: Algunos datos y documentos." *Cuadernos de Historia de España* 35–36 (1962): 274–314.

Aparisi Mocholi, Antonio. "La enseñanza en Madrid en el siglo XVIII." In *Ciclo de conferencias sobre Madrid en el siglo XVIII*, ed. Instituto de Estudios Madrileños del Consejo Superior de Investigaciones Científicas, 11–36. Madrid: Artes Gráficas Municipales, 1978.

Aragón, María Aurora. "Traducciones de obras francesas en la *Gaceta de Madrid* entre 1790 y 1799." In *Imágenes de Francia en las letras hispánicas*, ed. Francisco Lafarga, 261–69. Barcelona: Promociones y Publicaciones Universitarias, S.A., 1989.

Aram, Bethany. "Juana 'the Mad's' Signature: The Problem of Invoking Royal Authority, 1505–1507." *Sixteenth-Century Journal* 29, no. 2 (1998): 331–58.

Arce, Joaquín. "El conocimiento de la literatura italiana en la España de la segunda mitad del siglo XVIII." In *La literatura española del siglo XVIII y sus fuentes extranjeras*, 7–45. Cuadernos de la Cátedra Feijoo, no. 20. Oviedo: Universidad de Oviedo, 1968.

———. *La poesía del siglo ilustrado*. Madrid: Editorial Alhambra, S.A., 1980.

Arenal, Electa. "The Convent as Catalyst for Autonomy: Two Hispanic Nuns of the Seventeenth Century." In *Women in Hispanic Literature: Icons and Fallen Idols*, ed. Beth Miller, 147–83. Berkeley: University of California Press, 1983.

Arenal, Electa, and Stacey Schlau, eds. *Untold Sisters: Hispanic Nuns in Their Own Works*. Trans. Amanda Powell. Albuquerque: University of New Mexico Press, 1989.

Areta Armentía, Luis María. "Presencia de Jean-Jacques Rousseau en el País Vasco." *Boletín de la Institución Sancho el Sabio* 21 (1977): 371–99.

Ariza, Marquesa de. *Elogio de la Reyna N.S. formado por la Excelentísima Señora Marquesa de Ariza, socia de honor y mérito de la junta de señoras, leído en la junta pública de distribución de premios, celebrada por la Real Sociedad Económica de Madrid en 22 de enero de 1795*. Madrid. Imprenta de Sancha, 1795.

Artiñano, Pedro M. de. "Los encajes en España durante el reinado de los Borbones." *Arte Español: Revista de la Sociedad de Amigos del Arte* 6, no. 1 (1922): 61–87.

Artola, Miguel. *Los afrancesados*. Madrid: Alianza Editorial, 1989 [1953].

Ayala, Ignacio López de. "Papel sobre si las señoras deben admitirse como individuos de las Sociedades." In *Ilustración y educación: La Sociedad Económica Matritense*, ed. Olegario Negrín Fajardo, 176–83. Madrid: Editora Nacional, 1984.

Aymes, Jean-René, ed. *España y la Revolución francesa*. Barcelona: Editorial Crítica, 1989.

———. *La guerra de la independencia en España (1808–1814)*. 4th ed. Madrid: Siglo Veintiuno de España Editores, S.A., 1990.

———. "Las repercusiones politico-ideológicas de la Revolución francesa en España (1789–1795): Esbozo de síntesis." In *Repercusiones de la Revolución francesa en España,* ed. Celso Almuiña and Emilio de Diego, 31–64. Madrid: Hispagraphis, S.A., 1990.

Azcárate Ristori, José María de, Julián Gállego, Juan José Martín González, Antonio Bonet Correa, José Antonio Domínguez Salazar, and Ángel del Campo y Francés. *Obras maestras de la Real Academia de San Fernando: Su primer siglo de historia (exposición conmemorativa del 250 aniversario de su fundación).* Madrid: Real Academia de Bellas Artes de San Fernando, 1994.

Azcona, Tarsicio de. *Isabel la Católica: Estudio crítico de su vida y su reinado.* Madrid: Biblioteca de Autores Cristianos, 1993.

Barbeito Carneiro, María Isabel. "Feminist Attitudes and Expression in Golden Age Spain: From Teresa de Jesús to María de Guevara." In *Recovering Spain's Feminist Tradition,* ed. Lisa Vollendorf, 48–68. New York: Modern Language Association of America, 2001.

———. *Mujeres del siglo XVII entre Europa y Madrid.* Madrid: Ayuntamiento, 1990.

Barberá, Carmen. *La duquesa de Alba.* Barcelona: Editorial Planeta, S.A., 1995.

Barcía y Pavón, Ángel María. *Catálogo de la colección de dibujos originales de la Biblioteca Nacional.* Madrid: Tipográficos de la Revista de Archivos, Bibliotecas, y Museos, 1906.

Baretti, Joseph. *A Journey from London to Genoa, through England, Portugal, Spain, and France.* With an introduction by Ian Robertson. 2 vols. Sussex: Centaur Press Limited, 1970.

Barnes, Gwendolyn. "Enlightenment and Religious Oratory in Eighteenth-Century Spain." *Ideologies and Literature: Journal of Hispanic and Lusiphone Discourse* 3, no. 2 (1998): 115–84.

Baroja de Caro, Carmen. *El encaje en España.* Barcelona: Editorial Labor, S.A., 1933.

Barreno, María Luisa. "Bordadores de cámara y situación del arte de bordar en Madrid durante la segunda mitad del siglo XVIII." *Archivo Español de Arte* 47, no. 187 (1974): 273–300.

Basco Flancas, Ricardo. *Apoyo a la defensa de las mugeres, que escrivió El R. Mo P. Fr. Benito Feyjóo y crisis de la contra-defensa crítica que a favor de los hombres, y contra las mugeres, dió a luz temerariamente Don Laurencio Manco de Olivares, en dictamen que da de ella a una señora.* Madrid: Viuda de Blas de Villanueva, 1727.

Baum, Robert, II. "The Counter-Discourse of Josepha Amar y Borbón's *Discurso.*" *Dieciocho: Hispanic Enlightenment* 17, no. 1 (1994): 7–15.

Beckford, William. *The Journal of William Beckford in Portugal and Spain, 1787–1788.* Ed. Alexander Boyd. London: Rupert Hart-Davis, 1954.

Bédat, Claude. *Los académicos y las juntas, 1752–1808.* Madrid: Real Academia de Bellas Artes de San Fernando, 1982.

———. *L'académie des beaux-arts de Madrid: 1744–1808*. Toulouse: Association des Publications de l'Université de Toulouse, 1973.
Bell, David A. "The Public Sphere, the State, and the World of Law in Eighteenth-Century France." *French Historical Studies* 17, no. 4 (1992): 912–34.
Benito, María Pilar. "Los estados civiles de la mujer en el siglo XVIII a través de los textos literarios." In *Literatura y vida cotidiana: Actas de las cuartas jornadas de investigación interdisciplinaria*, 201–15. Zaragoza: Seminario de Estudios de la Mujer, Universidad Autónoma de Madrid, 1987.
Bennassar, Bartolomé. *The Spanish Character: Attitudes and Mentalities from the Sixteenth to the Nineteenth Century*. Berkeley: University of California Press, 1975.
Berg, Maxine. *The Age of Manufactures, 1700–1820*. London: Fontana Press, 1985.
Bilinkoff, Jodi. *The Avila of Santa Teresa: Religious Reform in a Sixteenth-Century City*. Ithaca: Cornell University Press, 1989.
———. "Elite Widows and Religious Expression in Early Modern Spain: The View from Avila." In *Widowhood in Medieval and Early Modern Europe*, ed. Sandra Cavallo and Lyndan Warner, 181–92. London: Longman, 1999.
Blackbourn, David, and Geoff Eley. *The Peculiarities of German History: Bourgeois Society and Politics in Nineteenth-Century Germany*. Oxford: Oxford University Press, 1984.
Blanco Soler, Carlos, Antonio Piga Pascual, and Manuel Pérez Petinto. *La duquesa de Alba y su tiempo*. Madrid: Ediciones y Publicaciones Españolas, S.A., 1949.
Bock, Gisela. *Women in European History*. Trans. Allison Brown. Oxford: Blackwell Publishers, 2002.
Boix, Felix. *Exposición de dibujos originales, 1750–1860*. Madrid: Imprenta Blass, 1922.
Bolufer Peruga, Mónica. "Actitudes y discursos sobre la maternidad en la España del siglo XVIII: La cuestión de la lactancia." *Historia Social* 14 (Fall 1992): 3–22.
———. "Escritura femenina y publicación en el siglo XVIII: De la expresión personal a la 'república de las letras.'" In *Género y ciudadanía: Revisiones desde el ámbito privado*, ed. Margarita Ortega et al., 197–223. Madrid: Instituto Universitario de Estudios de la Mujer, Universidad Autónoma de Madrid, 1999.
———. "Espectadores y lectoras: Representaciones e influencia del público femenino en la prensa del siglo XVIII." *Cuadernos de Estudios del Siglo XVIII* 5 (1995): 23–57.
———. "Galerías de 'mujeres ilustres' o el sinuoso camino de la excepción a la norma cotidiana (ss. XV–XVIII)." *Hispania* 60, no. 204 (2000): 181–224.
———. "La lactancia asalariada en Valencia a finales del siglo XVIII." *Saitabi* 43 (1993): 255–68.
———. "Máscaras femeninas en un periódico ilustrado: El *Diario de Valencia* (1790–1800)." *Estudis: Revista de Historia Moderna* 18 (1992): 199–215.

———. *Mujeres e ilustración: La construcción de la femininidad en la Ilustración española*. Valencia: Artes Gráficas, S.A., 1998.

———. "El plantel del estado: Educación física de las mujeres y los niños en la literatura del siglo XVIII." In *Mulheres, Trabalho e reproduçã: Attitudes sociais e políticus de protecção à vida*, ed. Mary Nash and Rosa Ballester, vol. 2, 57–75. Porto: Edições Afrontamento, 1996.

Bolufer Peruga, Mónica, and Isabel Morant Deusa. "Josefa Amar y Borbón: Une intellectuelle espagnole dans les debats de lumières." *Clio: Histoire, Femmes, et Sociétés* 13 (2001): 69–97.

———. "On Women's Reason, Education, and Love: Women and Men of the Enlightenment in Spain and France." *Gender and History* 10, no. 2 (August 1998): 183–216.

———. "Pedagogía y moral en el siglo de las luces: Las escritoras francesas y su recepción en España." *Revista de Historia Moderna* 20 (2002): 251–92.

Bordiga Grinstein, Julia. "Dramaturgas españolas de fines del siglo XVIII y principios del siglo XIX: El caso de María Rosa de Gálvez." Ph.D. diss., University of Pennsylvania, 1996.

———. "Panorama de la dramaturgia femenina española en la segunda mitad del siglo XVIII y principios del siglo XIX." *Dieciocho: Hispanic Enlightenment* 25, no. 2 (Fall 2002): 195–218.

———. "La rosa trágica de Málaga: Vida y obra de María Rosa de Gálvez." *Anejos de Dieciocho* 3 (2003): 1–223.

Boruchoff, David A., ed. *Isabel la Católica, Queen of Castile: Critical Essays*. New York: Palgrave Macmillan, 2003.

Bostic, Heidi. "The Light of Reason in Graffigny's *Lettres d'une Péruvienne*." *Dalhousie French Studies* 63 (Summer 2003): 3–11.

Bradley, James E., and Dale K. Van Kley, eds. *Religion and Politics in Enlightenment Europe*. Notre Dame, IN: University of Notre Dame Press, 2001.

Brown, Jonathan. "Academies of Painting in Seventeenth-Century Spain." In *Academies of Art: Between Renaissance and Romanticism*, ed. Anton W. A. Boschloo, 177–85. The Hague: SDU Uitgeverij, 1989.

Burns, Kathryn. *Colonial Habits: Convents and the Spiritual Economy of Cuzco, Peru*. Durham, NC: Duke University Press, 1999.

Buxó, María José, and Pedro Voltes. *Las mujeres en la historia de España*. Barcelona: Editorial Planeta, 1986.

Cabarrús, Francisco. "Memoria sobre la admisión y asistencia de las mujeres en la Sociedad Patriótica." In *Ilustración y educación: La Sociedad Económica Matritense*, ed. Olegario Negrín Fajardo, 150–56. Madrid: Editora Nacional, 1984.

Calderone, Antonietta. "Traducción y adaptación de piezas de tema americano en el teatro español del siglo XVIII." In *Teatro y traducción*, ed. Francisco Lafarga and Roberto Dengler, 83–93. Barcelona: Universitat Pompeu Fabra, 1995.

Calhoun, Craig, ed. *Habermas and the Public Sphere*. Cambridge: MIT Press, 1992.

Cambre Mariño, Jesús. "La Ilustración, la Revolución francesa y la reacción en España." *La Torre: Revista General de la Universidad de Puerto Rico* 5, supplement (1991): 91–108.

Campomanes, Pedro Rodríguez. *Discurso sobre el fomento de la industria popular*. Madrid: Don Antonio de Sancha, 1774.

———. *Discurso sobre la educación popular de los artesanos y su fomento*. Ed. Francisco Aguilar Piñal. Madrid: Editora Nacional, 1978.

———. "Memoria sobre la admisión de señoras, presentada a la Real Sociedad Económica de Amigos del País por el Conde de Campomanes el 18 de noviembre de 1775 sobre la admisión de las señoras en ella." In *La mujer ilustrada en la España del siglo XVIII*, ed. Paloma Fernández-Quintanilla, 154–57. Madrid: Ministerio de Cultura, 1981.

Camporredondo, María. *Tratado philosóphi-poético escótico, compuesto en siguidillas por Doña María Camporredondo (muger, y sobrina de Don Manuel de Camporredondo), natural, y vecina de la villa de Almagro*. Madrid: Miguel Escrivano, 1758.

Cano González, Rufino, and R. Clara Revuelta Guerrero. *Escuelas y talleres de la Sociedad Económica de Amigos del País de Valladolid (1783–1820)*. Valladolid: Secretariado de Publicaciones e Intercambio Editorial, Universidad de Valladolid, 2002.

Capel Martínez, Rosa María. "La mujer española en el siglo XVIII: Estado de la cuestión." In *Coloquio Internacional Carlos III y su siglo*, 511–17. Madrid: Universidad Complutense, Departamento de Historia Moderna, 1990.

———. "Mujer, sociedad, y literatura en el setecientos española." *Cuadernos de Historia Moderna* 16 (1995): 103–19.

Capella Martinez, Miguel. *La industria en Madrid: Ensayo histórico crítico de la fabricación y artesanía madrileñas*. 2 vols. Madrid: Artes Gráficas y Ediciones, S.A., 1962–1963.

Capmany y Suris de Montpalau, Antonio de. *Arte de traducir el idioma francés al castellano*. Ed. María del Carmen Fernández Díaz. Santiago de Compostela: Universidad de Santiago de Compostela, Servicio de Publicacións e Intercambio Científico, 1987.

Carande, Ramón. "El despotismo ilustrado de los 'Amigos del País.'" In *Siete estudios de historia de España*, 143–81. Barcelona: Ediciones Ariel, 1969.

Carrascosa Miguel, Pablo. "El teatro de Nicasio Alvarez de Cienfuegos y las ideas de la Ilustración." In *Repercusiones de la Revolución francesa en España*, ed. Celso Almuiña and Emilio de Diego, 645–75. Madrid: Hispagraphis, S.A., 1990.

"Carta de Don Juan Antonio Hernández de Larrea, á Doña Josepha Amar, diciendo su parecer sobre el discurso antecedente." *Memorial Literario* (Madrid), 7 (August 1786): 438.

Caso, María Catalina de, trans. *Modo de enseñar y estudiar las bellas letras, para ilustrar el entendimiento, y rectificar el corazón*, by Charles Rollin. 4 vols. Madrid: Imprenta del Mercurio, 1755.

Caso González, José Miguel. *De ilustración y de ilustrados*. Oviedo: Instituto Feijóo de Estudios del Siglo XVIII, 1988.
———. "La literatura de 1759 a 1808." In *El estado y la cultura (1759–1808)*. Vol. 1 of *La época de la Ilustración*. Historia de España, ed. José María Jover Zamora, no. 31. Madrid: Espasa-Calpe, 1988.
Cassirer, Ernst. *The Philosophy of Enlightenment*. Trans. C. A. Koelln and James P. Pettergrove. Boston: Beacon Press, 1955.
Castellano Castellano, Juan Luis. *Luces y reformismo: Las Sociedades Económicas de Amigos del País del reino de Granada en el siglo XVIII*. Granada: Imprenta Provincial, 1984.
Caveda y Solares, Rita, trans. *Cartas selectas de una señora á una sobrina suya, entresacadas de una obra inglesa impresa en Filadelfia, y traducidas al español por Doña Rita Caveda y Solares*. Madrid: García y Compañía, 1800.
Ceán Bermúdez, Juan Agustín. *Diccionario histórico de los más ilustres profesores de las Bellas Artes en España*. 5 vols. 1800. Reprint, Madrid: Reales Academias de Bellas Artes de San Fernando y de la Historia, 1965.
Chamorro, Bonifacio. "Jovellanos y las mujeres." *Letras: Revista del Hogar* 8, no. 85 (August 1944): 1–3.
Chartier, Roger. *The Cultural Origins of the French Revolution*. Trans. Lydia G. Cochrane. Durham, NC: Duke University Press, 1991.
———. *Lectures et lecteurs dans la France d'Ancien Régime*. Paris: Seuil, 1987.
———. *Passions of the Renaissance*. Trans. Arthur Goldhammer. Vol. 3 of *History of Private Life*, ed. Philipe Ariès and Georges Duby. Cambridge: Harvard University Press, 1989.
Checa Beltrán, José. "Opiniones dieciochistas sobre la traducción como elemento enriquecedor o deformador de la propia lengua." In *Traducción y adaptación cultural: España-Francia*, ed. María Luisa Donaire and Francisco Lafarga, 593–602. Oviedo: Universidad de Oviedo, 1991.
Checa Beltrán, José, J. A. Ríos, and I. Vallejo. *La poesía del siglo XVIII*. Historia de la Literatura Española, ed. R. de la Fuente, no. 26. Madrid: Ediciones Júcar, 1992.
Cienfuegos, Beatriz. *La Pensadora Gaditana*. Ed. Cinta Canterla. Cádiz: Publicaciones de la Universidad de Cádiz, 1996.
Clavijo y Fajardo, Joseph. *El Pensador*. Madrid: Joachin Ibarra, 1762.
Coe, Ada M. *Catálogo bibliográfico y crítico de las comedias anunciadas en los periódicos de Madrid desde 1661 hasta 1819*. The Johns Hopkins Studies in Romance Literatures and Languages, extra vol. 9. Baltimore: Johns Hopkins Press, 1935.
Coffin, Judith G. *The Politics of Women's Work: The Paris Garment Trades, 1750–1915*. Princeton: Princeton University Press, 1996.
Coolidge, Grace. "Families in Crisis: Women, Guardianship, and the Nobility in Early Modern Spain." Ph.D. diss., University of Indiana, 2001.
Cordoba y Pacheco, Sor María, trans. *Discursos espirituales y morales*, by P. César Calino. Málaga: Félix de Casas y Martínez, 1786.
Corteguera, Luis R. "The Making of a Visionary Woman: The Life of Beatriz

Ana Ruiz, 1666–1735." In *Women, Texts, and Authority in the Early Modern Spanish World,* ed. Marta V. Vicente and Luis R. Corteguera, 165–82. Aldershot: Ashgate, 2004.

Coughlin, Edward V. "The Polemic of Feijóo's 'Defensa de las mujeres.'" *Dieciocho: Hispanic Enlightenment* 9, nos. 1–2 (1986): 74–85.

Cox, R. Merritt. *Tomás de Iriarte.* Twayne's World Authors Series, 228. New York: Twayne Publishers, 1972.

Criado y Domínguez, Juan P. *Literatas españolas del siglo XIX: Apuntes bibliográficos.* Madrid: Imprenta de Antonio Pérez Dubrull, 1889.

Cruz Seoane, María. *Historia del periodismo en España.* 3 vols. Madrid: Alianza Editorial, 1983–1996.

Cruz Valenciano, Jesús. *Gentlemen, Bourgeois, and Revolutionaries: Political Change and Cultural Persistence among the Spanish Dominant Groups, 1750–1850.* New York: Cambridge University Press, 1996.

———. "Hidalgos, burgueses, libros, y libreros en Madrid, 1751." *Villa de Madrid* 26 (1988): 116–40.

Cubié, Juan Bautista. *Las mugeres vindicadas de las calumnias de los hombres: Con un catálogo de las Españolas, que mas se han distinguido en ciencias, y armas.* Madrid: Imprenta de Antonio Perez de Soto, 1768.

Cueto, Leopoldo Augusto de. *Poetas líricos del siglo XVIII.* Biblioteca de autores españoles desde la formación del lenguaje hasta nuestros días, no. 61. Madrid: Ediciones Atlas, 1952.

Curtis, Judith. "Anticipating Zilia: Madame de Graffigny in 1744." In *Femmes savantes et femmes d'esprit: Women Intellectuals of the French Eighteenth Century,* ed. Roland Bonnel and Catherine Rubinger, 129–54. New York: Peter Lang, 1994.

D'Abrantès, Duchesse. *Souvenirs d'une ambassade et d'un séjour en Espagne et en Portugal, de 1808 a 1811.* 2 vols. Paris: Ollivier, Libraire-Éditeur, 1837.

Darnton, Robert. *The Great Cat Massacre and Other Episodes in French Cultural History.* New York: Vintage Books, 1984.

Da Silva, Jose-Gentil. "La mujer en España en la época mercantil: De la igualdad al aislamiento." In *La mujer en la historia de España (Siglos XVI–XX): Actas de las II jornadas de investigación interdisciplinaria,* ed. Universidad Autónoma de Madrid, Seminario de Estudios de la Mujer, 11–33. Madrid: Ediciones de la Universidad Autónoma de Madrid, 1990.

Davis, Charles, and Paul Julian Smith, eds. *Art and Literature in Spain: 1600–1800: Studies in Honour of Nigel Glendinning.* London: Támesis Books Limited, 1993.

Deacon, Philip. "Portrait of an Eighteenth-Century Spanish Intellectual: Luis Joseph Velázquez." In *Art and Literature in Spain: 1600–1800: Studies in Honour of Nigel Glendinning,* ed. Charles David and Paul Julian Smith, 105–16. London: Támesis Books Limited, 1993.

———. "Vicente García de la Huerta y el círculo de Montiano: La amistad entre Huerta y Margarita Hickey." *Revista de Estudios Extremeños* 44, no. 2 (1988): 395–421.

Deane, Phyllis. *The First Industrial Revolution*. 2nd ed. Cambridge: Cambridge University Press, 1979.
Defourneaux, Marcelin. *Inquisición y censura del libros en la España del siglo XVIII*. Trans. J. Ignacio Tellechea Idigoras. Madrid: Taurus Ediciones, S.A., 1973.
———. "Les *Lettres péruviennes* en Espagne." *Mélanges offert a Marcel Bataillon par les Hispanistes Français, Bulletin Hispanique* 64 bis (1962): 412–23.
De Grazia, Victoria, ed. *The Sex of Things: Gender and Consumption in Historical Perspective*. Berkeley: University of California Press, 1996.
De Jean, Joan. Introduction to *Letters from a Peruvian Woman*, by Françoise de Graffigny. Trans. David Kornacker. New York: Modern Language Association of America, 1993.
Delpy, G. *L'Espagne et l'esprit européen: L'oeuvre de Feijoo (1725–1760)*. Paris: Librairie Hachette, 1936.
Demerson, Jorge. *La Real Sociedad Económica de Amigos del País de Avila (1786–1857)*. Avila: Imprenta de "El Diario de Avila," 1968.
———. *La Real Sociedad Económica de Valladolid (1784–1808): Notas para su historia*. Universidad de Valladolid, Departamento de Historia Moderna, Estudios y Documentos, 28. Valladolid: Gráficas Andrés Martín, 1969.
Demerson, Jorge, and Paula de Demerson. *La decadencia de las Reales Sociedades Económicas de Amigos del País*. Oviedo: Centro de Estudios del Siglo XVIII, Universidad de Oviedo, 1978.
Demerson, Paula de. *Catálogo de las socias de honor y mérito de la junta de damas matritense (1787–1811)*. Tirada Aparte de los Anales del Instituto de Estudios Madrileños, 7. Madrid: Raycar, S.A., 1966.
———. *La Condesa de Montijo, una mujer al servicio de las luces*. Madrid: Fundación Universitaria Española, 1976.
———. "Les écoles patriotiques de Madrid entre 1787 et 1808." *Cahiers du Monde Hispanique et Luso-Brésilien (Caravelle)* 13 (1969): 83–95.
———. "Las Escuelas Patrióticas de Madrid entre 1787 y 1808." In *Las Reales Sociedades Económicas de Amigos del País y su obra*, 191–205. San Sebastián: G. Izarra, 1972.
———. *María Francisca de Sales Portocarrero (Condesa del Montijo): Una figura de la Ilustración*. Madrid: Editora Nacional, 1975.
———. *Una mujer cirujano en tiempos de Carlos IV: Victoria de Félix*. Tirada Aparte de los Anales del Instituto de Estudios Madrileños, 9. Madrid: Raycar, S.A., 1973
———. *La Real Inclusa de Madrid a finales del siglo XVIII*. Madrid: Raycar, S.A., 1972.
Demerson, Paula de, Francisco Aguilar Piñal, and Jorge Demerson. *Las Sociedades Económicas de Amigos del País en el siglo XVIII*. San Sebastian: Gráficas Izarra, 1974.
Díaz-Plaja, Fernando. *Teresa Cabarrús: Una española en los destinos de la Revolución francesa*. Barcelona: Editorial Olimpo, 1943.
Diego, Estrella de. "La educación artística en el XIX: Todo menos pintoras. La

mujer profesora de dibujo." In *VI jornadas de investigación interdisciplinaria sobre la mujer: El trabajo de las mujeres: Siglos XVI–XX*, ed. Universidad Autónoma de Madrid, Seminario de Estudios de la Mujer, 227–38. Madrid: Imprenta de la Universidad Autónoma de Madrid, 1987.

———. *La mujer y la pintura del XIX español (Cuatrocientas olvidadas y algunas más)*. Madrid: Ediciones Cátedra, S.A., 1987.

———. "Nobles damas y mujeres pintoras: Una aproximación." In *El arte en las cortes europeas del siglo XVIII*, 237–42. Madrid: Comunidad de Madrid, 1989.

———. "Reales estudios y la educación artística de las niñas en la primera mitad del siglo XIX." In *Cinco siglos de arte en Madrid: III jornadas de arte*, ed. Departamento de Historia del Arte "Diego Velazquez," Centro de Estudios Históricos, Consejo Superior de Investigaciones Científicas, 377–82. Madrid: Editorial Alpuerto, S.A., 1991.

Diego, Estrella de, Juan Carrete, and Jesusa Vega. *Estampas españolas, grabado 1550–1820*. 2 vols. Catálogo del gabinete de estampas del Museo Municipal de Madrid. Madrid: Museo Municipal, 1985.

Diez de Armendariz, Antonio. *El nuevo para todos: Siete discursos*. Madrid: Imprenta de la Viuda de Manuel Fernandez, 1767.

Dillard, Heath. *Daughters of the Reconquest: Women in Castilian Town Society, 1100–1300*. Cambridge: Cambridge University Press, 1984.

Dinan, Susan Eileen. "Confraternities as a Venue for Female Activism during the Catholic Reformation." In *Confraternities and Catholic Reform in Italy, France, and Spain*, ed. John Patrick Donnelly and Michael W. Maher, Sixteenth-Century Essays and Studies, vol. 44, 191–213. Kirksville, MO: Thomas Jefferson University Press, 1999.

Discurso sobre el luxo de las señoras y proyecto de un traje nacional. Madrid: Imprenta Real, 1788. A facsimile edition: Madrid: Mondadori España, S.A., 1987.

Dobie, Madeleine. "'Language inconnu': Montesquieu, Graffigny, and the Writing of Exile." *Romanic Review* 87, no. 2 (1996): 209–24.

———. "The Subject of Writing: Language, Epistemology, and Identity in the *Lettres d'une Péruvienne*." *Eighteenth Century* 38, no. 2 (1997): 99–117.

Dock, Terry S. *Women in the Encyclopédie: A Compendium*. Madrid: J. Porrua Turanzas, 1983.

Domergue, Lucienne. *Censure et lumière dans l'Espagne de Charles III*. Paris: Éditions du CNRS, 1982.

———. *Jovellanos à la société économique des amis du pays de Madrid (1778–1795)*. Toulouse: France-Ibérie, 1971.

———. *Le livre en Espagne au temps de la Révolution Française*. Lyon: Presses Universitaires de Lyon, 1984.

———. "Penser les femmes, pensée des femmes dans l'Espagne des lumières." In *Femmes-philosophes en Espagne et en Amérique Latine*, ed. Lucienne Domergue, 11–25. Paris: Editions du Centre National de la Recherche Scientifique, 1989.

Dominguez Bordona, Jesús. *El arte de la miniatura española*. Madrid: Editorial Plutarco, S.A., 1932.

Dominguez Lazaro, Martín. "La educación en España en la segunda mitad del siglo XVIII." *Revista Española de Pedagogia* 43, no. 167 (1985): 71–89.

———. "Tres cartas de Mengs." *Archivo Español de Arte y Arqueología* 1 (1925): 226–28.

Dominguez Ortiz, Antonio. "La reconstrucción del estado español por los primeros Borbones." In *I Borbone di Napoli e i Borbone di Spagna*, ed. Mario Di Pinto, 385–405. Naples: Guida Editori, 1985.

Dominguez Salazar, José Antonio, José Enrique García Melero, Andrés Úbeda de los Cobos, Leticia Azcue Brea, and Elvira Villena. *Renovación, Crisis, Continuismo: La Real Academia de San Fernando en 1792*. Madrid: Real Academia de Bellas Artes de San Fernando, 1992.

Donahue-Wallace, Kelly. "*La casada imperfecta:* A Woman, a Print, and the Inquisition." *Mexican Studies* 18, no. 2 (2002): 231–50.

Donaire, María Luisa, and Francisco Lafarga, eds. *Traducción y adaptación cultural: Espana-Francia*. Oviedo: Universidad de Oviedo, 1991.

Dopico Black, Georgina. *Perfect Wives, Other Women: Adultery and Inquisition in Early Modern Spain*. Durham, NC: Duke University Press, 2001.

Dosi-Delfini, G. Gray de Cristoforis. "La dama defendente ovvero una tesi de laurea femminile del 1722." *Archivio Storico per le Province Parmensi* 36 (1984): 61–87.

Douthwaite, Julia V. *Exotic Women: Literary Heroines and Cultural Strategies in Ancien Régime France*. Philadelphia: University of Pennsylvania Press, 1992.

———. "Relocating the Exotic Other in *Lettres d'une Péruvienne*." *Romanic Review* 82, no. 4 (1997): 456–74.

Dupuis, Lucien. "Francia y lo Francés en la prensa periódica española durante la Revolución francesa." In *La literatura española del siglo XVIII y sus fuentes extranjeras*, 95–127. Oviedo: Universidad de Oviedo, 1968.

Earenfight, Theresa. *Queenship and Political Power in Medieval and Early Modern Spain*. Women and Gender in the Early Modern World Series. Aldershot: Ashgate, 2005.

Elizalde Armendariz, Ignacio. "Feijóo, representante del enciclopedismo Español." In *II Simposio sobre el Padre Feijóo y su siglo*, ed. Catedra Feijóo, vol. 1, 321–45. Oviedo: Centro de Estudios del Siglo XVIII, 1981.

Enciso Recio, Luis Miguel. "La reforma de la universidad española en la época de Carlos III." In *I Borbone di Napoli e i Borbone di Spagna*, ed. Mario Di Pinto, 191–239. Naples: Guida Editori, 1985.

Enders, Victoria Lorée, and Pamela Beth Radcliff, eds. *Constructing Spanish Womanhood: Female Identity in Modern Spain*. Albany: State University of New York Press, 1999.

Entrambasaguas y Peña, Joaquín de. "Tres notas para la historia del arte." *Revista de la Biblioteca, Archivo, y Museo del Ayuntamiento de Madrid* 6, no. 22 (1929): 215–20.

Equipo Madrid de Estudios Históricos. *Carlos III, Madrid, y la Ilustración.* Madrid: Siglo XXI de España Editores, 1988.

Erauso, Catalina de. *Memoir of a Basque Lieutenant Nun Transvestite in the New World.* Trans. Michele Stepto and Gabriel Stepto. Boston: Beacon Press, 1996.

Escolano Benito, Agustín. "Las escuelas de diseño y dibujo y la renovación de las artes industriales en la segunda mitad del siglo XVIII." In *Educación e ilustración en España: III coloquio de historia de la educación,* 442–50. Barcelona: Publicaciones del Departamento de Educación Comparada e Historia de la Educación, Universidad de Barcelona, 1984.

Espeja, Marquesa de, trans. *Compendio de la filosofía moral, escrito en lengua Italiana por D. Francisco María Zanotti, y traducido al español por la Marquesa de Espeja,* by Francisco María Zanotti. Madrid: D. Joaquin Ibarra, 1785.

Espina Garcia, Antonio. "María Isidra de Guzmán, la erudita." In *Seis vidas españolas (María Isidra de Guzmán, Diego de Torres Villarroel, María Luisa de Parma, Isidoro Máiquez, Lola Montes, Julián Romea),* 11–35. Madrid: Taurus Ediciones, S.A., 1967.

———. *Las tertulias de Madrid.* Ed. Óscar Ayala. Madrid: Alianza Tres, 1995.

Espinosa de los Monteros, Don Manuel. *Relación de los exercicios literarios, que la Señora Doña María del Rosario Cepeda y Mayo, hija de D. Francisco de Cepeda y Guerrero, Cavallero profeso del Orden de Calatrava, Alguacil mayor de la Inquisición, regidor perpetuo de esta ciudad, capitan de sus milicias y diputado de la Real Junta de Sanidad; y de la Señora Doña Isabel Mayo, actuó los días 19, 22, y 24 de septiembre del presente año desde las nueve, a las doce de la mañana de cada un día, teniendo solamente doce de edad, y poco menos de uno de instrucción en sus estudios.* Cádiz: Impresor Real de Marina, 1768.

Espinosa Martín, María del Carmen. "El retrato-miniatura de los regalos diplomáticos españoles en el siglo XVIII." In *El arte en las cortes europeas del siglo XVIII,* 263–68. Madrid: Comunidad de Madrid, 1989.

Ezquerra del Bayo, Joaquín. *La Duquesa de Alba y Goya: Estudio biográfico y artístico.* Madrid: Aguilar, 1959.

Ezquerra del Bayo, Joaquín, and Luis Pérez Bueno. *Retratos de mujeres españolas del siglo XIX.* Madrid: J. Cosana, 1924.

Feijoo y Montenegro, Benito Jerónimo. *Defensa de la mujer.* Ed. Victoria Sau. Barcelona: Icaria, 1997. Translated as *An Essay on Women; or, Physiological and Historical Defense of the Fair Sex* (London: W. Bingley, 1765); *An Essay on the Learning, Genius, and Abilities of the Fair Sex Proving Them Not Inferior to Man, from a Variety of Examples, Extracted from Ancient and Modern History* (London: D. Steel, 1774); and *Three Essays or Discourses on the Following Subjects, a Defense or Vindication of the Women, Church Music, a Comparison between Ancient and Modern Music* (London: T. Becket, 1778).

———. *Teatro crítico universal.* 7th ed. Ed. Angel Raimundo Fernández González. Madrid: Cátedra, 2002.

Fernanda de Tordesillas Cepeda y Sada, María Antonia, trans. *Instrucción de una señora christiana para vivir en el mundo santamente: Traducida del Francés al Español por Da. María Antonia Fernanda de Tordesillas Cepeda y Sada*, by Jacques Joseph Duguet. Madrid: Joachin Ibarra, 1775.

Fernández Gómez, Juan Fernando. "Tendencias de la traducción de obras francesas en el siglo XVIII." In *Traducción y adaptación cultural: España-Francia*, ed. María Luisa Donaire and Francisco Lafarga, 579–91. Oviedo: Universidad de Oviedo, 1991.

Fernández Pérez, Paloma. "Mujeres y burguesía en el Cádiz del siglo XVIII." In *La burguesía española en la edad moderna*, ed. L. M. Enciso, vol. 1, 281–98. Valladolid: Universidad de Valladolid, 1996.

———. *El rostro familiar de la metrópoli: Redes de parentesco y lazos mercantiles en Cádiz, 1700–1812*. Madrid: Siglo XXI de España Editores, 1997.

Fernández-Quintanilla, Paloma. "Una española ilustrada: Doña María Isidra Quintina de Guzmán y de La Cerda." *Tiempo de Historia* 5, no. 60 (November 1979): 96–105.

———. "La junta de damas de honor y mérito." *Historia 16* 5, no. 54 (October 1980): 65–73.

———. *La mujer ilustrada en la España del siglo XVIII*. Madrid: Ministerio de Cultura, 1981.

———. "Los salones de las 'damas ilustradas' madrileñas en el siglo XVIII." *Tiempo de Historia* 5, no. 52 (March 1979): 44–53.

———. "Un traje nacional femenino: Floridablanca quiso uniformar a las Españolas." *Historia 16* 3, no. 30 (October 1978): 115–21.

Fernández y Figuero, Magdalena, trans. *La muerte de Abel vengada: Tragedia en tres actos*, by Gabriel Le Gouvé. Madrid: Imprenta de la Viuda de Ibarra, 1803.

Fink De Backer, Stephanie L. "Widows at the Nexus of Family and Community in Early Modern Castile." Ph.D. diss., University of Arizona, 2003.

Fischer, Christian Augustus. *A Picture of Madrid: Taken on the Spot*. London: J. G. Barnard, 1808.

Floriano Cumbreño, Antonio C. *El bordado*. Barcelona: Editorial Alberto Martín, 1942.

Forniés Casals, José Francisco. *Fuentes para el estudio de la Sociedad y la Económica Aragonesas, 1776–1808: Documentos citados en las actas de la Real Sociedad Económica Aragonesa de Amigos del País*. Zaragoza: Diputación Provincial, Institución "Fernando el Católico," 1980.

———. *La Real Sociedad Económica Aragonesa de Amigos del País en el periodo de la Ilustración (1776–1808): Sus relaciones con el artesanado y la industria*. Madrid: Confederación Española de Cajas de Ahorros, 1978.

Fourny, Diane. "Language and Reality in Françoise de Graffigny's *Lettres d'une Péruvienne*." *Eighteenth-Century Fiction* 4, no. 2 (1992): 221–38.

Fox-Genovese, Elizabeth. "Women and the Enlightenment." In *Becoming Visible: Women in European History*, ed. Renate Bridenthal, 251–77. Boston: Houghton-Mifflin, 1987.

Fox-Lockert, Lucía. *Women Novelists in Spain and Spanish America.* London: Scarecrow Press, 1979.
Franco Rubio, Gloria A. "Educación femenina y prosopografía: Las alumnas del Colegio de las Salesas Reales en el siglo˙XVIII." *Cuadernos de Historia Moderna* 19 (1997): 171–81.
Freixa, Consol. *Los Ingleses y el arte de viajar: Una visión de las ciudades españolas en el siglo XVIII.* Barcelona: Ediciones del Serbal, 1993.
Freixa, Mireia. "Las mujeres artistas desde la Revolución francesa al fin del siglo." In *Historia del arte y mujeres,* ed. Teresa Sauret, 71–89. Málaga: Universidad de Málaga, 1996.
Frick Art Reference Library. *Spanish Artists from the Fourth to the Twentieth Century: A Critical Dictionary.* 4 vols. New York: G. K. Hall and Company, 1993.
Fuerte-Híjar, Marquesa de, trans. *Noticia de la vida y obras del Conde de Rumford, traducida del Francés, y presentada á la Sociedad Patriótica de Madrid.* N.p., n.d.
Galerstein, Carolyn L., ed. *Women Writers of Spain.* New York: Greenwood Press, 1986.
Gálvez, María Rosa. *Ali-Bek.* Madrid: En la Oficina de D. Benito García, y Compañía, 1801.
———. *Obras poéticas de Doña María Rosa Gálvez.* Madrid: Imprenta Real, 1804.
———. "Poesía—Oda: En elogio de las fumigaciones de morvó, establecidas en España á beneficio de la humanidad, de orden del Excelentísimo Señor Príncipe de La Paz." *Minerva o El Revisor General* 3 (1806): 3–10.
———. *"Safo," "Zinda," y "La familia a la moda."* Ed. Fernando Doménech. Madrid: Publicaciones de la Asociación de Directores de Escena de España, 1995.
———. "Viage al Teyde." *Variedades de Ciencias, Literatura, y Artes* (February 1805): 301–8.
———, trans. *Catalina, ó la bella labradora, comedia en tres actos,* by Amélie-Julie Caneille. Madrid: D. Benito García, y Compañía, 1801.
García Brocara, José Luis. *La Real Sociedad Económica Matritense de Amigos del País.* Madrid: Publicación de la Real Sociedad, 1991.
García Buñuel, Pedro Christian, ed. *Guión y synopsis cinematográfica de Luis Buñuel.* Teruel: Instituto de Estudios Turolenses, 1992.
García de León, María Encarnación. "Los prólogos de las traducciones de novelas en el s. XVIII." In *II simposio sobre el Padre Feijóo y su siglo,* ed. Catedra Feijóo, vol. 2, 483–94. Oviedo: Centro de Estudios del Siglo XVIII, 1983.
García Garrosa, María Jesús, and Germán Veba García-Luengos. "Las traducciones del teatro francés (1700–1835): Más impresos españoles." *Cuadernos de Estudios del Siglo XVIII* 1 (1991): 85–104.
García-Nieto París, María Carmen, ed. *Ordenamiento jurídico y realidad social de las mujeres, siglos XVI a XX: Actas de las cuartas jornadas de investigación interdisciplinaria.* Madrid: Universidad Autónoma de Madrid, 1986.

García Yebra, Valentín. *Traducción: Historia y teoría*. Madrid: Biblioteca Románica Hispánica, Editorial Gredos, 1994.
Gaselee, Stephen. "The Spanish Books in the Library of Samuel Pepys." *Supplement to the Bibliographical Society's Transactions* 2 (1921): 1–49.
Gay, Peter. *The Enlightenment: An Interpretation*. 2 vols. New York: Knopf, 1966–69.
Gelbart, Nina Rattner. *Feminine and Opposition Journalism in Old Regime France:* Le Journal des Dames. Berkeley: University of California Press, 1987.
Gerrard, Mary D. "Here's Looking at Me: Sofonisba Anguissola and the Problem of the Woman Artist." *Renaissance Quarterly* 47, no. 1 (1994): 74–101.
Gies, David Thatcher. *Nicolás Fernández de Moratín*. Twayne's World Authors Series, 558. Boston: Twayne Publishers, 1979.
Gies, David Thatcher, and Russell P. Sebold. *Ilustración y neoclasicismo: Primer Suplemento*. Historia y crítica de la literatura española, ed. Francisco Rico, no. 4. Barcelona: Editorial Crítica, 1992.
Giles, Mary E., ed. *Women in the Inquisition: Spain and the New World*. Baltimore: Johns Hopkins University Press, 1999.
Gil Novales, Alberto. "Burke en España." In *II simposio sobre el Padre Feijóo y su siglo*, ed. Catedra Feijóo, vol. 1, 63–75. Oviedo: Centro de Estudios del Siglo XVIII, 1981.
Glendinning, Nigel. "Influencia de la literatura inglesa en el siglo XVIII." In *La literatura española del siglo XVIII y sus fuentes extranjeras*, 47–93. Oviedo: Universidad de Oviedo, 1968.
——— . *A Literary History of Spain: The Eighteenth Century*. New York: Barnes and Noble, 1972.
Goetz, Rainer H. "The Problematics of Gender/Genre in *Vida i sucesos de la monja alférez*." In *Women in the Discourse of Early Modern Spain*, ed. Joan F. Cammarata, 91–107. Gainesville: University Press of Florida, 2003.
Goldman, Peter B. "Reading to Survive: Speculations on the *Plumista* and the Growth of Reading in Eighteenth-Century Spain." In *Pen and Peruke: Spanish Literature of the Eighteenth Century*, ed. Monroe Z. Hafter, 45–71. Michigan Romance Studies no. 12. Ann Arbor: Department of Romance Languages, University of Michigan, 1992.
Goldsmith, Elizabeth C., and Dena Goodman, eds. *Going Public: Women and Publishing in Early Modern France*. Ithaca: Cornell University Press, 1995.
Goldstein, Carl. *Teaching Art: Academies and Schools from Vasari to Albers*. Cambridge: Cambridge University Press, 1996.
Goncourt, Edmundo y Julio de. *La mujer en el siglo XVIII*. Trans. Alberto Insúa. Buenos Aires: Peuser, S.A., 1946.
González, Teresa. *El estado del cielo para el año de 1778. Arreglado al meridiano de Madrid. Pronóstico general con todos los aspectos de los planetas entre sí, y con la luna, el signo, y grado que ésta ocupa diariamente, y los eclypses de los dos luminares. Juicio astrológico en quanto à sucesos elementales, y cosecha de frutos*. Madrid: D. Manuel Martin, 1777.
González, Teresa. "Midwives in Early Modern Spain." In *The Art of Midwifery:*

Early Modern Midwives in Europe, ed. Hilary Marland, 95–114. London: Routledge, 1993.
González Mateos, María Victoria. "Una escuela madrileña de bordado." *Revista de la Biblioteca, Archivo, y Museo del Ayuntamiento de Madrid* 15, no. 53 (1946): 57–81.
González Mena, María Ángeles. "Bordados, pasamanerías, y encajes." In *Historia de las artes aplicadas e industriales en España*, ed. Antonio Bonet Correa, 389–422. Madrid: Ediciones Cátedra, S.A., 1982.
———. *Catálogo de encajes con una adición al catálogo de bordados.* Madrid: Instituto Valencia de Don Juan, 1976.
Goodman, Dena. "Julie de Lespinasse: A Mirror for the Enlightenment." In *Eighteenth-Century Women and the Arts*, ed. Frederick M. Keener and Susan E. Lorsch, 3–10. Contributions in Women's Studies, 98. New York: Greenwood Press, 1988.
———. "Public Sphere and Private Life: Towards a Synthesis of Current Historiographical Approaches to the Old Regime." *History and Theory* 31, no. 1 (1992).
———. *The Republic of Letters: A Cultural History of the French Enlightenment.* Ithaca: Cornell University Press, 1994.
Gordon, Daniel. "Philosophy, Sociology, and Gender in the Enlightenment Conception of Public Opinion" and "Daniel Gordon Responds to Sara Maza." *French Historical Studies* 17, no. 4 (Fall 1992): 882–911, 951–53.
Gouma-Peterson, Thalia, and Patricia Mathews. "The Feminist Critique of Art History." *Art Bulletin* 69, no. 3 (September 1987): 326–57.
Graffigny, Françoise de. *Letters from a Peruvian Woman.* 1752 ed., trans. David Kornacker. New York: Modern Language Association of America, 1993.
Graffigny, Madame de. *Lettres d'une péruvienne.* Geneva, 1777.
———. *Lettres d'une péruvienne.* 1752 edition, ed. Gianni Nicoletti. Bari: Adriatica Editrice, 1967.
———. *The Peruvian Letters, Translated from the French with an Additional Original Volume by R. Roberts.* London: T. Cadell, 1774.
———. "Suite des *Lettres d'une péruvienne*." In *Lettres d'une péruvienne*, ed. Gianni Nicoletti, 325–41. Bari: Adriatica Editrice, 1967.
Graham, Sandra Lauderdale. "Making the Private Public: A Brazilian Perspective." *Journal of Women's History* 15, no. 1 (2003): 28–42.
Greer, Germaine. *The Obstacle Race: The Fortunes of Women Painters and Their Work.* New York: Farrar, Straus, and Giroux, 1979.
Guttman, Myron. *Toward the Modern Economy: Early Industry in Europe, 1500–1800.* New York: Knopf, 1988.
Haakonssen, Knud, ed. *Enlightenment and Religion: Rational Dissent in Eighteenth-Century Britain.* New York: Cambridge University Press, 1996.
Habermas, Jürgen. *The Structural Transformation of the Public Sphere: An Inquiry into a Category of Bourgeois Society.* Trans. Thomas Burger and Frederick Lawrence. Cambridge: MIT Press, 1989.
Hageman, Jeanne Kathryn. "'Les Conversations D'Emilie': The Education of

Women by Women in Eighteenth-Century France." Ph.D. diss., University of Wisconsin, Madison, 1991.
Haidt, Rebecca. "*Los besos de amor* and *La maja desnuda:* The Fascination of the Senses in the *Ilustración.*" *Revista de Estudios Hispánicos* 29 (1995): 477–503.
——. *Embodying Enlightenment: Knowing the Body in Eighteenth-Century Spanish Literature and Culture.* New York: St. Martin's Press, 1998.
——. "The Name of the Clothes: *Petimetras* and the Problems of Luxury's Refinements." *Dieciocho: Hispanic Enlightenment* 23, no. 1 (Spring 2000): 71–75.
Hall, Catherine. "Private Persons versus Public Someones: Class, Gender, and Politics in England, 1750–1850." In *White, Male, and Middle Class: Explorations in Feminism and History,* 151–71. New York: Routledge, 1992.
Harris, Ann Sutherland, and Linda Nochlin. *Women Artists, 1550–1950.* New York: Knopf, 1976.
Harrison, Nicole. "Nuns and Prostitutes in Enlightenment Spain." *British Journal for Eighteenth Century Studies* 9 (1986): 53–60.
Hauben, Paul J. "White Legend against Black: Nationalism and Enlightenment in a Spanish Context." *Americas* 34, no. 1 (1977): 1–19.
Heller, Deborah. "Bluestocking *Salons* and the Public Sphere." *Eighteenth-Century Life* 22, no. 2 (1998): 59–82.
Heller, Nancy G. *Women Artists, an Illustrated History.* New York: Cross River Press, 1987.
Henshall, Nicholas. *The Myth of Absolutism: Change and Continuity in Early Modern European Monarchy.* New York: Longman, 1992.
Herr, Richard. *The Eighteenth-Century Revolution in Spain.* Princeton: Princeton University Press, 1958.
Herrera Navarro, Jerónimo. *Catálogo de autores teatrales del siglo XVIII.* Madrid: Fundación Universitaria Española, 1993.
Hertz, Deborah. *Jewish High Society in Old Regime Berlin.* New Haven: Yale University Press, 1988.
Hesse, Carla. *The Other Enlightenment: How French Women Became Modern.* Princeton: Princeton University Press, 2003.
Hickey y Pellizoni, Margarita. *Poesías varias sagradas, morales, y profanas ó amorosas: Con dos poemas épicos en elogio del Capitán General D. Pedro Cevallos, el uno dispuesto en forma de diálogo entre la España y Neptuno: Concluido éste, y el otro no acabado por las razones que en su prólogo se expresan; con tres tragedias francesas traducidas al castellano: Una de ellas la Andrómaca de Racine, y varias piezas en prosa de otros autores, como son algunas cartas dedicatorias, y discursos sobre el drama, muy curiosos é instructivos.* Madrid: Imprenta Real, 1789.
Hidalgo Ogayar, Ana María. "La mujer madrileña en Don Ramón de la Cruz: Literatura y realidad." *Anales del Instituto de Estudios Madrileños* 24 (1987): 269–86.
Hijano Pérez, María de los Angeles. "Prohibición y censura en España durante

la Revolución francesa." In *Repercusiones de la Revolución francesa en España*, ed. Celso Almuiña and Emilio de Diego, 165–74. Madrid: Hispagraphis, S.A., 1990.

Hogsett, Alice Charlotte. "Graffigny and Riccoboni on the Language of the Woman Writer." In *Eighteenth-Century Women and the Arts*, ed. Frederick M. Keener and Susan E. Lorsch, 119–27. Contributions in Women's Studies, 98. New York: Greenwood Press, 1988.

Holland, Elizabeth, Lady. *The Spanish Journal of Elizabeth Lady Holland*. Ed. Earl of Ilchester. London: Longmans, Green, and Company, 1910.

Howe, Elizabeth Teresa. "Zenobia or Penelope? Isabel la Católica as Literary Archetype." In *Isabel la Católica, Queen of Castile: Critical Essays*, ed. David A. Boruchoff, 91–102. New York: Palgrave Macmillan, 2003.

Hunt, Lynn. *The Family Romance of the French Revolution*. Berkeley: University of California Press, 1993.

Ilie, Paul. "Exomorphism: Cultural Bias and the French Image of Spain from the War of Succession to the Age of Voltaire." *Eighteenth-Century Studies* 9, no. 3 (1976): 375–89.

Imbille, Luis. "Memoria sobre la admisión de asociadas." In *Ilustración y educación: La Sociedad Económica Matritense*, ed. Olegario Negrín Fajardo, 150–56. Madrid: Editora Nacional, 1984.

Jaffe, Catherine. "From *Precieuses Ridicules* to *Preciosas Ridículas:* Ramón de la Cruz's Translation of Molière and the Problems of Cultural Adaptation." *Dieciocho: Hispanic Enlightenment* 24, no. 1 (Spring 2001): 147–76.

———. "Subject Pleasure: Writing the Woman Reader in Eighteenth-Century Spain." *Dieciocho: Hispanic Enlightenment* 22, no. 1 (Spring 1999): 35–59.

Jiménez Faro, Luzmaría, ed. *Poetisas españolas: Antología general*. Vol. 1 of *Hasta 1900*. Madrid: Ediciones Torremozas, 1996.

Johnson, Samuel. *Rasselas and Other Tales*. Ed. Gwin J. Kolb. Yale Edition of Works of Samuel Johnson Series, vol. 16. London: Yale University Press, 1990.

Jones, Joseph R. "María Rosa de Gálvez: Notes for a Biography." *Dieciocho: Hispanic Enlightenment* 18, no. 2 (Fall 1995): 173–86.

———. "María Rosa de Gálvez, Rousseau, Iriarte, y el melólogo en la España del siglo XVIII." *Dieciocho: Hispanic Enlightenment* 19, no. 2 (1996): 165–79.

Jordan, Constance. *Renaissance Feminism: Literary Texts and Political Models*. Ithaca: Cornell University Press, 1990.

Jovellanos, Gaspar Melchor de. "Informe dado á la junta general de comercio y moneda sobre el libre ejercicio de las artes." In *Obras publicadas e inéditas de Don Gaspar Melchor de Jovellanos*, ed. Candido Nocedal, vol. 2, 33–43. Madrid: Ediciones Atlas, 1952.

———. "Memoria sobre si se debían o no admitir las señoras en la Sociedad Económica de Madrid (1785)." In *Poesía, teatro, prosa*, 165–72. Madrid: Taurus Ediciones, S.A., 1979.

Joyes y Blake, Inés. "Apología de las mujeres." Appended to Samuel Johnson, *El*

príncipe de Abisinia: Novella. Trans. Inés Joyes y Blake. Madrid: Imprenta de Sancha, 1798.
Kagan, Richard L. "Prescott's Paradigm: American Historical Scholarship and the Decline of Spain." *American Historical Review* 101, no. 2 (1996): 423–46.
Kahiluoto Rudat, Eva M. "María Rosa Gálvez de Cabrera (1768–1806) y la defensa del teatro neoclásico." *Dieciocho: Hispanic Enlightenment* 9 (1986): 238–48.
———. "La mujer ilustrada." *Letras Femeninas* 2, no. 1 (Spring 1976): 20–33.
Kale, Steven D. *French Salons: High Society and Political Sociability from the Old Regime to the Revolution of 1848.* Baltimore: Johns Hopkins University Press, 2004.
Kaminsky, Amy Katz, ed. *Water Lilies: An Anthology of Spanish Women Writers from the Fifteenth through the Nineteenth Century.* Minneapolis: University of Minnesota Press, 1996.
Kavanagh, Thomas M. "Reading the Moment and the Moment of Reading in Graffigny's *Lettres d'une Péruvienne*." In *Eighteenth-Century Literary History*, ed. Marshall Brown, 136–58. Durham, NC: Duke University Press, 1999.
Kelly, Linda. *Women of the French Revolution.* London: Hamish Hamilton, 1987.
Kerber, Linda K. *No Constitutional Right to Be Ladies: Women and the Obligations of Citizenship.* New York: Hill and Wang, 1998.
———. *Women of the Republic: Intellect and Ideology in Revolutionary America.* Chapel Hill: University of North Carolina Press, 1980.
King, Willard F. *Prosa novelística y academias literarias en el siglo XVIII.* Anejos del Boletín de la Real Academia Española, no. 10. Madrid: Imprenta Silverio Aguirre Torre-Álvarez de Castro, 1963.
Kirkpatrick, Susan. *Las románticas: Women Writers and Subjectivity in Spain, 1835–1850.* Berkeley: University of California Press, 1989.
Kish, Kathleen. "A School for Wives: Women in Eighteenth-Century Spanish Theater." In *Women in Hispanic Literature: Icons and Fallen Idols,* ed. Beth Miller, 184–200. Berkeley: University of California Press, 1983.
Kitts, Sally Ann. *The Debate on the Nature, Role, and Influence of Woman in Eighteenth-Century Spain.* Lewiston: Edwin Mellen Press, 1995.
Krontiris, Tina. "Breaking Barriers of Genre and Gender: Margaret Tyler's Translation of *The Mirror of Knighthood* " *English Literary Renaissance* 28, no. 1 (1988): 19–39.
———. *Oppositional Voices: Women as Writers and Translators of Literature in the English Renaissance.* New York: Routledge, 1992.
Labalme, Patricia H., ed. *Beyond Their Sex: Learned Women of the European Past.* New York: New York University Press, 1980.
Labrador Herráiz, Carmen, and Juan Carlos de Pablos Ramírez. *La educación en los papeles periódicos de la Ilustración española.* Madrid: Ministerio de Educación y Ciencia, 1989.

Lafarga, Francisco. "Diderot et l'Espagne." In *Colloque International Diderot*, ed. Anne-Marie Chouillet, 395–401. Paris: Aux Amateurs de Livres, 1985.

———. *Imágenes de Francia en las letras hispánicas*. Barcelona: Promociones y Publicaciones Universitarias, S.A., 1989.

———. "La investigación sobre traducciones teatrales en el siglo XVIII: Estado actual y perspectivas." In *El teatro español del siglo XVIII*, ed. Josep María Sala Valldaura, vol. 2, 573–87. Lleida: Universitat de Lleida, 1996.

———. *Las traducciones españolas del teatro francés (1700–1835)*. Barcelona: Publicacions i Edicions de la Universitat de Barcelona, 1993.

———. *Voltaire en España: 1734–1835*. Barcelona: Edicions de la Universitat de Barcelona, 1982.

La Force, James Clayburn, Jr. *The Development of the Spanish Textile Industry, 1750–1800*. Berkeley: University of California Press, 1965.

Lamarche-Courmont, Hugary. "Lettres d'Aza." In *Lettres d'une péruvienne*, by Madame de Graffigny, ed. Gianni Nicoletti, 343–93. Bari: Adriatica Editrice, 1967.

Landes, Joan B. "The Public and the Private Sphere: A Feminist Reconsideration." In *Feminists Read Habermas: Gendering the Subject of Discourse*, ed. Johanna Meehan, 91–116. New York: Routledge, 1995.

———. *Women and the Public Sphere in the Age of the French Revolution*. Ithaca: Cornell University Press, 1988.

Langle de Paz, Teresa. "Beyond the Canon: New Documents on the Feminist Debate in Early Modern Spain." *Hispanic Review* 70, no. 3 (2002): 393–420.

Laqueur, Thomas. *Making Sex: Body and Gender from the Greeks to Freud*. Cambridge: Harvard University Press, 1990.

Lasala, Gregorio. "La Sociedad de Señoras." *Revista de la Escuela de Estudios Penitenciarios* 43 (1948): 82–88.

La Vopa Anthony J., and Lawrence E. Klein, eds. *Enlightenment in Europe, 1650–1850*. San Marino, CA: Huntington Library, 1988.

Le Gouvé, Gabriel. *La mort d'Abel en trois actes et en vers*. Paris: J. G. Mérigot, 1793.

Lehfeldt, Elizabeth A. "Discipline, Vocation, and Patronage: Spanish Religious Women in a Tridentine Microclimate." *Sixteenth-Century Journal* 30, no. 4 (1999): 1009–30.

———. "The Gender of Shared Sovereignty: Texts and the Royal Marriage of Isabella and Ferdinand." In *Women, Texts, and Authority in the Early Modern Spanish World*, ed. Marta V. Vicente and Luis R. Corteguera, 37–55. Aldershot: Ashgate, 2004.

———. *Religious Women in Golden Age Spain: The Permeable Cloister*. Women and Gender in the Early Modern World Series. Aldershot: Ashgate, 2005.

———. "Ruling Sexuality: The Political Legitimacy of Isabel of Castile." *Renaissance Quarterly* 53 (2000): 31–56.

———. "Spatial Discipline and Its Limits: Nuns and the Built Environment in

Early Modern Spain." In *Gender, Architecture, and Power in Early Modern Europe*, ed. Helen M. Hills, 131–49. Aldershot: Ashgate, 2003.

León, Fray Luis de. *La perfecta casada*. With a prologue by José López Navarro. Madrid: Ediciones Rialp, S.A., 1968.

Levacher de Valincourt, Madame. "Carta al Señor Don Francisco Cabarrús, Consejero de S.M. Católica, en respuesta al discurso que pronunció en la Real Sociedad Económica de los Amigos del País, establecida en Madrid, contra la admisión de las señoras mujeres en las sociedades literarias." *Espíritu de los Mejores Diarios Literarios que Se Publican en Europa* 17 (December 1787–29 December 1787): no. 73, 675–77; no. 74, 683–85; no. 75, 691–99; no. 76, 700–1; no. 77, 708–10.

Lewis, Elizabeth Franklin. "Feijoo, Josefa Amar y Borbón, and the Feminist Debate in Eighteenth-Century Spain." *Dieciocho: Hispanic Enlightenment* 12, no. 2 (1989): 188–99.

———. "Feminine Discourse and Subjectivity in the Works of Josefa Amar y Borbón, María Gertrudis Hore, and María Rosa Gálvez." Ph.D. diss., University of Virginia, 1993.

———. "Mythical Poetry or 'Monja romántica'?: The Poetry of María Gertrudis Hore." *Dieciocho: Hispanic Enlightenment* 16, nos. 1–2 (1993): 95–109.

———. "The Sensibility of Motherhood: Josefa Amar y Borbón's *Discurso sobre la educación física y moral de las mujeres*." *Eighteenth-Century Women: Studies in Their Lives, Work, and Culture* 2 (2002): 209–41.

———. *Women Writers in the Spanish Enlightenment: The Pursuit of Happiness*. Women and Gender in the Early Modern World Series. Aldershot: Ashgate, 2004.

Liss, Peggy K. *Isabel the Queen: Life and Times*. New York: Oxford University Press, 1992.

Llanos M., Bernardita. "Integración de la mujer al proyecto de la Ilustración en España." *Ideologies and Literature: Journal of Hispanic and Lusiphone Discourse* 4, no. 1 (1989): 199–223.

Llopis, Jesus, and María Victoria Carrasco. *Ilustración y educación en la España del siglo XVIII*. Valencia: Imprenta Martin, 1983.

López, François. "España y la Revolución francesa: Consecuencias inmediatas, repercusiones lejanas." In *Pen and Peruke: Spanish Literature of the Eighteenth Century*, ed. Monroe Z. Hafter, 115–34. Michigan Romance Studies no. 12. Ann Arbor: Department of Romance Languages, University of Michigan, 1992.

López Castán, Ángel. "Las escuelas femeninas de encajes en el Madrid ilustrado." In *La mujer en el arte español*, 265–70. Madrid: Consejo Superior de Investigaciones Científicas, 1997.

———. *Los gremios artísticos de Madrid en el siglo XVIII y primer tercio del siglo XIX: Oficios de la madera, textil y piel*. Madrid: Ediciones de la Universidad Autónoma de Madrid, 1991.

López-Cordón Cortezo, María Victoria. "La literatura religiosa y moral como conformadora de la mentalidad femenina (1760–1860)." In *La mujer en la historia de España (Siglos XVI–XX): Actas de las II jornadas de investigación interdisciplinaria*, ed. Universidad Autónoma de Madrid, Seminario de Estudios de la Mujer, 59–69. Madrid: Ediciones de la Universidad Autónoma de Madrid, 1990.

———. "Traducciones y traductoras en la España de finales del siglo XVIII." In *Entre la marginación y el desarrollo: Mujeres y hombres en la historia. Homenaje a María Carmen García-Nieto*, ed. C. Segura and G. Nielfa, 89–112. Madrid: Ediciones del Orto, 1996.

López Martinez, Asunción. *La Sociedad Económica de Amigos del País de Málaga*. Málaga: Grafima, Servicio de Publicaciones, Diputación Provincial de Málaga, 1987.

López Serrano, Matilde. *Presencia femenina en las artes del libro español*. Madrid: Fundación Universitaria Española, 1976.

López Torrijo, Manuel. "La formación de la mujer en la Zaragoza del XVIII (Dos Instituciones Religioso-Pedagógicas)." In *Educación e ilustración en España: III coloquio de historia de la educación*, 471–85. Barcelona: Publicaciones del Departamento de Educación Comparada e Historia de la Educación, Universidad de Barcelona, 1984.

———. "El pensamiento pedagógico ilustrado sobre la mujer en Josefa Amar y Borbón." In *Educación e ilustración en España: III coloquio de historia de la educación*, 114–29. Barcelona: Publicaciones del Departamento de Educación Comparada e Historia de la Educación, Universidad de Barcelona, 1984.

———. "La R.S.E. Aragonesa y la educación de la mujer." In *Educación e ilustración en España: III coloquio de historia de la educación*, 264–75. Barcelona: Publicaciones del Departamento de Educación Comparada e Historia de la Educación, Universidad de Barcelona, 1984.

Lougee, Carolyn. *"Le Paradis des Femmes": Women, Salons, and Social Stratification in Seventeenth-Century France*. Princeton: Princeton University Press, 1976.

Lunenfeld, Marvin. "Isabella I of Castile and the Company of Women in Power." *Historical Reflections* 2, no. 4 (1977): 207–29.

Luzán Claramunt de Suelves y Gurrea, Ignacio de. *Memorias literarias de Paris: Actual estado y methodo de sus estudios*. Madrid: Imprenta de Don Gabriel Ramirez, 1751.

———. *La poética, o reglas de la poesía en general*, ed. Russel P. Sebold. Barcelona: Editorial Labor, 1977.

Luzuriaga, María Josefa, trans. *Viage al interior de la China y Tartaria*, by George Stanton. Madrid: Sancha, 1798.

Lyte, Herbert O. *Spanish Literature and Spain in Some of the Leading German Magazines of the Second Half of the Eighteenth Century*. University of Wisconsin in Language and Literature, no. 32. Madison: University of Wisconsin Press, 1932.

MacArthur, Elizabeth J. "Devious Narratives: Refusal of Closure in Two

Eighteenth-Century Epistolary Novels." *Eighteenth-Century Studies* 21, no. 1 (1987): 1–20.

Manero Sorolla, María Pilar. "On the Margins of the Mendozas: Luisa de la Cerda and María de San José (Salazar)." In *Power and Gender in Renaissance Spain: Eight Women of the Mendoza Family, 1450–1650,* ed. Helen Nader, 113–31. Urbana: University of Illinois Press, 2004.

Maravall, José Antonio. "The Idea and Function of Education in Enlightenment Thought." In *The Institutionalization of Literature in Spain,* ed. Wlad Godzich and Nicholas Spadaccini, 39–99. Minneapolis: Prisma Institute, 1987.

Martínez Abelló, María, trans. *La estuarda en quatros actos.* Barcelona: Francisco Suriá y Burgada, n.d.

Martínez Medina, Africa. *Espacios privados de la mujer en el siglo XVIII.* Madrid: Horas y Horas, 1995.

Martínez y Salafranca, Miguel Juan. *Desagravios de la muger ofendida: Contra las injustas quexas de la Contradefensa crítica de D. Laurencio Manco de Olivares.* Madrid. Pedro Díaz, 1727.

Martín Gaite, Carmen. *Usos amorosos del dieciocho en España.* 5th ed. Barcelona: Editorial Anagrama, 1994. Trans. María G. Tomsich under the title *Love Customs in Eighteenth-Century Spain.* Berkeley: University of California Press, 1991.

Massardier-Kenney, Françoise. "Translation Theory and Practice." In *Translating Slavery: Gender and Race in French Women's Writing, 1783–1823,* ed. Doris Y. Kadish and Françoise Massardier-Kenney, 1–7. Kent, OH: Kent State University Press, 1994.

Matthews, Glenna. *The Rise of Public Woman: Woman's Power and Woman's Place in the United States, 1630–1970.* New York: Oxford University Press, 1992.

May, Florence Lewis. *Hispanic Lace and Lacemaking.* New York: Hispanic Society of America, 1939.

Maza, Sarah. "Women, the Bourgeoisie, and the Public Sphere: Response to Daniel Gordon and David Bell." *French Historical Studies* 17, no. 4 (Fall 1992): 935–50.

Mazaorini de Lleros, Rosa. "Décima." *Diario de Madrid,* 31 August 1794, 991–92.

———. "A mi balcon, y á mi anteojo: Oda." *Diario de Madrid,* 19 June 1796, 687–89.

———. "Octava y Soneto." *Diario de Madrid,* 11 September 1796, 1041–42.

———. "Oda." *Diario de Madrid,* 21 July 1796, 819–21.

McClendon, Carmen Chaves. "Josefa Amar y Borbón: A Forgotten Figure of the Spanish Enlightenment." In *Seven Studies in Medieval English History and Other Historical Essays Presented to Harold S. Snellgrove,* ed. Richard H. Bowers, 133–39. Jackson: University Press of Mississippi, 1983.

———. "Josefa Amar y Borbón: Essayist." *Dieciocho: Hispanic Enlightenment* 3, no. 2 (1980): 138–61.

———. "Josefa Amar y Borbón y la educación femenina." *Letras Femeninas* 4, no. 2 (Fall 1978): 3–11.

———. "Neojansenist Elements in the Work of Josepha Amar y Borbón." *Letras Femeninas* 7, no. 1 (1981): 41–48.

McNerney, Kathleen, and Cristina Enríquez de Salamanca. *Double Minorities of Spain: A Bio-Bibliographic Guide to Women Writers of the Catalan, Galician, and Basque Countries*. New York: Modern Language Association of America, 1994.

Meehan, Johanna, ed. *Feminists Read Habermas: Gendering the Subject of Discourse*. New York: Routledge, 1995.

Meijide Pardo, María Luisa. *La mujer de la orilla: Visión histórica de la mendiga y prostituta en las carceles galeras de hace dos siglos*. Sada, A Coruña: Edicios de Castro, 1996.

Melammed, Renée Levine. *Heretics or Daughters of Israel?: The Crypto-Jewish Women of Castile*. New York: Oxford University Press, 1999.

Meléndez Gayoso, Antonio. "La educación de la mujer y la Sociedad Económica de Amigos del País de Segovia." *Cuadernos de Historia Moderna y Contemporánea* 9 (1988): 139–66.

Menéndez Pelayo, M. *Biblioteca de traductores españoles*. Ed. Enrique Sánchez Reyes. Edición nacional de las obras completas de Menéndez Pelayo, vols. 54–57. Madrid: Consejo Superior de Investigaciones Científicas, 1952–1953.

Metzeltin, Miguel. "El difícil nacimiento del feminismo español: De Fray Luis de León a Adolfo Posada." In *España, teatro, y mujeres: Estudios dedicados a Henk Oostendorp*, ed. Martin Gosman and Hub. Hermans, 103–11. Amsterdam: Editions Rodopi, 1989.

Miguel Egea, Pilar de. "Breve semblanza de Ana María Mengs." In *IV Jornadas de Arte: El arte en tiempo de Carlos III*, ed. Departamento de Historia del Arte Diego Velázquez, Centro de Estudios Históricos, Consejo Superior de Investigaciones Científicas, 387–93. Madrid: Editorial Alpuesto, S.A., 1989.

Miller, Nancy K. "The Knot, the Letter, and the Book: Graffigny's *Peruvian Letters*." In *Subject to Change: Reading Feminist Writing*, ed. Nancy K. Miller, 125–61. New York: Columbia University Press, 1988.

Ministerio de Cultura. *Antonio Rafael Mengs, 1728–1779*. Madrid: Museo del Prado, 1980.

Moliner Prada, A. "La imagen de la Revolución francesa en la España de 1808." In *Repercusiones de la Revolución francesa en España*, ed. Celso Almuiña and Emilio de Diego, 251–66. Madrid: Hispagraphis, S.A., 1990.

Morales y Marín, José Luis. *Pintores cortesanos de la segunda mitad del siglo XVIII*. Colección de documentos para la historia del arte en España, 7. Madrid: Real Academia de Bellas Artes de San Fernando, 1991.

———. *Los pintores de la Ilustración*. Madrid: Centro Cultural del Conde Duque, 1988.

———. *Pintura en España, 1750–1808*. Madrid: Ediciones Cátedra, S.A., 1994.

Morel de Vindé, Madame. "Suite del 1797." In *Lettres d'une péruvienne*, by

Madame de Graffigny, ed. Gianni Nicoletti, 395–437. Bari: Adriatica Editrice, 1967.

Moron, Isabel María. *Buen amante y buen amigo*. Madrid: Librería del Castillo, 1790.

Moya, A. Morales. "La ideología de la ilustración española." *Revista de Estudios Políticos* 59 (1988): 65–105.

Munson, Elizabeth. "Walking on the Periphery: Gender and the Discourse of Modernization." *Journal of Social History* 36, no. 1 (2002): 63–75.

Nadal Oller, Jordi. *El fracaso de la revolucíon industrial en España*. Barcelona: Ariel, 1975.

Nader, Helen. *Liberty in Absolutist Spain: The Habsburg Sale of Towns, 1516–1700*. Baltimore: Johns Hopkins University Press, 1990.

———, ed. *Power and Gender in Renaissance Spain: Eight Women of the Mendoza Family*. Urbana: University of Illinois Press, 2004.

Negrín Fajardo, Olegario. *La educación popular en la España de la segunda mitad del siglo XVIII: Las actividades educativas de la Sociedad Económica Matritense de Amigos del País*. Madrid: Universidad Nacional de Educación a Distancia, 1987.

———. "Las escuelas de artes y oficios de la Sociedad Económica Matritense de Amigos del País (1775–1808)." In *La educación en la España contemporánea: Cuestiones históricas: Libro homenaje a Ángeles Galino*, 22–30. Madrid: Sociedad Española de Pedagogía, 1985.

———. *Ilustración y educación: La Sociedad Económica Matritense*. Madrid: Editora Nacional, 1984.

———. "Otras actividades educativas y culturales de la Sociedad Económica Matritense de Amigos del País (1775–1808)." *Revista Española de Pedagogía* 41, no. 159 (1983): 89–104.

———. "Pedagogía e ilustración españolas: El ideario educativo de los fundadores de la Sociedad Económica Matritense de Amigos del País." *Anales del Instituto de Estudios Madrileños* 18 (1981): 367–93.

Neira de Mosquera, Antonio. "La Doctora Guzman y La Cerda." In *Seminario pintoresco español: Lecturas de las familias*, ed. Angel Fernández de los Ríos, 188–90. Madrid: Oficinas y Establecimiento Tipográfico del Semanario Pintoresco Español y de la Ilustración, 1853.

Nelken, Margarita. *Las escritoras españolas*. Barcelona: Editorial Labor, S.A., 1930.

Nieto-Galan, Agustí. "The Images of Science in Modern Spain." In *The Sciences in the European Periphery during the Enlightenment*, ed. Kostas Gavroglu, 73–94. Dordrecht: Kluwer Academic Publishers, 1999

Nikulin, Nikolái, ed. *Anton Raphael Mengs*. Leningrad: Editorial de Artes Aurora, 1984.

Nipho, Francisco Mariano. "Asunto quinto, y duodécimo de los propuestos. ¿Si es conveniente sean sábias las mugeres?" In *Discursos eruditos de varios ingenios españoles, que (en desagravio de la patria ofendida por algunos*

escritores de moda) ofrecen sobre algunos asuntos de los propuestos en 4 de junio de 1763, 1–21. Madrid: Imprenta de Francisco Xavier Garcia, 1764.
Nochlin, Linda. "Why Have There Been No Great Women Artists?" Chap. 7 in *Women, Art, and Power and Other Essays*. New York: Harper and Row, 1988.
Offen, Karen. *European Feminisms, 1700–1950: A Political History*. Stanford: Stanford University Press, 2000.
———. "Reclaiming the European Enlightenment for Feminism: Or Prolegomena to Any Future History of Eighteenth-Century Europe." In *Perspectives on Feminist Political Thought in European History from the Middle Ages to the Present*, ed. Tjitske Akkerman and Siep Stuurman, 85–103. New York: Routledge, 1998.
Onaindía, Mario. *La construcción de la nación española: Republicanismo y nacionalismo en la Ilustración*. Barcelona: Ediciones B, 2002.
Oñate, María del Pilar. *El feminismo en la literatura española*. Madrid: Espasa-Calpe, S.A., 1938.
Ornstein, Jacob. "Misogyny and Pro-Feminism in Early Castilian Literature." *Modern Language Quarterly* 3 (1942): 221–34.
Ortega Costa, Milagros. "Spanish Women in the Reformation." In *Women in Reformation and Counter-Reformation Europe*, ed. Sherrin Marshall, 89–119. Bloomington: Indiana University Press, 1989.
Ortega López, Margarita. "La educación de la mujer en la Ilustración española." In *Simposium internacional sobre educación e ilustración: Dos siglos de reformas en la enseñanza*, 193–222. Madrid: Ministerio de Educación y Ciencia, 1988.
———. "Protestas de las mujeres castellanas contra el orden patriarchal privado durante el siglo XVIII." *Cuadernos de Historia Moderna* 19 (1997): 65–89.
———. "El siglo XVIII." In *Las mujeres de Madrid como agentes de cambio social*, ed. Margarita Ortega López, 3–55. Madrid: Instituto Universitario de Estudios de la Mujer, Universidad Autónoma de Madrid, 1995.
———. "Textos y pronunciamientos de mujeres en el antiguo régimen español." *Arenal* 1, no. 1 (1994): 117–35.
Orti y Brull, Vicente. *Doña María Manuela Pignatelli de Aragón y Gonzaga, Duquesa de Villahermosa*. 2 vols. Madrid: Viuda é Hijos de M. Tello, 1896.
Ortiz, Teresa. "From Hegemony to Subordination: Midwives in Early Modern Spain." In *The Art of Midwifery: Early Modern Midwives in Europe*, ed. Hilary Marland, 95–114. New York: Routledge, 1993.
Outram, Dorinda. *The Enlightenment*. Cambridge: Cambridge University Press, 1995.
Pageaux, D. H. "La 'Gaceta de Madrid' et les traductions espagnoles d'ouvrages français (1750–1770)." In *Studies on Voltaire and the Eighteenth Century: Transactions of the 2nd International Congress on the Enlightenment III*, ed. Theodore Besterman, vol. 62, 1147–68. Geneva: Institut et Musee Voltaire, 1967.

Pajares Infante, Eterio. "Samuel Richardson's Presence and Absence in Spain." *Revista Alicantina de Estudios Ingleses* 7 (1994): 159–70.
Palacios Fernández, Emilio. *La mujer y las letras en la España del siglo XVIII*. Madrid: Ediciones del Laberinto, S.L., 2002.
Palau y Dulcet, Antonio, and Agustín Palau Baquero. *Manual del librero hispanoamericano*. 28 vols. Barcelona: Librería Palau, 1948–1977.
Palma García, Dolores. "Las escuelas patrióticas creadas por la Sociedad Económica Matritense de Amigos del País en el siglo XVIII." *Cuadernos de Historia Moderna y Contemporánea* 5 (1984): 37–55.

———. "Las escuelas patrióticas de hilazas creadas en la villa de Madrid durante el reinado de Carlos III." *Anales del Instituto de Estudios Madrileños* 18 (1981): 443–55.
Parada, Diego Ignacio. *Escritoras y eruditas españolas (ó apuntes y noticias para servir á una historia del ingenio y cultura literaria de las mujeres españolas, desde los tiempos más remotos hasta nuestros días, con inclusión de diversas escritoras portuguesas é hispano-americanas)*. Madrid: Establecimientos Tipográficos de M. Minuesa, 1881.
Parada y Santín, José. *Las pintoras españolas*. Madrid: Imprenta del Asilo de Huérfanos del S.C. de Jesús, 1902.
Pardo Canalís, Enrique. *La Real Academia de San Fernando*. Madrid: Instituto de Estudios Madrileños del Consejo Superior de Investigaciones Científicas, 1989.

———. *Los registros de matrícula de la Academia de San Fernando de 1752 a 1815*. Madrid: Consejo Superior de Investigaciones Científicas, 1967.
Parker, Rozsika. *The Subversive Stitch: Embroidery and the Making of the Feminine*. New York: Routledge, Chapman, and Hall, 1989.
Parker, Rozsika, and Griselda Pollock. *Old Mistresses: Women, Art, and Ideology*. London: Routledge and Kegan Paul, 1981.
Pateman, Carole. "Feminist Critiques of the Public/Private Dichotomy." In *The Disorder of Women: Democracy, Feminism, and Political Theory*, 118–40. Cambridge, U.K.: Polity Press, 1989.
Pekacz, Jolanta T. *Conservative Tradition in Pre-Revolutionary France: Parisian Salon Women*. New York: Peter Lang, 1999.
Pérez Bueno, Luis. "En el Madrid del siglo XVIII: La artesanía del encaje y su enseñanza." *Revista de las Artes y los Oficios*, nos. 17–18 (October–November 1945): 27–39.
Pérez Sánchez, Alfonso E. "Las mujeres 'pintoras' en España." In *La imagen de la mujer en el arte español: Actas de las terceras jornadas de investigación interdisciplinaria*, ed. Universidad Autónoma de Madrid, Seminario de Estudios de la Mujer, 73–86. Madrid: Ediciones de la Universidad Autónoma de Madrid, 1984.
Pérez Sarrión, Guillermo. "Casual Poverty in the Spanish Enlightenment: Josefa Amar y Borbón and the Real Sociedad Económica Aragonesa de Amigos del País." *Dieciocho: Hispanic Enlightenment* 26, no. 2 (Fall 2003): 265–93.

Perinat, Adolfo, and María Isabel Marrades. *Mujer, prensa, y sociedad en España: 1800–1939*. Madrid: Centro de Investigaciones Sociológicas, 1980.
Pernil Alarcón, Paloma. "Carlos III y la formación profesional de la mujer." In *Educación y pensamiento*, 445–59. Vol. 3 of *Actas del Congreso Internacional sobre "Carlos III y la Ilustración,"* ed. Pablo Fernández Albaladejo. Madrid: Ministerio de Cultura, 1989.
Perry, Mary Elizabeth. "*Beatas* and the Inquisition in Early Modern Seville." In *Inquisition and Society in Early Modern Europe*, ed. Stephen Haliczer, 147–68. London: Croom Helm, 1987.
———. "From Convent to Battlefield." In *Queer Iberia: Crossing Cultures, Crossing Sexualities*, ed. Gregory Hutcheson and Josiah Blackmore, 394–419. Durham, NC: Duke University Press, 1999.
———. *Gender and Disorder in Early Modern Seville*. Princeton: Princeton University Press, 1990.
———. "Magdalens and Jezebels in Counter-Reformation." In *Culture and Control in Counter-Reformation Spain*, ed. Anne J. Cruz and Mary Elizabeth Perry, 124–44. Minneapolis: University of Minnesota Press, 1992.
Pevsner, Nikolaus. *Academies of Art: Past and Present*. Cambridge: Cambridge University Press, 1940.
Pocock, J. G. A. *Barbarism and Religion*. Vols. 1 and 2. Cambridge: Cambridge University Press, 1999.
Poirier, Roger. "'Biblioteca Selecta de las Damas': Its Cultural Significance." *Dieciocho: Hispanic Enlightenment* 7, no. 1 (1984): 28–41.
Polt, John H. R. *Gaspar Melchor de Jovellanos*. Twayne's World Author Series, 181. New York: Twayne Publishers, 1971.
———. *Poesía del siglo XVIII*. Madrid: Editorial Castalia, 1975.
Pombo y Robledo, Julian, trans. *Galería de mugeres fuertes*. 4 vols. Madrid: D. Benito Cano, 1794.
Portela Sandoval, Francisco José. *Noticias sobre algunos artistas que estudiaron en la Real Academia de Bellas Artes de San Fernando en tiempos de Carlos III*. Madrid: Alpuerto, 1989.
Puyol, Julio, ed., *Crónica incompleta de los Reyes Católicos (1469–1476)*, Madrid: Tipografía de Archivos, 1934.
Quadra, Antonio de la. "Memoria sobre que se dé ocupasion á las mugeres, que se suponen ociosas en Madrid, leída en la junta general de 14 de octubre de 1775." In *Memorias de la Sociedad Económica*, vol. 2, 14–19. Madrid: Don Antonio de Sancha, 1780.
Quintana, Manuel José. *Vidas de los españoles célebres*. 9th ed. Toulouse: Édouard Privat, 1930.
Quintero Atauri, Pelayo. "Ana Mengs." *Boletín de la Sociedad Española de Excursiones* 15 (1907): 13–15.
———. *Mujeres ilustres: Apuntes biográficos sobre las pintoras, Teresa Nicolau Parody y Ana María Mengs*. Madrid: Ibérica, 1907.
Quintina Guzmán y la Cerda, María Isidra. *Oración del género eucarístico, que hizo a la Real Academia Española la Excma. Señora Da. María Isidra*

Quintina, Guzman y La Cerda, hija de los Excmos. Señores Marqueses de Monte-Alegre, Condes de Oñate, y de Paredes, Duques de Naxera, &c. en el día 28 de diciembre del año de 1784, en que fue incorporada por socia de dicha Real Academia. Madrid: D. Joachin Ibarra, 1785.

―――. *Oración del género eucarístico que hizo a la Real Sociedad de Amigos del País de esta corte la Excelentísima Señora Doña María Isidra Quintina Guzmán y La Cerda, doctora en filosofía, y letras humanas, consiliaria perpetua, examinadora de cursantes en filosofía, y cathedrática honoraria de filosofía moderna en la Real Universidad de Alcalá. Socia de la Real Academia Española, y honoraria, y literata de la Real Sociedad Bascongada de los Amigos del País. En el día 25 de febrero del año de 1786 en que fue incorporada en esta real sociedad.* Madrid: Don Antonio de Sancha, 1786.

Rada y Delgado, Juan de Dios de la. *Mugeres célebres de España y Portugal.* 2 vols. Barcelona: Casa Editorial de Víctor Perez, 1868.

Radcliff, Pamela Beth. "Citizens and Housewives: The Problem of Female Citizenship in Spain's Transition to Democracy." *Journal of Social History* 36, no. 1 (2002): 77–100.

―――. "Imagining Female Citizenship in the "New Spain": Gendering the Democratic Transition, 1975–1978." *Gender and History* 13, no. 3 (2001): 498–523.

―――. "Women's Politics: Consumer Riots in Twentieth-Century Spain." In *Constructing Spanish Womanhood: Female Identity in Modern Spain,* ed. Victoria Lorée Enders and Pamela Beth Radcliff, 301–23. Albany: State University of New York Press, 1999.

Ramírez Martín, Susana María. "Proyección científica de las ideas de Tomás Romay sobre la vacuna de la viruela en la inclusa madrileña." *Asclepio* 54, no. 2 (2002): 109–28.

Real Academia de Bellas Artes de San Fernando. *Distribución de los premios concedidos por el Rey Nuestro Señor á los discípulos de las nobles artes, hecha por la Real Academia de San Fernando en la junta general de 23 de diciembre de 1753.* Madrid: D. Gabriel Ramirez, 1754.

―――. *Distribución de los premios concedidos por el Rey Nuestro Señor á los discípulos de las nobles artes, hecha por la Real Academia de San Fernando en la junta general de 22 de diciembre de 1754.* Madrid: D. Gabriel Ramirez, 1755.

―――. *Distribución de los premios concedidos por el Rey Nuestro Señor á los discípulos de las nobles artes, hecha por la Real Academia de San Fernando en la junta general de 25 de enero de 1756.* Madrid: D. Gabriel Ramirez, 1756.

―――. *Distribución de los premios concedidos por el Rey Nuestro Señor á los discípulos de las nobles artes, hecha por la Real Academia de San Fernando en la junta general de 6 de febrero de 1757.* Madrid: D. Gabriel Ramirez, 1757.

―――. *Distribución de los premios concedidos por el Rey Nuestro Señor á los discípulos de las nobles artes, hecha por la Real Academia de San Fernando en la junta general de 28 de agosto de 1760.* Madrid: D. Gabriel Ramirez, 1760.

———. *Distribución de los premios concedidos por el Rey Nuestro Señor á los discípulos de las nobles artes, hecha por la Real Academia de San Fernando en la junta general de 3 de junio de 1763.* Madrid: D. Gabriel Ramirez, 1763.

———. *Distribución de los premios concedidos por el Rey Nuestro Señor á los discípulos de las nobles artes, hecha por la Real Academia de San Fernando en la junta general de 3 de agosto de 1766.* Madrid: Imprenta de la Viuda de Eliseo Sanchez, 1766.

———. *Distribución de los premios concedidos por el Rey Nuestro Señor á los discípulos de las nobles artes, hecha por la Real Academia de San Fernando en la junta general de 12 de julio de 1769.* Madrid: Imprenta de la Viuda de Eliseo Sanchez, 1769.

———. *Distribución de los premios concedidos por el Rey Nuestro Señor á los discípulos de las nobles artes, hecha por la Real Academia de San Fernando en la junta pública de 5 de julio de 1772.* Madrid: D. Joachin Ibarra, 1772.

———. *Distribución de los premios concedidos por el Rey Nuestro Señor á los discípulos de las nobles artes, hecha por la Real Academia de San Fernando en la junta pública de 25 de julio de 1778.* Madrid: D. Joachin Ibarra, 1778.

———. *Distribución de los premios concedidos por el Rey Nuestro Señor á los discípulos de las nobles artes, hecha por la Real Academia de San Fernando en la junta pública de 14 de julio de 1781.* Madrid: D. Joachin Ibarra, 1781.

———. *Distribución de los premios concedidos por el Rey Nuestro Señor á los discípulos de las nobles artes, hecha por la Real Academia de San Fernando en la junta pública de 17 de julio de 1784.* Madrid: D. Joachin Ibarra, 1784.

———. *Distribución de los premios concedidos por el Rey Nuestro Señor á los discípulos de las nobles artes, hecha por la Real Academia de San Fernando en la junta pública de 4 de agosto de 1790.* Madrid: Imprenta de la Viuda de Ibarra, 1790.

———. *Distribución de los premios concedidos por el Rey Nuestro Señor á los discípulos de las nobles artes, hecha por la Real Academia de San Fernando en la junta pública de 20 de agosto de 1793.* Madrid: Imprenta de la Viuda de Ibarra, 1793.

———. *Distribución de los premios concedidos por el Rey Nuestro Señor á los discípulos de las nobles artes, hecha por la Real Academia de San Fernando en la junta pública de 13 de julio de 1796.* Madrid: Imprenta de la Viuda de Ibarra, 1796.

———. *Distribución de los premios concedidos por el Rey Nuestro Señor á los discípulos de las nobles artes, hecha por la Real Academia de San Fernando en la junta pública de 13 de julio de 1799.* Madrid: Imprenta de la Viuda de Ibarra, 1799.

———. *Distribución de los premios concedidos por el Rey Nuestro Señor á los discípulos de las nobles artes, hecha por la Real Academia de San Fernando en la junta pública de 24 de julio de 1802.* Madrid: Imprenta de la Viuda de Ibarra, 1802.

———. *Distribución de los premios concedidos por el Rey Nuestro Señor á los discípulos de las nobles artes, hecha por la Real Academia de San Fernando en la junta pública de 27 de julio de 1805.* Madrid: Imprenta de la Hija de Ibarra, 1805.

———. *Distribución de los premios concedidos por el Rey Nuestro Señor á los discípulos de las nobles artes, hecha por la Real Academia de San Fernando en la junta pública de 24 de septiembre de 1808.* Madrid: Impresor de Cámara de S.M., 1832.

———. *Guía del Museo de la Real Academia de San Fernando.* 2 vols. Madrid: Comunidad de Madrid, 1988.

———. *Reglamento interior de la Real Academia de Bellas Artes de San Fernando.* Madrid: Imprenta de San Francisco de Sales, 1914.

Real Academia Española. *Antología de poetisas líricas.* Madrid: Tipografía de la "Revista de Archivos, Bibliotecas, y Museos," 1915.

Recio, Roxana, ed. *La traducción en España, ss. XIV–XVI.* Anexos de Livius, I. León: Universidad de León, 1995.

Restout, Jean-Bernard. *Galerie françoise ou portraits des hommes & des femmes célèbres, qui ont paru en France.* Paris: Chez Hérissant le Fils, 1771.

Ringrose, David R. *Spain, Europe, and the "Spanish Miracle," 1700–1900.* Cambridge: Cambridge University Press, 1996.

Ríos Izquiedo, Pilar, and Ana Rueda Roncal. "Análisis de las normas jurídicas de la junta de damas de honor y mérito." *Torre de los Lujanes: Boletín de la Real Sociedad Económica Matritense de Amigos del País* 13 (September 1989): 151–61.

Rio y Arnedo, María Antonia, trans. *Cartas de Madama de Montier, recogidas por Madama le Prince de Beaumont,* by Madame le Prince de Beaumont. 3 vols. Madrid: Don Benito García, y Compañía, 1798.

Robb, Bonnie Arden. "The Easy Virtue of a Peruvian Princess." *French Studies* 46, no. 2 (1992): 144–59.

Robertson, John. "The Enlightenment above National Context: Political Economy in Eighteenth-Century Scotland and Naples." *Historical Journal* 40, no. 3 (1997): 667–97.

Rodrigo, Antonina. *Mujeres de España (Las silenciadas).* Barcelona: Plaza and Janes, S.A., 1979.

Rodríguez-Escudero, Paloma, ed. *Arte y mujer.* Bilbao: Servicio Editorial, Universidad del País Vasco, 1987.

Romero Masegosa y Cancelada, María, trans. *Cartas de una peruana, escritas en francés por Madame de Graffigny y traducidas al castellano con algunas correcciones, y aumentada con notas, y una carta para su mayor complemento por Doña María Romero Masegosa y Cancelada,* by Madame de Graffigny. Valladolid: Oficina de la Viuda de Santander, é Hijos, 1792.

Rosset, François. "Les noeuds du langage dans les *Lettres d'une péruvienne.*" *Revue d'Histoire Littéraire de la France* 96, no. 6 (1996): 1106–27.

Rosslyn, Wendy. "Making Their Way into Print: Poems by Eighteenth-Century Russian Women." *Slavonic and East European Review* 78, no. 3 (2000): 407–38.

Roulston, Christine. "No Simple Correspondence: Mme de Graffigny as 'Epistolière' and as Espistolary Novelist." *L'Esprit Créateur* 40, no. 4 (2000): 31–37.

———. "Seeing the Other in Mme de Graffigny's *Lettres d'une Péruvienne*." *Eighteenth-Century Fiction* 9, no. 3 (1997): 309–26.

Rubinger, Catherine. "A Might-Have-Been: Feminism in Eighteenth-Century France." *Atlantis* 15, no. 2 (1990): 59–68.

Rueda Roncal, Ana, Pilar Ríos Izquierdo, and María Esperanza Zábalo Rojas. "Carlos III y la junta de damas." In *Coloquio Internacional Carlos III y su siglo*, 683–98. Madrid: Universidad Complutense, Departamento de Historia Moderna, 1990.

———. "Carlos III y la junta de damas." *Torre de los Lujanes: Boletín de la Real Sociedad Económica Matritense de Amigos del País* 12 (1989): 113–25.

Ruiz Guerrero, Cristina. *Panorama de escritoras españolas*. Vol. 2. Cádiz: Universidad de Cádiz, Servicio de Publicaciones, 1997.

Saíz, María del Carmen. *Cabezas de las obras del Rafael de Urbino grabadas por María del Carmen Saíz, académica de mérito de la Real de S. Fernando*. N.p., 1816.

Salas, Xavier de. "Notas sobre el retrato de la 'Marquesa de Llano' por Mengs." *Archivo Español de Arte* 35, no. 140 (1962): 331–33.

Salgado, María A. "El autorretrato clandestino de Margarita Hickey, escritora ilustrada." In *l'autoportrait en Espagne: Litterature e peinture: Actes du Ive Colloque international d'Aix-en-Provence (6–7–8 decembre 1990)*, 133–47. Aix-en-Provence: Publications de l'Université de Provence, 1992.

———. "Reescribiendo el canon: Góngora y Margarita Hickey." *Dieciocho: Hispanic Enlightenment* 17, no. 1 (1994): 17–31.

———. "Women's Voices in Eighteenth-Century Hispanic Poetry." *Dieciocho: Hispanic Enlightenment* 11, no. 1 (1988): 15–26.

Saltillo, Marqués del. "Artistas Madrileños (1592–1850)." *Boletín de la Sociedad Española de Excursiones* 57 (1953): 137–243.

San Alberto, Vizconde de. *Los directores de la Real Sociedad Económica Matritense de Amigos del País y las presidentas de su junta de damas de honor y mérito*. Madrid: Talleres de "El Eco Franciscano," 1925.

Sánchez, Luis Alberto. "Una iluminista olvidada: Las 'Cartas peruanas' de Madame de Graffigny." *Cuadernos Americanos* 16, no. 3 (1957): 185–95.

Sánchez, Magdalena S. *The Empress, the Queen, and the Nun: Women and Power at the Court of Philip III of Spain*. Baltimore: Johns Hopkins University Press, 1998.

———. "Melancholy and Female Illness: Habsburg Women and Politics at the Court of Philip III." *Journal of Women's History* 8, no. 2 (Summer 1996): 81–102.

Sánchez-Blanco Parody, Francisco. *El absolutismo y las luces en el reinado de Carlos III*. Madrid: Marcial Pons, 2002.
———. *Europa y el pensamiento español del siglo XVIII*. Madrid: Alianza Editorial, 1991.
———. *La ilustración en España*. Ed. Akal Hipecu. Historia del pensamiento y la cultura no. 29. Madrid: Ediciones Akal, S.A., 1997.
———. *La mentalidad ilustrada*. Madrid: Taurus Ediciones, S.A., 1999.
Sánchez Cantón, D. Francisco Javier. *Mengs en España*. Madrid: Centro de Intercambio Intelectual Germano-Español, 1927.
Sánchez Ortega, María Helena. "La mujer, el amor, y la religión en el antiguo regimen." In *La mujer en la historia de España (siglos XVI–XX): Actas de las II jornadas de investigación interdisciplinaria*, ed. Universidad Autónoma de Madrid, Seminario de Estudios de la Mujer, 35–58. Madrid: Ediciones de la Universidad Autónoma de Madrid, 1990.
Sarasúa García, Carmen. *Criados, nodrizas, y amos: El servicio doméstico en la formación del mercado de trabajo madrileño, 1758–1868*. Madrid: Siglo Veintiuno de España Editores, S.A., 1994.
———. "La industria del encaje en el Campo de Calatrava." *Arenal* 2, no. 2 (July–December 1995): 151–74.
Sarrailh, Jean. *L'Espagne éclairée de la seconde moitié du XVIIIe siècle*. Paris: C. Klincksieck, 1954. Trans. Antonio Alatorre, as *La España ilustrada de la segunda mitad del siglo XVIII*. Madrid: Fondo de Cultura Económica, 1992.
Saviñon, Antonio, trans. *La muerte de abel, tragedia, en tres actos y en verso*, by Gabriel Marie Jean Baptiste Le Gouvé. Madrid: Imprenta de la Administración del Real Arbitrio de Beneficencia, 1803.
Scanlon, Geraldine M. "Revolución burguesa e instrucción femenina." In *Nuevas perspectivas sobre la mujer: Actas de las primeras jornadas de investigación interdisciplinaria*, ed. Universidad Autónoma de Madrid, Seminario de Estudios de la Mujer, 163–73. Madrid: Imprenta de la Universidad Autónoma de Madrid, 1982.
Schidlof, Leo R. *La miniature en Europe aux 16e, 17e, 18e, et 19e siècles*. Vol. 2. Austria: Akademische Druck—u. Verlagsanstalt, 1964.
Schulte, Henry F. *The Spanish Press, 1470–1966: Print, Power, and Politics*. Chicago: University of Illinois Press, 1968.
Schulz, Andrew. "Goya's Portraits of the Duchess of Osuna: Fashioning Identity in Enlightenment Spain." In *Women, Art, and the Politics of Identity in Eighteenth-Century Europe*, ed. Melissa Hyde and Jennifer Milam, 263–83. Aldershot: Ashgate, 2003.
Scott, Joan Wallach. *Gender and the Politics of History*. Gender and Culture Series. New York: Columbia University, 1988.
———. *Only Paradoxes to Offer: French Feminists and the Rights of Man*. Cambridge: Cambridge University Press, 1996.
———. "'A Woman Who Has Only Paradoxes to Offer': Olympe De Gouges Claims Rights for Women." In *Rebel Daughters: Women and the French*

Revolution, ed. Sara E. Melzer and Leslie W. Rabine, 102–20. Oxford: Oxford University Press, 1992.
Sebold, Russell P. "La pena de la hija del sol: Realidad, leyenda, y romanticismo." In *Estudios en honor a Ricardo Gullón,* ed. Luis T. Gonzalez-del-valle and Dario Villanueva, 295–308. Lincoln: Society of Spanish and Spanish-American Studies, 1984.
———. *El rapto de la mente: Poética y poesia dieciochescas.* 2nd ed. Barcelona: Editorial Anthropos, 1989.
Sempere y Guarinos, Juan. *Ensayo de una biblioteca española de los mejores escritores del reynado de Carlos III.* 6 vols. Madrid: Imprenta Real, 1785–1789.
———. *Historia del luxo, y de las leyes suntuarias de España.* 2 vols. Madrid: Imprenta Real, 1788.
Semprún, Ana Rosa. *Mengs. Los genios de la pintura,* 45. Madrid: Sarpe, D.L., 1982.
Serrano y Sanz, Manuel. *Apuntes para una biblioteca de escritoras españolas desde el año 1401 al 1833.* 2 Vols. Madrid: Impresores de la Real Casa, 1903. Reprinted in *Biblioteca de autores españoles desde la formación del lenguaje hasta nuestros días.* Vols. 268–71. Madrid: Ediciones Atlas, 1975.
Shafer, Robert Jones. *The Economic Societies in the Spanish World (1763–1821).* Syracuse, NY: Syracuse University Press, 1958.
Sheriff, Mary D. *The Exceptional Woman: Elisabeth Vigée-Lebrun and the Cultural Politics of Art.* Chicago: University of Chicago Press, 1996.
Sherwood, Joan. "El niño expósito: Cifras de mortalidad de una inclusa del siglo XVIII." *Anales del Instituto de Estudios Madrileños* 18 (1981): 299–312.
———. *Poverty in Eighteenth-Century Spain: The Women and Children of the Inclusa.* Toronto: University of Toronto Press, 1988.
Showalter, English, Jr. "The Beginnings of Madame de Graffigny's Literary Career: A Study in the Social History of Literature." In *Essays on the Age of Enlightenment in Honor of Ira O. Wade,* ed. Jean Macary, 293–304. Geneva: Librairie Droz, 1977.
———. "An Eighteenth-Century Best-Seller: *Les Lettres Péruviennes.*" Ph.D. diss., Yale University, 1964.
———. "Graffigny at Cirey: A Fraud Exposed." *French Forum* 21, no. 1 (1996): 29–44.
———. "A Woman of Letters in the French Enlightenment: Madame de Graffigny." *British Journal for Eighteenth-Century Studies* 1 (1978): 89–104.
Shubert, Adrian. *A Social History of Modern Spain.* A Social History of Europe Series. London: Routledge, 1992.
Simon Palmer, María del Carmen. *Escritoras españolas del s. XIX: Manual bio-bibliográfico.* Madrid: Editorial Castalia, 1991.
———. "La mujer madrileña del siglo XIX." In *Ciclo de conferencias sobre Madrid en el siglo XIX,* ed. Delegación de Cultura Instituto de Estudios Madrileños del Consejo Superior de Investigaciones Científicas, Ayuntamiento de Madrid. Madrid: Artes Gráficas Municipales, 1982.

———. "Las neurosis femeninas y la educación española." *Asclepio* 35 (1983): 327–42.
Smith, Bonnie G. *Changing Lives: Women in European History since 1700.* Lexington: D. C. Heath and Company, 1989.
———. *Ladies of the Leisure Class: The Bourgeoises of Northern France in the Nineteenth Century.* Princeton: Princeton University Press, 1981.
Smith, David. "Graffigny *Rediviva:* Editions of the *Lettres d'une Péruvienne* (1967–1993)." *Eighteenth-Century Fiction* 7, no. 1 (1994): 71–78.
———. "The Popularity of Mme de Graffigny's *Lettres d'une Péruvienne:* The Bibliographical Evidence." *Eighteenth-Century Fiction* 3, no. 1 (1990): 1–20.
Smith, Theresa Ann. "Fashioning the Enlightenment: The Proposal for a Female National Dress in Eighteenth-Century Spain." *Dieciocho: Hispanic Enlightenment* 23, no. 1 (Spring 2000): 76–85.
———. "New Visibility: Women and the Public Sphere in Eighteenth-Century Spain." Ph.D. diss., University of California, San Diego, 1999.
———. "Reconsiderando el papel de la mujer en la Real Academia de Bellas Artes de San Fernando." In *La mujer en el arte español,* 279–88. Madrid. Consejo Superior de Investigaciones Científicas, 1997.
———. "Writing out of the Margins: Women, Translation, and the Spanish Enlightenment." *Journal of Women's History* 15, no. 1 (Spring 2003): 116–43.
Sociedad Económica de Madrid. *Estatutos de la junta de socias de honor y mérito de la Real Sociedad Económica de Madrid.* Madrid: Imprenta de Sancha, 1794.
Socolow, Susan Migden. *The Women of Colonial Latin America.* Cambridge: Cambridge University Press, 2000.
Soria de Irisarri, Isabel. "La mujer en la época de Goya." *Boletín del Museo e Instituto "Camón Aznar"* 67 (1997): 123–42.
Soria Medina, Enrique. *La Sociedad Económica de Amigos del País de Osuna.* Sevilla: Gráficas del Sur, 1975.
Sorkin, David. "From Context to Comparison: The German Haskalah and Reform Catholicism." *Tel Aviver Jahrbuch für Deutsche Geschichte* (Israel) 20 (1991): 23–58.
———. "Reform Catholicism and Religious Enlightenment." *Austrian History Yearbook* 30 (1999): 187–219.
Spell, Jefferson Rea. *Rousseau in the Spanish World before 1833: A Study in Franco-Spanish Literary Relations.* Austin: University of Texas Press, 1938.
Spencer, Samia I., ed. *French Women and the Age of Enlightenment.* Bloomington: Indiana University Press, 1984.
Staniland, Kay. *Embroiderers: Medieval Craftsmen.* Toronto: University of Toronto Press, 1991.
Starr-LeBeau, Gretchen D. "Writing (for) Her Life: *Judeo-Conversas* in Early Modern Spain." In *Women, Texts, and Authority in the Early Modern Spanish World,* ed. Marta V. Vicente and Luis R. Corteguera, 57–72. Aldershot: Ashgate, 2004.
Stirling, Maxwell William. *Annals of the Artists of Spain.* Vol. 4. London: John C. Nimmo, 1891.
Stone, Marilyn, and Carmen Benito-Vessels, ed. *Women at Work in Spain: From the*

Middle Ages to Early Modern Times. New York: Peter Lang Publishing, 1998.
Street, Donald R. "The Economic Societies: Springboard to the Spanish Enlightenment." *Journal of European Economic History* 16, no. 3 (Winter 1987): 569–85.
Sullivan, Constance A. "A Biographical Note on Margarita Hickey." *Dieciocho: Hispanic Enlightenment* 20, no. 2 (1997): 219–29.
———. "Constructing Her Own Tradition: Ideological Selectivity in Josefa Amar y Borbón's Representation of Female Models." In *Recovering Spain's Feminist Tradition*, ed. Lisa Vollendorf, 142–59. New York: Modern Language Association of America, 1991.
———. "'Dinos, dinos quién eres': The Poetic Identity of María Gertrudis Hore (1742–1801)." *Pen and Peruke: Spanish Literature of the Eighteenth Century*, ed. Monroe Z. Hafter, 153–83. Michigan Romance Studies no. 12. Ann Arbor: Department of Romance Languages, University of Michigan, 1992.
———. "Las escritoras del siglo XVIII." In *La literatura escrita por mujer desde la edad media hasta el siglo XVIII*, 305–30. Vol. 4 of *Breve historia feminista de la literatura española (en lengua castellana)*, coord. Iris M. Zavala. Madrid: Dirección General de la Mujer, Consejería de Educación de la Comunidad de Madrid, 1997.
———. "Gender, Text, and Cross-Dressing: The Case of "Beatriz Cienfuegos" and *La Pensadora Gaditana*." *Dieciocho: Hispanic Enlightenment* 18, no. 1 (1995): 27–47.
———. "Josefa Amar y Borbón (1749–1833)." In *Spanish Women Writers: A Bio-Bibliographical Source Book*, ed. Linda Gould Levine, Ellen Engelson Marson, and Gloria Feiman Waldman, 32–43. Westport, CT: Greenwood Press, 1993.
———. "Josefa Amar y Borbón and the Royal Aragonese Economic Society." *Dieciocho: Hispanic Enlightenment* 15, nos. 1–2 (1992): 95–148.
———. "On Spanish Literary History and the Politics of Gender." *Journal of the Midwest Modern Language Association* 23, no. 2 (1990): 26–41.
———. "The Quiet Feminism of Josefa Amar y Borbón's 1790 Book on the Education of Women." *Indiana Journal of Hispanic Literatures* 2, no. 1 (1993): 49–73.
Surtz, Ronald E. "Morisco Women, Written Texts, and the Valencia Inquisition." *Sixteenth-Century Journal* 32, no. 2 (2001): 421–33.
———. *Writing Women in Late Medieval and Early Modern Spain: The Mothers of Saint Teresa of Avila*. Philadelphia: University of Pennsylvania Press, 1995.
Tato y Amat, Miguel. *La actual Sociedad Económica Matritense de Amigos del País: Lista general de socios por orden cronológico, alfabético y de categorias*. Madrid: Imprenta Izaguirre, 1935.
Tenorio Gómez, Pilar. *Las madrileñas del mil seiscientos: Imagen y realidad*. Madrid: Horas y Horas, 1993.

Thomas, Diana M. "The Book Trade in Ibarra's Madrid." *The Library* 5 (1983): 335–58.
Thomas, Downing A. "Economy and Identity in Graffigny's *Lettres d'une Péruvienne*." *South Central Review* 10, no. 4 (1993): 55–72.
Tolivar Alas, Ana Cristina. "El teatro de Racine en la España de los primeros Borbones." In *Teatro y traducción*, ed. Francisco Lafarga and Roberto Dengler, 59–70. Barcelona: Universitat Pompeu Fabra, 1995.
Tolosa, Marquesa de, trans. *Tratado de educación para la nobleza, escrito por un eclesiástico de París*. Madrid: Imprenta de Manuel Álvarez, 1796.
Tomlinson, Janis A., ed., *Goya: Images of Women*. New Haven: Yale University Press, 2002.
Tormo, Elías. *La visita a las colecciones artísticas de la Real Academia de San Fernando*. Madrid: Hauser y Menet, 1929.
Tortosa Linde, María Dolores. *La Academia del Buen Gusto de Madrid (1749–1751)*. Granada: Universidad de Granada, Departamento de Filología Española, 1988.
Townsend, Joseph. *A Journey through Spain in the Years 1786 and 1787; With Particular Attention to the Agriculture, Manufactures, Commerce, Population, Taxes, and Revenue of That Country; and Remarks in Passing Through a Part of France*. 3 vols. London: C. Dilly, 1792.
Trouille, Mary Seidman. *Sexual Politics in the Enlightenment: Women Writers Read Rousseau*. The Margins of Literature Series. Albany: State University of New York Press, 1997.
Truant, Cynthia Maria. "The Guildswomen of Paris: Gender, Power, and Sociability in the Old Regime." *Proceedings of the Annual Meeting of the Western Society for French History* 15 (1988): 130–38.
———. "Parisian Guildswomen and the (Sexual) Politics of Privilege: Defending their Patrimonies in Print." In *Going Public: Women and Publishing in Early Modern France*, ed. Elizabeth C. Goldsmith and Dena Goodman, 46–61. Ithaca: Cornell University Press, 1995.
Úbeda de los Cobos, Andrés. *La Academia y el artista*. Cuadernos de Arte Español, 33. Madrid: Información y Revistas, D.L., 1992.
———. *Pintura, mentalidad, e ideología en la Real Academia de Bellas Artes de San Fernando: 1741–1800*. 2 vols. Madrid: Universidad Complutense de Madrid, 1988.
Urzainqui, Inmaculada. "Anuncios y reseñas de traducciones de obras inglesas en la prensa española del siglo XVIII." In *Scripta in memoriam José Benito Álvarez-Buylla Álvarez (1916–1981)*, 313–32. Oviedo: Universidad de Oviedo, 1986.
———. "Hacia una tipología de la traducción en el siglo XVIII: Los horizontes del traductor." In *Traducción y adaptación cultural: España-Francia*, ed. María Luisa Donaire and Francisco Lafarga, 623–38. Oviedo: Universidad de Oviedo, 1991.
Valis, Noël, and Carol Maier. *In the Feminine Mode: Essays on Hispanic Women Writers*. Lewisburg: Bucknell University Press, 1990.

Van Gorp, Hendrik. "Translation and Literary Genre: The European Picaresque Novel in the 17th and 18th Centuries." In *The Manipulation of Literature: Studies in Literary Translation,* ed. Theo Hermans, 136–48. London: Croom Helm, 1985.

Vega, Jesusa. "Los inicios del artista: El dibujo base de las artes." In *La formación del artista de Leonardo a Picasso: Aproximación al estudio de la enseñanza y el aprendizaje de las bellas artes,* 1–29. Madrid: Real Academia de Bellas Artes de San Fernando, 1989.

Velasco, Sherry M. *The Lieutenant Nun: Transgenderism, Lesbian Desire, and Catalina de Erauso.* Austin: University of Texas, 2000.

———. "Visualizing Gender on the Page in Convent Literature." In *Women, Texts, and Authority in the Early Modern Spanish World,* ed. Marta V. Vicente and Luis R. Corteguera, 127–48. Aldershot: Ashgate, 2004.

Vicente, Marta V. "La documentación gremial: El trabajo de las mujeres en la modernidad." In *Nuevas preguntas, nuevas miradas: Fuentes y documentación para la historia de las mujeres (Siglos XIII-XVIII),* ed. Margarita María Birriel Salcedo. Granada: Universidad de Granada, 1992.

———. "Textual Uncertainties: The Written Legacy of Women Entrepreneurs in Eighteenth-Century Spain." In *Women, Texts, and Authority in the Early Modern Spanish World,* ed. Marta V. Vicente and Luis R. Corteguera, 183–95. Aldershot: Ashgate, 2004.

Vicente, Marta V., and Luis R. Corteguera, eds. *Women, Texts, and Authority in the Early Modern Spanish World.* Aldershot: Ashgate, 2004.

Vidal Galache, Florentina. *Bordes y bastardos: Una historia de la Inclusa de Madrid.* Madrid: Compañía Literaria, 1995.

Villota, Paloma de. "El siglo de la Ilustración y la capacidad intelectual de la mujer." In *Mujeres y hombres en la formación del pensamiento occidental,* ed. Virginia Maqueira D'Angelo, vol. 2, 185–96. Madrid: Ediciones de la Universidad Autónoma de Madrid, 1989.

Vives, Juan Luis. *De los deberes del marido.* In *La mujer cristiana: De los deberes del marido y Pedagogía pueril,* ed. and trans. Lorenzo Riber. Madrid: M. Aguilar, 1944.

———. *The Education of a Christian Woman: A Sixteenth-Century Manual.* Ed. and trans. Charles Fantazzi. Chicago: University of Chicago Press, 2000.

Vollendorf, Lisa. *The Lives of Women: A New History of Inquisitional Spain.* Nashville: Vanderbilt University Press, 2005.

———. "'No Doubt It Will Amaze You': María de Zayas's Early Modern Feminism." In *Recovering Spain's Feminist Tradition,* ed. Lisa Vollendorf, 103–20. New York: Modern Language Association of America, 2001.

———. *Reclaiming the Body: María de Zayas's Early Modern Feminism.* Oxford: Oxford University Press, 2001.

———, ed., *Recovering Spain's Feminist Tradition.* New York: Modern Language Association of America, 2001.

Voltaire. "Zaïre." In *Repertoire général du théatre français,* vol. 10, 189–280. Versailles: L'Imprimerie de J.-A. Lebel, 1813.

Waldmann, Susan. *Goya and the Duchess of Alba*. Munich: Prestel-Verlag, 1998.
Ward, Bernardo. *Proyecto ecónomico en que se proponen varias providencias, dirigidas á promover los intereses de España, con los medios y fóndos necesarios para su plantificación*. 3rd ed. Madrid: Ibarra, 1782.
Weber, Alison. *Teresa of Avila and the Rhetoric of Femininity*. Princeton: Princeton University Press, 1990.
———. "The Three Lives of the *Vida:* The Uses of Convent Autobiography." In *Women, Texts, and Authority in the Early Modern Spanish World*, ed. Marta V. Vicente and Luis R. Corteguera, 105–25. Aldershot: Ashgate, 2004.
Weckel, Ulrike. "A Lost Paradise of a Female Culture? Some Critical Questions Regarding the Scholarship on Late Eighteenth- and Early Nineteenth-Century German Salons." Trans. Pamela E. Selwyn. *German History* 18, no. 3 (2000): 310–36.
Weinreb, Ruth Plaut. "*Emilie* or *Emile?* Madame d'Epinay and the Education of Girls in Eighteenth-Century France." In *Eighteenth-Century Women and the Arts*, ed. Frederick M. Keener and Susan E. Lorsch, 57–66. Contributions in Women's Studies, 98. New York: Greenwood Press, 1988.
Weissberger, Barbara F. "'A tierra, puto!': Alfonso de Palencia's Discourse of Effeminacy." In *Queer Iberia: Crossing Cultures, Crossing Sexualities*, ed. Gregory Hutcheson and Josiah Blackmore, 291–324. Durham, NC: Duke University Press, 1999.
———. "'Deceitful Sects': The Debate about Women in the Age of Isabel the Catholic." In *Gender in Debate from the Early Middle Ages to the Renaissance*, ed. Thelma Fenster and Clare A. Lees. New York: Palgrave, 2002.
———. *Isabel Rules: Constructing Queenship, Wielding Power*. Minneapolis: University of Minnesota Press, 2004.
Whitaker, Daniel S. "Absent Mother, Mad Daughter, and the Therapy of Love in *La Delirante* of María Rosa Gálvez." *Dieciocho: Hispanic Enlightenment* 16, nos. 1–2 (1993): 167–76.
———. "Clarissa's Sisters: The Consequences of Rape in Three Neoclassic Tragedies of María Rosa Gálvez." *Letras Peninsulares* 5, no. 2 (1992): 239–51.
———. "Darkness in the Age of Light: *Amnón* of María Rosa Gálvez." *Hispanic Review* 58, no. 4 (1990): 439–53.
———. "An Enlightened Premiere: The Theater of María Rosa Gálvez." *Letras Femeninas* 19, nos. 1–2 (1993): 21–32.
———. "*Los figurones literarios* of María Rosa Gálvez as an Enlightened Response to Moratín's *La comedia nueva*." *Dieciocho: Hispanic Enlightenment* 11, no. 1 (1988): 3–14.
———. "Introduction to *Safo*." *Dieciocho: Hispanic Enlightenment* 18, no. 2 (1995): 189–210.
———. "La mujer ilustrada como dramaturga: El teatro de María Rosa Gálvez." In *Actas del X Congreso de la Asociación Internacional de Hispanistas*, ed. Antonio Vilanova, 1551–59. Barcelona: PPU, 1992.

Wiesner, Merry. *Women and Gender in Early Modern Europe.* Cambridge: Cambridge University Press, 1993.
Wolfgang, Aurora. "Intertextual Conversations: The Love-Letter and the Footnote in Madame de Graffigny's *Lettres d'une Péruvienne.*" *Eighteenth-Century Fiction* 10, no. 1 (1997): 15–28.
Wollstonecraft, Mary. *A Vindication of the Rights of Woman.* Ed. Ashley Tauchert. London: Everyman, 1995.
Woodford, Charlotte. "Women as Historians: The Case of Early Modern German Convents." *German Life and Letters* 52, no. 3 (1999): 271–80.
Yebes, Condesa de. *La condesa-duquesa de Benavente: Una vida en unas cartas.* Madrid: Espasa-Calpe, S.A., 1955.
Zanotti, Francesco Maria. "Compendio de la filosofia moral, escrito en lengua italiana por Francisco Maria Zanotti, y traducido al español por la Marquesa de Espeja." *Memorial Literario* (Madrid) (November 1786), 335.
Zavala, Iris M., coord. *Breve historia feminista de la literatura española (en lengua castellana).* 6 Vols. Madrid: Dirección General de Educación de la Mujer, Consejería de la Comunidad de Madrid, 1993–2000.

Index

Absolute monarchy, 5, 8
Academia de Buen Gusto, 45–46, 50
Academia de San Carlos (Valencia), 71
Académico de honor, 53. *See also* Real Academia de Bellas Artes de San Fernando
Académico de mérito, 53. *See also* Real Academia de Bellas Artes de San Fernando
Académie de Peinture et Sculpture (Paris), 51–52
Académie Française, 40
Academy of Fine Arts of San Fernando. *See* Real Academia de Bellas Artes de San Fernando
Academy of Good Taste, 45–46, 50
Academy of Noble Arts (Valladolid), 71
Adultery, 25
Aguayo, Joaquina Domínguez de, 137
Aguirre y Rosales, Cayetana, 128
Alba, Duchess of, 1
Alcudía, Duke of, 174
Alderete, Mariana, 42
Almagro, Diego de, 189
Almanacs, 122–24
Almarico, 29
Almodóvar, Duchess of, 137
Altamira, Marquise of, 137
Alvarado Lezo Pacheco y Solís, Josefa de, 181
Álvarez de Cienfuegos, Nicasio, 46
Amar y Borbón, Josefa: biography of, 43–44; on female education, 150–51, 154; membership in Aragonese Economic Society, 99–100, 175–76, 235n93; membership in Madrid Economic Society, 111, 137; new scholarship on, 7; translations of, 99; on women's admission to the Madrid Economic Society, 2, 87, 98–105, 107; on women's auxiliary status in *junta de damas*, 111–12, 130, 134
Amazons, 32, 95, 97
Andrade, Domingo de, 142
Angel of the house, 197
Anguissola, Sofonisba, 33
Aquinas, Thomas, 123
Aranda, Countess of, 138
Arcos, Duchess of, 43, 50, 54, 59, 65, 74
Ardanaz y Centellas, Jaime, 35–36
Arguellada, Ventura de, 142
Aristotle, 28, 29
Ariza, Marquise of, 134, 151–54, 164
Armendaríz y Samaniego, Juana Regis, 55, 59, 138
Arteaga y Palafox, María Teresa de, 67
Astrauli, María Luisa, 175
Asturias, 76, 78
Atlantic trade, 9, 21
Augustine, 29, 124, 129
Avila, 175
Avila, Manuel de, 120–21
Ayala, Mariana Fariña de, 138
Ayerbe, Marquise of, 2, 137
Ayerbe, Marquis of, 53, 175
Ayudantas, 164

299

Azcona y Valanza, María Agustina de, 54, 58–59

Bacon, Francis, 28, 29, 33
Bails, Benito, 122–24
Basco Flancas, Ricardo, 36–38
Bayle, Pierre, 28
Beatas, 23
Beaufort, Countess of, 175
Beltrán, Felipe, 164
Benalúa, Countess of, 43, 137
Benavente, Count-Duchess of: admission to Economic Societies, 87, 91, 105, 129, 137, 175; dedications to, 49, 129; palace of, 48; participation in *junta de damas*, 129, 171; *tertulia* of, 1, 42, 47–50, 129; titles of, 43
Bermudo, Marquise of, 137
Bertoni, Gertrudis, 54, 56
Betencourt y Molina, María, 137
Bible: in debates on women, 19, 34, 79; source for catalogues of women, 120. See also Eve
Bigamy, 25
Bisbal, Casilda, 71
Black Legend, 179–80, 187–90, 194–96
Bolufer Peruga, Mónica, 7, 9, 36
Borbón, María Josepha de, 137
Borbón, María Victoria de, 137
Borbonesa (dress design), 83–86. See also Dress code for women
Bordonaba, Antonia de, 135
Bosarte, Isidoro, 57
Bouligni del Pizarro, Clementina, 71
Bóveda, Marquise of la, 71
Briteño, María, 168
Burriel, María Josepha, 138

Caba, Florinda, 30–31
Cabarrús, Francisco: critics of, 98–104; as reformer, 96; on women's admission to Madrid Economic Society, 87, 96–99, 107, 231–32n79
Cádiz, 21, 44, 127, 172
Camarasa, Marquise of, 138
Campomanes, Pedro Rodríguez: on women and industry, 76–78, 79–80, 162; on women and the Madrid Economic Society, 87, 90–91, 93, 95, 104
Campuzano, María, 68
Cañas, María Josefa de, 137
Canillejas, Marquise of, 138
Capmany y de Montpalau, Antonio de, 27
Caraza y Ofarril, Ana, 138
Carolina (dress design), 83–84, 86. See also Dress code for women
Caron, María Josefa, 54, 71–72
Caro y Sureda, María, 71
Carpio, Countess of, 2, 137
Carranque, María Luisa, 54, 61, 71
Carriera, Rosalba, 51
Casaflórez, Countess of, 138
Casas, Engracia de las, 71
Caso, María Catalina de, 38, 42
Castillo y Calvo, Agustina, 168
Castrillo, Marquise of, 50, 135
Castro Terreño, Countess of, 138
Catalogues of women, 33–34, 89, 103, 120
Catherine of Aragon, 23
Catholic Church, and censorship, 115. See also Religion
Catholicism: as stagnating force, 3, 179, 195; calls for reform of, 47, 180, 190–96. See also Religion
Caveda y Solares, Rita, 128
Cavendish, Margaret, 27
Ceán Bermúdez, Juan Agustín, 56, 65–66
Censorial petitions, 13, 27, 38, 112–25, 155–56
Cepeda y Mayo, María del Rosario, 44, 137, 146
Cereta, Laura, 33
Cervantes, Miguel de, 17, 23, 27, 95
Cerviño y Pontejos, María de la Concepción, 175
Cevallos Guerra, Francisca de, 54
Charles II, 9
Charles III, 9, 13, 75, 78, 106, 111
Charles IV, 10, 47, 126–27, 134, 158–60
Charrière, Madame de, 185–86

Chastity, 25
Cheste, Baroness of, 71
Child rearing, 153, 157–61
Choiseul, Duchess of, 45
Cifuentes, Francisco Gerónimo, 142–45
Citizenship: and civic education of women, 152; in France, 8; passion and, 180; passive, 87; rank-based notions of female, 13, 74, 80, 84–87, 95, 149, 162, 177; rights vs. responsibilities of, 8; Spanish debates on, 8, 11, 86, 112, 147, 154, 196. *See also* Civic motherhood
Civic motherhood, 149–57, 161–62, 176–77
Clavijo y Fajardo, José, 38, 81
Codes, Simon de, 141
Colonial expansion, 179–80, 187–90, 194–96; impact on women, 21
Concordia Marón, Teresa, 69
Condillac, Etienne Bonnot de, 114–15
Constitution of Cádiz, 8, 11
Consumption: of foreign products, 81–82; national importance of, 75, 81–84, 86, 89, 154; as part of household economy, 151–52
Contraminz, Countess of, 55
Convent of the Descalzas Reales, 22
Convents: as sites of empowerment, 22; as suffocating, 103, 151, 191; in work of María de Zayas y Sotomayor, 27. *See also* Convent schools
Convent schools, 44, 184
Córdoba, Martín de, 20
Correas, María, 168
Cortes y Konock, Luisa Sanz de, 54, 64
Cortina y Morales, Josefa Díez de la, 138
Costilla y Jaraba, María Jacoba, 55, 58
Council of Castile, 115
Council of Trent, 123
Counter-Reformation, 25
Crenne, Hélisenne de, 27
Cross-dressing, 21
Cruz, Ramón de la, 48
Cudero, Cristina, 168
Cueva, Beltrán de, 20

Cueva y Alcedo, María Gertrudis de la, 64, 67
Curadoras, 160, 167–68
Curtis, Judith, 182

Defense of Women (Feijoo y Montenegro), 12, 17; impact of, 17–18, 41, 95, 197; as reference point, 102. *See also* Feijoo y Montenegro, Fray Benito Jerónimo
Demerson, Jorge, 175
Demerson, Paula de, 131, 148
Descartes, René, 28, 33, 36
Desvallo Coronela, Josepha, 67
Diario de Madrid (newspaper), 160, 165, 172, 180
Díaz González, Santos, 125
Diderot, Denis, 17
Diego, Estrella de, 51
Diez, Margarita, 165, 168
Dolores Miranda, María de los, 175
Dolores Veytía, María Josefa de los, 137
Domingo Carbonero, María, 68
Don Quixote (Cervantes), 17, 23, 95
Douthwaite, Julia V., 188
Dowries, 94, 163–64
Dress code for women, 80–86, 130–31, 139
Duménes, Vicente, 165
Durán, Cipriana, 68

Economic reforms, 78, 96
Economic Societies: origins of, 75–76; as royal project, 9. *See also Junta de damas*; Real Sociedad Económica de Granada; Real Sociedad Económica Matritense de Amigos del País
Economy. *See* Industry
Education. *See* Women's education
Elizabeth I, 20
Embroidery, 139, 162–63, 164–70, 172
Empress María, 22
Encyclopédie (Diderot), 17
England, 4, 6, 20, 26, 51, 61, 190
Engraving, by women artists, 62, 69
Enlightenment: burgeoning public discourse of, 1, 40; cooperation between

Enlightenment *(continued)*
  monarch and reformers, 9, 40, 76;
  definition of, 4–5; democratic principles embodied in, 136; impact of
  Feijoo on, 28, 39; lack of, 6; religion
  and, 5–6; women's centrality to, 7, 98
Enrile y Alcedo, María Magdalena de, 67
Enrique IV, 19–20
Épinay, Madame d', 150
Equality: definitional issues, 4–5;
  difference and, 12, 14; in Economic
  Society debates, 75, 88, 91, 96, 102–3; Feijoo and, 18, 28–29, 32–34, 38–39; Zayas and, 26. *See also* Universal rights
Erauso, Catalina de, 21, 25
Escobedo y Velasco, María Dolores, 67
Escritor sin Título, El (Romea y Tapia), 81
Escuela de bordados, 139, 162–63, 164–70, 172
Escuela de San Andrés, 141
Escuelas patrióticas, 94, 130, 139, 141, 162–65, 170
Española (dress design), 83–84, 86. *See also* Dress code for women
Espeja, Marquise of la, 43, 114–15, 137
Espíritu de los Mejores Diarios Literarios que Se Publican en Europa, 99
Estala, Pedro, 115–16
Estepa, Marquise of, 50, 54, 59, 71
Estrados, 90
Euripides, 30
Eve: and women's intellectual curiosity, 102–3; and women's subordination, 19, 24, 30–31, 34–35, 37–38. *See also* Bible
Ezpeleta, Isabel de, 54, 56
Ezpeleta, Juan Bautista de, 115, 125

Fadejas, Manuela, 167
Farel, Teresa, 168, 170
Feijoo y Montenegro, Fray Benito Jerónimo: critics of, 35–36, 97; impact of, 17, 28–29, 39, 41, 72, 88, 197; as reference point, 102; supporters of, 36–37; on women, 28–39, 95, 101, 103. *See also Defense of Women; Teatro crítico universal*
Female public: *junta de damas* and, 112–13, 129, 140, 147–48, 172, 176–77; women writers and, 112, 127–29, 183
Fénelon, François, 38
Ferdinand (of Aragon), 18, 20; in Feijoo, 31
Ferdinand VI, 9, 43
Fernandez de Cordóva, María Magdalena, 67
Fernandez Diez, Andrés, 173
Fernández-Quintanilla, Paloma, 171
Fernán Nuñez, Countess of, 137
Ferrer, Micaela, 71
Figueroa y Montalvo, María Loreto, 138
Floridablanca, Count of: dismissal of, 10; *junta de damas* and, 130–31, 133, 135, 175
Fonte, Moderata, 27
Foreign books in Spain, 28, 48, 76, 150. *See also* Translation; Translators
Foundling home, 2, 157–61, 163
France: citizenship and, 8; and French Revolution, 10–11; historiography of, 3–4; intellectual connections to, 44–45, 47–48, 75; royal academies in, 40, 51, 64; salons in, 2, 12, 41–42, 75; women writers, 89; as yardstick of Enlightenment, 5–7, 9, 89, 126
Franco dictatorship, 3, 6
Freixa, Mireia, 62
French Revolution, 5, 8, 10–11
Frías, María Josefa de, 68
Frías y Uceda, Duchess of, 139
Fuentenueva, Countess of, 139
Fuerte-Híjar, Marquise of: *junta de damas* and, 137, 143, 154–55, 171, 174; *tertulia* of, 2, 42, 46, 50

Galazzo, Ana María, 68
Galicia, 76, 78
Gálvez, Matilde de, 67
Gálvez de Cabrera, María Rosa, 43, 124–27, 143, 181
García, Antonio Allen, 122

García, Balbina, 167
García, Juan Agustín, 165
García, Manuel, 46
García, María Luisa, 68
García, Santiago, 160
Gardner, Ava, 1
Gay, Peter, 5
Gender history, 3
Geoffrin, Madame, 45
Gerona, Eulalia, 71
Gilabert, María Lucia, 55, 71
Girón, Manuela, 68
Glendinning, Nigel, 40
Godoy, Manuel, 10–11, 47
Goldsmith, Elizabeth C., 113
Goldstein, Carl, 62
Gómez de Castro Aragón, María de las Mercedes, 117–21, 124
González, Teresa, 122–24
Goodman, Dena, 2, 42, 113
Goughi y Quilty, Elena, 55, 57–58, 64
Goya, Francisco de, 1–2, 48, 63–64
Graffigny, Madame de, 179–96, 198
Granada, 175
Greer, Germaine, 69
Guerrero, María, 137
Guevara Vasconcelos, José de, 87, 91–92, 96
Guilds, 78
Gutiérrez, Vicenta, 168
Gutiérrez Bueno, Pedro, 46

Habermas, Jürgen, 3
Herbas, Petra Pedregal de, 139
Hernández de Larrea, Juan Antonio, 99–100, 175–76
Hernández de Morejón, Magdalena, 114
Herr, Richard, 10, 17, 46
Hertz, Deborah, 42
Hickey y Pellizoni, Margarita, 116, 127–28
Holland, Lady, 46, 48
Honor, cult of, 23, 26, 31
Honorary directors, 59, 74. *See also* Real Academia de Bellas Artes de San Fernando
Household economy, 151–54
Huarte de San Juan, 29

Huéscar y Arcos, Duchess of, 43, 50, 54, 59, 65, 74
Hueva, Bárbara María de, 54, 56, 65
Hunt, Lynn, 5
Hurtado de Mendoza, María Juana, 55, 56, 64
Hust, Countess of, 138

Ibarra, Joaquín, 46
Idleness, of women, 76–80, 88–90, 93–96, 195
Imbille, Luis de, 87, 93–94
Inclusa, 2, 157–61, 163
Industry: and female-appropriate work, 78–79, 90, 162, 225–26n14; impact of foreign imports on, 81–82, 163; *junta de damas* and, 139, 162–74, 176–77; women as consumers of Spanish, 83; women's participation in, 75–80, 162–71, 225–26n14
Infanta Doña María Isabel, 55
Inheritance practices, 22, 78
Inquisition, 1, 3, 23, 47, 191
Iriarte, Tomás de, 48–49
Isabel I: acclamation ceremony of, 20, 25; ascension of, 18; dispute over throne, 19; in Feijoo, 31; marriage of, 18; reference to, 97, 103

Jácome y Ricardos, María del Rosario, 137
Jansenism, 47
Jara de Soto, Clara, 27, 182
Jefferson, Thomas, 5
Jesús, Mariana de, 23
Johnson, Samuel, 128
Journal des Débats, Le (periodical), 48
Journal des Modes, Le (periodical), 48
Jovellanos, Gaspar Melchor de: Charles IV and, 10; on circumscribed role for women, 112; Count-Duchess of Benavente and, 48; Countess of Montijo and, 46; on guilds, 78; on women and industry, 78–80, 162; on women's admission to Madrid's Economic Society, 87, 90, 92–93, 96, 98–100, 104, 155
Joyes y Blake, Inés, 128–29

Juana (la Beltraneja), 19–21
Judaism, women and religious tradition of, 23
Junta de damas, 129–47, 148–77, 197–98; agenda of, 14, 149; auxiliary status of, 91–92, 104–7, 111–13, 130–31, 134, 142–45; dress code proposal and, 130–31; first meeting of, 129; formation of, 2, 105–7; membership dues and, 93–94, 135; as mothers to the nation, 149, 176–77; place within Economic Society at large, 130–47, 158; role beyond Madrid, 171–77; schedule of, 2, 129–30, 148–49; as space for female action, 112; statutes of, 13, 113, 132–41, 145, 150; women's education and, 139–40, 146–47, 162–71. *See also* Economic societies; Real Sociedad Económica Matritense de Amigos del País
Justiniana y Peñaflorida, María Concepción, 68

Kauffmann, Angelica, 51, 61
Kerber, Linda, 2
Kitts, Sally Ann, 7, 101, 104
Krontiris, Tina, 178

Labille-Guiard, Adélaïde, 51
Lace-making school, 162–63, 168–70
Lainz, Josepha, 168
Lalemant, Pierre, 116
Lamarche-Courmont, Hugary de, 186
Landes, Joan, 4–5, 41–42
Lavauguyon, Antonia de, 54
La Vopa, Anthony, 6
Lehfeldt, Elizabeth, 20, 22
Lemos, Countess of. *See* Sarría, Marquise of
León, Fray Luis de, 23–25, 38
Lerma, Duke of, 22
Letrado class, 43
Levacher de Valincourt, Madame, 87, 98–105, 107
Lezo y Garro, María Casilda de, 68
Liberal ideology, 4, 11–12. *See also* Universal rights

Licenses for publication, 114–15. *See also* Censorial petitions
Lille, Carlota, 172
Limpieza de sangre, 23
Listenois Beaufremont, Princess of, 54, 59, 64
Litz, María Josepha, 172
Llano, Marquise of, 137
Locke, John, 161, 184
Lope de Vega, 25
López, Josepha, 168
López de Ayala, Ignacio, 87–89
López de Porras, Rita, 2, 172
Losada y Portocarrero, Teresa, 137, 143
Louis XIV, 9
Lucía de Jesús, 23
Lugo, 175
Luisa María, Princess, 67
Luna, Álvaro de, 19
Luxury, 80–83, 130, 139, 151–52, 154, 185, 187
Luzán, Ignacio de, 45
Luzuriaga, María, 115–16

MacArthur, Elizabeth J., 185–86
Macía, María del Carmen, 68
Macpherson, James, 182
Madison, James, 5
Madrid, 40, 76, 159, 171
Madrid Royal Economic Society of Friends of the Country. *See* Real Sociedad Económica Matritense de Amigos del País
Madrileña (dress design), 83–86. *See also* Dress code for women
Maecenas, 121
Mahón, Duchess of, 139
Maja desnuda (Goya), 1–2
Malebranche, Nicolas, 28, 33
Manco de Olivares, Laurencio, 35–38
Mañer, Salvador José, 35
Manuel, Miguel de, 143
Manzanares, Petrona, 167
Margaret of Austria, 22
Margaret of the Cross, 22
María Luisa, wife of Charles IV, 10–11, 137, 166–67

Marín, Manuel José, 74, 87, 89–91, 93–95, 104, 162
Marin, Michel-Ange, 128
Marriage: in Feijoo, 34; impact of *luxo* on, 82; Isabel and, 20–21; in the law, 25; León's views on, 24; as one of women's few options, 151, 185; rejection of, 185–87, 191; Vives's views on, 24–25
Martínez, Martín, 37
Martínez y Salafranca, Miguel Juan, 37–38
Martín Gaite, Carmen, 42, 90
Martin y Abril, Catalina, 67, 175
Massardier-Kenney, Françoise, 178
Masson le Golft, Mademoiselle le, 137
Matriarchy, 78, 208n28
Mayans y Pastor, Josefa, 71
Medinaceli y Santistevan, Duchess of, 68
Medina Conde, Cristóbal (pseud. Tiburcio Cascajales), 36
Meléndez, Ana, 1, 54, 65, 69, 71
Meléndez, Clara, 69
Meléndez, Francisca Efigenia, 55, 69–70, 71
Meléndez, Francisco Antonio, 53, 69
Meléndez, Josef Agustin, 69
Meléndez, Luis, 69
Meléndez, Miguel Jacinto, 69
Meléndez Valdés, Juan, 47
Mémoires de Trévoux (periodical), 17
Memorial Literario (periodical), 98–100, 127–28, 180
Menéndez, Clara, 54
Mengs, Ana María, 1, 7, 55, 64, 66, 69, 71
Mengs, Anton Raphaël, 58, 66
Mercure de France (periodical), 17, 98
Michel, Dorotea, 64, 67
Michel, Pedro, 64
Mill, John Stuart, 78, 91
Milton, 104
Miñano y Ramírez, María Eugenia, 71
Miranda, Countess of, 138
Miret, María Paula, 68

Miscegenation, fear of, 23
M. O., 80–86, 89, 130–31, 226–27n28
Mondragón, María Reguera de, 175
Montealegre, Marquise of, 137
Montepío de hilazas, 170–71
Montesquieu, Baron of, 183
Montiano y Luyando, Agustín de, 45
Montijo, Countess of: on dress code, 131; education of, 44; on female citizenship, 155–56; and Inclusa, 157–60; and *junta de damas*, 130, 137, 148, 150–51, 174; *tertulia* of, 2, 42, 46–47, 50
Morant Deusa, Isabel, 9
Moratín, Leandro Fernández de, 48, 117–18
Moratín, Nicolás Fernández de, 116
Morel de Vindé, Madame, 186
Moreno, María Josepha Ester de, 138
Moser, Mary, 51, 61
Mosti, Faustina, 54, 61
Mosti, Manuela, 54, 61
Motherhood: Isabel I and, 21; as natural duty of women, 97; rejection of, 185; and women as educators of children, 80, 149; women's education and, 104, 149–57. *See also* Civic motherhood; Republican Motherhood
Muñoz de Torres, Bartolomé, 118, 120, 125–26

Naked Maja, The (Goya), 1
Napoleon, 1, 11, 114, 167
Nasarre y Ferriz, Antonio, 46
Navagero, Andres, 21
Negrín Fajardo, Olegario, 163–64
Newton, Isaac, 28
Nieto, Josef, 165–67, 170
Nieulant, Countess of, 138
Nochlin, Linda, 61
Novales, Josepha, 68
Nuns, economic power of, 22

Olivieri, Faraona María Magdalena, 54, 56–57, 71
O'Reylli, Countess of, 137
O'Reilly, Rosa, 138

Osuna, 175
Osuna, Count-Duchess of. *See* Benavente, Count-Duchess of
Osuna, Duke of, 53, 87

Padilla, María, 172
Palacios, Jacinta, 168
Palacios, Marquise of, 137
Palafox, Antonio, 47
Palafox y Portocarrero, María Ramona, 55, 64–65
Palazuelos, Viscountess of, 137
Panes y Mangino, María Josepha, 138, 168
Parada y Santín, José, 51, 71
Parreño, Isabel, 138
Partible inheritance, 22
Passion, 101, 180, 192, 194–96
Patriarchy: critics of, 19, 179; as dominant paradigm, 23–25, 199; questioning of, 208n28
Patriotism, 82–86, 111, 149, 155, 158
Pelayo, 78
Peñafiel, Marquise of, 138
Peñaflorida, Count of, 75
Pensador, El (Clavijo y Fajardo), 81
Pepys, Samuel, 26
Pérez, Isabel, 165–67, 170
Pérez Caballero, Angela, 54
Pérez de Ocampo, María, 22
Perez García, Joseph, 117–20
Perfecta casada, La (León), 23–25, 38
Periodical press: Economic Society debate in, 75, 87, 98–100, 107; growth of, 40; women writers and, 180–81
Perry, Mary Elizabeth, 21
Philip II, 52, 169
Philip III, 22, 169
Philip V, 9, 40
Physiocrats, 77
Pizan, Christine de, 20, 27, 30
Pizarro, Francisco, 189
Pocock, J. G. A., 5
Poetry, 45–46, 116, 126, 197
Pon, Felipa, 168
Pontejos, María Ana de, 137
Porcel y Salablanca, José Antonio, 45

Porres de Sotelo, María de las Mercedes, 139
Portago, Marquise of, 138
Pougens, Charles, 48
Prada, María Concepción, 68
Preciado, Catherina Cherubini, 54, 71
Priego, María Francisca, 68
Prieto, María, 1, 54, 56, 65, 69
Private sphere, 4
Producers, women as, 75–80
Public exhibitions, 41, 62–64, 66–68
Public presence of women, 99, 107; concerns over, 88, 98; risks of "going public," 175–83, 195; women's embrace of, 88, 112, 114, 117–29
Public sphere: definition of, 4, 6; Economic Society and, 9; feminist critiques of, 4; women's history and, 5

Quadra, Antonio de la, 77
Quadra, María de la, 68
Querelle des femmes. *See* Woman question, the
Quintanilla, Antonia, 67
Quintano y Bonifax, Manuel, 116–17
Quintina Guzmán y la Cerda, María Isidra, 87, 91, 105–6, 129, 137, 175
Quipus, 181–82, 193
Quiros, Francisca Bernaldo de, 68

Rada, María, 165–67, 170
Rada y Aguirre, D. Joseph de, 38
Ramón y Ripalda, María Vicenta, 71
Rank: elite character of Spain's *ilustradas*, 43–45, 135; rank-based notions of female citizenship, 13, 74, 80, 84–87, 95, 149, 162, 177
Raón y Mariño, Francisca, 138
Reading public, 40, 112
Real Academia de Bellas Artes de San Fernando, 50–72, 74–75, 89, 197; creation of, 41, 50–53; dismissal of women's admission, 51–52; figures on women's admission, 1, 53; importance of, in art world, 52; opportunities for women in, 41; and participation of nonmembers, 64–65, 67–68

Real Academia de Jurisprudencia de Santa Bárbara, 41
Real Academia de la Historia, 41, 51
Real Academia Española de la Lengua, 40, 50, 123
Real Academia Médica Matritense, 41, 51
Real Escuela de Bordados al Cuidado de la Sociedad Económica de Esta Corte, 139, 162–63, 164–70, 172
Real Monasterio de Monjas Salesas, 44
Real Sociedad Económica de Amigos del País de Osuna, 175
Real Sociedad Económica de Granada, 175
Real Sociedad Económica Matritense de Amigos del País: debate over women's admission, 12–13, 74–75, 87–105; structure of, 130; women's admission to, 2, 105–7, 111–13. *See also Junta de damas*
Religion: myth of Enlightenment secularism, 5–6; reform and, 47, 180, 190–96; women's education and, 152, 165–66; women's writings on, 114
Republican Motherhood, 14, 80. *See also* Civic motherhood
Republic of Letters: in Spain, 40; women's participation in, 43, 116, 129, 181
Retamora, Rita Martin de, 68
Río y Arnedo, María Antonia de, 180
Roberts, R., 186, 190
Rodríguez, Gabriela, 168
Rodríguez, Ramón Carlos, 87
Rodríguez del Padrón, Juan, 19
Rojas, Josefa de, 170
Roman, Marta, 168
Romea y Tapia, Cristóbal, 81
Romero Masegosa y Cancelada, María, 179–96, 198
Rosa, Phelipa de la, 165
Rosa del Monte, Marquise of, 42
Royal academies, creation of, 40
Royal Aragonese Economic Society, 99–100, 175–76

Royal Economic Society of Friends of the Country. *See* Economic societies; Real Sociedad Económica Matritense de Amigos del País
Royal Spanish Language Academy, 40
Rousseau, Jean-Jacques, 28, 98, 182
Roxas y Velarde, María de, 138
Royal Academy of Fine Arts of San Fernando. *See* Real Academia de Bellas Artes de San Fernando
Roza, Felipa la, 137
Ruiz de la Prada, Rosa, 71
Ruiz y Careaga, 165–66
Ryan, Mary P., 4

Sabatier, Francisca, 68
Sabatini, María Ana, 55, 64
Sabuco de Nantes, Oliva, 33
Saint-Lambert, Jean-François, 180
Saíz, María del Carmen, 62, 64
Saldueña, Count of, 46
Salonnières, scholarship on, 2, 42
Salons, scholarship on, 41–42, 212–13n2
Salvador Carmona, Juan Antonio, 46, 64
Salvador Carmona, Manuel, 66
San Andrés, 162, 164
San Bartolomé, Marquise of, 139
Sancha, Antonio, 46
San Christóbal, María Rafaela de, 137
San Ginés, 162, 164
San Martín, 162
San Miguel de Perá, Baroness of, 138
San Román, Countess of, 139
San Sebastián, 162
Santa Cruz, Marquise of, 54, 59, 64, 70–71, 138
Santa Cruz de Merlín, María de las Mercedes, 139
Santa Eufemia, Countess of, 137
Santa Fé, Duchess of, 139
Santareli, Juan Antonio, 36
Santisteban, Duchess of, 50
Sarrailh, Jean, 175
Sarría, Marquise of, 42, 45–46, 49–50
Scholasticism, 28

Seix y Páez, Catalina, 138
Sempere y Guarinos, Juan, 39, 106
Seville, 21
Sherwood, Joan, 160–61
Smith, Adam, 77
Social utility, of admitting women to the Madrid Economic Society, 88–91, 104, 112, 147
Sociedad Bascongada de los Amigos del País, 75
Socios/Socias. See *Junta de damas*; Real Sociedad Económica Matritense de Amigos del País
Someruelos, Marquise of, 137, 165
Sonora, Marquise of, 137, 153
Sorkin, David, 6
Soto y Urgujo, Luisa, 68
Spain: absolute monarchy in, 5; cooperation between monarch and Enlightenment reformers, 9, 40, 76; Enlightenment project in, 3; fissures in, 11; foundational myth of, 30–31; gender and modernization of, 3, 7, 13, 75–80, 86–88, 125, 129, 131, 147, 148; history of conquest, 179–80, 187–90, 194–96; monarchical history, 9–11, 19–21; Muslim conquest of, 30–31, 77–78, 89; myth of decline, 3, 6–7; nineteenth-century instability, 11; religion and, 5
Spanish Succession, War of, 9
Spilimberg, Irene de, 33
Statutes: of the Economic Society, 132, 136; of the embroidery school, 162–63; of the *junta de damas*, 113, 132–41, 145, 150; of the lace-making school, 163, 168
Sul, Ana María, 168
Sullivan, Constance, 99–100
Supernumerario, 53. See also Real Academia de Bellas Artes de San Fernando
Superunda, Countess of, 173

Teatro crítico universal (Feijoo y Montenegro), 17, 28, 35, 40

Teresa de Jesús of Avila, Santa, 22
Tertulias, 40–42, 45–50; definition of, 2, 40; as frivolous gatherings, 42, 90; hosts of, 42; impact of, 75; as instrument of women's education, 45; in nineteenth century, 197; role of women as hosts, 41, 49, 213–14n4; women as attendees, 50
Teruel y Montezuma, Josepha Marsilla de, 67
Texada Hermoso y de la Buria, María Ignacio de, 67
Tirado, María, 168
Tolosa, Marquise, 116–17
Tordesillas Cepeda y Sada, María Antonia Fernanda de, 180
Toro, 20
Torrecilla, Marquise of, 137
Torrejón, Countess of, 138
Torrepalma, Countess of, 132, 134, 137, 143, 150, 151–52, 156
Torrepalma, Count of, 46
Torres, Ana, 71
Tourneaux, Nicolás, 47
Translation, as means to publication, 14, 178–83, 195
Translators, women, 38, 99, 114–17, 126, 128, 178–83
Trastámara, Countess of, 138
Trent, Council of, impact on female religious, 22
Trúllas, Countess of, 132, 134, 137, 143, 150, 151–52, 156
Tudor, Mary, 23
Tully, Ana, 138
Two-sex model, 29

Ugarte, Francisca Cepeda de, 138
Ulorix, Margarita, 168
United States, 4
Universal rights: rejection of, 156; role in fostering women's activities, 5, 74, 112, 148. See also Equality; Liberal ideology
Urries y Pignatelli, Mariana, 54, 59–60

Urrutia, Ana Gertrudis de, 54
Utility. *See* Social utility

Vaca, Beatriz Montiel de, 138
Valdeolmos, Marquise of, 143, 167
Valencia, Marcela de la, 55, 71
Valenzuela y Pizarro, María Dolores, 67
Valladolid, 22, 71, 174
Valoría, Viscountess of, 174
Varo Gil, Andrea de, 138
Vega, Garcilaso de la, 188
Velasco, Juana Antuner de, 68
Velasco y Escobedo, María Gertrudis de, 138
Viegas, Simon de, 143
Vigée LeBrun, Elisabeth, 51
Villafranca, Marquise of, 55, 62–63, 71, 138
Villahermosa, Duchess of, 44–45
Villalobos, Countess of, 138
Villalobos, Count of, 140
Villa López, Marquise of, 137
Villamonte, Countess of, 138
Villarino, Isidora, 67
Villaverde, Marquise of, 54
Villena, Enrique de, 19
Virgil, 104, 121, 124, 129
Virginity, cult of honor and, 23
Vives, Juan Luis, 23–25, 38
Vizurrun de Azanza, María del Pilar, 68
Vollendorf, Lisa, 27

Wet-nursing, 153, 157–58, 160
Widows, patronage of, 22
Wiesner, Merry, 169
Wollstonecraft, Mary, 80, 150
Woman question, the: *junta de damas*'s writings as part of, 150–57; persistence of negative views on women, 35–36, 93, 97–98, 111; shifts in thought, 41, 73, 74, 149; in Spain, 18, 28

Women artists: and the academy, 41, 52; common mediums of, 62, 69; in families of artists, 64, 66, 69; and genre limitations, 61–62, 69, 169–70; training of, 52, 61–62, 69, 169–70
Women's bodies: as determiners of women's role, 155, 158–59, 161; and inequality, 33, 37; physical inferiority of, 29; as proof of moral superiority, 19; two-sex model, 29
Women's council. *See Junta de damas*
Women's education, 42–45; civic, 152; during Counter-Reformation, 25; in female-appropriate industries, 79–80, 90, 162–71; *junta de damas* and, 139–40, 149–57; lack of, as reason for women's status, 26, 32, 79, 103, 179, 183–85, 195; in *tertulias*, 45; in work of Zayas, 26. *See also* Motherhood
Women's history: broadening definitions in, 8–9; history of, 3; public sphere and, 4; in Spain, 6
Women's intellectual abilities, 32–34, 35
Women writers, 113–29; censorial petitions of, 13, 27, 38, 112–25, 129; and challenges of public exposure, 113–14, 178–83, 195; figures on, 114; texts of *junta de damas* as, 150–57

Ximera, Countess of la, 175

Ybañez de la Rentería, María Manuela, 67–68

Zamora, Francisco de, 45
Zayas y Sotomayor, María de, 25–28, 30, 182
Zebriada y Zerezeda, Judas Joseph, 172
Zilleruelo, Marquise of, 138
Zurana, Andres, 142–43

STUDIES ON THE HISTORY OF SOCIETY AND CULTURE

Victoria E. Bonnell and Lynn Hunt, Editors

1. *Politics, Culture, and Class in the French Revolution,* by Lynn Hunt
2. *The People of Paris: An Essay in Popular Culture in the 18th Century,* by Daniel Roche
3. *Pont-St-Pierre, 1398–1789: Lordship, Community, and Capitalism in Early Modern France,* by Jonathan Dewald
4. *The Wedding of the Dead: Ritual, Poetics, and Popular Culture in Transylvania,* by Gail Kligman
5. *Students, Professors, and the State in Tsarist Russia,* by Samuel D. Kassow
6. *The New Cultural History,* edited by Lynn Hunt
7. *Art Nouveau in Fin-de-Siècle France: Politics, Psychology, and Style,* by Debora L. Silverman
8. *Histories of a Plague Year: The Social and the Imaginary in Baroque Florence,* by Giulia Maria Calvi
9. *Culture of the Future: The Proletkult Movement in Revolutionary Russia,* by Lynn Mally
10. *Bread and Authority in Russia, 1914–1921,* by Lars T. Lih
11. *Territories of Grace: Cultural Change in the Seventeenth-Century Diocese of Grenoble,* by Keith P. Luria
12. *Publishing and Cultural Politics in Revolutionary Paris, 1789–1810,* by Carla Hesse
13. *Limited Livelihoods: Gender and Class in Nineteenth-Century England,* by Sonya O. Rose
14. *Moral Communities: The Culture of Class Relations in the Russian Printing Industry, 1867–1907,* by Mark D. Steinberg
15. *Bolshevik Festivals, 1917–1920,* by James von Geldern
16. *Venice's Hidden Enemies: Italian Heretics in a Renaissance City,* by John Martin
17. *Wondrous in His Saints: Counter-Reformation Propaganda in Bavaria,* by Philip M. Soergel
18. *Private Lives and Public Affairs: The Causes Célèbres of Prerevolutionary France,* by Sarah Maza

19. *Hooliganism: Crime, Culture, and Power in St. Petersburg, 1900–1914,* by Joan Neuberger
20. *Possessing Nature: Museums, Collecting, and Scientific Culture in Early Modern Italy,* by Paula Findlen
21. *Listening in Paris: A Cultural History,* by James H. Johnson
22. *The Fabrication of Labor: Germany and Britain, 1640–1914,* by Richard Biernacki
23. *The Struggle for the Breeches: Gender and the Making of the British Working Class,* by Anna Clark
24. *Taste and Power: Furnishing Modern France,* by Leora Auslander
25. *Cholera in Post-Revolutionary Paris: A Cultural History,* by Catherine J. Kudlick
26. *The Women of Paris and Their French Revolution,* by Dominique Godineau
27. *Iconography of Power: Soviet Political Posters under Lenin and Stalin,* by Victoria E. Bonnell
28. *Fascist Spectacle: The Aesthetics of Power in Mussolini's Italy,* by Simonetta Falasca-Zamponi
29. *Passions of the Tongue: Language Devotion in Tamil India, 1891–1970,* by Sumathi Ramaswamy
30. *Crescendo of the Virtuoso: Spectacle, Skill, and Self-Promotion in Paris during the Age of Revolution,* by Paul Metzner
31. *Crime, Cultural Conflict, and Justice in Rural Russia, 1856–1914,* by Stephen P. Frank
32. *The Collective and the Individual in Russia: A Study of Practices,* by Oleg Kharkhordin
33. *What Difference Does a Husband Make? Women and Marital Status in Nazi and Postwar Germany,* by Elizabeth D. Heineman
34. *Beyond the Cultural Turn: New Directions in the Study of Society and Culture,* edited by Victoria E. Bonnell and Lynn Hunt
35. *Jazz, Rock, and Rebels: Cold War Politics and American Culture in a Divided Germany,* by Uta G. Poiger
36. *The Frail Social Body: Pornography, Homosexuality, and Other Fantasies in Interwar France,* by Carolyn J. Dean
37. *Blood and Fire: Rumor and History in Colonial Africa,* by Luise White
38. *The New Biography: Performing Femininity in Nineteenth-Century France,* edited by Jo Burr Margadant

39. *France and the Cult of the Sacred Heart: An Epic Tale for Modern Times,* by Raymond Jonas

40. *Politics and Theater: The Crisis of Legitimacy in Restoration France, 1815–1830,* by Sheryl Kroen

41. *On the Postcolony,* by Achille Mbembe

42. *Fascist Modernities: Italy, 1922–1945,* by Ruth Ben-Ghiat

43. *Women Writing Opera: Creativity and Controversy in the Age of the French Revolution,* by Jacqueline Letzter and Robert Adelson

44. *Popular Theater and Society in Tsarist Russia,* by E. Anthony Swift

45. *Beyond the Pale: The Jewish Encounter with Late Imperial Russia,* by Benjamin Nathans

46. *The View from Vesuvius: Italian Culture and the Southern Question,* by Nelson J. Moe

47. *The Three-Piece Suit and Modern Masculinity: England, 1550–1850,* by David Kuchta

48. *The Emancipation of Writing: German Civil Society in the Making, 1790s–1820s,* by Ian F. McNeely

49. *Obstinate Hebrews: Representations of Jews in France, 1715–1815,* by Ronald Schechter

50. *An Ottoman Tragedy: History and Historiography at Play,* by Gabriel Piterberg

51. *The Family on Trial in Revolutionary France,* by Suzanne Desan

52. *Producing Desire: Changing Sexual Discourse in the Ottoman Middle East, 1500–1900,* by Dror Ze'evi

53. *The Emerging Female Citizen: Gender and Enlightenment in Spain,* by Theresa Ann Smith

Compositor:	BookMatters, Berkeley
Text:	10/13 Aldus
Display:	Aldus
Printer and binder:	Sheridan Books, Inc.

UNIVERSITY OF ST. THOMAS LIBRARIES

WITHDRAWN
UST
Libraries

HQ 1693 .S64 2006
Smith, Theresa Ann, 1971-
The emerging female citizen

DATE DUE